American Literary Scholarship
1970

American Literary Scholarship

An Annual / 1970

Edited by J. Albert Robbins

Essays by John C. Broderick, Nina Baym, Merton M. Sealts, Jr., Bernice Slote, Hamlin Hill, Robert L. Gale, Michael Millgate, William White, J. A. Leo Lemay, M. Thomas Inge, Patrick F. Quinn, Warren French, James H. Justus, Richard Crowder, A. Kingsley Weatherhead, Walter J. Meserve, John T. Flanagan, G. R. Thompson.

Duke University Press, Durham, North Carolina, 1972

© 1972, Duke University Press. Library of Congress Catalogue Card number 65–19450. I.S.B.N. 0–8223–0270–5. Printed in the United States of America by Heritage Printers, Inc.

Foreword

If you chance to be one who, as an individual, depends greatly upon the prompt appearance of the *MLA International Bibliography*, you can imagine the problems which have faced the contributors and editor of this year's volume of *American Literary Scholarship*. As I have indicated earlier, we must rely upon this important and unique resource. There is no substitute for it. In more normal times we would have had advance galley proof of the American literature segment of the bibliography in March or April, but this past year the bibliography, always an increasingly complex operation, embraced the computer with initially disastrous results. At this writing, the bibliography still is not available and the appearance of *ALS 1970*, approximately on schedule, is a tribute to the resourcefulness of the contributors. We are especially indebted to Professor Jackson R. Bryer of the University of Maryland, who superintends the American section of the bibliography, for he rose to our need and provided us with a specially typed copy of his card file. Without this special help the year's work would have been far less complete. One should note, also, that what Professor Bryer provided was, at that time, a tentative listing. This means that some important items may be overlooked this year which might have been included under more normal circumstances.

To those of you who belong to the American Literature Section of the Modern Language Association and routinely receive copies of *American Literary Scholarship*, we recently asked for your views on the series. We solicited your comments to gain some sense of what these readers think of the effort, and to gather your suggestions for changes or improvements. The comments have been gratifying, for an overwhelming majority of respondents have told us that the series is of substantial utility. The recurrent word is "indispensable." I was especially gratified by many comments on the quality of the writing. To cite only two, one person notes that "the wit and perceptiveness of the reviews make reading *ALS* a pleasure" and another says, "What really amazes me is that it produces year after year such a high quality of writing."

Finally I would like to remind readers that the person who conceived, organized, and edited the series for the first five years is Professor James Woodress of the University of California, Davis. Several spoke to this point, including one person who feels that "The original idea for the *ALS* series was nothing less than inspired."

The opinion poll has helped to give us a sense of our academic readership. We urge all readers to volunteer unsolicited comments and suggestions whenever you feel the urge to express yourself. This "feedback," whether favorable or critical, will be especially useful to the several contributors, who, in time of stress, may wonder if what they are doing is worth the effort.

J. Albert Robbins

Indiana University

Table of Contents

Key to Abbreviations

A-A / Klaus Lanzinger, ed., *Americana-Austriaca: Beiträg zur Amerikakunde*, Vol. 2 (Vienna, Wilhelm Braumüller)
ABC / *American Book Collector*
ABR / *American Benedictine Review*
AForum / *African Forum: A Quarterly Journal of Contemporary Affairs*
Agenda
AH / *American Heritage*
AL / *American Literature*
ALR / *American Literary Realism, 1870–1910*
ALS / *American Literary Scholarship: An Annual*
American Dreams / David Madden, ed., *American Dreams, American Nightmares* (Carbondale, So. Ill. Univ. Press)
Americana Norvegica / Sigmund Skard, ed., *Americana Norvegica: Norwegian Contributions to American Studies*, Vol. 2. (Philadelphia, Univ. of Pa. Press, 1969)
AN&Q / *American Notes and Queries*
AQ / *American Quarterly*
Arcadia (Berlin)
ArlQ / *Arlington Quarterly*
ArQ / *Arizona Quarterly*
Art and Error / Ronald Gottesman and Scott Bennett, ed., *Art and Error: Modern Textual Editing* (Bloomington, Ind. Univ. Press)
AtM / *Atlantic Monthly*
ATQ / *American Transcendental Quarterly*
AW / *American West*
AWR / *The Anglo-Welsh Review* (Pembroke Dock, Wales)
BB / *Bulletin of Bibliography*

BC / *Book Collector*
Black World (formerly *Negro Digest*)
BNYPL / *Bulletin of the New York Public Library*
BRMMLA / *Bulletin of the Rocky Mountain Modern Language Assn.*
Brotéria
BS / *Black Scholar* (San Francisco)
BSCB / *Birmingham-Southern College Bulletin*
BSUF / *Ball State University Forum*
Cabellian / *The Cabellian: A Journal of the Second American Renaissance*
Calamus (Tokyo)
CalR / *Calcutta Review*
CE / *College English*
CEA / *CEA Critic* (College English Assn.)
CEAA / Center for Editions of American Authors
CEAAN / *Center for Editions of American Authors Newsletter* (MLA)
Celebration / Richard H. Rupp, *Celebration in Postwar American Fiction, 1945–1967* (Miami, Fla., Univ. of Miami Press)
CentR / *The Centennial Review* (Mich. State Univ.)
CimR / *Cimarron Review* (Okla. State Univ.)
Cithara (St. Bonaventure Univ.)
CL / *Comparative Literature*
CLAJ / *CLA Journal* (College Language Assn.)
CLS / *Comparative Literature Studies*
CO / *Chronicles of Oklahoma*
ColQ / *Colorado Quarterly*
Comentário (Rio de Janeiro)
CompD / *Comparative Drama*

ConL / Contemporary Literature
ConnR / Connecticut Review
Courier / The Courier (Syracuse Univ.)
CP / Concerning Poetry (Western Wash. State Coll.)
CR / The Critical Review (Melbourne, Sydney)
CRAS / Canadian Review of American Studies (Montreal)
Crit / Critique: Studies in Modern Fiction
Criticism (Wayne State Univ.)
Critique (Paris)
CritQ / Critical Quarterly
CWCP / Contemporary Writers in Christian Perspective (Grand Rapids, Mich., William B. Eerdmans)
D&T / Drama and Theatre (State Univ. Coll. of N. Y., Fredonia)
Dædalus
DAI / Dissertation Abstracts International
DeltaR / Delta Review (Miss. State Coll.)
Discourse (Concordia Coll.)
DR / Dalhousie Review
EA / Etudes anglaises
EAL / Early American Literature
ECS / Eighteenth-Century Studies (Univ. of Calif., Davis)
Edda (Oslo)
EDB / Emily Dickinson Bulletin
EigoS / Eigo Seinen [The Rising Generation] (Tokyo)
EIHC / Essex Institute Historical Collections
EJ / English Journal
ELH / ELH, Journal of English Literary History
ELLS / English Literature and Language (Tokyo)
ELN / English Language Notes (Univ. of Colo.)
Encounter (London)
ER / English Record
ES / English Studies
ESQ / Emerson Society Quarterly
Essays / Thomas G. Burton, ed. *Essays in Memory of Christine Burleson in Language and Liter-*

ature by Former Colleagues and Students (Johnson City, Research Advisory Council, East Tenn. State Univ., 1969)
ETJ / Educational Theatre Journal
Expl / Explicator
FH / Frankfurter Hefte
FHA / Fitzgerald-Hemingway Annual, edited by Matthew J. Bruccoli and C. E. Frazer Clark, Jr.
FJ / Faculty Journal (East Stroudsburg State Coll.)
Forms of Lyric / Reuben A. Brower, ed., *Forms of Lyric: Selected Papers from the English Institute* (New York, Columbia Univ. Press)
GaR / Georgia Review
Genre (Univ. of Ill. at Chicago Circle)
Hasifrut (Tel-Aviv Univ.)
HC / The Hollins Critic (Hollins Coll., Va.)
HLB / Harvard Library Bulletin
HMPEC / Historical Magazine of the Protestant Episcopal Church
HSL / Hartford Studies in Literature
HudR / Hudson Review
Husson Rev / Husson Review (Husson Coll.)
IEJ / Indiana English Journal
IEY / Iowa English Yearbook
IF / Indiana Folklore
Indian Essays / Sujit Mukherjee and D. V. K. Raghavacharyulu, eds., *Indian Essays in American Literature: Papers in Honour of Robert E. Spiller* (Bombay, Popular Prakashan)
IndL / Indian Literature (New Delhi)
IowaR / Iowa Review (Univ. of Iowa)
JA / Jahrbuch für Amerikastudien
JAF / Journal of American Folklore
JAMA / Journal of the American Medical Association
JAmS / Journal of American Studies
JHS / Journal of Historical Studies (Princeton, N.J.)
JGE / Journal of General Education
JLN / Jack London Newsletter

JMiH / *Journal of Mississippi History*
JML / *Journal of Modern Literature*
(Temple Univ.)
JPC / *Journal of Popular Culture*
JPH / *Journal of Presbyterian History*
JRUL / *Journal of the Rutgers
University Library*
JSH / *Journal of Southern History*
Judaism
KAL / *Kyushu American Literature*
(Fukuoka, Japan)
KanQ / *Kansas Quarterly*
KFQ / *Keystone Folklore Quarterly*
KFR / *Kentucky Folklore Record*
KuL / *Kunst und Literatur*
Kyoritsu Essays / *Collected Essays by
the Members of the Faculty,
Kyoritsu Women's Junior College,*
no. 13 (Kyoritsu, Japan)
L&P / *Literature and Psychology*
(Univ. of Hartford)
Lang&S / *Language and Style*
LanM / *Les Langues Modernes*
LaS / *Louisiana Studies*
LaUR / *Lakehead University Review*
(Port Arthur, Ontario)
LauR / *Laurel Review* (West
Virginia Wesleyan Coll.)
LC / *Library Chronicle* (Univ. of Pa.)
LCrit / *Literary Criterion* (Univ. of
Mysore)
LE&W / *Literature East and West*
LHR / *Lock Haven Review* (Lock
Haven State College, Pa.)
LHY / *Literary Half-Yearly*
(Univ. of Mysore)
LitM / *Literary Monographs*, Vol. 3
(Madison, Univ. of Wis. Press)
LJ / *Library Journal*
LWU / *Literatur in Wissenschaft
und Unterricht* (Kiel)
Markham Rev / *Markham Review*
(Wagner Coll.)
MASJ / *Midcontinent American
Studies Journal*
MD / *Modern Drama*
Medieval Literature / Jerome Mandel
and Bruce A. Rosenberg, eds.,
*Medieval Literature and Folklore
Studies* (New Brunswick, N. J.,
Rutgers Univ. Studies)
MFR / *Mississippi Folklore Register*

MFS / *Modern Fiction Studies*
MHSB / *Missouri Historical Society
Bulletin*
MichA / *Michigan Academician*
Midway
MinnR / *Minnesota Review*
MissQ / *Mississippi Quarterly*
MLA / Modern Language Assn.
MLQ / *Modern Language Quarterly*
Modern American Poetry / Jerome
Mazzaro, ed., *Modern American
Poetry: Essays in Criticism* (New
York, David McKay Co.)
*Mosaic: A Journal for the Comparative
Study of Literature and Ideas*
MPS / *Modern Poetry Studies*
(Buffalo, N. Y.).
MQR / *Michigan Quarterly Review*
MR / *Massachusetts Review*
MSE / *Massachusetts Studies in
English*
MTJ / *Mark Twain Journal*
N&Q / *Notes and Queries*
NALF / *Negro American Literature
Forum*
NAS / *Norwegian-American Studies*
(Northfield, Minn.)
NCarF / *North Carolina Folklore*
NCF / *Nineteenth-Century Fiction*
NEG / *New England Galaxy*
NegroD / *Negro Digest*
NEMLA-N / *New England Modern
Language Association Newsletter*
NEQ / *New England Quarterly*
NH / *Nebraska History*
NJH / *New Jersey History*
NLH / *New Literary History*
NM / *Neuphilologische Mitteilungen*
NMW / *Notes on Mississippi Writers*
NOQ / *Northwest Ohio Quarterly*
Novel: A Forum on Fiction
NS / *Die neueren Sprachen*
NY / *New Yorker*
NYFQ / *New York Folklore
Quarterly*
NYHSQ / *New York Historical So-
ciety Quarterly*
NYRB / *New York Review of Books*
NYTBR / *New York Times Book
Review*
Oberon

PAAS / *Proceedings of the American Antiquarian Society*

PAH / *Perspectives in American History*

PAPS / *Proceedings of the American Philosophical Society*

PBSA / *Papers of the Bibliographical Society of America*

PCP / *Pacific Coast Philology*

PE&W / *Philosophy East and West* (Honolulu)

Person / *The Personalist*

PH / *Pennsylvania History*

Phylon

PLL / *Papers on Language and Literature*

PMHB / *Pennsylvania Magazine of History and Biography*

PMLA / *PMLA, Publications of the Modern Language Association*

PN / *Poe Newsletter* (Wash. State Univ.)

PR / *Partisan Review*

Private Dealings / David J. Burrows, Lewis M. Dabney, Milne Holton, Grosvener E. Powell, *Private Dealings: Eight Modern American Writers* (Stockholm, Almqvist and Wiksell)

Project Occult / George R. Petty, Jr., and William M. Gibson, *Project Occult: The Ordered Computer Collation of Unprepared Literary Text* (New York, New York Univ. Press)

Prose (New York, N.Y.)

PrS / *Prairie Schooner*

PS / *Pensiero e Scuola* (Chieti, Italy)

PsychiatricQ / *Psychiatric Quarterly*

QH / *Quaker History: Bulletin of the Friends Historical Assn.*

QJLC / *Quarterly Journal of the Library of Congress*

QJS / *Quarterly Journal of Speech*

QQ / *Queen's Quarterly*

Renascence

Rendezvous: Journal of Arts and Letters

Review / *The Review, A Magazine of Poetry and Criticism* (London)

RKHS / *Register of the Kentucky Historical Society*

RLC / *Revue de littérature comparée*

RLM / *La revue des lettres modernes*

RLV / *Revue des langues vivantes*

RMS / *Renaissance and Modern Studies* (Univ. of Nottingham)

RR / *Romanic Review*

RS / *Research Studies* (Washington State Univ.)

S&S / *Science and Society*

SA / *Studi americani*

SAB / *South Atlantic Bulletin*

SAQ / *South Atlantic Quarterly*

SBL / *Studies in Black Literature* (Mary Washington College of the Univ. of Va.)

SCB / *South Central Bulletin*

SCN / *Seventeenth-Century News*

SCR / *South Carolina Review* (formerly *Furman Studies*)

SEL / *Studies in English Literature, 1500–1900*

SELit / *Studies in English Literature* (English Literary Society of Japan, Univ. of Tokyo)

Serif / *The Serif* (Kent State Univ., Ohio)

SF&R / Scholars' Facsimiles and Reprints (Gainesville, Fla.)

SFQ / *Southern Folklore Quarterly*

Shaken Realist / Melvin J. Friedman and John B. Vickery, eds., *The Shaken Realist: Essays in Modern Literature in Honor of Frederick J. Hoffman* (Baton Rouge, La. State Univ. Press)

Shenandoah

SHR / *Southern Humanities Review*

SIR / *Studies in Romanticism*

SlavR / *Slavic Review* (Seattle)

SLitI / *Studies in the Literary Imagination* (Ga. State Coll.)

SLJ / *Southern Literary Journal*

SLN / *Sinclair Lewis Newsletter*

SNNTS / *Studies in the Novel* (N. Tex. State Univ.)

SoQ / *The Southern Quarterly* (Univ. of So. Miss.)

SoR / *Southern Review*

SoRA / *Southern Review: An Australian Journal of Literary Studies* (Univ. of Adelaide)

Sou'wester (So. Ill. University, Edwardsville)

Spirit: A Magazine of Poetry (Seton Hall Univ.)

SR / Sewanee Review

SSF / Studies in Short Fiction

SSJ / Southern Speech Journal

StAR / St. Andrews Review (St. Andrews Presbyterian Coll.)

StQ / Steinbeck Quarterly (formerly *Steinbeck Newsletter*)

Studies (Dublin)

Style

Sur (Buenos Aires)

Survival of Poetry / Martin Dodsworth, ed., *The Survival of Poetry: A Contemporary Survey* (London, Faber and Faber)

SWR / Southwest Review

SWS / Southwest Writers Series (Austin, Texas, Steck-Vaughn Co.)

SXX / Secolul XX (Bucharest)

TCL / Twentieth Century Literature

TD / Theatre Documentation (New York)

TDR / The Drama Review

TFSB / Tennessee Folklore Society Bulletin

The Forties / Warren French, ed., *The Forties: Fiction, Poetry, Drama* (Deland, Fla., Everett / Edwards, 1969)

Themes and Directions / Ray B. Browne and Donald Pizer, eds., *Themes and Directions in American Literature: Essays in Honor of Leon Howard* (Lafayette, Ind., Purdue Univ. Studies, 1969)

Thoth (Syracuse Univ.)

Thought

THQ / Tennessee Historical Quarterly

TJQ / Thoreau Journal Quarterly

TLS / Times Literary Supplement (London)

TN / Theatre Notebook

TQ / Texas Quarterly (University of Texas)

TransR / Transatlantic Review (London)

TriQ / Tri-Quarterly

TS / Theatre Survey

TSB / Thoreau Society Bulletin

TSL / Tennessee Studies in Literature

TSLL / Texas Studies in Literature and Language

TUSAS / Twayne United States Authors series (New York, Twayne Publishers)

UCQ / University College Quarterly (Michigan State Univ.)

UHQ / Utah Historical Quarterly

UMPAW / University of Minnesota Pamphlets on American Writers

Under the Sign of Pisces: Anaïs Nin and her Circle (Ohio State Univ.)

UR / University Review (Kansas City, Mo.)

UTMS / University of Tulsa Monograph Series

UTQ / University of Toronto Quarterly

VH / Vermont History

VLit / Voprosy literatury (Moscow)

VMHB / Virginia Magazine of History and Biography

VQR / Virginia Quarterly Review

WAL / Western American Literature

WF / Western Folklore

WGCR / West Georgia College Review

WHR / Western Humanities Review

WMQ / William and Mary Quarterly

WR / Western Review

WSinL / Wisconsin Studies in Literature (Oshkosh)

WWR / Walt Whitman Review

Yankee (Dublin, N. H.)

YR / Yale Review

Part I

1. Emerson, Thoreau, and Transcendentalism

John C. Broderick

In 1970 "scholarship that matters" was not abundant concerning Emerson, Thoreau, and the Transcendentalists, despite the numerous entries eligible for inclusion in a comprehensive checklist. A few substantial articles, another volume in the exemplary edition of Emerson's journals, and one or two contributions off the beaten track—these constitute the items indispensable to future study. One characteristic of American scholarship for the year was its preoccupation with the poetry of the Transcendentalists, that of Emerson, Thoreau, and Jones Very in particular.

Meriting special attention is the unique and handsomely presented *Thoreau Gazetteer* by Robert F. Stowell, edited by William L. Howarth (Princeton, Princeton Univ. Press). It is a domestic and contemporary counterpart to John F. Christie's *Thoreau as World Traveler*. Included are reproductions of Thoreau's own maps, contemporary maps which provide visual orientation for his numerous journeys, some photographs by Herbert Gleason which illuminate scenes described in Thoreau's journal, informative headnotes, a chronology of Thoreau's travels, and a seemingly all-inclusive index of place names, likely to be one of its most serviceable features. (The volume bears little resemblance to the portfolio of maps and reproductions issued privately by Stowell in 1948.) Though not without some slips (it is the Geography and Map Division at the Library of Congress, not vice versa, a mistake that occurs four out of five times), it well deserves its designation as a supplement to *The Writings of Henry David Thoreau*, a CEAA edition now being prepared for publication, also by the Princeton University Press. In addition to the benefits which students of Thoreau are certain to derive from the publication, *A Thoreau Gazetteer* is a "picture book" which competes favorably with the Sierra Club volume, *In Wildness Is the Preserva-*

tion of the World, though their attractions are complementary, not identical.

i. Texts, Editions, Bibliographies

Volume 8 of *The Journals and Miscellaneous Notebooks of Ralph Waldo Emerson* (Cambridge, Harvard Univ. Press), though actually published early in 1971, carries a 1970 imprint date, entitling it to consideration in this report. Volume 8 is a companion volume to its predecessor and overlaps it in date and topical interest. From the technical standpoint, the recovery of numerous erased passages (especially of verse) is notable. These include, for example, the earliest lines in response to the death of Emerson's son Waldo. The movement from acquiescence to skepticism and turmoil (from "The Method of Nature" to "Experience") is the acknowledged pattern of these years (1841–1843), but there is no consecutivity apparent in this volume. Emerson's mind moved by fits and starts, and no easy formulation does justice to its complexities. There are surprising features to these journals. Considering the fact that the years covered by volume 8 are identical with Thoreau's first residence in Emerson's home, the younger man's relative absence from the journals is strange, almost spooky. Margaret Fuller, Bronson Alcott, even Edmund Hosmer are more nearly pervading presences than the young man to whom he was supplying room and board for services rendered. To follow up these and other questions about Emerson's life and work, the Harvard edition of the journals is making itself indispensable. The editors (particularly the chief editor, William H. Gilman) continue to deserve our laurels (and rhodoras too, for that matter).

Gilman has restated the "original rationale" of the edition in *CEAAN* 3:26–27.[1] Since that "original rationale" varies in a few respects from some fixed principles of the CEAA, the Emerson editors deposit lists of unreported normalizations in designated libraries. A counterpart statement by J. Lyndon Shanley in *CEAAN* 3:24–25 concerning the edition of Thoreau's journal now in preparation indicates an approach entirely different from that of the Emerson editors. The Thoreau editors will provide "a complete and accurate transcription in clear-text of what Thoreau first wrote in the manuscript notebooks

---

1. A more elaborate *apologia* for the editorial method, which appeared in *EAL* in 1971, will be noticed in the next volume of *ALS*.

that constitute the *Journal*" without indication of revisions in the text itself and not all revisions in the apparatus. (Editors of Thoreau's journal, struggling with the vagaries of his script, may find comfort in the analysis of Thoreau's handwriting by Lynn and Bill Lee, New York graphologists, in *TSB* 113:4–5, who describe it as "an arcadian linear hand composed of angles and thread, without a trace of the softening garland.")

Lauriat Lane's " 'Civil Disobedience': A Bibliographical Note" (*PBSA* 63[1969]:295–96) has implications concerning its interpretation as well. In its first printing ("Resistance to Civil Government," *Aesthetic Papers*, 1849), the specific account of the night in jail was set off from the rest of the essay typographically. In its posthumous printing in *A Yankee in Canada* (1866), the same passage was set in reduced type. This separation has not been uniformly observed in later editions, with the result that the special character of that portion of the essay is obscured.

The Merrill Checklist of Ralph Waldo Emerson, compiled by Alfred R. Ferguson (Columbus, Ohio, Charles E. Merrill), is a brief and selective listing. The quarterly checklists of comment on Thoreau continue to appear in *TSB*, all issues.

ii. Biography, Literary History, Sources and Influence

Except for *Emerson, Our Contemporary* by the late August Derleth (London, Crowell-Collier Press), aimed at juveniles, there are no book-length biographies to report and few biographical studies of any kind.[2] "The Severity of the Ideal: Emerson's 'Thoreau,' " by Leonard Neufeldt (*ESQ* 58:77–84), however, addresses itself to a fundamental biographical question, the rift between Emerson and Thoreau, which began in the 1840s, intensified in the 1850s, and was only partially resolved in the months before Thoreau's death. Neufeldt dates Emerson's cooling toward Thoreau from the mid-1840s, about the time Thoreau moved to Walden, and relates it to the skeptical mood which was beginning to change Emerson's philosophy and conduct of life and the essays of that period. In brief, Emerson

2. An exception is George E. Bell, "Emerson and Baltimore: A Biographical Study" (*Maryland History Magazine* 65:331–68), which provides many details of local history organized around Emerson's visits of 1827, 1843, 1859, and 1872. There is also some discussion of Emerson's views of the South.

came to doubt moral absolutism just at the moment Thoreau chose to enact it in dramatic ways at Walden Pond and Concord jail. Neufeldt provides a fresh reading of Emerson's funeral eulogy of Thoreau, demonstrating its ironic detachment from the subject and rejection of Thoreau's implacability. He has also studied to good effect the manuscript of the address (in the Huntington Library), the revisions of which validate his thesis.

J. Wade Caruthers, in "Who Was Octavius Brooks Frothingham?" (*NEQ* 43:631–37), provides a brief general review of the life and work of the man who was the link between Channing, Parker, and Emerson and modern Unitarian thought, if indeed he does not rival these "giants" in the American intellectual tradition.

Amerika: Vision und Wirklichkeit, edited by Franz H. Link (Frankfurt, Athenäum Verlag, 1968), contains a general essay by Walther Fischer, "Henry David Thoreau (1817–1862), der Dichter des *Walden-Sees* (1854)," pp. 97–113. Fischer emphasizes Thoreau's relation to his own time and the unique opportunities afforded by relaxation of the last fetters of Puritan restraint. Thoreau's genius resides in the combination of the practical and romantic (the wagon which he hitched to a star was a New England vehicle). Although he seriously overestimated his own narrow environment, even that form of local patriotism had a beneficial effect on his writing, which betrays nothing unclear or uncertain. He came at a unique moment for genuine national literary performance.

Jesse Bier, "Weberism, Franklin, and the Transcendental Style" (*NEQ* 43:179–92), is also interested in the times of Emerson and Thoreau and finds in their work "the last clear literary reflex of the Protestant ethic and the spirit of capitalism." Although their writings represent a development away from "a strict Franklinian pragmatism and a narrow cost-analysis of experience," they do not transcend the ethic which they inherited, as their vocabularies and styles show. They are "brothers in the flesh" with Franklin. Both Emerson and Thoreau speak in terms of cost, work as a calling, a belief in self-improvement, and a dedication to life-experiment. Bier neglects to make use of the most sophisticated analysis of Thoreau's view of economic man, *After Walden* (1957) by the late Leo Stoller, an oversight which is especially surprising because part of Stoller's book was originally published in *NEQ*.

A less ambitious venture in literary history is Bernard Rosenthal,

"*The Dial*, Transcendentalism, and Margaret Fuller" (*ELN* 8:28–36). Rosenthal thinks it a mistake to construe *The Dial*, especially those issues of 1840–1842, as the journal of the American Transcendentalists. It was the journal of Margaret Fuller, an interpretation supported by the volume of her personal contribution, by her rejection of Thoreau's *The Service* and other contributions urged upon her by Emerson, and by the change in character in *The Dial* when Emerson succeeded her as editor. The point is granted, but it is hardly one that has been entirely overlooked. (See *ALS 1969*, p. 14, s.v. Hopkins and Poger, not to mention George Willis Cooke's *Historical and Biographical Introduction to "The Dial"* [1902].)

It is difficult to overestimate the importance to New England Transcendentalism of the publication in 1829 of James Marsh's edition of Coleridge's *Aids to Reflection*, with Marsh's own influential "Preliminary Essay." According to John J. Duffy ("Problems in Publishing Coleridge: James Marsh's First American Edition of *Aids to Reflection*," *NEQ* 43:193–208), Marsh had serious misgivings about the effect his edition might have among leaders of the conservative theological establishment. He sought to disarm criticism in advance, sought to secure reviews from Francis Wayland and others, and solicited from Coleridge himself some ammunition with which to defend himself against criticism. Ironically, Marsh failed of acceptance during his lifetime only with those, such as Archibald Alexander and Charles Hodge, whom he had assiduously courted.

Among source studies, Georg Fridén's "Transcendental Idealism in New England" (*NM* 69[1968]:256–71) is a general review on an elementary level, but with a good command of literary scholarship on the subject, of classical, European, Oriental, and American sources of transcendental ideas. More limited is Ernest J. Moyne, "Thoreau and Emerson: Their Interest in Finland" (*NM* 70[1969]:738–50), which gathers various references by the two writers to Finland and things Finnish. Most of the article concerns Thoreau's interest in Peter Kalm and his citation of Kalm in *A Yankee in Canada*, "Chesuncook," and *Cape Cod*.

In "The Hindu Matrix of *Walden*: The King's Son" (*CL* 22:303–18) William Bysshe Stein argues that chapter 2 of *Walden* ("Where I Lived and What I Lived For") recapitulates Thoreau's "mastery of the successive states of Yoga." The imagery of awakening which dominates the chapter, Stein believes, has been understood in too limited a fashion. It is actually a mode of the Self's awakening, as typified by the story of the King's son, which he regards as a climax of the chapter. The Hindu lore which presumably underlies Thoreau's achievement, he derived from William Ward's *View of History*, reprinted by Stein (see *ALS 1967*, p. 6.)[3] According to David G. Hoch, "Thoreau's Source for the Story of the King's Son," *TJQ* 2:10–12, Thoreau probably read the *Sankhya Karika* in the Harvard library.

The "King's Son" bids fair to rival "the artist of Kouroo" among the dramatis personae of *Walden* subject to scholarly exegesis. He also occupies a central place in the argument of Joseph R. Millichap, "Plato's Allegory of the Cave and the Vision of *Walden*" (*ELN* 7:274–82). That story, the allusion to Mammoth Cave which precedes it, the references to Plato in "Reading"—all these seem to Millichap to entitle *The Republic* to more acknowledgement than it has received as a source of aesthetic concepts by which Thoreau conveys his discovery of a new self-image.

In an article of equal interest to students of Melville and of the Transcendentalists, Herschel Parker discusses "Melville's Satire of Emerson and Thoreau: An Evaluation of the Evidence" (*ATQ* 7:61–67), specifically in *The Confidence-Man*. Parker admits that the case was too broadly put by its original spokesman, Egbert S. Oliver, but a case exists, based on letters, marginalia, family history, and other evidence, some of which was not available to Oliver or to Elizabeth Foster. Parker's article is a specific reply to Sidney P. Moss (see *ALS 1968*, pp. 9, 39–40). Conclusion: Melville *was* anti-transcendental and *did* satirize Emerson and Thoreau in *The Confidence-Man*. Q.E.D.

Two brief notes (*ESQ* 58:111, 157–59) provide additional verification of Emerson's influence upon Emily Dickinson and Robert Frost. Finally, there is interest of a negative kind in Morton Nirenberg, *The Reception of American Literature in German Periodicals, 1820–1850* (Heidelberg, Carl Winter). The Transcendentalists, who must have been the chief sponsors of German literature during the period, had no reception in German periodicals, which were hospitable to Cooper, Irving, Paulding, and even Lydia M. Child, but, to judge from Nirenberg's discussion, not Margaret Fuller, Theodore Parker, or Emerson.

3. I was unable to see Stein's essay, "The *Yoga* of *Walden*: Chapter I (Economy)," *LE&W* 13[1969]:1–26.

iii. Criticism: Poetry

There seems to be a renewed interest in the poetry of the Transcendentalists. This may be the result of the central place accorded Emerson in Hyatt H. Waggoner's *American Poets from the Puritans to the Present* (Boston: Houghton Mifflin, 1968), a work which has not, I believe, received the discussion it merits in *ALS*. Its discovery of Emersonian influences and echoes in both likely and unlikely twentieth-century poets will invite corroborative and corrective studies. Its persuasive discussion of Emerson's merits as a poet will undoubtedly lead to more detailed reconsiderations of the poetry.

One scholar who has enlarged understanding of Emerson's poetry whether it was momentarily in or out of fashion is Carl F. Strauch. In "The Mind's Voice: Emerson's Poetic Styles" (*ESQ* 60:43–59), he identifies a number of styles and traces their origins. For some basic techniques Emerson is indebted to Sampson Reed (correspondence), Milton (the Miltonic catalog line), and Wordsworth (the clipped line to open, break, or close a passage of blank verse). Also of great importance was the Bardic tradition, which led Emerson to experiment with gnomic, runic lines in "Hamatreya," the ode to Channing, and others. Strauch regards Emerson's poetry as experimental, both in the verse and in larger poetic techniques. The poetic masks which he created (Uriel, Merlin, Saadi) permitted him to achieve distance from emotions and feelings of considerable immediacy. There is also in Emerson's verse the bemused Yankee—the predecessor of Frost. Emerson's development as a poet, according to Strauch, was a development in style and voice, not in vision. He succeeds (as in "Uriel" and "The Snow Storm") when the technique works.

In a general essay, "The Poetry of Henry David Thoreau" (*ESQ* 61:1–26), also published separately by Transcendental Books, Arthur L. Ford places Thoreau "somewhere between Emerson's prescription and Whitman's practice—often conventional and hesitant, nevertheless a step in the direction of freedom and innovation." A reader coming to Ford's essay from a reading of Strauch, however (as in a *seriatim* reading of *ESQ* he would), will find it difficult to regard Thoreau's poetry as freer or more innovative than that of Emerson. Ford's discussion is most helpful perhaps in discussing Thoreau's tetrameters and the rationale of his fondness for puns and paradoxes. The young Thoreau, we know, wrote a great deal of poetry, a practice which he almost abruptly stopped in the early 1840s. Lauriat Lane, Jr., in "Finding a Voice: Thoreau's Pentameters" (*ESQ* 60:67–72), believes that he did so because the rhythms of his verse grew so close to his prose rhythms that he could no longer keep the two separated. Lane does not discount the obvious explanations (the advice of friends, the attraction to science, and so on), but invites attention to literary influences by pointing out how Thoreau's last poems are in the *Walden* mode and voice. Mary S. Mattfield's emendation for Thoreau's Poem No. 189 (in Bode's edition) (*CEA* 33,i:10–12), should find acceptance. She suggests "eaves were rabbeted" for "caves were rabitted." Neither Bode nor Mattfield, apparently, has actually examined the manuscript in the Huntington Library.

The most active student of transcendental poetry in 1970 was Carl Dennis, who published essays on Thoreau's poetry (*ESQ* 58: 101–09), on Emerson's poetry (*ESQ* 58:139–53), and on Jones Very's poetry (*NEQ* 43:250–73). (There was also an essay on *Walden* which employed the same theoretical framework, "The Balance of *Walden*" [*TJQ* 2:19].) All of these derive from a dissertation discussed in *ALS 1967*, pp. 5–6. The essay on Very, "Correspondence in Very's Nature Poetry," is the most substantial of the four. Dennis sees a unity of theory and practice among the major transcendental poets. Whereas the British Romantics held two different and even contradictory conceptions of the mind's relation to nature (nature as beneficent active force or nature as passive matter to be shaped by the creative imagination), the Transcendentalists were remarkably consistent. The key to the transcendental aesthetic is "correspondence." The poet does not impose meaning on the world; he discovers it by an act of sympathy. Of the three, Very is clearest, for reasons not necessarily to the theoretical credit of his poetry, for Emerson is frequently ambiguous as nature itself is ambiguous. Thoreau is most concerned with nature as language.

iv. Criticism: Prose

In 1939 Henry Nash Smith introduced the question of "vocation" to consideration of Emerson's "The American Scholar." The intervening publication of the early lectures and the journals and miscellaneous notebooks has made possible a more detailed and sophisticated analysis of the strata underlying the essay's surface. This has now been provided in Merton M. Sealts, Jr.'s "Emerson on the Scholar, 1833–1837" (*PMLA* 85:185–95). The key antecedents are the lecture series on natural history, reflecting the enthusiasm for science with which Emerson returned from France; the lecture series on biography, in which no scientist appeared, indicating Emerson's realization that science was not his answer; the series on English literature, suggestive of Emerson's growing admiration of the Miltonic truth-teller, a role to which he began to aspire; *Nature*, with its stress on originality and creativity; and the essay on education, the natural preliminary to "The American Scholar." Although the manuscript of the address has not survived, more than one-third of it is traceable to journal and lecture passages, making possible the kind of reconstruction of the method of composition, which Sealts's article provides.

The relationship of early lectures to later essays and of Bacon to both is the subject of Ralph C. LaRosa, "Bacon and the 'Organic Method' of Emerson's Early Lectures" (*ELN* 8:107–14). Emerson's early admiration for Bacon is well known, but by the time of his 1835 lecture Emerson found fault with Bacon's essays as "a vast collection of proverbs," lacking in organic method. Emerson nevertheless admired such *sententiae* and accumulated them in his own journals for later use. (LaRosa lists some of these in "Emerson's Sententiae in *Nature*," *ESQ* 58:153–57.) Although Emerson attempted to achieve an organic, progressive arrangement in his lectures, balancing appeals to the Understanding and the Reason, his lecture audiences responded most to the individual *sententiae*. Because the essays could be prepared without reference to the requirements of the audience, they are more successful in achieving the balance Emerson sought. (William M. Wynkoop, *Three Children of the Universe: Emerson's Views of Shakespeare, Bacon, and Milton* [see *ALS 1966*, pp. 7–8], had already gone over some of this ground, though not precisely in the same way.)

Emerson's prose style and method were also the subject of R. A. Yoder, "Emerson's Dialectic" (*Criticism* 11[1969]:313–28) and Alfred S. Reid, "Emerson's Prose Style: An Edge to Goodness" (*ESQ* 60:37–42). Reid sees in Emerson's aphoristic style evidence of an inspirational though doctrinaire personality. Yoder's article refutes W. T. Harris, Blair and Faust, et al. on a Platonic dialectic in the

essays. He finds various structures: "parallel dichotomies" ("The
Over-Soul"); thesis-antithesis ("Compensation"); variations on a
theme ("Experience").

The styles of both Emerson and Thoreau (and Carlyle as well)
are subjected to a linguistic analysis by Donald Ross, Jr., in "Composition as a Stylistic Feature" (*Style* 4:1–10). The exhibits are "Discipline" in *Nature* and "Solitude" in *Walden* (plus the brief chapter
on Morrison's Pill in *Past and Present*). Thoreau is considered the
most idiosyncratic of the three stylists since he does not employ the
usual lexical, grammatical, or rhetorical unifying devices for his
chapter. In fact, "Solitude" seems disorganized until the next-to-last
paragraph which pulls the chapter together by repeating all the key
words used earlier (some of which are virtually unique to this chapter). Ross adjudges Emerson the most formal of the three in his use
of rhetorical devices such as "lexical equivalent chains" (pronouns
and their antecedents). This is an interesting approach, and the discussion of Thoreau's method is genuinely illuminating. The remarks
on Emerson are less useful since *Nature* (despite its importance) is
not a typical specimen of Emerson's mature style. With its "firstlies"
and so on it seems more the last example of a pulpit style even then
being transcended.

Among several studies of Thoreau's prose style, that of Eugene F.
Timpe goes beyond the impressionistic and subjective. In "Thoreau's
Developing Style" (*ESQ* 58:120–23), he analyzes three manuscripts
of the Sir Walter Raleigh essay plus the version which appeared in
A Week on the Concord and Merrimack Rivers. In his revisions, Thoreau sought a studied natural movement and poetic order. He was
also preoccupied with diction and imagistic precision.

According to Edward L. Galligan, "The Comedian at Walden
Pond" (*SAQ* 69:20–37), *Walden* is a comedy because 1) it is optimistic and has a happy ending; 2) it has many funny things in it;
3) it has a comic hero; 4) it has a comic vision and comic strategies.
Galligan's avowed purpose is to combat Perry Miller and Sherman
Paul, who have taken insufficient account of Thoreau's self-ridiculing
gestures and images. The essential need is to distinguish Thoreau
from the hero of the book ("I"). Although gracefully and vigorously
presented, this analysis adds nothing to Charles Anderson's in *The
Magic Circle of Walden* (1968), to say nothing of the essays of Joseph Moldenhauer and others even earlier. M. Thomas Inge, "Tho-

reau's Enduring Laugh" (*TJQ* 2,iv:1–9), also seeks to salvage Thoreau's reputation as a wit, assuming it to be neglected.[4]

There are three other studies of Thoreau's style. Kenneth Kurtz, "Style in *Walden*" (*ESQ* 60:59–67), points out two styles, literal for description and figurative for philosophical portions. William Reger, on the other hand, argues in "Beyond Metaphor" (*Criticism* 12:333–44), that *Walden* ought to be read as "matter-of-fact statement." On the face of it, "*Walden* is a book about farming." Reger's impatience with symbol hunting may appeal even to those unwilling to adopt so stringent a view of *Walden*. Carl Nelson offers a brief linguistic study of the unifying "O" sound in "Sound Knowledge in *Walden*" (*TJQ* 2, iii:1–6), associating it with Hindu sound meditation.

v. Criticism: Ideas

What are the essential characteristics of American transcendental literature? For a generation or more, the grand triumvirate of organicism, dynamism, and diversitarianism have reigned, with one or another of the troika in momentary command. To the extent that a consensus prevailed, it owed much to the early studies of A. O. Lovejoy, to the theoretical framework for organicism provided by Stephen Pepper in *World Hypotheses* (1942), and to the practical criticism of Morse Peckham, Richard P. Adams, and others. Peckham enunciated his view of Romantic literature in 1951 and a decade later modified it significantly. Now Richard Adams, whose first publication in 1952 was an application of Peckham's formulations to American writing, recants slightly. "I now feel," he writes in "Permutations of American Romanticism," (*SIR* 9:249–68), "that the fundamental impulse of romanticism was the shift from staticism to dynamism, and that organicism was mainly a means of control, a defense against chaos, and a technical resource for writing, rather than an article of belief." When held as an article of belief, organicism led to inevitable contradictions of the sort which Adams outlined in 1969 (see *ALS 1969*, p. 7). All writers in F. O. Matthiessen's pantheon, therefore, contradicted themselves, "Emerson and Whitman most frankly and cheerfully, Thoreau less frankly, Hawthorne and Melville less cheerfully." To accept such a view will require the surrender of some

4. Evidence of Thoreau's drollery concerning coats-of-arms is presented in *TSB* 110:1 and 113:1–2.

treasured heirlooms, among them several notable interpretive articles by Adams himself. Not everyone will be willing to do so, however hospitable they may be to change. They will nevertheless wish to consult Adams's survey (which includes twentieth- as well as nineteenth-century writers).

According to Raymond Gardella, "The Tenets and Limitations of Emerson's All-Conscious Man" (*ABR* 21:375–88), the principal tenet was the priority of consciousness. The principal limitation was a failure to acknowledge man's finitude as well as his relationship with the infinite. Emerson was suspicious of all communication, except with the Universal Mind. Emerson's ethics are thereby vitiated by the "impregnable wall of defense against the finitudes of existence" created by self-reliance.

Thoreau's ethical view fares much better in the hands of Robin Linstromberg and James Ballowe, "Thoreau and Etzler: Alternative Views of Economic Reform" (*MASJ* 11:20–29). Analyzing "Paradise (to be) Regained" in the context of economic thinking of the time, the authors assert that Thoreau approaches a "viable resolution to the materialist-idealist debate in reform."

The somewhat surprising disparity between Thoreau's attacks on social and economic exploitation on the one hand and his distant treatment of the actual poor known to him is the subject of Thomas Woodson's "Thoreau on Poverty and Magnanimity" (*PMLA* 85:21–34). It is a wide-ranging essay which begins with an analysis of the neglected or misunderstood "Complemental Verses" at the end of "Economy" in *Walden* and concludes with the John Brown essays, which romanticize and mythicize Brown but show less searching sense of his character than three lines of Melville's "The Portent." According to Woodson, the "Complemental Verses" merely carry forward the discussion of philanthropy with which "Economy" ends. They do not provide equal time for rebuttal of Thoreau's point of view. In the Thomas Carew masque from which the verses are taken, Mercury rejects the pretensions of Poverty because Poverty is insufficiently magnanimous. Thoreau accepted the Elizabethan concept of magnanimity but modified it by romanticizing the actual poor, such as Minott, Rice, and Johnny Riordan, who appear in his writing as "the prince in disguise," "the royal changeling," etc. This romantic impulse governs "Civil Disobedience" as well. In the later essays, however, and especially those dealing with John Brown, Thoreau reveals the limitations of his art. The characterizations in those essays lack any dimension of tragic magnanimity, which a writer such as Melville was able to provide.

Two lesser studies deserve mention. Blakeney J. Richard, "Emerson and Berkeleian Idealism" (*ESQ* 59:90–96), points out Emerson's interest in Berkeley and similarities in their philosophies. Thoreau's anticipation of twentieth-century thinking on the value of leisure is outlined in a somewhat literal minded study by Isadore Becker, "Thoreau's Princely Leisure," (*Husson Rev* 3:161–67).

vi. Dissertations

As yet there is, perhaps regrettably, no consensus among contributors to *ALS* concerning the weight to be given the scholarly output recorded in each year's *Dissertation Abstracts*. Without descending to the cant of "trends," however, we can learn much from this source about what corners of well-ploughed fields seem to graduate students (and their advisers) to merit further cultivation and even anticipate some future harvests.

There were fifteen relevant dissertations in *DAI* for 1970, with the following symmetrical distribution: five on Emerson, five on Thoreau, two on general topics involving several American writers, in one of which Thoreau figures and Emerson in the other, and three in other disciplines, again one involving Emerson, one Thoreau, and one the Unitarian Transcendentalists generally.

The five dissertations on Emerson concern themselves, primarily, with components of Emerson's thought: Peter Anthony Obuchowski, "The Relationship of Emerson's Interest in Science to His Thought" (30:3914A–15A); John Edward Schamberger, "Emerson's Concept of the 'Moral Sense': A Study of Its Sources and Its Importance to His Intellectual Development" (31:1292A); and Carl Martin Lindner, "Ralph Waldo Emerson: The Conceptualization of Experience" (31:1233A–34A). Even Arlen Jay Hansen, "Emerson's Poetry of Thought" (30:3944A), seems almost equally interested in tenor and vehicle. Only "Emerson's Prose Style: His Created World" by Phyllis Brown Burke, (30:4937A), is fundamentally a study of Emerson's art.

The five on Thoreau, on the other hand, are all concerned with various phases of his literary artistry. Of these, two emerge from Kent State and two from Oklahoma, not known heretofore for Thoreau studies, and one (just recorded from 1967) from Columbia, where several important Thoreau dissertations were prepared in the 1950s and 1960s under the direction of Lewis Leary. "Annals and Perennials: A Study of Cosmogonic Imagery in Thoreau" by David George Hoch (30:5446A), is a study of oriental influences on his art. The concerns of the others are evident from their titles: Robert James Demott, " 'The Eccentric Orbit': Dimensions of the Artistic Process in Henry David Thoreau's Major Writings" (30:5405A–06A); Robert Kedzie Thomas, "The Tree and the Stone: Time and Space in the Works of Henry David Thoreau" (31:1776A); Emmett Loy Phillips, "A Study of Aesthetic Distance in Thoreau's *Walden*" (30:3953A); and Rosemary Whitaker, "*A Week on the Concord and Merrimack Rivers*: An Experiment in the Communication of Transcendental Experience" (31:737A).

The hero of *Walden* figures in "The Continuing Encounter: Studies of the American Romantic Hero" by Todd Michael Lieber (30:3911A), and Emerson is paired with Poe in "The Dialectic of Death in Poe, Dickinson, Emerson, and Whitman" by James Michos Hughes (31:1280A). "Emerson's Philosophy of Rhetoric" is the subject of a speech dissertation by Roberta Kay Cloer (31:848A). "The Reading Interests of Thoreau, Hawthorne, and Lanier" by Dennis Neil Ribbens (31:777A), is a library science dissertation, complete with "multiple radices" and other jargon. Finally, "American Unitarians, 1830–1865: A Study of Religious Opinion on War, Slavery, and the Union," a history dissertation by Charles Richard Denton (30:5373A–74A), is based on extensive research in published and unpublished sources.

vii. Miscellaneous

In 1970 Kenneth W. Cameron published two large compendia of the type for which he is well known. One of them, *Transcendental Reading Patterns* (Hartford, Transcendental Books), provides library charging lists from Harvard and the Athenaeum for a number of writers. There are more than 1000 titles for Theodore Parker and George Ripley and more than 2000 for James Freeman Clarke. Some of these are quite suggestive. For example, in the last quarter of 1840, shortly before launching Brook Farm, Ripley borrowed from the Athenaeum a dozen or more books on farming (Agricola's letters, and the *New England Farmer*, among others). *Contemporary Di-*

mension: An American Renaissance Literary Notebook of Newspaper Clippings (Hartford, Transcendental Books) is just that, based on an actual notebook kept by an unknown compiler from 1875 to 1895. Fully one-third of the entries have to do with James Russell Lowell, but there are ten or twelve other writers represented also. Transcendental Books also published separately some of the symposia prepared for publication in the *Emerson Society Quarterly*.

It is impossible to keep up with the active field of scholarly reprints these days. At least three publishers have brought out reprint editions of John Weiss, *Life and Letters of Theodore Parker*, for example. Nevertheless, such reprints form an important adjunct to current literary scholarship and one for which we may be properly grateful.

In a recent review of an anthology of Thoreau criticism published in 1969, Lawrence Buell questions the range and perceptiveness of commentary about Thoreau (*NEQ* 44[1971]:323–25). The libel is undoubtedly just. Criticism of Thoreau lags behind that of his great contemporaries, despite the large number of scholars and critics writing about him. One may hope that the new edition of his works and journal will have the same kind of beneficial effect that the publication of Emerson's journals and lectures has had. If it does, the elaborate mechanism of CEAA editions will have more than justified itself.

Library of Congress

2. Hawthorne

Nina Baym

The year's work on Hawthorne includes two interpretive books, a substantial collection of critical reviews written by his contemporaries, a volume of the Centenary edition (*Our Old Home*), a special number of *Studies in the Novel*, as well as something like a dozen dissertations, the same number of brief notes, and perhaps thirty articles. Arlin Turner edited a collection of critical essays for the Merrill Studies series, and Hyatt H. Waggoner reissued his *Selected Tales and Sketches* (Holt) with an updated introduction. The Garrett Press reprinted Hawthorne's biography of Franklin Pierce, with a foreword by Richard G. Robey. Much of the year's new material—as is perhaps inevitable when the quantity is so great—rephrases or rearranges interpretations already current, or provides at the most some minor variation on a moot point; at the same time, there is evidence of vigor and informed exploration in the criticism. The notes are concerned, as notes always are, with sources, parallels, and explications of brief cruxes, and I shall mostly omit them from the discussion which follows. The dissertation titles suggest, in the main, traditional approaches to Hawthorne criticism, and they will not be considered here. Some 1969 articles which escaped the bibliographer's net last year will be taken up in this review.

i. Texts, Reputation, Life, Bibliography

The 1970 volume of the Centenary edition (Columbus: Ohio State Univ. Press) is *Our Old Home*, the collection of sketches about England which Hawthorne worked up from material in his notebooks for publication in the *Atlantic*. The 342-page text is preceded by more than a hundred pages of textual introduction, and more than 140 of textual appendices. The editors take the first edition of *Our Old Home* as their copy text, finding it superior both to the separately published articles in the *Atlantic* as well as to the extant manuscripts for those articles. The superiority is a matter of very small detail; there are no exciting textual cruxes. The drama of the edition is supplied, as in previous Centenary volumes, by the performances of the compositors, who are ranked according to the quantity of material they set and the percentage of errors they made.

The battle over the Centenary edition is certainly familiar to students of Hawthorne, and shows no signs of abating. A good history of the controversy, as well as an excellent overview of Hawthorne scholarship since the revival launched by Randall Stewart, may be found in Buford Jones's comprehensive "Hawthorne Studies: The Seventies" (*SNNTS* 2:504–18). A stunning attack on the edition is John Freehafer's "*The Marble Faun* and the Editing of Nineteenth-Century Texts" (*SNNTS* 2:487–503). Freehafer attacks the Centenary edition on its own terms; i.e., editorial competence, consistency, and sensitivity. He elaborates on four major defects in the edition: "(1) tendentious and narrow analysis of internal bibliographic evidence, without regard to pertinent external evidence; (2) inattention to pertinent linguistic and lexicographic evidence; (3) 'normalization' of variants which often runs counter to Hawthorne's artistic and linguistic intentions; and (4) adherence to a predetermined editorial practice which is not adequate to deal successfully with the special problems in editing *The Marble Faun*." The main problem, shared by many nineteenth-century American works, is that *The Marble Faun* was published first in England and then in America, and that Hawthorne changed the text with an eye to his American audience. Because of this, Freehafer argues, it is incorrect to regard either edition as the "right" one and to use it exclusively as a copy-text. Most importantly, Hawthorne wrote a post-script for the British, and a conclusion for the American, text. These are quite different, but the editors arbitrarily select the British post-script as Hawthorne's final word, and "omit all but the first and last words of a paragraph peculiar to the 'Conclusion' (467.9), which may be the most important variant passage in the book." Again, Freehafer finds the editors' normalizations a mishmash, sometimes introducing obsolete spellings where Hawthorne's were current, and sometimes unjustifiably modernizing the text. In sum, he says, "a critic who tried to judge Hawthorne's linguistic habits, style, and artistic intentions from the sham Briticisms, false personifications, pretentious capitals, and miscorrections in the Centenary *Marble Faun* could come to odd,

erroneous, and unflattering conclusions." This may well be the most
significant article written on the subject thus far.

J. Donald Crowley has edited a collection of reviews of Hawthorne's work which were written by his contemporaries, many of
which were presumably read by Hawthorne himself. The book, entitled *Hawthorne: The Critical Heritage* (New York: Barnes and
Noble), contains in all over 140 items, some of which are prefaces
and letters of Hawthorne's, to show the extent to which his views of
his work mirrored those of his critics. The interplay between Hawthorne and his reviewers is fascinating, and we are reminded of the
extent to which Hawthorne directed his writings towards the artic-
ulate responses of his readers. The image of Hawthorne the shy,
retiring, morbid, and dreamy man emerges as the cooperative creation of the critics and the author. This image, so often called "feminine" by critics of his own day, in contrast to what they took to be
the aggressive, outgoing, "masculine" temperament of the new nation, was at once Hawthorne's burden and his refuge. Another work
about Hawthorne's literary reputation is an article by Morton Nirenberg on "Hawthorne's Reception in Germany" (*JA* 15:141–61),
which studies German literary histories and periodicals of the period
from 1850 to 1914. Nirenberg concludes that, although Hawthorne
was known in Germany after 1851 (the year *The Scarlet Letter* was
translated), he never became popular, largely because German critics interpreted him as a sort of minor German author. He was not
American enough, in their view; his writing was too Continental.

*Hawthorne's Son: The Life and Literary Career of Julian Haw-
thorne* (Columbus: Ohio State Univ. Press), by Maurice Bassan,
devotes one chapter to Julian's life up to the time of his father's
death. The senior Hawthorne emerges as a sympathetic, loving, and
non-demanding parent, quite unlike the typical Victorian father.
The son's feelings for him seem genuine and uncomplicatedly warm.
Benjamin Lease's "Hawthorne and 'A Certain Venerable Personage':
New Light on 'The Custom-House'" (*JA* 15:201–07) revises the
commonly held opinion that Hawthorne's butt in "The Custom-
House" was the nefarious Upham, who engineered his dismissal. He
demonstrates that Hawthorne's target was a certain William Lee, a
custom-house official whose life fits the details of Hawthorne's sketch
very closely. This is a useful contribution. C. E. Frazer Clark, Jr.'s
article "Posthumous Papers of a Decapitated Surveyor: *The Scarlet*

Letter in the Salem Press" (*SNNTS* 2:395–419) provides a montage of reviews and notices of Hawthorne's work from Salem newspapers. His purpose is to demonstrate that Hawthorne's dismissal from the custom-house was news "because Hawthorne was newsworthy." Clark certainly demonstrates that Hawthorne was a big frog in the local pond; his leap to the conclusion that Hawthorne's loss of a job was a national scandal seems unwarranted.

Clark also prepared a bibliographical pamphlet in the Merrill Checklist series (Columbus, Ohio, Charles E. Merrill). This is highly selective but presents some useful information—notably the date and place of first publication of all Hawthorne's short works. If these dates were well known, critics and students might the better avoid such egregious errors as that committed by Q. D. Leavis in her famous article, "Hawthorne as Poet" (1951) where she called "Young Goodman Brown," by virtue of its intrinsic excellence, a late story. A compact and yet extensive checklist of criticism and scholarship has been compiled by Maurice Beebe and Jack Hardie (*SNNTS* 2:519–87); as of this moment, it is the most up-to-date bibliographical aid available.

ii. General Criticism

The two books on Hawthorne published this year present striking contrasts in approach, and taken together they testify to the remarkable "openness" of Hawthorne, his adaptability to an enormous range of critical modes. Interpretation in general is dedicated to the task of "closing" an author, eliminating or at least limiting the range of statements which may be acceptably made about him. A criticism which acknowledged Hawthorne's openness instead of accepting it only as a challenge to be surmounted, and which devoted itself to the causes of that openness, would be revolutionary indeed, but at the moment there are no signs of such an approach.

Nathaniel Hawthorne: An Approach to an Analysis of Artistic Creation, by Jean Normand (trans. by Derek Coltman, foreword by Henri Peyre; Cleveland, Press of Case Western Reserve Univ.) has an organization which may be confusing and irritating to readers accustomed to the linear clarity of the English and American expository manner. Normand's method cycles the same materials through changing perspectives. The result appears both repetitious and frag-

mented. To find out what he has to say about *The Scarlet Letter*, for
example, one must read the entire book, abstract the numerous references to the novel, and piece them together. The book is divided into
three sections: a highly selective biography which aims to point out
the origins of Hawthorne's particular perspectives on experience; a
discussion of the creative process as exemplified in his writings and
his writing habits (about which too little is known to build a good
study); and finally a discussion of the recurring properties—styles,
symbols, techniques of the finished products. Throughout his book
Normand stresses an archetypal fiction of which all Hawthorne's
works are supposed to be a part. This fiction is a sort of night journey,
wherein the hero seeks the father in a quest which leads necessarily
into and then beyond the womb. By reentering the mother (cavern,
dark room, and so on) the hero receives an influx of energy which
fits him for manhood, but only by leaving the "motherland" for the
"fatherland" can he attain his true identity, which is male. This fiction
has three characters—the terrible yet redeeming father, the wonderful yet treacherous mother, and the hesitating son. On the basis of
this pattern, Normand proposes that Hawthorne had a significant
"female component" (whatever that might be) to his nature, and
suffered severe psychological conflict because of it. Normand also
derives from this pattern a profoundly conservative social ethic
which he attributes to Hawthorne, one that is hierarchical, aristocratic, puritanical, authoritarian, and patriarchal. Hawthorne's ever-
present sense of guilt is attributed to his secret longing to linger with
the mother, which also accounts for the particularly violent way in
which women are repudiated in the stories. This analysis suffers
severely from the facile assumptions on which it serenely, even ar-
rogantly, rests: that male and female are inherently antithetical
psychological types, givens of one's biological makeup, and that the
precise structure of these types is well known. At this juncture in
time, when the socially conditioned character of sexual roles is the
subject of much study and speculation, Normand's assumptions seem
outmoded. On the other hand, his stylistic analysis is extremely impressive and constitutes some of the best work that has been done
on Hawthorne. Normand is particularly good in his exposition of the
visual quality of Hawthorne's imagination. He makes much of Hawthorne's painterly and "cinematic" techniques. In effect he demonstrates that Hawthorne's imagination is a visual, rather than a verbal,

instrument, the images preceding the specific verbal meanings which are later attached to them. This fact may possibly explain why those who discuss Hawthorne's style find it hard to stick to his language. For all his grace and elegance of phrase, Hawthorne's language is a translation of anterior material.

In contrast to Normand's Hawthorne, all complexity and chaos, John Stubbs's Hawthorne is a man of clarity and light. *The Pursuit of Form: A Study of Hawthorne and the Romance* (Urbana, Univ. of Ill. Press) offers the proposition that Hawthorne's successful fiction is characterized by the streamlining of human experience to the point where it retains some feel of complexity but acquires even more strongly a sense of order and organization. Working within the well-developed nineteenth-century genre of romance (not to be confused with the genres invented by Richard Chase or Northrup Frye) Hawthorne structures his protagonists' dilemmas in a dialectical fashion. Stressing his own artifice in doing so, he calls attention to the organizing mind of the artificer. The result of all this is distance, order, clarity. Stubbs analyzes the four major romances with a view to pointing out their chief artificing devices. The main concern of the works he takes to be the need of the hero, an outsider, to affirm his tie to the procession of life, "however repellent or illusory that procession may appear to him." Within this frame, Stubbs proposes no striking new readings; interpretation is not his concern. In *The Scarlet Letter*, Hawthorne's chief device is to oppose a conventional emblematic pair: the dark Puritan (Chillingworth) against the fair (Hester). In *The House of the Seven Gables* he creates distance by using a comic pair, Hepzibah and Clifford, to burlesque the sins of the Pyncheons and the virtues of the lovers. *The Blithedale Romance* is distanced by an irony which is created when its tragic events are channeled through the perspective of its bumbling, stupid narrator. *The Marble Faun,* an experiment in mythmaking, uses the artifices of dream. In all these discussions, the conscious mind of the artist is seen to leave its imprint on material precisely to the extent that it makes that material artificial. This is a knowledgeable, generous, firmly written book. Yet the neatness of its presentation implies an orderliness in Hawthorne's mind which many readers will find lacking in their own experience of the author. The simple polarity of experience and artifice is, I feel, inadequate to Hawthorne's art. Because the experience dealt with in Hawthorne's writings is so often inner rather than outer, it partakes in its own nature of the nature of artifice; conversely, because Hawthorne's "artifices" are so often the unconscious artifices of fantasy, dream, wish, or fear, rather than the conscious artifices of dialetic, comedy, or irony, one cannot maintain a clear distinction between his subject and his treatment, as Stubbs attempts to do. In a sense this book represents a return to a new-critical stance that has been gradually disappearing from Hawthorne studies, with its assumptions of the perfection of the work, and the thoroughly aware controlling mind of the maker.

Among articles on Hawthorne dealing with general themes, Lee Schneiderman's "Hawthorne and the Refuge of the Heart" (*ConnR* 3:83–101), though not especially original, is certainly the most ambitious, for it attempts nothing less than a complete synthesis of Hawthorne's life and works. The guiding thesis of his interpretation is that Hawthorne perceived evil in men's hearts, but needed to believe in their normalcy and reasonableness. His perceptions of evil led to his greatness, the belief in reason was responsible for his failures, chief of which is his inability to create truly tragic situations. Another general article is "Hawthorne, the Hippie, and the Square" by Earl M. Hinton (*SNNTS* 2:425–39) which is concerned with making a contact between Hawthorne and certain contemporary lifestyles. Since, from one view, the hippie is a latter-day Romantic, and since Hawthorne may be considered a Romantic of an earlier age, the connection is easily established. But Hinton rather overdoes Hawthorne's great stress on peace and love. Hawthorne's idea of saving love was a far narrower, more singular emotion than the encompassing emotion indicated by the peace sign, and he was neither for nor against peace or war so much as detached from such massive questions. Moreover, Hinton's ideas about hippies seem to have been drawn from conversations with a handful of students; and few students, regardless of their self-images, are really hippies. On the hippies, Hinton is so facile as to be almost irresponsible.

Carroll D. Laverty, "Some Touchstones of Hawthorne's Style" (*ESQ* 60:30–36) demonstrates the difficulty of the topic, for Laverty spends all his time talking about Hawthorne's themes and ideas. An earnest theological article is Sheila Dwight's "Hawthorne and the Unpardonable Sin" (*SNNTS* 2:449–58). Drawing her evidence from Matthew, who says that he who speaks against the Holy Ghost will not be forgiven, Dwight argues that the only unpardonable sin is to destroy the dwelling place of the spirit within. Since articles of this kind proceed by splitting hairs, it seems fair to counter in kind: there is no evidence that by the Holy Ghost Matthew meant the spirit within, nor does any sin in Hawthorne's canon correspond to speaking against the Holy Ghost, which is specifically what Matthew says. The question of the unpardonable sin has been run into the ground; it owes much of its longevity to the reluctance of critics who, religious themselves, are unwilling to accept the basically atheological cast of Hawthorne's speculations about evil and the human heart.

Richard H. Fogle, "Hawthorne's Pictorial Unity" (*ESQ* 55[1969]: 71–76), writes about Hawthorne's descriptions of landscape. Hawthorne subscribes to a classical rather than a romantic version of the doctrine of *ut pictura poesis*, the idea that poetry like painting takes its power from the harmonious fusion of parts. Because the fusion in Hawthorne's descriptions is produced more by analysis than by image, Fogle classifies Hawthorne as a rationalist rather than symbolist author. Darrel Abel, " 'A More Imaginative Pleasure': Hawthorne on the Play of Imagination" (*ESQ* 55[1969]:63–71), discusses Hawthorne's view of imagination with attention to his metaphors of play for imaginative activity, and plaything for work of art. He says that for Hawthorne imagination is activity rather than product, and in order to be a veritable work of art the product must always refer back to the activity that produced it. An imperfect object is more suggestive than a perfect one, which seems self-contained, and therefore the imperfect object is preferred as an art object. This theory is drawn largely from Hawthorne's comments on painting, and Abel draws back from applying it to Hawthorne's own works. Instead of finding Hawthorne's suggestiveness in his imperfection, he finds it in his multiplicity of meanings. Despite this final inconsistency, the article is stimulating. William L. Hedges, in "Irving, Hawthorne, and the Image of the Wife," (*ATQ* 5:22–26) looks at one of Hawthorne's images of woman by comparing Priscilla to Irving's wife in his sketch of that name. Both of these display amazing fortitude in sustaining overwhelming reverses of fortune, and thrive on love in contrast to man's somewhat more scattered and unstable nature. Conventional nineteenth-century images of femininity stand behind both Irving's and Hawthorne's depiction, which Hedges calls a "post-lapsarian Eve," a non-tempting though carnal wife and mother, and finally a "grotesque born of dread and desire." Hedges does not note that where Irving is thoroughly enraptured by the image, Hawthorne is a good deal more skeptical about it. Still, this is a study in an important and underworked area. It derives from Fiedler, but is more free of its own myths than is Fiedler.

iii. Long Romances

Articles appeared on all five of Hawthorne's finished romances. Leo B. Levy, in "*Fanshawe*: Hawthorne's World of Images" (*SNNTS* 2:440–48) discusses the villain, Butler, in terms of the psychological complexity of the portrait, and he shows how even at this very early stage Hawthorne could manipulate landscape to reflect and express emotional and moral states. His discussion shows that there is more in this novel than the conventional piece of melodrama which some see it to be. Nina Baym's "Passion and Authority in *The Scarlet Letter* (*NEQ* 43:209–30) attempts a fresh reading of this much-read book, and essentially moves back to an earlier critical generation's understanding of Hawthorne as a Romantic. Beginning from the (demonstrated) premise that Hawthorne's Puritans are a distortion of historical reality, the article interprets *The Scarlet Letter* in a wholly secular framework. Dimmesdale and Hester are seen as two transgressors of a purely social code. They feel guilt to the extent that they have internalized the prohibitions of their community, and no absolute moral issues are implicated in their "sin." The society is repressive and authoritarian in nature, and condemns their act because of its passionate and self-expressive essence. Hester, the freer spirit, tries earnestly to accept the social judgment which is pinned upon her, but eventually in faithfulness to her inner nature must reject the social interpretation of her deed. Conversely, Dimmesdale tries for long years to resist the guilt feelings which eventually overwhelm him and to which he capitulates with his confession and death. Pearl and Chillingworth are interpreted as projections of the "sin" as perceived respectively by Hester and Dimmesdale: for Hester, the deed is beautiful, wild energy; for Dimmesdale it is loathsome error. An article by Robert Stanton, "*The Scarlet Letter* as Dialectic of Temperament and Idea" (*SNNTS* 2:474–86) comes to many of the same conclusions as Baym, though it is differently organized. Stanton describes the basic contrast in *The Scarlet Letter* as between two temperaments, one "emanative" and the other "introceptive." Two philosophies—romanticism and Puritanism—represent articulations suitable to the two temperaments, and the novel is a sort of minuet among these four givens. As does Baym, Stanton sees Pearl and Chillingworth as projections of the psyches of the main characters rather than characters in their own right. He finds Hawthorne attracted to Hester's emanative temperament and Dimmesdale's Puritan philosophy both, and he attributes the melancholy tone of the work to his realization that they are not compatible.

Two minor articles on *The Scarlet Letter* are James G. Janssen's "Dimmesdale's 'Lurid Playfulness' " (*ATQ* 1[1969]:30–34) wherein the author argues that Hawthorne marks the stages in Dimmesdale's progress away from prideful hypocrisy by the character's outbursts of grotesque humor, and Rosemary Stephens's " 'A' is for 'Art' in *The Scarlet Letter*" (*ATQ* 1[1969]:23–27) which takes up the familiar idea that the letter symbolizes art and applies it with methodical completeness to virtually every episode in the book. This is ingenious, but implies an allegorical rigidity too narrow for the novel. One example will set the tone: the fact that Hester takes off the letter when she goes back to Europe, but resumes it when she returns to Boston at the book's conclusion, means that "the American artist is finding a place abroad, but in America the artist is still an outcast."

For *The House of the Seven Gables* Nina Baym also proposed a new reading. "Hawthorne's Holgrave: The Failure of the Artist-Hero" (*JEGP* 69:584–98) quarrels with almost every previous interpretation of the novel except Rudolph von Abele's, and takes exception to his idea that the book is a failure. According to Baym, Pyncheon and Maule represent the forces of repression and expression, and their struggle to possess the house is equal to a struggle for possession of the self by opposed psychological drives. Hawthorne's historical myth of the origins of the quarrel shows that he identifies the true self with Maule, for Pyncheon is a criminal (though legal) usurper. Outlawed, the forces represented by Maule turn perverse and destructive, but in Holgrave a more healthy kind of art and creativity seems prefigured. Unfortunately, the necessary death of Pyncheon implicates Holgrave in the bleak system of guilt and atonement which pervades society, and his victory is Pyrrhic since he becomes, in essence, a Pyncheon. The secondary but important figure of Clifford is taken to represent another kind of distortion of art at an extreme from the perverse wizard Maule: a sterile aestheticism, a passive imitation of artistry which is really infantile appetite. Both the wizard and Clifford show what happens to art in a repressive, authoritarian society. Hawthorne's pretense that the book's ending is happy indicates his desire to ally himself at the last minute with the conservative and orthodox views that were attacked throughout the romance. Quite a different view of the ending is argued by Frank Battaglia in "*The* (Unmeretricious) *House of the Seven Gables*" (*SNNTS* 2:468–73). Battaglia quotes from several of Hawthorne's letters to show that the book was intended from the beginning to end happily; therefore, he claims, the ending was not conceived of as a sop to public opinion. This is a non sequitur. Letters in which Hawthorne claims that the cheer of *The House of the Seven Gables* is more natural to his temperament than the gloom of *The Scarlet Letter* may be taken literally, as Battaglia takes them; they may also be taken as disingenuous, or simply as a case of mistaken self-analysis. In any event, Battaglia seems not to realize that the critical objection to the ending has nothing to do with when or how Hawthorne planned it out.

A third important article on *The House of the Seven Gables* is Lewis B. Horne's "Place, Time, and Moral Growth in *The House of the Seven Gables*" (*SNNTS* 2:459–67). This is argued like a syllogism: moral growth depends on the recognition of horrors within the self and the ability to accept them and then pass on. The house is the physical representation of these horrors in the Pyncheon family. Therefore, moral growth in the surviving members of the family is measured by the nature of their relationship to the house—crucially, their ability to get out of it. Moreover, there are really three houses in the novel, corresponding to different stages of moral development: the prelapsarian cottage of the first, innocent Maule, the house of sin and decay which is the house of the title, and finally Judge Pyncheon's country estate, which implies mature regeneration. Julian Smith's "A Hawthorne Source for *The House of the Seven Gables*" (*ATQ* 1[1969]:18–19) points out some interesting resemblances between the novel and the "Legends of the Province House": in both a house is central, and in both the devices of mirrors, pictures, a curse, a ghostly procession, figure prominently. Of course these are the paraphernalia of Hawthorne's imagination in general; the similarities between Alice Pyncheon and Lady Eleonore, Esther Dudley and Hepzibah are more striking.

Only one article of substance appeared on *The Blithedale Romance*, and that was Alfred H. Marks, "Ironic Inversion in *The Blithedale Romance*" (*ESQ* 55[1969]:95–102). Marks proposes that in reality Zenobia is the victim, and Priscilla the calculator and bewitcher in the novel, precisely the reverse of what is asserted by Miles Coverdale about the two women. But Coverdale is hampered in his perceptions by his male prejudices. Aided and abetted by these prejudices in Coverdale and Hollingsworth, Priscilla contrives to make the pure and womanly Zenobia appear sullied, while she passes her own questionable past off as one of spotless innocence. Priscilla, Marks says, stands for woman's downtrodden state, while Zenobia represents an emancipatory effort. Marks has been anticipated by two articles of which he seems unaware, that by Allan and Barbara Lefcowitz (see *ALS 1966*, p. 21) and that by Nina Baym (see *ALS 1968*, p. 27), but his final statement that the novel puts Hawthorne squarely on the side of the feminists is both strong and right.

Leo B. Levy has published an article on *The Marble Faun* in his continuing study of Hawthorne and the picturesque. "*The Marble Faun*: Hawthorne's Landscape of the Fall" (*AL* 42:139–56) seems to me the least successful of this impressive series, because it does not see how Hawthorne has transcended his own categories. Art for Hawthorne, Levy claims, is an idealist impulse expressed in representations of nature. This impulse cannot be expressed through the Italian landscape of Rome or of the countryside, so imbued are these with evil and decay. In Italy, then, art loses its importance and is repudiated. But in America art is saved through Hilda and Kenyon, who observe without participating in the fall which has destroyed art in Europe. However it can be argued that the art which *The Marble Faun* repudiates is precisely that kind of art, "idealistic" art, which is represented by Hilda and Kenyon. *The Marble Faun* is instinct with Hawthorne's despairing sense of the greatness of art of the past, and his recognition that its greatness stems from its ability to encompass areas of human life—sex and evil—which contemporary art ignores. Levy does not recognize that the category of landscape is less relevant to *The Marble Faun*, despite the enormous quantity of description, than is the portrait both in statuary and painting. The centrality of the human face and form in Hawthorne's discussions of art in *The Marble Faun* implies a conception of art expanded beyond the picturesque. Moreover, Levy accepts Hilda un-

critically as Hawthorne's spokesman, even though he recognizes that
her views are simple-minded. Clare R. Goldfarb, in "The Marble
Faun and Emersonian Self-Reliance" (ATQ 1[1969]:19–23) has produced a much cruder article which is nevertheless right in its contention that The Marble Faun shows that without exposure to Europe
and experience, American art will be stunted, shallow, and imperfect.
She takes the book as a counter to Emerson's demand for a "pure"
American literature. Spencer Hall, in "Beatrice Cenci: Symbol and
Vision in The Marble Faun" (NCF 25:85–95) considers the meaning
of the Cenci portrait. He finds it a mediating symbol between the two
heroines, who are united in their mutual resemblance to the portrait.
Even though Hilda remains sinless, she experiences the grief of sin,
and this emotion establishes a common sisterhood between her and
Miriam. Thus some of the initial rigid dichotomies of the story are
dissolved, and Beatrice incarnates "Hawthorne's most mature and
complex vision of human experience."

iv. Shorter Works

The well-worked-over stories continued to be worked over, but
there were also some less frequently seen subjects of analysis this
year. For example, Darrel Abel wrote " 'A Vast Deal of Human Sympathy': Idea and Device in Hawthorne's 'The Snow Image' " (Criticism 4:316–32). Abel claims that the story combines the masculine
symbolism of the imagination (snow) with the feminine symbol of
actualizing power (needlework) to produce the snow image itself, a
"visible figure of ideal imaginations." This is interesting, but stops
far short of what Hawthorne really does in the story. The image is
actually produced by children, under the sympathetic eye of their
mother. There is nothing to indicate that snow is masculine; indeed
the father, identified with business and common sense, is also symbolized by the fire which melts the snow-child. It would seem that
Abel is willing to concede some part of the imaginative process to
the feminine principle, but he is unable to relinquish all of it to
women and babes. This, however, is what the story does. Sheldon
W. Liebman's "Ambiguity in 'Lady Eleanore's Mantle' " (ESQ 58:
97–101) develops the significance of the story's Dr. Clarke, the revolutionary democrat who gives Gervayse Helwarth the wine which he
in turn gives Eleanore. Liebman suggests that the wine is poisoned,

and draws a parallel to the machinations of Baglioni in "Rappaccini's Daughter." A note of interest by George Monteiro, "A Nonliterary Source for Hawthorne's 'Egotism; Or the Bosom Serpent'" (*AL* 41: 575–77) cites a case reported in the *New England Magazine* (a journal which Hawthorne read) of a woman with an eel in her stomach. Thus Monteiro suggests, "facts" that Hawthorne is assumed to have invented may well have been true facts, so far as he knew. The larger significance of this note has to do with the extent to which Hawthorne was a pure fantasist. Another interesting note is by Richard VanDerBeets and Paul Witherington. Called "My Kinsman, Brockden Brown: Robin Molineux and Arthur Mervyn" (*ATQ* 1 [1969]:13–15), it demonstrates close resemblances between Hawthorne's story and the opening chapters of Brown's novel.

"Young Goodman Brown" came in, as always, for more than its share of articles, which monotonously puzzle over the moral point of the story without contributing much new insight. Walter J. Paulits, in "Ambivalence in 'Young Goodman Brown'" (*AL* 41:577–84), explains that Brown's action is *ambivalent* because he is attracted to the Devil but regrets leaving Faith; it is *ambiguous* because it conjoins good (revulsion against evil) with bad (rejection of knowledge). Besides the semantic hair-splitting, this interpretation assumes what needs to be shown—that the acquisition of knowledge is necessarily good. Allison Ensor's "'Whispers of the Bad Angel': A *Scarlet Letter* Passage as a Commentary on Hawthorne's 'Young Goodman Brown'" (*SSF* 7:467–69) parallels Brown's and Hester's cases because both are prompted to think evil of others. Because Hawthorne says that Hester is prompted by a "bad angel," Ensor maintains that Brown too is so prompted. There is less parallelism than Ensor claims, however, because the psychological reasons behind their similar desires are opposite. Hester wants to feel that others are sinners as she is; Brown wants to feel that all *except* himself are evil. Hester, that is, wants company; Brown, solitude. Reginald Cook, in "The Forest of Goodman Brown's Night: A Reading of Hawthorne's 'Young Goodman Brown'" (*NEQ* 43:473–81) defines the tale as a night-journey in which Brown willfully mistakes illusions for realities. The whole journey expresses a desire for self-punishment, Cook says, and the story serves as a moral warning to readers to do better with their own lives.

"A Reading of Nathaniel Hawthorne's 'The Gentle Boy'" by

William A. Tremblay (*MSE* 2:80–87) is a rather disjointed article discussing the deletions made in the 1832 *Token* version of the tale when Hawthorne collected it in the 1837 volume of *Twice-Told Tales*. Since Tremblay can find no overall pattern in the excisions, he is unable to contribute to his announced purpose of clarifying Hawthorne's artistic intentions in the story. At the same time, the quoted deletions are interesting and readers without access to the *Token* might want to take a look at the article to see them. Lewis B. Horne, in "The Heart, the Hand, and 'The Birthmark'" (*ATQ* 1[1969]:38–41) suggests that the hand on Georgiana's cheek is less the mark of her own than of her husband's mortal heart—it is he who has laid a fatal grip on her soul. Finally, Robert Plank's "Heart Transplant Fiction" (*HSL*, 2:102–12) considers "Ethan Brand" in the context of concern generated by the recent wave of heart transplants. Along with Wilhelm Hauff's "Das kalte Herz," he claims, Hawthorne's tale is a symbolic description of a heart transplant, wherein the loss of a heart is equated with the loss of decent, normal human feeling. In a Freudian conclusion he asserts that the anxiety generated by the feeling that the loss of a heart is equal to losing one's humanity may easily regress, "appear as castration anxiety" and "coalesce with the Oedipus complex." Readers will be hard put to find this thesis demonstrated for "Ethan Brand," however.

University of Illinois

3. Melville

Merton M. Sealts, Jr.

Although 1969 marked a new high in the quantitative output of the Melville industry, 1970 has more than matched it. Last year I counted ninety-six individual items exclusive of dissertations either published during 1969 or not previously reported in the annual MLA bibliographies. This year the corresponding tally is ninety-five, but the number of dissertations has soared: a year ago, *Dissertation Abstracts* listed ten new dissertations concerned wholly or partly with Melville; this year there are twenty-three. Again in 1970, as in 1969, two American journals published what in effect are Melville issues: the Summer *Arizona Quarterly* carries seven Melville items; for the Summer *American Transcendental Quarterly* Raymona Hull arranged a symposium on works from *Pierre* to *Billy Budd* consisting of her own prefatory essay, "After *Moby Dick*: Melville's Apparent 'Failures'" (*ATQ* 7:4), and eighteen articles, half of them on the tales. Melville also inspired three poets, as attested by John Bennett's prize-winning volume, *The Struck Leviathan: Poems on "Moby Dick"* (Columbia, Univ. of Mo. Press), and other individual pieces by J. Joseph Leonard ("Melville's Lima," *ArQ* 26:100) and Stephen Tudor ("Four for Melville," *ESQ* 59:3). Many of the shorter articles of 1970 are brief notes of interest mainly to specialists; the major contributions during the year appeared in the form of edited texts, reference works, and monographs, sixteen in all, which therefore deserve special attention here. As in 1969, I am omitting any consideration of dissertations, not only to conserve space but also because their most important findings are likely to be reported in print and noted in future chapters of *ALS*.

i. Books

Two more volumes of the Northwestern-Newberry edition of Melville, edited by Harrison Hayford, Hershel Parker, and G. Thomas Tanselle, were published in 1970: *Mardi* and *White-Jacket* (Evanston, Northwestern Univ. Press). The respective Historical Notes, by Elizabeth S. Foster and Willard Thorp, are compendiums of essential information about the composition and publication of the two books and their sources, structure, and critical reception. Textual apparatus assembled by the editors completes each volume, as in their three predecessors in the new edition.

For his *Selected Poems of Herman Melville, A Reader's Edition* (New York, Random House) Robert Penn Warren chose seventy-five items, from "Jonah's Song" in *Moby-Dick* to "Billy in the Darbies," including nineteen extracts from *Clarel*. Editorial commentary occupies nearly half the volume. The introduction is an augmented version of Warren's major essay of 1967, "Melville's Poems" (see *ALS 1967*, pp. 40–41, 43); following the texts are a hundred pages of additional notes that consider individual poems in relation to the entire Melville canon, thus providing a conspectus of Warren's estimate of Melville's total artistic achievement. This is a fine book, at once a superior classroom text and a significant contribution to Melville studies by a distinguished poet and critic. Two other volumes primarily designed for student use are *Melville's South Seas, An Anthology*, edited by A. Grove Day (New York, Hawthorn Books), which "attempts to reveal the richness of Melville's presentation of Pacific life," and *Great Short Works of Herman Melville*, a revised version now edited with an introduction by Warner Berthoff (New York, Harper and Row) and improved by the provision of new and better texts ranging from "The Town-Ho's Story" to *Billy Budd, Sailor*.

Described in a foreword by Harrison Hayford as "the first published book of pure reference devoted to Melville's writings," Robert L. Gale's *Plots and Characters in the Fiction and Narrative Poetry of Herman Melville* (Hamden, Conn., Archon Books, 1969) does for students of Melville what Gale's companion volumes have already done for students of Hawthorne and Henry James, providing chronologies of the author's life and works, summaries of plots, and lists of "named or namable characters"—1039 in Melville's fiction and another 398 in his narrative poetry. In *"Moby-Dick" as Doubloon: Essays and Extracts (1851–1970)* (New York, Norton) Hershel Parker and Harrison Hayford have made "the fullest collection of criticism ever assembled on an American literary work," thus providing the basic evidence for studying the book's reception and early critical history; an annotated list of books and articles on *Moby-Dick*, from 1921 to

1969, concludes the volume. Another collection of essays, *The Merrill Studies in "Billy Budd"*, compiled by Haskell S. Springer (Columbus, Ohio, Charles E. Merrill), aims not at completeness but at a representative sampling, in terms of twenty-five well chosen selections, of the "hundreds" of commentaries on *Billy Budd* published between 1924 and 1967. Two reprinted books should also be noted here: Nathalia Wright's *Melville's Use of the Bible* (New York, Octagon, 1969), and Merton M. Sealts, Jr.'s *Melville as Lecturer* (Folcroft, Pa., Folcroft Press).

Among new monographs, *The Tailoring of Melville's "White-Jacket"* by Howard P. Vincent and *The Poetry of Melville's Late Years* by William Bysshe Stein are considered in sections ii and vii below, respectively. Other works by Maurice Friedman, Leon F. Seltzer, and Kingsley Widmer study Melville as a forerunner of twentieth-century thought and art: Friedman strikes their common keynote in remarking that modern man "knows existence emptied of God and himself as alienated and divided. Melville shows the world in which modern man now finds himself." Friedman's book, *Problematic Rebel: Melville, Dostoievsky, Kafka, Camus* (Chicago, Univ. of Chicago Press) is a revised version of a volume first published in 1963; it incorporates two essays previously noticed in *ALS 1963* (p. 38) and *ALS 1966* (p. 33). The chapters devoted to Melville, which make up about a fifth of the book (pp. 49–148, 437–41), focus primarily on *Moby-Dick* with some additional consideration of "Bartleby," *The Confidence-Man*, and *Billy Budd*. Instead of attempting to survey Friedman's sensitive reading of all four works or to explicate his special terminology—e.g., Ahab as "Modern Promethean" and Ishmael as "Modern Exile"—I quote here a representative passage dealing with the "ever-shifting point of view" in *Moby-Dick:*

> By going all the way with Ahab and at the same time turning back with Ishmael and by holding the tension of these two opposing points of view within the form of *Moby Dick* itself, Melville creates an artistic meaning and balance great enough to contain his questions, great enough, too, not to attempt an answer. Melville's point of view comprehends both Ishmael's point of view and Ahab's without being identical with either, or being a moderate balance between them such as we find in "The Try-Works." The golden mean is not the moral of this

whaling voyage in which Melville, as well as his characters, risked being eternally stoved in. In so far as there is *one* point of view in the book, it is that which holds in tension Ahab's and Ishmael's conflicting directions of movement. [pp. 439–40]

Friedman regards Melville himself as being "of surer tragic stature than Ahab, because more human," calling him "the man who in his life and his art held in tension Ishmael's 'wisdom that is woe' and Ahab's 'woe that is madness.'" But Melville could not sustain the tension after *Moby-Dick*, Friedman concludes, pointing to "the bitterness of *Pierre* and *The Confidence-Man*, the intolerable solitude of 'Bartleby,' and the ironic resignation of *Billy Budd*."

In *The Vision of Melville and Conrad, A Comparative Study* (Athens, Ohio Univ. Press) Leon F. Seltzer, contending that as artists Melville and Conrad "responded to human experience in essentially the same way," characterizes their vision of man as "really not so much tragic as ironic or absurd." His monograph, the outgrowth of a doctoral dissertation (see *ALS 1968*, p. 49), discusses the literary techniques of the two men as reflecting their radical skepticism, or "nihilism": thus they purposefully invert traditional symbolic connotations; they leave fictional endings "open"; they often employ rhetoric "not to mitigate our confusion but to justify it—or, in fact, add to it"; they abandon the omniscient point of view for a far more restricted one that makes the narrator's role central in their works. Both as artists and as thinkers they are more "modern" than most of their contemporaries; as moralists, they "appear indirectly to recommend" a kind of behavior that Seltzer considers "generally existential." Terminology similar to Seltzer's—"existential," "absurd," and especially "nihilist"—also turns up in the third book of this grouping, Kingsley Widmer's *The Ways of Nihilism: A Study of Herman Melville's Short Novels* (Los Angeles, Ward Ritchie Press, for the California State Colleges). But where Seltzer writes tentatively of Melville's nihilism as something akin to his "discouraged agnosticism," Widmer vigorously insists that to regard Melville as "an American existential nihilist" who found in nihilism the "resolution" of his "tormented unbelief" is "the only attitude that makes sense of much of his work." This deliberately "contentious" book "uses" Melville and his fiction to exemplify conditions in contemporary America which in Widmer's opinion "demand and need nihilism" as a prerequisite to their eradication. The result is a tract for the times rather than the usual scholarly inquiry. Obviously disenchanted with conventional literary study and its practitioners, Widmer offers his book as a "corrective" of what he was taught "in classroom and library" about Melville and about literature generally.

The core of Widmer's study, treating *Billy Budd*, "Benito Cereno," and "Bartleby" in that order, is a "redevelopment" of his previously published essays on those works (see *ALS 1968*, pp. 40–41, 45–46; *ALS 1969*, p. 44); new introductory and concluding chapters round out the discussion. On the whole the three stories qualify as "major documents of 'modernism'"; at some points in the argument, however, Widmer is obliged to confront Melville himself as a recalcitrant nineteenth-century figure whose ideas on race and revolution appear by no means as enlightened or unequivocal as a twentieth-century activist would prefer. The stories are seen as variations on a common pattern involving "a figure of authority and his victim, a sacrificial image of human pathos." Collectively they constitute "an attack on the legitimacy of all authority" and on "our prevalent views on order and legitimacy"; their "nihilistic implications," in this single-minded interpretation,

> deny ameliorist possibilities. This essentially leaves us with the logic of "nothing less." Nothing less will save the innocent Billy Budds, and make just the Captain Veres, than the practical abolition of the eighteenth century British navy, and whatever goes with it. Nothing less than a full revolution will free Babo's blacks, and liberate Captains Cereno and Delano from moral manicheanism, and all that goes with it. Nothing less than the transformation of a whole mode of consciousness and lifestyle will save the Bartlebys from suicide, and the benevolent rationalists from bad faith, and much that goes with it in our civilization. Melville so constructed, so perceived, his moral situations that no alternate choice, no mere reform of an institution or redemption of a moral flaw, would answer the fated annihilations. These stories rightly terrify because of what we would have to choose to go beyond such nihilism. [pp. 135–36]

Three other books, by Alan Lebowitz, Martin Leonard Pops, and John Seelye, all less pyretic than Widmer's, share a common emphasis on recurrent patterns in Melville's life and work, though their approaches differ considerably. Lebowitz addresses Melville's major writings through 1857 in *Progress into Silence: A Study of Melville's Heroes* (Bloomington, Ind. Univ. Press). In *Typee, Omoo,* and *Mardi,* according to Lebowitz, Melville develops one of his two persistent character-types, "the innocent who pursues dark knowledge"; with *Redburn* he initiates a twofold scheme, involving his young neophyte with "a direct forerunner of Ahab" in Jackson, and by the time of *Moby-Dick* his dominant concern has become "the complex relation" between the neophyte and a "Promethean" hero. "Essentially Melville had only the two characters, Ishmael and Ahab," Lebowitz contends, "and only the one story"; when in *Pierre, Israel Potter,* and *The Confidence-Man* "that story gives out and the characters disappear—the younger into disillusionment, the older into the oblivion of history and dream—the fiction-writing stops." Excluding the short stories, Lebowitz distinguishes three triadic groupings within Melville's first nine books: within each group, he holds, the first "novel" regularly "thrusts the basic story outward," the second brings the hero homeward "not notably changed," and the third "represents a major effort of synthesis." These recurrent patterns reflect Melville's own "continuing personal development . . . that culminates, finally, in a denial of his art, a lengthy, willful silence" after 1857. As for the books themseves, all but *Moby-Dick* are "variously flawed": Lebowitz, a practicing novelist, "cannot read the early works with pleasure," he considers the last three novels "a letdown," and his word for both *Mardi* and *The Confidence-Man* is "tedious."

Martin Pops covers a larger canvas in *The Melville Archetype* (Kent, Ohio, Kent State Univ. Press), studying Melville's writings from the juvenilia of 1839 to the late poetry and *Billy Budd.* As in his earlier dissertation (see *ALS 1968,* p. 48), Pops regards Melville as essentially "a religious artist"—"a heterodox Christian" whose correlative personal quests "for the Sacred, for the realization of soul," and "for sexual fulfillment" carried his fictional heroes "outside the boundaries of formal worship, toward the sacramental modes of romanticism, primitivism, and, ultimately, that archetypal experience C. G. Jung called individuation." His analysis of the successive works as reflections of Melville's own "interior life" supports a heavy burden of both Freudian and Jungian terminology. Here is his outline of the later stages of Melville's spiritual progress:

Ishmael's Epilogue expresses Melville's last vision of earthly transcendence; *Pierre* . . . , his first metaphysical descent, into fire; the stories . . . , the resistance of souls to their season in hell. But these tales could not forestall a still deeper progress, into the spiritual dryness of *The Confidence-Man* [a "nihilistic novel"]. And then for a while Melville stopped writing altogether. . . . Without an integrative vision of this world and the next, Melville's prose becomes a silent instrument, and his Long Quietus will not end until *Billy Budd* grants what *The Confidence-Man* had denied. Hence one significance of the poetry. For . . . the poems are a purgatorial medium through which Melville rediscovered his original dialectic and which allowed him to celebrate Billy's Ascension in his most authentic voice. [pp. x-xi]

As the last sentence suggests, a reading of *Billy Budd* as comedy, in Northrop Frye's sense of the term, is crucial to Pops's entire interpretation of both the life and the works. In the hanging scene, he is persuaded, "a miracle is taking place," Billy being a realization of the god who "dies and rises again." Thus Pops regards the story as the final episode in a fourfold "quest-myth" that also embraces romance, tragedy, and irony, the modes of Melville's earlier fiction. By following an analogous pattern, Melville's life similarly "transcends tragedy," according to Pops, and therefore it too "approaches the most distinguished of all art-forms, the divine comedy."

Melville: The Ironic Diagram by John Seelye (Evanston, Northwestern Univ. Press) also surveys Melville's writings from 1839 to 1891 in terms of "the questing impulse that gives the narratives their characteristic form," but this book, shorter than *The Melville Archetype*, concentrates on the design of the fiction and poetry rather than the psychology of their author. Unlike those critics who impose conclusive interpretations on Melvillean ambiguities, Seelye finds "no absolute center of value in Melville's work to which one may refer, no moral standpoint against which to measure the declarations of his characters." Instead, he proposes a Melville "impelled by his uncertainties to create forms which would encompass them." As in an earlier version of his first chapter (see *ALS 1967*, pp. 30–31), what Seelye calls "The Ironic Diagram" involves opposing forces figured by *lines* and *circles*, lines being kinetic and circles static: "If the line represents a voyage in the world of the mind, so the circle represents the limits of inquiry." In some works the linear element—the story, the quest—is dominant; others are primarily cyclical. According to Seelye's analysis, both the stature of Melville's heroes and the linear aspect of the diagram diminish after *Moby-Dick*, but the diagram itself "persists through the many changes of narrative form and style . . . , ending with his last uncompleted work." In *Billy Budd* it is "the personality of Captain Vere" rather than that of Billy which captures Seelye's attention, the characterization being "at once a tour de force of stylistic indirection and a psychomachia of diagrammatic conflict."

If Seelye and Pops are right, the basic patterns in Melville's work, whether archetypal or otherwise, are discernible even before *Typee*, continue well beyond *The Confidence-Man* (where for Lebowitz "the fiction-writing stops"), and inform the poetry as well as the prose. As the divergences in their interpretations suggest, the issue of how to read the later work that culminates in *Billy Budd* is the determining factor in any account of the grand design, whatever the temperament and allegiances of the individual critic. Here Seelye parts company not only with Pops, who sees the pattern concluding with an affirmation, but with Widmer, who hears only a recurrent NO! in thunder. What Seelye says of the tensions that meet in Vere is comparable to Friedman's words about *Moby-Dick*: that Melville "creates an artistic meaning and balance great enough to contain his question, great enough, too, not to attempt an answer." But when applied to Melville's later writing this is a controversial evaluation, Friedman himself being one of the critics who writes of *Billy Budd* in terms of its author's ironic resignation rather than of sustained creative tension.

ii. Before *Moby-Dick*

Publication of the first volumes of the Northwestern-Newberry edition may be generating a renewed interest in Melville's works before *Moby-Dick*. Six articles of 1970 deal briefly and somewhat narrowly with *Redburn* or *White-Jacket;* a seventh, "The Art of Melville's *Typee*" by Paul M. Witherington (*ArQ* 26:136–50), has kinder words for Melville's craftsmanship than did Charles Anderson's essay of last year (see *ALS 1969*, pp. 37–38). Unlike Anderson, Witherington is willing to call *Typee* a novel, at least of an experimental sort, because "it openly searches for forms with which to convey the increasing complexity of its ideas." His study provides a detailed analysis of the book in terms of structure and theme, concluding with a defense of its ending.

Howard P. Vincent's "long encounter" with *White-Jacket* (see *ALS 1968*, p. 35), which began with an interpretative essay of 1949, has now culminated in an engrossing book, *The Tailoring of Melville's "White-Jacket"* (Evanston, Northwestern Univ. Press). As in *The Trying-Out of "Moby-Dick"* Vincent once again demonstrates Melville's practice of "literary appropriation," showing in detail how skillfully he used a wide variety of source materials "to structure and to fill out" a work that "grew almost at random." The stitching of the jacket itself, as the title character describes it, Vincent takes to be Melville's "conscious metaphor of the very process of composition," the "patches" representing his miscellaneous borrowings. What Melville wrote so hurriedly in 1849 he at first intended only as "a potboiler amusingly informative," a "documentary" of shipboard life resembling the various sailors' reminiscences he was pillaging, according to Vincent; unlike Lebowitz, or Witherington on *Typee*, Vincent does not see the book as a "novel." But the writing of 1849 prepared the way for the greater work of 1850 and 1851: as Melville, in Vincent's words, "became aroused by his insight into his materials, his book exploded on him—as the whaling voyage more furiously exploded into *Moby-Dick*—and upset the orderly and unambitious documentary."

iii. Moby-Dick

The articles of 1970 on *Moby-Dick* are relatively few in number and somewhat limited in both scope and importance. But among those of more general interest, "The Unshored World of *Moby Dick*" by Graham Burns (*CR* 13:68–83) is probably the best discussion of the sea in Melville's book since the appearance of Auden's *The Enchaféd Flood* in 1951. Burns is especially concerned with Melville as a stylist, offering a perceptive critical discussion of the strengths and weaknesses of Ishmael-Melville's prose and studying the author's "only partly controlled habit of creative opportunism" as it affects his use of nautical materials. On balance, the " 'infinite perspectives' of the sea-world" as Melville depicts it in contrast to the land have both positive and negative attributes, Burns concludes; they encourage Ishmael's personal growth, but at the same time they "carry a threat that retrospectively converts the containment and constriction of the land into an ambiguous comfort." In a mythological reading of the book, Harry Slochower ("The Quest for an American Myth: *Moby Dick*," in *Mythopoesis: Mythic Patterns in the Literary Classics* [Detroit, Wayne State Univ. Press], pp. 223–45) also finds its art to be "uneven" and its major elements "*not* . . . unambiguous." Both Burns and Slochower have more to say than can be conveniently summarized here concerning Melville's mythic patterning; Slochower goes farther in speculating about the "secret psychological burden" that he sees affecting Melville and his characters and in relating *Moby-Dick* to American history and experience. In writing the book, he thinks, Melville "at once continues the American Myth of unlimited possibilities and expresses disenchantment with it" and through Ahab "gives us both the threat and the promise of the American quest."

A different approach, raising the question of whether *Moby-Dick* is a tragedy, and if so, of what kind, is that of Julian Rice in "*Moby-Dick* and Shakespearean Tragedy" (*CentR* 14:444–68). Applying the theories of tragedy formulated for the drama by Isadore Traschen, Rice argues that *Moby-Dick* qualifies as a genuine tragedy in Traschen's sense by its imaginative rendering of various attitudes toward a universe that is itself to be regarded as tragic. "As in all tragedy," Rice observes, "the totality of meaning, though pessimistic, is held short of total bleakness . . . by the magnificent dignity of Ahab and the ability of a good character to endure." Although Rice finds Melville sympathetic to Ahab and his views, he sees him offering in Ishmael an alternative to Ahab's fate that represents "a less tragic but morally tenable means of life and perception."

Ishmael's way of telling his story illustrates a particular narrative mode that Barry A. Marks considers common to Melville, Thoreau, and Whitman, analyzing it with special reference to *Moby-Dick* in his "Retrospective Narrative in Nineteenth Century American Literature" (*CE* 31:366–75). Like the narrators in *Walden* and "Song of Myself," Ishmael appears to be telling two stories simultaneously, one about his past experience and the other about "a narrator's *telling* about his past." Marks discerns in all three works a relationship in both shape and meaning between the "writing-time story," as he calls it, and "its related past-time story," growing out of the narrator's "significantly patterned search for efficacious speech." The "writing-time story," he notes, is employed to show "directly and immediately meanings which the author despairs of being able to communicate by conventional language and literary forms."

iv. Pierre

Melville's shift from a first-person to a third-person narrator in his next book after *Moby-Dick* is the point of departure for three differing studies of *Pierre*. Bert C. Bach in "Narrative Technique and Structure in *Pierre*" (*ATQ* 7:5–8) distinguishes "six major episodes" in which this "self-conscious" narrator not only breaks into the first person but also undermines critical assumptions about his supposed omniscience by revealing his lack of knowledge concerning Pierre's thoughts and motives. Alan Holder in "Style and Tone in Melville's *Pierre*" (*ESQ* 60:76–86) traces the critical disagreements about the book to its "astonishing tonal discontinuities"; his ensuing analysis of major segments of the narrative attempts "to establish a clear auctorial intention when such can be textually supported" and "to indicate how the style (or styles) creates the tonal breaks and ambiguities." He concludes that there are "major inconsistencies in Melville's handling of his materials," particularly in the later chapters, which cause the book's ultimate "collapse into contradictions and fragments," as he puts it.

Melville's supposed loss of control in *Pierre* is disputed, however, in the most ingenious—if not the most convincing—article of the year: Raymond J. Nelson's "The Art of Herman Melville: The Author of *Pierre*" (*YR* 59:197–214). Proposing a new reading that will demonstrate not only the basic unity of the book but also "the function of its blatant literary excesses," Nelson begins by denying that Melville was writing autobiographically in *Pierre*, as some critics have assumed. The work is "about" literature, he argues, rather than "about" Herman Melville; moreover, its tone is "much more comic than has been generally recognized." As in *Don Quixote*, which Nelson takes to be Melville's chief model, "a morally superior person" is "influenced by contemporary romanticism . . . until he turns his life into a literary role, becomes a tragic hero, and destroys himself." More specifically, Melville's purpose is "to bring the reader into the mind of a young man as he becomes insane"—and to accomplish this objective, Nelson argues, *he makes Pierre the narrator of his own story.* In other words, "the staggeringly uneven romance is his. *Pierre* is the book he is writing in his frigid room." This is the idea that controls the narrative material and explains the action—especially that of the second half of the story, where Holder and others locate most of Melville's supposed technical shortcomings; Nelson thinks that none of the events following Pierre's arrival in the city actually take place "except in the mind of Pierre." Moreover, Nelson distinguishes two time schemes in the book, just as in the typical "retrospective narrative" discussed by Marks, with its "past-time story" and "writing-time story." What Nelson calls "the true time" in *Pierre* commences at the Apostles as Pierre begins writing about his past in order to explain his present predicament, experiencing "an increasing inability to do so as he comes closer to himself in time." As the two times become one time, so Pierre's book and Pierre's life "become one and the same thing"; he projects his own death in his writing, according to Nelson, because he sees himself as a tragic hero, and "it is in the nature of tragic heroes to die."

v. Tales

If sheer quantity is any measure, Melville's tales of the 1850s were clearly the center of critical attention in 1970, on the evidence of no less than twenty-six articles—too many to be looked at individually here. With the exception of "The 'Gees," every one of his contributions to the magazines receives at least a passing glance. The notes and articles are of varying length and significance, ranging from a source-study by Beryl Rowland, "Melville's Waterloo in 'Rich Man's Crumbs'" (*NCF* 25:216–21), which calls attention to certain curious factual errors in Melville's sketch, to several appreciative essays that survey either the six *Piazza Tales* or the magazine pieces in general. In one of the latter articles, "A Quiet Crusade: Melville's Tales of the Fifties" (*ATQ* 7:8–12), Marie A. Campbell sees the fall of innocence as a recurrent theme in these works, "the real tragedy of Melville's characters" being "the failure to mature, to be regenerated by the experience undergone." Like Friedman and Seelye, she emphasizes Melville's duality of focus: on both his protagonist and his antagonist, or upon the protagonist and narrator; his own vision, she thinks, encompasses both poles.

The diversity of approach to the stories is well illustrated by three readings of "Bartleby," the first of Melville's magazine stories to be published. According to Donald M. Fiene, the title character "really was meant by Melville to be an incarnation of Christ" and the tale itself was designed as an allegory dramatizing the apocalypse ("Bartleby the Christ," *ATQ* 7:18–23). What John Seelye detects in the story, however, is a series of satirical thrusts at Melville's own contemporaries: Irving and the Whigs in the complacent attorney; the Transcendentalists, as sketched in Emerson's essay about them, in Bartleby himself ("The Contemporary 'Bartleby,'" *ATQ* 7:12–18). But Gordon E. Bigelow, taking "Bartleby" to be a symbolist story by a symbolist writer, finds it embodying no fixed references or explicit allegorical meanings; on the contrary, it is "implicit with the same ambiguity and mystery as life itself, with that inscrutability which fascinated and appalled Melville during his whole career" ("The Problem of Symbolist Form in Melville's 'Bartleby the Scrivener,'" *MLQ* 31:345–58).

There is a similar division of opinion about "Benito Cereno," the subject of eight essays that differ primarily in their handling of the issue of slavery as Melville treats it in the story. Mason I. Lowance, Jr., who has reservations about Melville's artistry, reads "Benito Cereno" as "an ironic narrative that depicts the illusions and ambiguities of evil's mask"; its thematic tension arises not from the presence of slavery, he thinks, but rather from the contrast of "Don Benito's corrupted innocence and Captain Delano's innocent naïveté" ("Veils and Illusions in 'Benito Cereno,'" *ArQ* 26:113–26). Charles Nicol, however, like an increasing number of recent critics, holds that "slavery is the evil"; in his view, Melville himself, "while sympathetic to the plight of the slaves, is generally unsympathetic toward Babo's revolt because it merely gives another turn to the circle of bloodshed" ("The Iconography of Evil and Ideal in 'Benito Cereno,'" *ATQ* 7:25–31). Richard E. Ray is dissatisfied with interpretations that see the story as either a study of pure evil or a condemnation of slavery; he takes its central figure to be Babo, portrayed as an unusually intelligent leader "doing his duty" when the opportunity presents itself ("'Benito Cereno': Babo as Leader," *ATQ* 7:31–37). And Peter Hays, though agreeing with those who consider "Benito Cereno" to be "Melville's contribution to the attack on slavery," prefers to emphasize its wider implications as "an attack on all forms of moral blindness and prejudice, whether perpetrated by nations, religions, or individuals." In his "Aristotelian reading" of the story Hays focuses attention on the title character as a tragic hero who finally achieves a self-realization that is denied Captain Delano; he gives relatively little attention to Babo. Hays is troubled by "the transcribed depositions," which for him detract from "the tone and mood" of the narrative though they contribute to its unity of theme—the difficulty of true perception—by revealing the obtuseness of officialdom ("Slavery and *Benito Cereno*: An Aristotelian View," *EA* 23:38–46).

What may well be the most significant of the essays on the short fiction is Jean Fagan Yellin's "Black Masks: Melville's 'Benito Cereno'" (*AQ* 22:678–89), which assumes that Melville intended specifically to evoke contemporary recollections, not only of "the black insurrection that occurred in Santo Domingo in the last decade of the 18th century" but also of the more recent revolt in Virginia led by Nat Turner. In her reading the narrative "projects a shifting triad of figures"—Delano, Cereno, and Babo—recognizable by magazine readers of the day "as Yankee, Slaveholder, and Negro. Through them, Melville probes the problem of reality and the nature of evil. The particular reality and the specific evil in 'Benito Cereno' involve their relationships as blacks and whites, as masters and slaves." The structure of the story comprises the American's observations, the Spaniard's chronicle, and the ensuing dialogue between them; the Negro's viewpoint "is unexpressed. Without the black perspective, ambiguity is inevitable." In summary, she holds that "Melville used well established literary versions of the Negro as happy slave, unfortunate victim and exotic primitive, displayed their falseness, and destroyed them," thus revealing "the stereotyped faces worn by Negroes in our fiction to be masks."

As several other articles show, the relation of Melville's fiction to his reading of Hawthorne is receiving continued attention. In writing "The Piazza," according to Hyatt H. Waggoner, "Melville was both remembering Hawthorne and defining their differences"; like Helmbrecht Breinig (see *ALS 1968*, p. 42), Waggoner suggests "The Old Manse" as the "inspiration" of "The Piazza" if not its actual source ("Hawthorne and Melville Acquaint the Reader with Their Abodes," *SNNTS* 2:420–24). Edward H. Rosenberry, though he too writes in terms of Melville's "organic assimilation" of Hawthorne's work rather than his use of it "as an absolute source," argues convincingly that elements of both "I and My Chimney" and "The Apple-Tree Table" derive from a recollection or a rereading of *Mosses from an Old Manse* ("Melville and His *Mosses*," *ATQ* 7:47–51). Irving Malin regards "The Bell-Tower" as "an ironic inversion of 'The Artist of the Beautiful'": both stories concern "The Faustian drive in art," but Owen Warland is a genuine artist and Bannadonna is a mechanician —like Ahab, Malin suggests ("The Compulsive Design," *American Dreams*, pp. 58–75). And Marvin Fisher, in "Focus on Herman Melville's 'The Two Temples': The Denigration of the American Dream" (*American Dreams*, pp. 76–86), thinks that Melville's diagnosis of "pathological alienation and sterility" in that diptych is not only reminiscent of Hawthorne's tales but like Emerson's Divinity School Address as well.

vi. Israel Potter, The Confidence-Man

After the recent flurry of critical interest in *Israel Potter* and *The Confidence-Man*, discussion of these works in articles of 1970 seems relatively slight, being confined mainly to short notes on somewhat minor points. The current disposition to look for something other than "gloom and futility" in the latter book is reflected in an essay by Paul McCarthy (*ATQ* 7:56–61) which singles out as "Affirmative Elements in *The Confidence-Man*" Melville's treatments of Pitch, "the most important moral character," and such other figures as the boy peddler, the barber, and the merchant. In emphasizing Pitch, like D. Nathan Sumner and Merlin Bowen (see *ALS 1968*, p. 43; *ALS 1969*, p. 48), McCarthy argues that he combines the best qualities of both the Easterner and the Westerner; through Pitch, he thinks, Melville is suggesting that "the country may regain a sense of direction, at least a greater awareness of both its potentialities and responsibilities."

Melville's "ultimate confidence-man, the cosmopolitan," is the subject of a provocative essay by Frank Jaster ("Melville's Cosmopolitan: The Experience of Life in *The Confidence-Man: His Masquerade*," *SoQ* 8:201–10) that identifies him as "neither Satan nor Satan's emissary," as many commentators have argued, but rather as "a symbolic representation of life itself." The cosmopolitan "meets all who come his way in the manner in which they ask to be met," Jaster explains. While the other characters react to their own reflection as they see it in him, he himself remains wholly indifferent. "He confronts man and reflects whatever is in man. The only demand is the confrontation." In the final chapter of the book, which Jaster interprets as synthesizing all the confrontations of its predecessors, the cosmopolitan as Life meets two other archetypal characters, "the old man as Victim" and "the youth as Cynic"; as the book closes "it is life that leads the living out from the decay of the darkened room," with its smell "of death," into "either more darkness or, perhaps, into light." If, as one begins to suspect, "there is nothing behind the endlessly changing masks" of the confidence-man—i.e., of life, Jaster concludes, "then the only hope for the salvation of humanity must come from within man himself."

vii. *Clarel* and Other Poems

The various poetic fruits of Melville's travels in Italy early in 1857 are the principal concerns of two commendable articles reflecting the continuing Italian interest in Melville: "Le poesie 'italiane' di Herman Melville" by Cristina Giorcelli (*SA* 14[1968]:165–91) and "Melville dinanzi al Risorgimento ed alla Guerra di Secessione" by Elémire Zolla (*Italia e Stati Uniti nell'età del risorgimento e della guerra civile*, Florence, La Nuova Italia, 1969, pp. 7–18). In "Melville's *Clarel*: Dynamic Synthesis" (*ATQ* 7:67–76) Joseph G. Knapp interprets that poem as "a continued dissonance struggling toward a harmony" that is ultimately achieved only in the imagery. What the imagery reveals to Father Knapp is "a certitude that is learned only through suffering—which is real even though infra-conceptual." Melville, he thinks, came to accept a kind of Christianity offering "not a blueprint for social utopia but a promise of the same fate that befell its founder." In "Clarel's Rejection of the Titans" (*ATQ* 7:76–81), Vincent S. Kenny, noting an increasing "social skepticism" in Melville, holds that the poem "enunciated Melville's final word on the Rebel's plan of action in a man-o-war world": the failures of Celio, Mortmain, and Ungar, whom Kenny regards as comparable in their monomania to Taji, Ahab, and Pierre, are presented, he thinks, as object lessons for the title character.

John Marr, Timoleon, and the other verse written after *Clarel* are the works explicated by William Bysshe Stein in *The Poetry of Melville's Late Years: Time, History, Myth, and Religion* (Albany: State Univ. of N.Y. Press), a book incorporating four of Stein's previous articles along with new materials. Between *Clarel* and *John Marr*, Stein believes, Melville "resolved a tormenting psychological and spiritual crisis," not in the religious terms emphasized by Pops and Knapp but by renouncing "all modes of abstract thought," along with "the code of nihilistic individualism developed in *Moby Dick, Mardi*, and *Pierre*"—as Kenny also suggests—and by repudiating "constrictive Protestant Christianity with its fear of the unholy flesh." His resulting creative activity "served to exorcise all the disillusionments of his young adulthood," according to Stein, who sees as "the main problem" of the poetry "its bewildering discordance and unconventionality." Melville, he argues, developed a "revolutionary" poetic method to accommodate his mature vision of experiential reality. Thus the world he depicts in *John Marr*

> reflects the cold neutrality of nature, the setting of life in which the absence of God is as self-evident as the inevitability of suffering and death. This fact inspires literally hundreds of chortling blasphemies on the absurdity of belief in a supernatural power. A kind of Freudian in his old age, Melville also relates the basic insecurity of experience to unsuspected psychosexual anxieties and disturbances which are induced by the frustrations of hope and desire. Moreover, he couches these insights in patterns of mythic imagery which embrace the now commonly recognized archetypes of the unconscious. In short, his relentless focus on the inherent disorder of things coincides with his antipoetic rhetorical practices. [pp. 13–14]

Stein's "psychoanalytic interpretations" of individual poems, "Freudian, Jungian, and sometimes plainly Steinian," develop these generalizations.

viii. Billy Budd, Sailor

A half-dozen essays illustrate the usual variety of critical approaches to *Billy Budd*, several of them again raising the issues of Melville's modernity and his affiliations with existentialism. In an illuminating comparison of Melville's handling of historical materials with Stephen Crane's, Toby Fulwiler holds in "The Death of the Handsome Sailor: A Study of *Billy Budd* and *The Red Badge of Courage*" (*ArQ*

26:101–12) that "Melville remains forever linked to the romantic past while Crane strikes out toward the existential future." Fulwiler is concerned with the relation between content and form in the two works: "When Crane's world split apart," he writes, "the fictional technique he used went along with it"; *Billy Budd*, though it "may be 'modern'" in offering "an obviously symbolic narrative, but an ambiguous resolution," remains "traditional" in its characterization, narrative point of view, and presentation of theme. Other criticism of 1970 is more narrowly focused, with the role of Captain Vere receiving primary attention. A politically oriented study by Jon M. Kinnamon sees Melville calling upon his readers to face the very dilemma confronting Vere, forcing them to choose between competing political ideals: those of Hume and Rousseau or those of Hobbes and Burke ("*Billy Budd*: Political Philosophies in a Sea of Thought," *ArQ* 26:164–72). Man must decide whether his responsibility is to "the welfare of society" or "his private sense of what is moral"; Vere's stand, abjuring private judgment on Billy in order to insure maintenance of social order, Kinnamon classifies as "essentially Hobbesian."

Two other critics whose orientation is existentialist differ both with Kinnamon and with one another in evaluating Vere's action. Philip D. Ortego, tracing what he calls "The Existential Roots of *Billy Budd*" (*ConnR* 4,i:80–87), argues that Melville is presenting no absolute truth or moral example in the story but "simply trying to show what man is: his own victim, not God's." He probes "the question of moral responsibility" in terms of the death of Billy: Vere cannot escape the consequences of his choice, having the option of "an alternate punishment for Billy Budd," but his fellow officers, the chaplain, and even Billy himself must also share the responsibility, since each man is responsible for his own actions even though he "will grasp at any pretext to avoid moral responsibility." Marjorie Dew ("The Prudent Captain Vere," *ATQ* 7:81–85) holds that Vere alone "has existentially taken upon himself the full guilt for the decision against Billy"; in doing so he "creates himself." Thus Vere—and through Vere, Melville himself—"accepts his fate," Mrs. Dew argues, but not "with satisfaction or in peace." On the contrary, he is led to assume responsibility for maintaining order in the belief that "ordinary men must not be allowed to endure freedom of decision, freedom that God has not equipped them to handle," for "freedom is

an affliction that only the few can bear." The result: "Vere's knowledge of human nature and the consciousness of having taken on himself God's function burn him to his death."

Vere's decision, according to still another analysis of *Billy Budd*,
was "relevant to his vision of the world," but among the several different interpretations of reality set forth in the story Vere's "is most
at odds with the narrator's." This is the contention of Edward A.
Kearns in "Omniscient Ambiguity: The Narrators of *Moby-Dick* and
Billy Budd" (*ESQ* 58:117–20); B. A. Yoder, in "Poetry and Science:
'Two Distinct Branches of Knowledge' in *Billy Budd*" (*SoRA*
3[1969]:223–39), goes farther than Kearns in characterizing that
narrator, regarding him as "a modern historian" who "accepts the
limitations of a scientific outlook" but "would like to read a deeper,
'prophetic' meaning into the events he recounts." His "character and
assumptions," Yoder thinks, "are much like Melville's own"; his "conflict between poetic and scientific insight"—a conflict characteristic of
nineteenth-century religious thought—is reflected also in the contrast
between Nelson's "poetry of action" and the professionalism of Vere,
who in Yoder's eyes lacks "a poetic sense." Yoder approaches the story
itself as a "gloss on historical Christianity" comparable to a poem by
Emily Dickinson, seeing in Billy's death "a type of the crucifixion,
the kind of extraordinary experience . . . from which great religions
grow. . . . Billy's example lives best as a ballad in the memory of the
sailors, all but inaccessible to the historians of this world."

One incidental feature of Yoder's essay is a running argument,
conducted mainly in his footnotes, with what he calls the "rather
plausible and accommodating new view of *Billy Budd*" which interprets the story as an unresolved moral dilemma and sees Vere as
making "an existential choice." Against this view, which he finds
represented in the work of Berthoff, Hayford and Sealts, and Brodt-
korb, he prefers to follow such critics as Willett, Casper, and Withim
in their unfavorable estimates of Vere. "If we must choose in darkness, let us choose like the poets whose imaginative light strikes
through the forms, not like Vere whose narrowing light only reflects
them—that, Romantic and anti-phenomenalistic as it is, is what I
think Melville is saying," Yoder affirms; in his reading as in Fulwiler's,
Melville appears more of a romantic traditionalist than an existential
modernist.

ix. Miscellaneous

In "An Attempt at a Union List of Editions of Melville, 1846–91" (*BC* 19:333–47), Richard Colles Johnson, the bibliographical associate of the editorial team directing the Northwestern-Newberry edition, reports information concerning the various editions and printings gathered for their preparation of a critical text of Melville and for Professor Tanselle's projected Melville bibliography. Another item of bibliographical interest, a machine-prepared collation of two texts of "Bartleby" (in *Putnam's Monthly* and *The Piazza Tales*), is reported in appendix B of *Project Occult*.

Hershel Parker, one of the Northwestern-Newberry editors who has been active in locating previously uncollected reviews of Melville's various works, has turned up significant English notices of *Mardi, The Whale,* and *Israel Potter* ("Three Melville Reviews in the London *Weekly Chronicle,*" *AL* 41:584–89). In another article Parker summarizes a detailed comparison of many original reviews with the findings previously reported by Hugh W. Hetherington in *Melville's Reviewers* (1961); Parker's dismaying conclusion is that this "supposedly definitive study of Melville's critical reception is all but unusable for any serious scholar" ("A Reexamination of *Melville's Reviewers,*" *AL* 42:226–32). A third article by Parker, "Melville's Satire of Emerson and Thoreau: An Evaluation of the Evidence" (*ATQ* 7:61–67; see corrections, 9[1971]:70), takes issue with recent remarks by Sidney P. Moss on Melville's response to the Transcendentalists (see *ALS 1968*, pp. 39–40), charging Moss with "an imperfect knowledge of Melville's works, Melville's life, and Melville scholarship." Readers will draw their own conclusions about the two studies from the evidence and reasoning presented on each side; as for Melville himself, I am still persuaded, as I put it in 1968, that his "attitude toward Transcendentalism and especially Emerson was 'ambivalent' rather than flatly hostile."

Melville's explicit references to Robert Burton, from 1839 to 1857, and the influence of Burton on his writing from *Mardi* through *The Confidence-Man* are the concerns of Nathalia Wright in "Melville and 'Old Burton,' with 'Bartleby' as *An Anatomy of Melancholy*" (*TSL* 15:1–13); she sees "Bartleby" as Melville's "most concentrated study of melancholy," the work which in theme and in form "perhaps owes most" to Burton's *Anatomy.* Janis Stout, in "Melville's Use of the Book of Job" (*NCF* 25:69–83), supplements earlier studies of Job and *Moby-Dick* by Miss Wright and C. Hugh Holman, examining both verbal allusions and thematic parallels to Job in the entire body of Melville's work. Although granting that "the significance one sees in Melville's development of the Job theme depends finally on one's interpretation of *Billy Budd*," she finds in his changing use of the Job story "an index of his progression from questioning to bitter defiance to resigned acceptance of the irrational necessity of evil."

A different view of Melville (and of *Billy Budd*) is taken by Charles Wayne Miller, who devotes a chapter of his book surveying the history of the American military novel to "Herman Melville and the Dissection of the Military World: A Warning to America" (*An Armed America: Its Face in Fiction*, New York, New York Univ. Press, pp. 29–52). Miller's discussion begins with *Israel Potter*, moves on to *White-Jacket* and *Billy Budd*, and concludes with a glance at *Battle-Pieces* as "a most fitting introduction to the fiction of the Civil War." He sees Melville as "a prime innovator" who surpasses the pioneering Cooper not only in characterization but also in his use of the military novel "as a vehicle for serious thought concerning American political and social evils." Miller specifically credits him with being the first of our novelists "to concentrate his attention on the fate of the common man within a military structure," "to analyze that structure as a microcosm of the authoritarian state," and "to mention seriously the possibility that such a form of government ever could gain power in the United States."

Four pairs of "doubled" characters in Melville receive the attention of Robert Rogers in *A Psychoanalytic Study of the Double in Literature* (Detroit, Mich., Wayne State Univ. Press). Rogers sees Ishmael and Ahab as "subject doubles" who "play the friendly role of secret sharers." He regards "Bartleby" as "a personal allegory" involving "another narrator-double composite," as in *Moby-Dick*; the "tragicomedy" of their relationship "symbolizes the despondency which Melville must have felt at the rejection by the public of his masterpiece," and the story itself "is, among other things, a piece of sublimation through fantasy" on the part of its author (see pp. 37–70). *Pierre*, according to Rogers, illustrates in the protagonist's relations with Lucy and Isabel as "object doubles" the way in which his "libidinal stream" separates "into love for fair maidens and femmes fatales" as a result of his "insuperable ambivalence . . . toward his mother" (see pp. 133 37). And *Billy Budd* is a "psycho-machia" taking place within "the composite mind of Billy-Claggart whose parts (one that of the rebellious, heterosexually-oriented son [Billy] and the other that of the loyal, homosexually-oriented son [Claggart]) may be said to be enacted on an oedipal stage before the eyes of the father, Vere, who combines both the tender and punishing aspects of the psychological father" (see pp. 146–60; a previous version is noticed in *ALS 1964*, p. 39).

A rewarding exploratory essay by Maurita Willett, "The Silences of Herman Melville" (*ATQ* 7:85–92), places Melville in still another perspective, examining the importance of Silence in authors he is known to have read, notably Shakespeare and Carlyle, and indicating the remarkable range and variety of the idea in his own writings. The study concludes with a suggestive comparison, observing that "Thoreau could live comfortably with Silence and the absolutes; Melville could not. Like God, like Truth, Silence was for him a siren with a silver voice, a 'Spirit-spout' luring him on to nothing or to the ultimate experience."

University of Wisconsin–Madison

4. Whitman and Dickinson

Bernice Slote

Whitman continues to stride massively ahead in publications, with Dickinson following along a little to the side and some distance behind him. Between them this year they bring (not counting, for the most part, reprints, anthologies, and dissertations) eighteen new monographs and books or portions of books and more than a hundred articles and reviews. It may be needful for some scholars to sit quietly for awhile, and read.

i. Whitman

a. **Bibliography, collections, biography.** "The proof of a poet is that his country absorbs him as affectionately as he has absorbed it": so Whitman concluded the 1855 *Preface* to *Leaves of Grass*. With the acquisition of the superb Charles E. Feinberg Whitman Collection by the Library of Congress, it is possible to think of Whitman as a kind of national treasure, held in Washington and thus absorbed into the symbolic heart of America. The story of the preservation of Whitman papers and memorabilia, the collecting and evaluating genius of Feinberg, and the final expansion of holdings in the Library of Congress is vividly told by John C. Broderick in "The Greatest Whitman Collector and the Greatest Whitman Collection" (*QJLC* 27:109–27). This "unparalleled collection"—which includes more than three thousand letters by and to Whitman and more than a thousand manuscripts—is suggested by the list of items included in the May 1969–January 1970 Library of Congress sesquicentennial exhibit ("Walt Whitman: The Man and the Poet," *QJLC* 27:171–76). Although Charles E. Feinberg has gallantly called Walt Whitman himself the greatest collector of Whitman materials, no one will deny that scholars owe a tremendous debt to Feinberg, who through a lifetime has with great energy and good judgment accumulated an American heritage.

Although it is unlikely that much new writing will be found to add to the Whitman canon, we do look to William White for miscellaneous notes on unpublished letters and other materials with a biographical interest. In "Some New Whitman Items" (*PrS* 44:47–55) he presents what may be "the earliest known verse by the author of *Leaves of Grass*"; four letters between Sam Stanley and Whitman; and four others to John Burroughs, John Addington Symonds, and W. Hale White. Two routine notes to R. Spence Watson are added (*WWR* 16:122), and an unrecorded, unpublished 1807 letter from Whitman's mother is given in text and holograph ("Mrs. Walter Whitman, Sr., Writes to Her Son," *WWR* 16:63–64). The full text of a letter to Josiah Child (June 1879), known previously only in summary, is presented by Florence B. Freedman (*WWR* 16:55–57). And a few more facts are gathered in: the date of Louis Tasistro's death (1886) gleaned from Whitman's *Daybook*, and references to Whitman in recent editions of John Jay Chapman's *Works* and A. Bronson Alcott's *Letters* (William White, "Tasistro and the *Daybook*," *WWR* 16:89–90; and "Alcott and Chapman Revisited," *WWR* 16:90–91).

There is little of the more esoteric bibliographical news, except Josiah Q. Bennett's account of a variant state of one leaf (the dropping of an "I") in the second gathering of the 1855 *Leaves of Grass* ("Whitman Loses His Ego; or, 'Not I, said the fly,'" *Serif* 7,i:35–36). Serials catalogues can add *Calamus*, a new "Walt Whitman Quarterly," published in Japan but written in English, and edited by William L. Moore of the International Christian University, Tokyo. Many of the articles used are reprints, but often new personal statements by the authors add interest. The dependable Whitman bibliography, compiled by William White, continues in each issue of the *Walt Whitman Review*.

Most scholars are well aware that Whitman not only collected Whitmaniana but helped to write it, too—with or without a signature. One example is Whitman's rather thorough involvement in the writing of his first biography, and the extent of that help is explored by Harold Jaffe in "Richard Maurice Bucke's *Walt Whitman*" (*Serif* 7,i:3–10). After at last being able to examine and collate the manuscript, Jaffe concludes that "not only did the poet write numerous passages, he assiduously revised nearly every page, and made frequent suggestions to Bucke about the inclusion or deletion of other material." As he worked on the book, Whitman "greatly improved

Bucke's manuscript" and in so doing illuminated certain aspects of himself: "his self-aggrandizement. . .; his fear of appearing in any way effeminate; his occasional overcautiousness." Finally, there is "the overall deception implied in his revising another man's book and disguising it" (though to anyone who knows how even today some inadequate scholarly work is metamorphosed by the editors of scholarly presses, this last concealment will not seem so unusual a sin). In "Whitman on Himself: An Unrecorded Piece" (*PLL* 6:202–05), William White presents an apparently unpublished essay found in the form of page proof (or it may be an offprint) among Whitman's papers and now in the Feinberg Collection: "Foreign Criticism on an American Poet." Style and circumstance point to Whitman as the author of this review of French and English notices about the American poet.

The most substantial new work on Whitman has been on his journalism, notably in Thomas L. Brasher's *Whitman as Editor of the "Brooklyn Daily Eagle"* (Detroit, Mich., Wayne State Univ. Press). This book, perhaps the most important for scholars among the longer studies of 1970, reviews in detail the two years (1846–1848) in which Whitman as editor wrote steadily for the *Eagle* on politics, business, urban problems, slavery, religion, literature, drama, and the other arts, thus furnishing a microcosm of American city life and Whitman's thinking in the years before he wrote *Leaves of Grass*. The material is organized and discussed under general topics. Not all selections are printed in full but there are many extended excerpts with a running commentary on their content and briefer references to other statements and to Whitman's life. (We have, for example, glimpses of Whitman going with four hundred Sunday schoolers, most of them children, to a picnic in Jamaica, or taking the ferry at the bottom of Fulton Street, or enjoying "The Marseillaise" at a New York band concert.) Mr. Brasher estimates that most—perhaps four-fifths—of the material in the book has not been previously reprinted. He has gone to the files of the newspaper directly, has worked from the complete primary sources, and has been able to correct a number of misconceptions. Although Whitman's journalistic work on the *Eagle* was usually conventional, he was a responsible editor, concludes Brasher—"a journalist who enjoyed his profession, took it seriously, and devoted it to an earnest purpose." Moreover, Whitman was educating not only his readers but himself: many of his ideas in

Leaves of Grass are here in embryo form. There are extensive notes and an index.

Two articles by Herbert Bergman consider Whitman's journalism as a whole. He sees the newspaper work contributing "a distinctively *American* perspective" to Whitman's thinking, and conjectures that the editor may have become a poet because he needed an editorial platform ("The Influence of Whitman's Journalism on *Leaves of Grass*," *ALR* 3:399–404). Bergman's problems in assembling Whitman's journalistic writings will be poignantly familiar to anyone who has attempted such a project—problems of authenticating authorship, determining accurately the facts about the history of a newspaper, sorting out contradictory evidence, locating missing files, or allowing for irremediable gaps ("On Editing Whitman's Journalism," *WWR* 16:104–09). But sometimes things do go right. In research for the journalism volumes of *The Collected Writings of Walt Whitman* (which he and William White are preparing), Professor Bergman discovered a file of the Hempstead *Inquirer* containing the long-missing first three "Sun-Down Papers." These Whitman essays are printed in full in an article by Bergman and White ("Whitman's Lost 'Sun-Down Papers,' Nos. 1–3," *ABC* 20,iv:17–20).

Several books or portions of books have primarily a biographical interest, though the story of a life always touches the works. The variety of approaches in biography may be illustrated first by the new edition of Emory Holloway's *Whitman: An Interpretation in Narrative*, noted here because of the new, second preface by the author (New York, Biblo and Tannen, 1969). In this preface the author speaks of an unpublished two-volume expansion and revision of his 1926 book which has been deposited in the Berg Collection of the New York Public Library and can be used there. Certainly Emory Holloway's conclusions about Whitman are important to all scholars who have followed him. Whitman's enduring power, Holloway suggests, comes from his largeness and flexibility, his blending of the conservative and radical, and Whitman's impact is credited to "his sphericity, his roundedness, his stable center of gravity." The edition has a list of errata but is otherwise unchanged from the 1926 printing. Another view of Whitman is through a focused collection of poems, *The Tenderest Lover: The Erotic Poetry of Walt Whitman*, edited with an introduction by Walter Lowenfels (New York, Delacorte Press). The poems are, of course, love poems in many senses, but even though they have been fragmented out of the fabric of *Leaves* they do not seem to be denigrated by such an emphasis or culling-out. In his generally fair introduction the editor comments on the revolutionary nature of *Leaves of Grass*, and for biographical context submits new evidence on two women in Whitman's life—Ellen Eyre (a letter shows that she had "a passing affair with Whitman") and Nelly O'Connor, the wife of Whitman's friend William D. O'Connor (according to another letter of 1870 she was in love with Walt). The editor observes, however, that there were no enduring relationships with women. He also presents what he terms "love letters" from Civil War soldiers.

Although it is aimed at a young—or general—audience, Barbara Marinacci's *O Wondrous Singer!* (New York, Dodd, Mead) is well written, knowledgeable, and worth recommending to older students, though for serious scholarship it would need to be read more critically. Even if the book is an introduction, it is not brief, using passages from the poetry extensively to blend Whitman's life with his work. It has a good section of photographs and reproductions of manuscript and book pages, a selected bibliography, a section identifying poetry quotations, and an index. A narrower consideration of biography and background is given in a section of Joan D. Berbrich's *Three Voices from Paumanok: The Influence of Long Island on James Fenimore Cooper, William Cullen Bryant, Walt Whitman* (Port Washington, N.Y., Ira J. Friedman, 1969, pp. 111–96), a study which explores the history of the area Whitman knew in his youth and what in his early experience helped to make Long Island a microcosm of the United States.

b. **Criticism: general.**   In the miscellany of critical portraits, general observations, and analyses of ideas or structures, two short essays were especially satisfying to read. One is a refreshing look at Whitman by the late Italian poet, novelist, and critic Cesare Pavese, whose 1933 essay, "Interpretation of Walt Whitman, Poet," has at last been made available in English by Edwin Fussell in his translation of Pavese's *American Literature: Essays and Opinions* (Berkeley, Univ. of Calif. Press, pp. 117–41). Pavese's writing is colorful and vigorous; whatever he says *seems* new, at least ("He did not make the primitive poem he dreamed, but the poem of this dream"). Pavese sees Whitman's writing in two periods—poetry at first and then later the prose—

which is prose, he says, even when it is printed as poetry. He defines the "form" of Whitman's poetry in terms of the line, the oratorical "period" of breath; the pattern is that of successive individual periods complete in themselves because of their movement, not their idea. In this sense lines are not fragments; they are valuable for "their eloquent flow, where every line is a complete whole, with its own harmonies and its own significance. It could be said that Walt Whitman thinks in lines." The highs and lows of his music, then, are "the highs and lows of his imaginative state." Pavese understands *Leaves of Grass* to be one identity, one process: the "Children of Adam" and "Calamus" poems are all "the same old hymn to the perfect Whitmanian individual," and Whitman "never sings America: he sings himself intent on discovering America."

The other article is Alfred Kazin's "The Great American Poet" (*NYRB* 15,vii:42–46). Though directed particularly to *Specimen Days and Collect* (and intended as the introduction to a reissue of that book by David R. Gotline), it is a vignette of the man, and more. Kazin writes of Whitman with eloquence and the perception possible only with wide knowledge, so that he can expand from significant detail to complex relationships. The semiautobiographical *Specimen Days* includes Whitman's notes on his youth, on his experiences during the Civil War, on travel and nature, but Kazin finds the Washington sketches especially revealing. It was Whitman's chief desire, he says, to join himself and his created persona to the sacred cause of the Union in the Civil War. He describes the book's "slower, more ruminative style," its realism of detail, its immediacy, and Whitman's "love of documenting the masses." There is something in every paragraph.

Any book which looks at the whole of *Leaves of Grass* is evidence of some major commitment by a Whitman scholar. With Gay Wilson Allen, any new book profits from the whole of a scholar's assimilated knowledge. *A Reader's Guide to Walt Whitman* (New York, Farrar, Straus and Giroux) is a general review of ideas, interpretations, editions of *Leaves of Grass*—a book designed to introduce and not to conclude.

An important Whitman study (copyrighted in 1970 though released later) is Thomas Edward Crawley's *The Structure of "Leaves of Grass"* (Austin, Univ. of Texas Press). In the first sections of the main body of the book Professor Crawley defines Whitman's organic principle and his role as poet-prophet, then demonstrates by many quotations that the persona of *Leaves of Grass* has the role of a Christ-like prophet. This, he concludes, is "the most fully developed and frequently recurring symbol in *Leaves of Grass.*" It is a cosmic figure, however, symbolical and mystical rather than historical, and unifies the book by fusing the personal, religious, and national themes. Whitman's persona as the humanistic poet-prophet Christ is harmoniously developed with his other, national theme of a symbolic American democracy. Although one is always uneasy in the face of another determined effort to find a Christ-figure in literature (nothing leaps more surely from the page than the passages which support what we want to prove), Professor Crawley's case is reasonably stated and too complex to be ignored. The third major section of the book, a structural analysis of *Leaves of Grass*, is based on the 1881 edition; though different in some details from other notable analyses of the book by Malcolm Cowley, James E. Miller, Jr., and others, it is like them in asserting the unity and deliberate arrangement of the book. A particular contribution, however, is Crawley's consistent tracing of the double "unfolding of poet and nation," themes supported by recurring symbols and relationships within and between groups of poems. The final chapter, on the evolution of *Leaves of Grass*, shows the "organic" growth by analysis of changes in the content and arrangement of each new edition. This useful book has an appendix listing "Passages of Religious Significance in Whitman's Works," a bibliography, and an index.

Several articles on *Leaves of Grass* should be considered with these books. Another view of Whitman's handling of his work is the fine article by Robin P. Hoople, " 'Chants Democratic and Native American': A Neglected Sequence in the Growth of *Leaves of Grass*" (*AL* 42:181–96), in which he analyzes with clarity and conviction the importance of that group of poems as "Whitman's assessment of contemporary American democracy" and as demonstrating the carefully wrought internal structure of Whitman's book. The poems in this sequence, added to the 1860 edition as a unit but dispersed in later editions, reflect the political tensions of the pre-Civil War years. They show "a sense of time present, of current reality and of profound urgency, all tempered by Whitman's unquenchable capacity to create visions."

Richard D. McGhee's "*Leaves of Grass* and Cultural Development" (*WWR* 16:3–14) is a good review of Whitman's progression through successive editions of *Leaves of Grass*; however, since it is based on the "construct" defining nineteenth-century development which Morse Peckham outlines in *Beyond the Tragic Vision*, and since Peckham had studied Whitman, it is perilously close to proving the critic by the poet the critic observed. Nevertheless, the subheads provided for each edition of *Leaves of Grass* in sections of the article describe the changing redirections of the book and show the nature of Whitman's creative and personal development: "Discoverer" (1855), "Explorer" (1856), "Redeemer" (1860), "Illusion and Reality" (1867), "Vistas of Invention" (1871–1872), "The Spirit of Style" (1876), and "The Style of Spirit" (1881). The sequence of emphases may indeed be archetypal culturally and creatively for Whitman's age. With an appropriately modern note Roger H. Sykes discusses the motifs of "passage" in several Whitman poems and relates these ways of spanning space to man's leap to the moon (" 'Seeking the Spheres to Connect,' " *Calamus* 3:20–25).

The great diversity in subject and treatment found in the shorter general articles on Whitman may be illustrated by *Papers on Walt Whitman*, edited by Lester F. Zimmerman and Winston Weathers (Tulsa, Okla., UTMS). The first piece is a group of poems, "Seven Considerations of Whitman's Creative Spirit" by Winston Weathers (pp. 1–5); the titles of the other five papers suggest their content: "Whitman and the English Writers" by Herbert Howarth (pp. 6–25); "The Second *Leaves of Grass* (1856): A Re-Evaluation" by Lester Goodson (pp. 26–34); "Whitman's Mechanical Muse" by Roy R. Male (pp. 35–43); "Walt Whitman and the Tradition of the Organic" by Lester F. Zimmerman (pp. 44–55); and "The Oratorical Stance and Whitman's Early Poetry" by C. Carroll Hollis (pp. 56–79). The monograph is dedicated to the late Professor Goodson. Some of these articles gain weight in combination with others. Lester Goodson's discussion in *Papers* of the 1856 edition and his article in the *Walt Whitman Review* (16:45–50), "Whitman and the Problem of Evil," both deal with the union of opposing or separate elements. In 1856 Whitman added poems that show the importance of the "Other" ("You, whoever you are") and thus stressed the uniting of poet-reader identities. The entire spiritual journey of the *Leaves* is "to make one identity of poet and reader." Evil, too, combines with good and "contributes its share to a schematized whole." Roy R. Male's article in *Papers* describes Whitman's organic principle, first in terms of a machine (like the printing press) with parts in composition; but it is also a "verbal artifice" and gains the illusion of life by his emphasis on the oral quality of language, the voice. *Leaves of Grass* was a "break-out from the world of print to the world of sound." Other details of Whitman's emphasis on the spoken word and the involvement of the reader are developed in an overlapping article (several sections are repeated), his "Whitman's Radical Utterance" (*ESQ* 60:73–75). C. Carroll Hollis's article in *Papers* strongly reinforces our interest in the oral elements in *Leaves of Grass* with a thorough and convincing analysis of the effect of the oratorical style of Whitman's poetics. As Whitman's youth coincided with "the high period of oratory in this country," so his early poetry took the tone of the platform and the "wander-teacher" described in an essay of 1857; but the later poems like "Passage to India," observes Professor Hollis, replace the call to the open road with words for a private journey.

Perhaps it is to be expected that brief articles dealing with Whitman's ideas be nebulous, repetitive, for Whitman does not submit easily to compression and close analysis in a prose statement. A number of articles, then, are more variations on the liturgy than new perceptions. And often writers dealing in these Whitman generalities do not stop long enough to read closely and quote carefully. In "Whitman as Social Theorist: Worker in Poetics and Politics" (*WWR* 16: 41–45), for example, R. Galen Hanson makes the sound point that Whitman saw society as pluralistic with social change determined by individual genius, but supports it with inaccurate quotations from *Democratic Vistas* (one is completely garbled and quite destroys the reader's confidence). Inaccurate quotations and vague references also mar David W. Marcell's "The Two Whitmans and *Democracy in America*" (the reference of the italicized words is not clear), included in *Challenges in American Culture*, edited by Ray B. Browne, Larry N. Landrum, and William Bottorff (Bowling Green, Ohio, Bowling Green Univ. Popular Press, pp. 178–89). Here the conclusion that during the Civil War Whitman's concept of democracy shifted from a trust in the common man, with each "Self" a poet, individual and universal, to an "elitism" in which a special class of poets is advocated, is based rather precariously on relating quite different works, contrasting "Song of Myself" and the 1855 *Preface* to *Leaves of Grass* with *Democratic Vistas*, published in 1871 (though not written in that year as is assumed in the essay). Moreover it ignores Whitman's almost determined selectivity before the Civil War, in his repeated definitions of "the greatest poet" in the 1855 *Preface* ("He is not one of the chorus"), and, in the 1860 *Leaves of Grass*, his call for "a new brood" of "Poets to come"—just as in *Democratic Vistas* he called for "a class of bards" who will carry on Whitmanian unity and write what is really *American* in literature.

There is a scholarly debate over Arthur Golden's review of Edwin H. Miller's *Walt Whitman's Poetry* (see *ALS 1969*, p. 65). Under the title of "Whitman and Psychoanalytic Criticism:" we have "A Response to Arthur Golden" by Stephen A. Black and "A Reply" by Arthur Golden (*L&P* 20,ii:79–92), who defends himself against the charge that his review "seriously misrepresents" Miller's book. My judgment while refereeing is that Golden wins.

c. **Criticism: individual poems.**   The only poem with more than one substantial article is, of course, "Song of Myself." Helge Normann Nilsen in "The Mystic Message. Whitman's 'Song of Myself'" (*Edda* 69[1969]:400–09), sees the type of mystical experience in the poem as different from that of ascetics and the categories outlined by Evelyn Underhill (and followed by James E. Miller, Jr., in describing an "inverted mystical experience" in *A Critical Guide to "Leaves of Grass"*). The overall structure of "Song of Myself," says the author, is "the gradual process of merging of self and reality, of ever-larger inclusion and identification." Some divisions of the poem are indicated though not in great exactness. The second article is by Elizabeth Phillips, "'Song of Myself': The Numbers of the Poem in Relation to Its Form" (*WWR* 16:67–81). The argument in this carefully exact study is that Whitman worked out a nearly mathematical arrangement by which certain pivotal lines occur in a discernible pattern. The "seven clusters or masses of lines" balance each other so that the poem is "symmetrical in its main disposition" but with "a bold asymmetry" which gives it vitality. There are indeed certain repetitions of key lines and figures at the numerically ordered points, notably themes of the grass, the body and soul, the I and you. The central lines in clusters also are said to have syntactical significance. While I am as yet unwilling to suspend my disbelief (the resemblance of such line-counts to Baconian ciphers is inescapable), Professor

Phillips may well be right and her pattern deserves a considered look.

There are two briefer notes on "Out of the Cradle Endlessly Rocking." Jon C. Stott suggests that there may be a possible parallel between the mockingbird's song and "Whitman's own organic manner of creation" ("The Mocking-Bird in 'Out of the Cradle,'" *WWR* 16:119–20), and Joseph M. DeFalco examines revisions in the 1867 version of the poem which play on echoes from "The Raven" and contrast Whitman's optimism with Poe's pessimism ("Whitman's Changes in 'Out of the Cradle' and Poe's 'Raven,'" *WWR* 16:22–27).

A half dozen other articles give attention to the poems. Richard P. Sugg traces a circular pattern in the symbolic movement of "A Broadway Pageant" ("Whitman's Symbolic Circle and 'A Broadway Pageant,'" *WWR* 16:35–40). "Mixed Tone in 'Cavalry Crossing a Ford,'" by Richard Allan Davison (*WWR* 16:114–17), notes a shift from a romantic to a realistic view of war in the descriptive language of the poem. John H. Matle has a good reading of the 1892 form of "I Sing the Body Electric" ("The Body Acclaimed," *WWR* 16:110–14), which he calls "at once lyrical and epic," a poem which presents the old idea that the physical gives rise to the spiritual but in "a poetic idiom peculiarly Whitman's." The last two lines of "A Sight in Camp" emphasize "the essential divinity of the common man," says James T. F. Tanner in "A Note on Whitman's 'A Sight in Camp'" (*ESQ* 58:123–24). In "Whitman's Vision of the Past in 'The Sleepers'" (*WWR* 16:86–89) Joyce Kornblatt gives a good explication of the poem, which she sees as uniting visions of the archetypal, historical, and personal poet in varying attitudes that together make a whole vision. Lyle Domina reviews the symbols and theme of "When Lilacs Last in the Dooryard Bloom'd" ("Whitman's 'Lilacs': Process of Self-Realization," *ESQ* 58:124–27) and sees the poem as "the reconciliation of the opposites of life and death, which is possible only through the poet's awareness of his transcendent nature." He compares "Lilacs" and "Song of Myself" as they show this process.

***d.* Sources, relationships, influence.** Some of the most interesting source studies during the past few years have been on Indian literature and philosophy, by Indian scholars, who of course bring a special competence to the subject. Now added to V. K. Chari's *Walt*

Whitman in the Light of Vedantic Mysticism (see *ALS 1964*, pp. 47–48) and O. K. Nambiar's *Walt Whitman and Yoga* (see *ALS 1967*, pp. 53–54) we have a long, detailed, and stimulating—to many it will be fascinating—study of Whitman's Indian sources, *The Roots of Whitman's Grass* (Rutherford, N.J., Fairleigh Dickinson Univ. Press), by T. R. Rajasekharaiah of Karnatak University. The sources are confined to material in English either mentioned by Whitman or available to him in the libraries he used before 1855. Mr. Rajasekharaiah is most successful in the early sections of the book when he reviews and treats quite fairly all of the problems in identifying what Whitman may have used; he is weakest in his later arguments for sources in specific passages that to an uncommitted reader can be no more than parallels—and some of those very tenuous ones. The parallels do enlarge our understanding of Indian ideas, and the author's enthusiasm is admirable. But one cannot accept the implication that most of Whitman's concepts and much of his language derived directly from Indian philosophy and literature when the passages given as evidence seem, to a Western reader, vivid reminders of the Bible and Blake, to name only two other possible sources. And we might also consider Whitman's suggestions of "sources" in "Song of Myself" (section 41): "Magnifying and applying come I / . . . Taking myself the exact dimensions of Jehovah, / Lithographing Kronos, . . . / Buying drafts of Osiris"—and also including Monito, Allah, Odin, and Mexitli. Yet, I am quite persuaded at this moment that Whitman's term "leaves of grass" grew from descriptions of the sacred leaves of *cusa* grass— unlike Gay Wilson Allen who in his introductory note doubts this point. The book has valuable notes and abstracts of some of the major articles and accounts referred to in the text, but a serious handicap in using the book is that there is no full bibliography of the works of and about Indian literature and philosophy that Whitman is said to have had available. Some lists are included in the text in early chapters, but even there some items are given without publisher and date. There is, however, a detailed but much less useful "Select Bibliography" of Whitman's works, as well as an equally detailed and familiar list of books and articles about him. Some miscellaneous errors can eventually be corrected (it is John Addington Symonds, not Symmonds; William Sloane Kennedy's book is *The Fight* [not *The Flight*] *Against the World*; *Start with the Sun* is written, not edited, by Miller, Shapiro, and Slote). Certainly *The Roots of Whitman's*

Grass is worth careful attention by Whitman scholars, though they may perversely take what the author has sometimes used for a "boxing in" of Whitman's thought and poetry and make of it a rich expansion.

Among other articles on Indian relationships V. Sachithanandan (Annamalai University, Madras) argues in "Whitman and the Serpent Power" (*WWR* 16:50–55) against O. K. Nambiar's link of Whitman and Sri Ramakrishna (in *Walt Whitman and Yoga*), holding that section 5 of "Song of Myself" shows a different kind of mystical vision—"cosmic, not acosmic," and that Whitman is "a theistic Vedantist who sings of the imminent and not of the transcendent aspect of the greater self." Om Prakash Sharma's "Walt Whitman and the Doctrine of Karman" (*PE&W* 20:169–74) finds Indian concepts in *Leaves of Grass* and shows particularly Whitman's use of *karmic* ideas of the oneness of time, the law of causality, the doctrine of reincarnation.

Whitman's larger personal context in history includes those to whom he first listened, those he touched on the way, and those who have lately found him alive and rising from beneath their bootsoles in more and more of contemporary life. The definition of such relationships is never simple. He was, for example, influenced by Elias Hicks and Quakerism and by Thomas Paine's "democratic faith," but he also diverged from both of them in many ways. Two excellent articles give abundant material on these two relationships: Lawrence Templin in "The Quaker Influence on Walt Whitman" (*AL* 42:165–80) shows that he was little affected by his Quaker background, except for his "Quaker intuition" and the Quakers' humanitarian concern, diverging mainly from their dualism; yet he greatly admired the power of the Quaker preacher Elias Hicks. Margaret M. Vanderhaar discusses "Whitman, Paine, and the Religion of Democracy" (*WWR* 16:14–22). Though Whitman's universe was organic, Paine's mechanistic, they shared many ideas; both had a supreme concern for human liberty and "were united in the central beliefs of the Enlightenment."

Several articles are concerned with Whitman's influence on other writers and thinkers—and that influence seems to be more and more apparent, and diverse. Lewis Leary points out the striking use of elements from "Out of the Cradle Endlessly Rocking" throughout Kate Chopin's *The Awakening* and elsewhere in her work. Perhaps, he suggests, she used Whitman allusions to convey "nuances which in the 1890's she might not openly express" ("Kate Chopin and Walt Whitman," *WWR* 16:120–21). And P. A. Doyle in "Whitman and Sean O'Faolain" (*WWR* 16:117–19) quotes references to Whitman from work of the Irish critic and novelist. In a longer study, James T. F. Tanner discusses William James's serious interest in Whitman, who symbolized for him "the emancipated and sympathetically tolerant human figure." James quoted Whitman, explicated a poem ("To You") in *Pragmatism*, and in general understood and admired him ("Walt Whitman and William James," *Calamus* 2:6–23). Responses to Whitman are recorded in a lecture (tentatively dated 1930) by the sociologist Robert Ezra Park, which is reprinted and discussed by Florence B. Freedman ("A Sociologist Views a Poet," *WWR* 16:99–104), and expressed in numerous poems and statements by other writers, described by Alice Moser Claudel in "Poems as Laurels for Walt Whitman" (*WWR* 16:81–86). Among these are works of Swinburne, the Nicaraguan poet Rubén Darío, and Stephen Vincent Benét. Readers looking for some leaves of humor might like to check the story of Whitman's appearance in an Art Young cartoon and some verses by Arthur Guiterman in John S. Mayfield, "Walt Whitman, Theodore Roosevelt, and 'The New Inferno'" (*Courier* 35:19–23).

Informative comments and appreciations continue to come from other countries. Manoj Das in "The Good Gray Poet and the Last Great Rishi" (*IndL* 12[1969],iii:87–91) reports Sri Aurobindo's view of Whitman as "a splendid forerunner." Two reprints are of special interest—one a 1904 essay by R. Takayama, "A Japanese Estimate of Walt Whitman" (*Calamus* 2:1–5), which sees Whitman as prophet, and a translation by Frank J. Corliss, Jr., of an article by M. Mendel'son, "He Dreamed of the Brotherhood of People," first published in *Pravda*, 30 May 1969 (*WWR* 16:57–59). And there is a perceptive look at the Russian poet Vladimir Mayakovsky, often described as in the Whitman tradition. In "Mayakovsky and Whitman: The Icon and the Mosaic" (*SlavR* 28:416–25) Dale E. Peterson says that although both were bardic poets with personae who spoke of the "religion of comradeship," the literary connection between the two is superficial; they are different in content, poetic forms, and their personae. He includes analyses of several Mayakovsky poems.

Critics continue to look for perspectives by grouping and relating American writers, among themselves and in the world. It is not usual to relate Whitman and T. S. Eliot. James E. Miller, Jr., did so in 1958 with "Whitman and Eliot: The Poetry of Mysticism," later collected in *Quests Surd and Absurd* (1967), and he is now joined by Philip Hobsbaum of the University of Glasgow with "Eliot, Whitman and American Tradition" (*JAmS* 3[1969]:239–64). Though he discusses a good many other writers, Mr. Hobsbaum's chief point is that T. S. Eliot was an American, not an English, poet, and that his literary ancestors were not those French poets he claimed for himself but his American predecessor, Whitman. Whitman is well-illustrated and analyzed, and two other important points are made: that critics in England have failed to give Whitman his due, partly because he did not have a proper interpreter, and that many twentieth-century American writers have been "evading their destiny" (Robinson, Ransom, Santayana). Others like Aiken, Pound, Stevens, Lowell stand clearly in "a definable American tradition in poetry."

That Whitman is recognizably contemporary, even to the new generation, is illustrated in several student essays which are explained by their titles: Kazuko Okamoto, "On One's Self: An Address to University Students in Rebellion" (*Calamus* 1[1969]:6–23); Katie Clarke, "Poets, Orators, Singers: Come" (*Calamus* 2:24–33); and two eloquent pieces included in an appendix in Walter J. Slatoff's *With Respect to Readers: Dimensions of Literary Response* (Ithaca, N.Y., Cornell Univ. Press, pp. 191–207): Sylvia Lewis, "Impressions of Emily Dickinson" (a comparison of Dickinson and Whitman); and James Moody, "Whitman."

In this year's work some of the best writing, by the most distinguished of Whitman scholars, and on the most provocative topics can be found in two collections. The first is *The Artistic Legacy of Walt Whitman: A Tribute to Gay Wilson Allen*, edited with a foreword by Edwin Haviland Miller (New York, New York Univ. Press). It begins with Oscar Cargill's "Gay Wilson Allen: A Tribute" (pp. 1–7). Ned Rorem offers notes on the poetry of music, "Words Without Song" (pp. 9–19), and his musical settings for Whitman's "As Adam Early in the Morning" and "O You Whom I Often and Silently Come" are reproduced on the front and back inside cover pages. Max Kozloff in "Walt Whitman and American Art" (pp. 29–53) discusses Whitmanesque relationships with artists such as Eakins, John Marin, Jackson Pollock, Claes Oldenburg, and architects such as Buckminster Fuller, as well as Whitman's use of "subject matter similar to that used by other American artists." A section of illustrations from American artists complements the article. Edwin Haviland Miller goes into more detail with "The Radical Vision of Whitman and Pollock" (pp. 56–71)—they "altered the American landscape and American consciousness fundamentally." Robert Duncan speaks for the poet in "Changing Perspectives in Reading Whitman" (pp. 73–102). Preceded by twenty-four pictures and drawings of Whitman is an article by Gay Wilson Allen, "The Iconography of Walt Whitman" (pp. 127–52), in which he makes his selection of his four favorite "icons" or images of Whitman. They are, briefly, the "Christ likeness," a composite of the 1854 bust and the 1855 *Leaves of Grass* portrait; the "wound dresser," or the Brady Whitman of 1863; the "Moses" photograph of 1869; and the "Laughing Philosopher" in the Cox photograph of 1887. Also included in the book is "'A Backward Glance: A Bibliography of Gay Wilson Allen" (pp. 153–60).

A second important collection is *Walt Whitman in Our Time*, edited with an introduction by William White as a supplement to the *Walt Whitman Review* (Detroit, Mich., Wayne State Univ. Press). It presents four papers from a symposium at Wayne State University: Roy P. Basler, "Walt Whitman in Perspective" (pp. 5–8), William Meredith, "Whitman to the Poet" (pp. 9–11)—on Whitman's "formal influence" in his "slow but total franchise of free verse" and the more subtle influence of Whitman's notion of identity and the relevant (or individual) form; Edwin Haviland Miller, "And Gladly Edit" (pp. 13–16)—a recounting of the principles of an editor; and James E. Miller, Jr., "Whitman: Dead or Alive?" (pp. 17–20)—on the way one hears from both outside and inside the world of books and intellectual discoveries that Whitman is indeed alive and well and sounding out his barbaric yawp over the rooftops of America.

ii. Dickinson

a. **Bibliography.** The most important publication in Dickinson studies for 1970 was *Emily Dickinson: An Annotated Bibliography*, edited by Willis J. Buckingham (Bloomington, Ind. Univ. Press). An impressively complete, accurate, and usable compilation, the Buckingham bibliography is indispensable for scholars and often entertaining for browsers. I have tentatively counted 2610 separate numbered entries. In addition to the expected sections on works by and

about Dickinson (including reviews), the foreign language material
is extensively covered, plus theses (though this list is incomplete),
juvenile literature, fiction and drama based on Dickinson's life, other
tributes in poetry, exhibitions, recordings, films, and more. Cross-
references and annotations help throughout. Especially valuable is
the index of explications for each poem. By this list, the most discussed poems are "Because I Could Not Stop for Death" with thirty-
three explications and "I Heard a Fly Buzz—When I Died" with
twenty-six. With this volume and other recent bibliographies by
Susan Freis and Sheila Clendenning, Emily Dickinson begins to be
encircled, if not completely understood.

Superseded by the Buckingham bibliography in sheer size but
still very useful because of its annotations and introductory review
of other bibliographies is William White's "Emily Dickinsoniana: An
Annotated Checklist of Books about the Poet" (*BB* 26[1969]:100–
04). Continuing checklists appear in the *Emily Dickinson Bulletin*,
edited by Frederick L. Morey, who had three notes on foreign material in 1970: Italian (*EDB* 12:7–13), French (*EDB* 13:51–56), and
Germanic (*EDB* 14:58–66). Nearly lost among all the formal lists
and notations are a brief note by Olivia Dickinson Gooch on the four
extant Emily Dickinson pictures ("Likenesses of ED," *EDB* 14:77),
a summary by Robert B. Laurence of the history of publication and
criticism of Dickinson's letters ("The Mind Alone," *EDB* 15:94–102),
and sprightly personal comment by William White in "The Tyranny
of Book Collecting: Emily Dickinson" (ABC 21,i:9).

b. **Biography.** Viewing the writer through the refracted lens of his
work is common enough, but when a life is as private, as undefined,
as that of Emily Dickinson and the work so cryptic and alluring, the
known fragments become charged, magnetic, inviting more than the
usual conjectures and curiosity about the writer. Although a reader
might not always agree with everything he says (and some might be
offended), John Cody's "Metamorphosis of a Malady: Summary of
a Psychoanalytic Study of Emily Dickinson" (*HSL* 2:113–32) deserves study, even though one is disturbed by simplistic answers to
problems of creativity. Dr. Cody's thesis is that Emily Dickinson felt
rejected by her mother and that such a privation, sublimated later in
her life when the daughter was responsible for the care of the paralyzed mother, had much to do with the substance and intensity of

her poetry. Earlier articles by Dr. Cody not previously noted in *ALS* discussed related analyses, holding that Emily Dickinson's two years of difficulty with her eyes was psychosomatic, "a late manifestation in an already existing pattern of stress and suffering" ("Watchers up-on the East: The Ocular Complaints of Emily Dickinson," *Psychi-atricQ* 42[1968]:548–76), and that her images of hunger and thirst show "a famished search for affection" ("Emily Dickinson and Na-ture's Dining Room," *MQR* 7[1968]:249–54). Cynthia Chaliff has also written on this point, but her article, "ED as the Deprived Child" (*EDB* 13:34–43), adds little to Dr. Cody's statement. Although Dr. Cody presents a great deal of material from the letters, the poems, and other known events to support his thesis that Emily Dickinson was profoundly affected by a sense of estrangement from her mother, most readers will have reservations, on the grounds that he begins with a statement taken secondhand and without the context—Higgin-son's report to his wife that Emily said, "I never had a mother"—and that he goes entirely too far in cataloging genius when he suggests that with a different mother Emily would have been satisfied, conven-tional, and—without the void—no poet at all.

c. Criticism: general.   Two new studies aim for a general biograph-ical-critical introduction to Dickinson. One is the excellent forty-seven-page pamphlet *Emily Dickinson* (UMPAW 81[1969]), by Denis Donoghue of University College, Dublin. Admirably compact yet easy and eloquent in style, this short work strikes one as the kind of sound, perceptive, revealing introduction every writer should have. Professor Donoghue touches some of the critical matters in Dickinson —her strange sensibility, which required little reality; her special area of feeling—"the preappointed pain, how we choose it, the conse-quences of the choice"; the apocalyptic element in her imagination. His final praise is for "those poems in which Emily Dickinson's sensi-bility encounters the great moral universals: love, pain, loss, doubt, death. What happens to the universals, what happens to the sensi-bility: the poems which give this double drama are among the great-est poems in the language." Less individually perceptive but sound, and capably written for a more general audience, is the thirty-three-page section (plus fourteen pages of poems) in Rosemary Sprague's study of five American poets, *Imaginary Gardens* (Philadelphia, Chilton Book Co., 1969, pp. 1–48). (The other poets discussed are

Amy Lowell, Sara Teasdale, Edna St. Vincent Millay, and Marianne Moore.)

In *Emily Dickinson and Riddle* (DeKalb, No. Ill. Univ. Press, 1969), Dolores Dyer Lucas directs her attention to the cryptic elements in the poetry, combining a study of poems, letters, and life. Although she uses Paull F. Baum's definition of "riddle" as a "calculated deception" in which "the resemblance is submerged in deliberate ambiguity or obscurity," Mrs. Lucas does not stay closely to the traditional "riddle" form but includes many Dickinson poems that ask questions, or allow for more than one answer, or suggest mysteries. The somewhat forced organization sees first "the speaker" as a questioning child (here there is a good survey of Dickinson's ambivalent view of nature); then "the subject" as, characteristically, the mystery of death; "the audience" as Dickinson's correspondents; and "the wider audience" as posterity, the world, or "you." Mrs. Lucas sees Dickinson in her "strategy for immortality" meeting the modern world on many grounds, especially cinematic techniques, visual images, and time-space relationships. The riddles were her "artistic ordeal," and came to be a ritualistic search for the meaning of existence.

A smoothly written, condensed little book by Salamatullah Khan of Aligarh Muslim University has some valuable insights from the Indian point of view: *Emily Dickinson's Poetry: The Flood Subjects* (New Delhi, Aarti Book Centre, 1969; Mystic, Conn., Lawrence Verry). The "flood subjects" are those to which Emily Dickinson returned again and again, and we therefore find chapters on nature, love, divine love, death, immortality, and herself. Some observations are familiar: her attention to seasons and elemental forces, her peculiar angle of vision, her qualities of both exact observation and omission in scenes, a metaphysical handling of love, death as a suitor, the tension of both faith and doubt about immortality; but throughout are good notes on a number of poems and frequent references to Dickinson's orientation. She has, says the author, a rapport with the Indian reader and in addition to likenesses with the lyrics of *Rig Veda*, he notes that some death lyrics are like the songs of Kabir, and her bridal poems of divine love like the devotional songs of Mira Bai. Although the *Rig Veda* is available in English, both of the latter Indian writers are still untranslated.

Related to Mrs. Lucas's discussion of Dickinson's use of "riddle"

and to Denis Donoghue's point on the drama of sensibility's encounter with universals, is an excellent article by David Porter, "Emily Dickinson: The Poetics of Doubt" (*ESQ* 60:86–93). Mr. Porter
concentrates chiefly on illustrating an important element in the Dickinson poetics—language used to effect "an inversion, producing not
uncritical discovery but chilling estrangement," going from the familiar acceptance to sudden turns of mood and understanding. The
drama is the movement, the structural shift: "Poems alter beneath
our eyes, slip to a perspective quite different from the disarming ones
with which they begin." This is the "slantness" of Emily Dickinson's
telling, it comes from "the remorseless drama of the questioning consciousness." Dislocation in the poem, both open and subtle, and a
craft which enabled Dickinson to convey through several "linguistic
layers" various "levels of belief and doubt," are convincingly illustrated. With a poetic consciousness "posed incessantly on the threshold of faith," says Mr. Porter, "poetry is what she did to her doubt."

In another general article on her poetics, "Emily Dickinson as a
Latter-Day Metaphysical Poet" (*ATQ* 1[1969]:77–81), C. J. Fisher
illustrates from the poetry points of correspondence with those
seventeenth-century poets (like Vaughan, Crashaw, Donne) termed
"metaphysical" by Samuel Johnson. Metaphysical characteristics are
"concentration of thought" ("The Soul Selects Her Own Society—"),
the conceit as a controlling image ("My Life Had Stood—a Loaded
Gun"), epigrams (of which there are many delightful examples); the
unexpected startling line and abrupt opening ("I Felt a Funeral in
My Brain"). Whether or not she consciously used the techniques of
the seventeenth-century metaphysicals, Mr. Fisher concludes quite
fairly that Emily Dickinson wrote in that tradition.

Relating imagery to ideas, Cynthia Chaliff in an article not previously noted in *ALS*, "The Psychology of Economics in Emily Dickinson" (*L&P* 18[1968]:93–100), observes that though in some poems
Dickinson consciously criticizes the "acquisitive society," in others
where there is less conscious use of economics she "has in fact
introjected the capitalistic system and has made it part of her own
psychological dynamics." Economic terms—money, trade, possession
—"become symbols for emotional needs" and the poet becomes a
capitalist by metaphors of buying, acquiring, or possessing love,
friends, and the riches of the poet-creator.

***d*. Criticism: individual poems.** Although numerous single poems
are discussed in the books on Dickinson described above, few articles
are so limited. The most interesting one is Robert E. Lowrey's
" 'Boanerges': An Encomium for Edward Dickinson" (*ArQ* 26:54–
58), which offers sound proof for his conclusion that in "I Like to
See It Lap the Miles" Emily Dickinson's description referred both to
a locomotive and—in the last stanza with "Boanerges," or "the Son of
Thunder"—to her father, Edward Dickinson. Not only was he the
president of the Amherst, Belchertown and Palmer Railroad, but
according to a newspaper account of 1862, their locomotive was re-
named for him. The poem is dated by Thomas H. Johnson as "about
1862," and it is quite possible that Emily Dickinson did praise "Edward Dickinson," locomotive and man.

Two notes take issue with or add to Simon Tugwell's interpretation of "The Soul Selects Her Own Society" (see *ALS 1969*, p. 75).
Will C. Jumper (*Expl* 29:item 5) contends that "divine Majority"
does not mean "coming of age" (as Father Tugwell interpreted it)
but is from Thoreau's phrase in *The Duty of Civil Disobedience*,
"Any man more right than his neighbors, constitutes a majority of
one," and means the Soul, not the speaker. He also relates references
in the second stanza to "an ironic combination of the folktales of 'The
Querulous Princess' and 'The King and the Beggar Maid' " and considers "valves" to be the shells of a mollusc. The truth of the poem is
"the logical outcome of carrying Emersonian Self-Reliance to its
ultimate conclusion, isolation." Elizabeth Bowman (*Expl* 29:item 13)
argues that if, according to Tugwell, the surface meaning seems only
"a rather trite, comfortable truth," a deeper reading, including linguistic analysis, may show disapproval; that "divine majority" is
ironic, the poet condemning the disapproved behavior by the image
of the shut door, or the closed mind. The poem is thus "a portrait
of bigotry."

Some relationships are suggested. Mario L. D'Avanzo in "Emily
Dickinson's and Emerson's 'Presentiment' " (*ESQ* 58:157–59) follows
what others have said more generally, that Dickinson's view of nature
is darker, more fatalistic than Emerson's, but illustrates it with parallel images from the poet's "Presentiment . . ." and the essayist's
last paragraph in "The Over-Soul." Dickinson is startled; Emerson accepts. Dan McCall's " 'I felt a funeral in my brain' and 'The Hollow

of the Three Hills'" (*NEQ* 42[1969]:432–35) shows that Dickinson's poem and Hawthorne's short story have similar themes (guilt and dread) and use similar images (sounds of voices, mourners, bread, coffin, bell). Concluding that Dickinson undoubtedly used the story, the writer pairs the two works as "remarkable chapters in the story of what Hawthorne called 'the anxiety that had long been kindling' in the New England mind."

e. **Miscellaneous.**   To bring Emily Dickinson back home from the mysteries of old New England or the metaphysicals and to retrieve her spirit from the psychoanalyst's couch for a walk at our side, we might note a personal memoir of a visit to Amherst by the late Winfield Townley Scott, written in 1954 but only recently published as "A Ballet of Emily Dickinson" (*EDB* 15:88–91). His delight and involvement with Emily Dickinson, as Amherst records her in the imagination, is contagious.

University of Nebraska

5. Mark Twain

Hamlin Hill

The most newsworthy Mark Twain story of the year 1970 would have taxed the ingenuity of Gilbert and Sullivan: imagine Mark Twain writing a 400-page harangue against his secretary Isabel Lyon in the form of a letter to William Dean Howells. Imagine the former attorney for the Mark Twain Estate "giving away" this document after Mark Twain's death so that its very existence was unknown until the Henry W. and Albert A. Berg Collection purchased it for $25,000 when it came to light in 1970. Then imagine a cluster of claims to the "ownership" of this document—a legal deposition which one would presume continued to belong to the Mark Twain Estate in spite of the attorney's magnificent generosity—claims which have submerged the physical document in litigation and prevented scholarly access to it. Twain himself would undoubtedly have loved every minute of the comic opera, but some of the rest of us must wonder whether "Mark Twain" and "boondoggle" are developing some kind of special affinity!

Otherwise, it was a year in which more orthodox proceedings emphasized the earlier writings to a degree unusual for the past few annual reports, and a year in which the humorist's societal and communal views received special attention.

i. Textual and Bibliographical

Mark Twain scholars may dimly recollect that a decade ago—long before the Howells, Irving, Crane, and Simms editions were conceived or in production—there was some discussion of an edition of the standard works of Mark Twain. There are probably still people who believe that any year now a volume or two of *The Works of Mark Twain* will come off the press (there are probably still people who believe that Ambrose Bierce is alive and well in Mexico), but it is worth noting at least briefly that 1970 was not the year. The closest

we came was an article of Louis J. Budd's on " 'Baxter's Hog': The
Right Mascot for an Editor (With CEAA Standards) of Mark
Twain's Political and Social Writings" (*CEAAN* 3:3–10), which uses
an especially elusive allusion of the humorist's as the starting-point
for discussing some of Budd's dilemmas in annotating and editing
the political writings, and which, in the process, offers a defense of
the Center for Editions of American Authors against the criticism
of the New Left.

Karl Kirali's "Two Recently Discovered Letters by Mark Twain"
(*MTJ* 15,iii:1–5) reproduces the texts of a disclaimer Twain wanted
published, together with a covering letter to Jerome B. Stillson, a
New York City journalist. In the New York *Tribune* for 19 January
1875, Twain was quoted as approving the performance of Kate Field
in his play "Colonel Sellers." His public disclaimer, which was presumably not printed, points out that his remark was based on hearsay
and had "been considerably improved & strengthened" in Miss Field's
use of it. "Mark Twain to Chatto & Windus: Two Unpublished Letters" (*CEAAN* 3:1–2) publishes the texts of two short letters (both
dated 22 July 1897, from Weggis, Austria) complaining about the
copy editing and proofreading of the English edition of *Following
the Equator*. Henry Duskis has edited "Serious Wilkins in Boston"
(*Yankee* 34,vi:79,179–83), an account of a visit to Boston by a critical
outsider—originally published in the Buffalo *Express* with no evidence then or now that it was written by Mark Twain.

The single text of special note was a new edition of *Huckleberry
Finn* (Glenview, Ill., Scott, Foresman; edited by James L. Bowen
and Richard VanDerBeets) with a short survey of book-length studies of Mark Twain since the late 1940s by Edgar M. Branch, titled
"Mark Twain Scholarship: Two Decades." Following are forty one-
paragraph abstracts of articles about *Huck* ranging over the same
two decades, many of the synopses prepared by the authors of the
original articles.

ii. Biography

Howard Baetzhold's *Mark Twain and John Bull: The British Connection* (Bloomington, Ind. Univ. Press) is a book so wide-ranging in
its scope that it is difficult to decide whether to include it as a biog-

raphy or a book of criticism. Its main organization is chronological, however, tracing with minute detail Mark Twain's mercurial relationship to Englishmen and England. Baetzhold shows that the humorist's response to England did not suggest disaffection until the early 1880s, reaching anglophobic proportions in 1883, partly as a response to Matthew Arnold. The irritation which produced the literary pearl *A Connecticut Yankee* is studied exhaustively, and Baetzhold concludes that "during the first few months of 1890, the breach between Clemens and England gaped its widest." From that point on, as his views shifted, the relationship mellowed; and although he railed at monarchy and colonialism, the Oxford degree capped a returning admiration for things British. In the midst of this tracing of Mark Twain's temperament, Baetzhold writes the most thorough study of the sources of *A Connecticut Yankee*, probes more painstakingly than anyone else the influence of Lecky, Carlyle, Kipling, and FitzGerald upon Mark Twain's writing, and analyzes most of the major works of the Clemens canon. (Indeed, occasionally—as in the extended examination of books which constitute what Baetzhold calls Mark Twain's "discussion with Lecky"—one needs to be reminded of the basic subject of the volume.) *Mark Twain and John Bull* concludes with an immensely helpful survey of the English literature which Mark Twain is known to have used in his own writing, from occasional references to Chaucer through to the nineteenth-century novelists. Baetzhold's research and documentation are so thoroughly and admirably precise that one wonders whether any major British source, influence, or allusion remains undiscovered.

Keith Coplin proposes in "John and Sam Clemens: A Father's Influence" (*MTJ* 15,i:1–6) that John Marshall Clemens was "a failure as a man, a husband, and, most important to this study, a father." As a result, "almost every father [in Mark Twain's fiction] has been either a weak, ineffectual man or a tyrannical, overpowering one, but the striking common denominator is that all of them have been failures as fathers." Tom Sawyer is fatherless but his behavior suggests that he is seeking the approval of a father-figure. In *Huckleberry Finn*, of the three father-figures (Pap, Jim, and Colonel Grangerford —but why not Uncle Silas?), only Jim, ironically at the opposite social pole from John Marshall Clemens, is loving, sympathetic, and affectionate. By contrast, Ralph Gregory, "John A. Quarles, Mark Twain's

Ideal Man" (*MHSB* 25[1968]:229–35) provides a biographical sketch of the uncle of whom Samuel Clemens said, "'I have not come across a better man than he was."

Kenneth T. Reed writes a detailed account of Mark Twain's lecture the evening of 20 July 1895 in "Mirth and Misquotation: Mark Twain in Petoskey, Michigan" (*MTJ* 15,ii:19–20). He includes an interview with the Petoskey *Resorter*, in which the reporter interjected some aspersions on the project of a newspaper competitor. Both J. B. Pond, manager of the tour, and Clemens wrote letters of denial, the latter claiming, "I don't like being used as a waste pipe for the delivery of another man's bile."

Two relatively pointless reminiscences of Mark Twain by contemporaries have been printed. Allison Ensor, "A Clergyman Recalls Hearing Mark Twain" (*MTJ* 15,iii:6), reprints in full the brief recollection by Joseph H. Newton of Mark Twain's address to the St. Louis Press Club in 1902; and Paul A. Doyle, "Henry Harper's Telling of a Mark Twain Anecdote" (*MTJ* 15,ii:13), summarizes without printing a letter of Harper's of 20 May 1895, in which Harper attests to Mark Twain's delight at hearing of the death and funeral of an imposter in Melbourne, Australia.

Amy Chambliss documents "The Friendship of Helen Keller and Mark Twain (*GaR* 24:305–10), a brief and mutually admiring acquaintance which is abstracted here principally from Paine's biography. And, finally, Philip Butcher, "Mark Twain's Installment on the National Debt" (*SLJ* 1[1969]:48–55) identifies Warner Thornton McGuinn as the Negro whom Clemens assisted through Yale Law School; McGuinn was later a prominent Baltimore attorney.

iii. General Criticism

Thomas Blues in *Mark Twain and the Community* (Lexington, Univ. of Ky. Press) suggests three stages in Mark Twain's fiction as it explores the relationship of the individual with his society. In the four novels before *Connecticut Yankee*, "he provided his hero with a victory over the community that in no way endangered his relations with it, a compromise resolution that permitted triumph without alienation." Colonel Sellers is a "harmless but triumphant visionary"; Tom Sawyer succeeds in manipulating "a community which willingly capitulates to his selfish desires for awed and reverent attention";

Edward and Tom Canty illustrate that falsely gained power is a betrayal of the community and that "the price one pays is disillusionment and moral isolation." And when Huck comes dangerously close
to revolt from the community Twain reintroduces Tom and makes
"Huck's rebellion against the community pointless and harmless."
Hank Morgan is torn between drives for improving the level of the
Arthurian community and for gaining vast personal power; because
he cannot control his own urge to domination, and because the community violently opposes his "reform," the Yankee destroys civilization and himself. In his final chapter, Blues examines the "old man"
archetype, who explodes the illusions of younger people and unveils
the community in its true light as a "destructive force, lacking dignity
and love, unworthy of . . . confidence." Brief explications of *The
American Claimant, Joan of Arc, The Mysterious Stranger, Pudd'n-
head Wilson*, and "The Man That Corrupted Hadleyburg" show the
old man as communal iconoclast and also show "the darkest truth of
all, the truth of man's pathetic inability to survive self-knowledge."
The book is small, but the views cogent and provocative—especially
so since they center upon Mark Twain's fiction rather than the mass
of factual and autobiographical data which might dilute this study.

Thomas Werge discusses "Mark Twain and the Fall of Adam"
(*MTJ* 15,ii:5–13) in a group of later works. Werge sees Twain's use
of the Adam archetype serving three functions: "as a figure to parody
Biblical and religious themes," "as a symbol, with Eve, of natural
innocence, uncorrupted goodness and reciprocal love," and "as the
original fallen man, the archetype of the human condition, in whose
corruption and sin we are all deeply bound." The article then transforms itself into a lengthy analysis of "Hadleyburg" as a parable of
universal corruption—a fairly common observation by now. Jay Martin's "Mark Twain: The Fate of Primitivity" (*SLJ* 2:123–37) is an
essay-review of five books about Mark Twain published in 1969,
which expands into a consideration of the humorist's attempt to
retain "primitivity," deliberately seeking basically factual modes of
writing, transcending time and space, and avoiding "the contrast
between the inevitability of human corruption and the unattainabil-
ity of Satanic freedom."

At this point, Maxwell Geismar's *Mark Twain, An American
Prophet* (Boston, Houghton Mifflin) ought to receive some serious
commentary, but it is simply impossible to take the book seriously.

It is so uniformly bad that there is no place to begin. The syntax and prose style of the volume are grating and intrusive. The factual errors would take pages to tabulate (for example, Huck and Jim are called "the two boys" on p. 74, as if Geismar is ignorant of the fact that Jim is grown, married, and has children; and Geismar does not *seem* like the sort that would call grown black men "boy"). The plot-summaries with lengthy quotations from the originals which provide the structure of the bulk of the book are modeled upon high-school theme assignments. The attacks on Van Wyck Brooks, Leslie Fiedler, Charles Neider (at last someone has taken Neider seriously!), F. R. Leavis, and Justin Kaplan—apparently the only Mark Twain critics Geismar knows—are hysterical, obsessive, and completely gratuitous. The central thesis, that Twain "did not have the split personality which is commonly attributed to him, nor all the frustration and repression and mental conflict which goes along with that" is refuted constantly throughout the book (see especially pp. 68, 145–46, and 250). Its insights—the strong values in the later works, the positive aspects of Mark Twain's philosophy, and the curious insistence that Mark Twain never said "nigger" in his own voice—are "proved" merely through repetition. In short, it is an unfortunate book desperately in need of revision, compression, and clarity.

Paul L. Kegel, in "Henry Adams and Mark Twain: Two Views of Medievalism" (*MTJ* 15,iii:11–21), wins the Tears-and-Flapdoodle Award for 1970. Among its various observations: *Connecticut Yankee* is a travel-book; we accept the authenticity of *The Prince and the Pauper* because it is a children's book. Adams, Kegel tells us, is a historian and Mark Twain writes "sheer fiction." Finally, the two writers present opposite versions of the Middle Ages and the reader must "settle for the balanced view."

E. P. Dutton has reissued a new paperback of the 1933 text of Van Wyck Brooks's *The Ordeal of Mark Twain*, with a breathless introduction in which James R. Vitelli assembles quotations from recent scholarly works to show that Brooks's thesis is still alive, indeed vindicated (there is an especially inept "courtroom trial" analogy which extends much too long in the introduction as it assembles its evidence). The point, which Vitelli seems to miss, is not that Mark Twain was not a complex personality with conflicts of major proportions (many of them between his artistic and mercantile instincts), but that these conflicts did not reach quite the clinically schizophrenic level which Brooks implied.

iv. Earlier Works

R. Bruce Bickley, Jr., examines two brief items from the *Territorial Enterprise* and two from the *Call* in "Humorous Portraiture in Twain's News Writing" (*ALR* 3:395–98) to suggest their relationship to the humorist's use of realism. C. Merton Babcock compiles a collection of burlesque recipes from the Notebooks, the Buffalo *Express* and *A Tramp Abroad* in "Mark Twain's Chuck Wagon Specialties" (*WAL* 5:147–51), but to no discernible purpose.

In a study marred by its haphazard structure, Harold T. McCarthy studies "Mark Twain's Pilgrim's Progress: *The Innocents Abroad*" (*ArQ* 26:249–58). McCarthy contemplates the differences between Mark Twain's and the Pilgrims' attitudes toward the Holy Land and biblical authority, underscoring the Pilgrims' hypocrisy and the Bible's unreliability. Lewis Leary's "More Letters from the *Quaker City*" (*AL* 42:197–202) reprints three letters of Daniel D. Leary, a part-owner of the ship, who made the voyage but did not mention Mark Twain in his correspondence. The three communications do provide background information on the Yalta meeting with the Emperor of Russia and on the sanctimoniousness of the Pilgrims; and Leary says of one of Mark Twain's perennial enemies, "[Captain] Duncan is a psalm singing hypocrite in my opinion, very fond of bunkum."

In "*Roughing It* as Retrospective Reporting" (*WAL* 5:113–19), John D. McKee provides an overview of *Roughing It* which unfortunately does not make enough of its theme and title—that the 37-year-old Mark Twain writing the travel book had matured significantly over the 26-year-old central character of the work. C. Merton Babcock's "Mark Twain as 'A Majority of One'" (*UCQ* 15,iv:3–7) probably belongs with *Roughing It* as sensibly as anywhere else. It is the collection of some acts of violence Mark Twain witnessed in his childhood, two of which were converted to literary use in *Roughing It* and *Huckleberry Finn*. It also discusses Slade from *Roughing It* and includes a few generalizations about Mark Twain's admiration of men of courage.

Elmo Howell's "In Defense of Tom Sawyer" (*MTJ* 15,i:17–19) proposes that *Huckleberry Finn* is greater than *Tom Sawyer* "only because the range and variety of Huck's experience is greater than Tom's." Unlike Huck, Tom is a "fine, good-natured fellow, a natural leader, willing to fight to maintain his standing, but never a bully. He is generous and fair according to the code of his elders; and most important of all he has . . . elemental goodness of heart." Colonel Grangerford is the "elder" cited as a model-figure, so it is unfortunate that Tom Sawyer never met that gentleman; and conveniently ignored are Huck's attempts to help the three thieves on the *Walter Scott*, the Wilks girls, and, most of all, Jim. Howell's defense of Tom manages to ignore the kinds of traits that make Tom reprehensible and his conduct dubious to contemporary eyes, without establishing a convincing case that such conduct would have been proper to Tom's "elders."

v. Huckleberry Finn

As usual, *Huckleberry Finn* received more critical attention than any other single work (although *Pudd'nhead Wilson* is gaining more notice every year). And, as usual, the *Huckleberry Finn* items range from the ridiculous to the sublime.

John Hakac describes, excessively, "*Huckleberry Finn*: A Copy Inscribed in 1903" (*ABC* 20,iv:7–9) which bears the inscription, "None genuine without this label on the bottle: Mark Twain."

Two articles discuss *Huckleberry Finn* as a source for more recent American fiction. Stuart L. Burns's "St. Petersburg Re-Visited: Helen Eustis and Mark Twain" (*WAL* 55:99–112), charts similarities in Eustis's novel *The Fool Killer* (1954); and Stewart Rodnon's interest is self-explanatory: "*The Adventures of Huckleberry Finn* and *Invisible Man*: Thematic and Structural Comparisons" (*NALF* 4:45–51).

Robert E. Lowery, breaking no new ground, notices that the word *Grangerford* suggests landed farmers; *Shepherdson*, cattlemen always on horseback. Although Mark Twain condemns both clans in the feud, this naming suggests the "struggle between the settler who tills the land and establishes a community and a tradition and the nomad who wanders the grass lands with his herds" ("The Grangerford-Shepherdson Episode: Another of Mark Twain's Indictments of the Damned Human Race" [*MTJ* 15,i:19–20]). Joseph H. Harkey wrings at least as much etymology out of a six-letter word as one could want in "When Huck Finn Smooched That Spoon" (*MTJ* 15,ii:14), suggesting that Twain might unconsciously have used "a word colored with anti-semitism"—because *smouch* is not only a synonym for *steal* but also a pejorative noun for a Jewish peddler. Langdon Elsbree's "Huck Finn on the Nile" (*SAQ* 69:504–10) is a reminiscence of a year's teaching in Egypt—*Huckleberry Finn* was one of the books—but the article has almost nothing to do with Mark Twain's novel.

Neil Sapper offers useful insights in "'I Been There Before': Huck Finn as Tocquevillian Individual" (*MissQ* 24:35–45). Sapper suggests that Tocqueville's definition of individualism as "a mature and calm feeling, which disposes each member of the community to sever himself from the mass of his fellows, and to draw apart with his family and friends; so that . . . he willingly leaves society at large to itself," applies to Huck in his departing from Pap, from Jackson's Island, and in his deciding to go to hell. Joel Jay Belson contemplates "The Nature and Consequences of the Loneliness of Huckleberry Finn" (*ArQ* 26:243–48), and concludes that loneliness—or "lonesomeness" in Huck's own language—is equated with boredom and, more importantly, with melancholy and despair. The latter value of the word finally becomes a philosophical stance when Huck's loneliness becomes concealment and isolation from his society.

Harold P. Simonson synthesizes several familiar views in his "*Huckleberry Finn* as Tragedy" (*YR* 59:532–48), concluding that "Huck's painful rebirth which culminates in Chapter 31 does not deliver him from a world of complexity and finiteness but, instead, thrusts him squarely into it. His is the loss of innocence, not the American Adam's recovery of it. His is the decision to be a man, not the Adamic freedom to remain a child." Simonson provides an indisputably pessimistic reading of the novel—in which the prison stands as the central metaphor—but one in which *tragedy* has loose rather than classic and strict definitions.

Alan Trachtenberg's "The Form of Freedom in *Adventures of Huckleberry Finn*" (*SoR* 6:954–71) is at once the most provocative and the most elusive article on *Huckleberry Finn* for 1970. It is the theme of freedom which Trachtenberg wishes to examine; that "form of freedom" is significantly expressed through a single voice. But that voice has a dual function: "At the outset we learn that Huck is teller

as well as actor, that we are listeners as well as witnesses of action."
But somehow, the participant-recollector duality in the novel has
parallels with oral story-telling and "high" art. Finally (on p. 960)
Trachtenberg announces that "my discussion will focus on this double role, will attempt to assess Huck's role as the verbalizer of the
narrative in order to assess his role as a character within the narrative." Among the serious implications of such a line of inquiry are
the questions, "Does Huck actually catch the same implications [as
the reader in the chapter 31 decision]? Does he know and understand
exactly what he is saying?" More generally, "Has he learned what
we have learned as witnesses, overhearers, of his conflict? Can we
be sure, here or at the end of the book, that we are not extrapolating
from our own lessons in expecting Huck to share our recognitions?"
Next, as the outgrowth of an answer to these questions, the article
asks whether Huck is a "guileful" deadpan narrator or simply ignorant. (Does he, for example, really approve the Grangerfords' taste
in home-decorating?) But guile implies duplicity and dishonesty—
traits we do not expect from Huck; and sheer ignorance reduces
Huck and leaves the reader "exploiting our sense of superiority and
condescending toward him." Trachtenberg finally concludes that
Mark Twain "seriously doubted the possibilities of personal freedom
within a social setting. He seems to have taken freedom as true only
when absolute and abstract, outside time." In an article so fertile
with insights and original perceptions, one hopes—perhaps unfairly—
for more concrete conclusions and a lengthier explication of the very
significant "dual voices" problem in the narration.

vi. Later Works

William K. Spofford in "Mark Twain's Connecticut Yankee: An Ignoramus Nevertheless" (*MTJ* 15,ii:15–18) shows perceptively that
Twain intended Hank and his revolution to fail. Hank's character is
basically unsympathetic, showing a "dehumanizing brutality." He
measures progress in the most superficial terms, enthusiastically in-
terpreting any material "improvement as synonymous with cultural
advancement." His version of "democracy" transforms him into "a
despot, and not particularly enlightened at that." Finally, his own
lack of perception of the significance of training results in the collapse of his republic. Spofford may ignore a little too easily the sim-

ilarities between the personalities of Mark Twain and Hank, the villainous ignoramus, but the article marshalls strong evidence for its argument. Kenneth Andersen's "Mark Twain, W. D. Howells, and Henry James: Three Agnostics in Search of Salvation" (*MTJ* 15,i:13–16) suggests that in *A Connecticut Yankee, A Hazard of New Fortunes*, and *The Ambassadors*, each author confronts a similar problem: a central character, dubious of heavenly salvation, attempts to reach a form of earthly salvation by persevering in some "appointed moral task even at the cost of sacrificing all that was dear to him." Hank Morgan fails to achieve salvation, however, because he is too short-sighted to see "the consistent ironies that he creates" or to "evaluate the past (in this case the future) which he left."

John A. Burrison's monograph *"The Golden Arm," The Folk Tale and Its Literary Use by Mark Twain and Joel C. Harris* (Atlanta, Ga. State Univ. Research Paper 19 [1968]) traces the folk tale throughout several hundred years and thirty-eight variant versions, concluding that it is of white origin and ineffective as written literature. Burrison compares and contrasts Twain's version (originally in *How to Tell a Story* in 1892) with "Uncle Remus's" version with silver dollars on the corpse's eyes as the stolen object.

After outlining basic similarities of a critical sort between Aristotle and Twain, Philip C. Kolin lists those aspects of *Pudd'nhead Wilson* which satisfy Aristotle's definition of tragedy ("Mark Twain, Aristotle, and Pudd'nhead Wilson" [*MTJ* 15,ii:1–4]): (1) it is complex rather than episodic, (2) it contains many reversals of intention and recognitions producing changes from ignorance to knowledge by "natural means," (3) the maxims serve the function of a Chorus, and (4) Pudd'nhead himself is a model of the tragic hero. Slightly similar is Mark D. Coburn's "'Training is Everything': Communal Opinion and the Individual in *Pudd'nhead Wilson*" (*MLQ* 31:209–19). Coburn suggests that Dawson's Landing serves the communal role of a Chorus, dispensing or withholding the approval which major characters seek—including Wilson himself, who "exemplifies Twain's growing conviction that every man's need of communal respect is so great that the individual will necessarily be as foolish and shortsighted as the society that surrounds him."

Also "communal" in its interests is George M. Spangler's *"Pudd'nhead Wilson*: A Parable of Property" (*AL* 42:28–37). Neither racial problems nor environmental determinism provides a viable theme for Twain's novel; but "the idea of property, more particularly the obsession with property as a vitiating and reductive influence on human beings" is satisfactory. The existence of blacks as mere property initiates the action and closes it when Tom cannot be imprisoned because of the pleas of the heirs of Percy Driscoll's estate. Tom is motivated solely by economic concerns, a foil to Pudd'nhead, who is dissociated from "material success." Roxy mediates between the two, acquiescing to Tom's value-system but redeeming herself "by her capacity for love, self-sacrifice, and moral awareness."

Two brief notes comment upon specific sections of *Pudd'nhead.* In "The Point of Pudd'nhead's Half-A-Dog Joke" (*AN&Q* 8:150–51), C. Webster Wheelock notes, as have others, that the joke is emblematic of Southern culture, in which a man *may* own a person who is part black. Stuart A. Lewis, "Pudd'nhead Wilson's Election" (*MTJ* 15,i:21), notes that unless the reader remembers Wilson's courtroom triumph from "Those Extraordinary Twins," Wilson's election as mayor of Dawson's Landing seems to suggest that "the position [is] so unrewarding and trivial that only the town fool was fit for it."

John Tuckey notes in "Hannibal, Weggis, and Mark Twain's Eseldorf" (*AL* 42:235–40) that, as several hitherto unpublished passages from the notebooks corroborate, Eseldorf was at least a mixture of Hannibal and Weggis, Austria, where Mark Twain was residing in 1897, just prior to beginning "The Chronicle of Young Satan"—the earliest *Mysterious Stranger* fragment. Ellwood Johnson's "Mark Twain's Dream Self in the Nightmare of History" (*MTJ* 15,i:6–12) is a reading of *The Mysterious Stranger* in terms of Emerson's philosophical concepts of Reason and Understanding. "Structurally, *The Mysterious Stranger* divides dialectically into thesis, antithesis, and synthesis. . . . The thesis says that man's history is determined by the scope of his beliefs (dreams); the antithesis says that history is determined by the cause-and-effect relationship between events over which man has no control." Such a reading makes the solipsistic and individualistic conclusion a resolution in favor of the former, as *dream, idea,* and *thought* become synonymous terms and "the outer world is only an extension of the inner world." Such a reading would gain immensely, of course, if it were possible to show Clemens's knowledge of the philosophies of Emerson or Kant or Hegel.

Ronald J. Gervais explores a similar line of thought as Jay Martin (above). In "*The Mysterious Stranger*: The Fall as Salvation" (*PCP*

5:24–33), he looks at the "angelic" rather than the "satanic" proportions of the character of Philip Traum. "An innocent devil has come to an already fallen world, and offered it the salvation of complete knowledge, a second fall which alleviates the suffering and guilt caused by the partial knowledge acquired in the first fall."

Robert A. Rees compares "*Captain Stormfield's Visit to Heaven* and *The Gates Ajar*" (*ELN* 7:197–202). Although Elizabeth Stuart Phelps's *The Gates Ajar* was not a literal model for Stormfield's plot, Mark Twain borrowed the idea of the ludicrousness of the white-robes-and-hymn-singing concept, the idea that unheralded humans may become more outstanding angels than persons of renown, and in several other fairly insignificant ways.

John Tuckey examines *The Mysterious Stranger, Three Thousand Years among the Microbes*, and *What Is Man?* in "Mark Twain's Later Dialogue: The 'Me' and the Machine" (*AL* 41:532–42). Tuckey suggests that these later writings continue to debate "whether man is essentially an automated or an autonomous being." In these works, Twain defines the essential "me" which he preserves and saves as well as he can. Perhaps, as the Old Man says in *What Is Man?*, this essence is the Soul, alleviating pure mechanism. Mark Twain was never able to choose between the two alternatives: "he was in the last analysis not confirmed in despair, not barred from seeing and representing human life as having value and significance."

University of Chicago

6. Henry James

Robert L. Gale

The quantity of Jamesian scholarship fell off in 1970 when compared with that of 1969 and even a little earlier, but 1970 can boast of several high-quality items. Viola Hopkins Winner's *Henry James and the Visual Arts* is one of the finest books ever published on a special aspect of James. Critics who notably treated individual works by James include Taylor Stoehr on politico-linguistic aspects of *The Princess Casamassima*, Philip L. Nicoloff on ambiguity in "Louisa Pallant," Alan W. Bellringer on the objective center of *The Tragic Muse*, Philip M. Weinstein on contrasting imaginations in *The Sacred Fount*, and Jane P. Tompkins on parenthetical statements in "The Beast in the Jungle." Two other essays deserve commendation here. They are Robert Garis's needed adverse criticism of Leon Edel's ongoing biography of James, and Raymond Thorberg's comparative study of James and Edmond About.

i. Manuscripts, Bibliography, Biography

New manuscript material is presented in two articles. Richard Cary in "Henry James Juvenilia: A Poem and a Letter" (*CLQ* 9:58–62) discusses the meager extant hints that James wrote a little poetry, and prints for the first time a twenty-eight-line poem (with one line missing) which begins "I cannot see the truth of love / I cannot feel the hope of life" and which exists only in a penciled copy by Mrs. Thomas Sergeant Perry. Cary rightly calls the effort "a mixture of adolescent bleakness, alienation, and melodrama." Then he prints a touching little note addressed by James (c. 1850) to a cousin. These juvenile items are both in the Colby College Library collection of James memorabilia. The same collection, according to J. Seelye Bixler's "James Family Letters in Colby College Library" (*CLQ* 9:25–47), also contains letters from Henry James, Sr., and his half-brother, the Rev. William James, fifty-two letters from the novelist's brother William, sixteen from William's wife Alice, two from their brother Robertson, one from their sister Alice, and a dozen from the novelist. Bixler prints several letters for the first time but none by Henry James.

Charles H. Nilon's *Bibliography of Bibliographies in American Literature* (New York, Bowker, pp. 105–08) provides a convenient though not complete or entirely up-to-date list of more than fifty sources of bibliographical information on James. *Russian Studies of American Literature: A Bibliography,* compiled by Valentina A. Libman, translated by Robert V. Allen, and edited by Clarence Gohdes (Chapel Hill, Univ. of N.C. Press, 1969, p. 110), has a list of six items on "Genri Dzheims." In *Art and Error,* pp. 279–300, William M. Gibson and George R. Petty, Jr., describe "Project Occult: The Ordered Computer Collation of Unprepared Literary Text," a "project designed to increase the accuracy and efficiency of collating." In their book on the subject, *Project Occult,* they present in Appendix C variant readings found in a collation of the first London edition and the revised New York edition texts of "Daisy Miller." In "Perpetuated Misprints" (*TLS* 4 Jun:613) Brian Pearce points out several of the "worst" printer's errors appearing in certain editions of *Washington Square* and reproduced in subsequent ones. Simon Nowell-Smith in "Texts of *The Portrait of a Lady,* 1881–1882: The Bibliographical Evidence" (*PBSA* 63[1969]:304–10) collates early printed texts of *The Portrait of a Lady,* including the two magazine texts, "to determine . . . the order in which those texts may be said to have come into being"; prints a five-column table to "show . . . the progression of errors and corrections . . . in the successive texts"; and concludes with a "genealogy of the texts" down to and including that of the New York edition. George Monteiro's "James and His Reviewers: Some Identifications" (*PBSA* 63[1969]:300–04) adds "pertinent information to the explanatory headnotes" in Roger Gard's *Henry James: The Critical Heritage* (London, Routledge and Kegan Paul; New York, Barnes and Noble, 1968).

Unusual biographical information is provided by Charles E. Burgess, who in "Henry James's 'Big' Impression: St. Louis, 1905" (*MHSB* 27:30–63) presents information about James and St. Louis. Sources of information are *The American Scene, The Bostonians,* and letters. James liked the city and in *The American Scene* compared it favorably with Philadelphia. Burgess suggests that St. Louis would

have figured importantly in James's projected but unwritten sequel
to *The American Scene*. Burgess also ingeniously reconstructs James's
activities in St. Louis early in March 1905, comments on several of
the intellectual leaders of the city whom James must have met, and
reprints a pamphlet called *Henry James: A Colloquy*—an abridged
transcript of James's formal conversation with members of the University Club of St. Louis on March 8, 1905. This "colloquy," which
Burgess analyzes splendidly, is a priceless record of James's conver-
sational manner and wit, and of his opinions on many of his contemporaries. Burgess has given us the last word on James and St.
Louis, in a far-ranging, significant, and engagingly written essay.

Of the many reviews of Leon Edel's *Henry James: The Treacherous Years, 1895–1901* (Philadelphia, Lippincott, 1969) Robert Garis's
"Anti-Literary Biography" (*HudR* 23:143–53) is the most noteworthy. It is an indictment of Edel's approach and critical ability.
Garis rejects Edel's thesis, that the failure of *Guy Domville* dealt
James a spiritual wound and caused him to regress emotionally even
as he advanced technically. Edel's evidence—James's purchase of
Lamb House, and his "Turn of the Screw," *The Spoils of Poynton*,
and *What Maisie Knew*—Garis reads differently from beginning to
end. He concludes that Edel is melodramatic, inconsistent, self-
serving, naïve, unseeing, and inaccurate, and that his theories are
distorted, absurd, and nonsensical. Garis also criticizes Edel for his
"lack of interest in James's language" and closes thus: "Edel's biography is a waste of time . . . . Worse: the strange prestige his incapac-
ity to argue the case has nevertheless won him may discourage better
minds from trying." A more temperate reviewer is Mildred E. Hart-
sock, who in "Biography: The Treacherous Art" (*JML* 1:116–19)
offers this balanced evaluation: "When the biographer writes as the
artist he is, he puts James before us with vivid warmth; when he
writes like the amateur psychiatrist, he exacerbates with a constrictive glibness." Appropriate here is mention of Stuart N. Hampshire's
chapter called "Henry James" in his *Modern Writers and Other Essays* (New York, Knopf, pp. 96–101). Hampshire sees the Edel of
Henry James: The Middle Years, 1882–1895 (Philadelphia, Lippincott, 1962) as a Jamesian character trying—probably without ultimate
success—to discern the figure in the carpet of the life of his subject,
who is also a Jamesian character, self-masking in attitude. Hampshire
depicts James as "a professional, rather than a priest, of art," and

compares his progress to "the foundation of a great American manufacturing fortune: there is the same ruthless planning and egoism, the same pride in output."

Light on an earlier controversial biography, *The Pilgrimage of Henry James* by Van Wyck Brooks (New York, Dutton, 1925), is shed by *The Van Wyck Brooks-Lewis Mumford Letters: The Record of a Literary Friendship, 1921–1963*, ed. Robert E. Spiller (New York, Dutton). The letters reveal, amid trivial comments on James, that Brooks was uneasy while he wrote the biography, set it aside for a while, and called one draft of it "a tract." James R. Vitelli in *Van Wyck Brooks* (New York, Twayne, 1969) interestingly calls *The Pilgrimage of Henry James* "a psychological novel in the manner of Henry James himself," shows that Brooks's first book of memoirs (*Scenes and Portraits*) resembles James's *Small Boy and Others*, and surveys opinions concerning James's expatriation expressed by reviewers of Brooks.

Herbert F. Smith in *Richard Watson Gilder* (TUSAS 166) includes discussion and speculation about the professional relationship of James and Gilder, the distinguished assistant editor of *Scribner's Monthly Magazine* and then editor of its successor, the *Century Monthly Magazine*. Shortly after the *Century* began serializing James's unpopular *Bostonians*, Gilder suggested that the novelist use "something of Tourgenieff's condensation" in later installments. Thereafter, James published no more fiction in the *Century*. Smith hypothesizes that Gilder knew his subscribers were too middle-class to appreciate James's fiction, that Gilder preferred James's non-fiction, and that Gilder probably "discriminated against James . . . because of a complex of feelings about James's success as a writer and his voluntary expatriation from America."

ii. Sources, Parallels, Influence

James was frequently compared and contrasted with other American writers. In a heavily academic essay called "*Roderick Hudson*: James' *Marble Faun*" (*TSLL* 11:1427–43), Sanford E. Marovitz attempts to show that "the themes, the settings, several of the primary characters, and, to a large extent, the methods of construction are very similar" in Nathaniel Hawthorne's late romance and James's early novel. Kenneth Andersen in "Mark Twain, W. D. Howells, and

Henry James: Three Agnostics in Search of Salvation" (*MTJ* 15:13–16) too briefly compares and contrasts the heroes of *A Connecticut Yankee in King Arthur's Court, A Hazard of New Fortunes,* and *The Ambassadors,* each of whom is alone, is transported to an alien society, seeks salvation here and now, is described in religious imagery, and concerns himself with freedom and selfishness in a world in which only the senses teach us. Kenneth S. Lynn in a brilliant article entitled "Howells in the Nineties" (*PAH* 4:27–82) demonstrates among a dozen more central matters that "In the twilight years of the *fin de siècle,* when Mark Twain, Henry James, and Henry Adams were all searching their imaginations for symbols of failure," Howells also felt bleak and in addition self-distrustful as he wrote well but too much, and became more and more strangled by material comforts, which James urged him to give up. William C. Fischer, Jr., in "William Dean Howells: Reverie and the Nonsymbolic Aesthetic" (*NFC* 25:1–30) incidentally contrasts Howells's "graphic" style and James's "symbolic uses of language that reach behind appearance to metaphorical meanings." Throughout his *Henry Blake Fuller* (TUSAS 175) John Pilkington, Jr., places pertinent references to both Howells and James; discusses Fuller's essay called "Howells or James?," in which Fuller, though he admired James's skill as an "idealistic" writer and partly envied him his life, sided with Howells because of his realistic treatment of American subjects; and concludes that "the difference which he [Fuller] noted between Howells and James offered a remarkable parallel to his own predicament; in fact, in the analogy he drew between them lay the core of his own dilemma." David Cheshire and Malcolm Bradbury in "American Realism and the Romance of Europe: Fuller, Frederic, Harland" (*PAH* 4:285–310) include passing references to James, mostly in connection with the preference of Fuller and Harold Frederic for Howells over James. Cheshire and Bradbury also note similarities between Frederic's *Damnation of Theron Ware* and James's *Roderick Hudson,* quote Henry Harland's intense praise of James, and discuss the debt of Harland's popular novel *The Cardinal's Snuff-Box* to James. Margaret B. McDowell in "Edith Wharton's Ghost Stories" (*Crit* 12:133–52) mentions that Mrs. Wharton believed "the effects which the writer should strive for in the supernatural tale resemble those of James . . . ." In his *Willa Cather* (New York, Pegasus) James Woodress tells us that Willa Cather learned "a disciplined artistry" from

James, who, however, also exerted a partly unfortunate influence on her at least until she published "The Enchanted Bluff." In eight or ten short critical essays, written in the late 1890s and conveniently reprinted in *The World and the Parish: Willa Cather's Articles and Reviews, 1893–1902*, ed. William M. Curtin (Lincoln, Univ. of Nebr. Press), Willa Cather always writes with intense respect of James's fiction as exhibiting superlative craftsmanship. Samuel French Morse in *Wallace Stevens* (New York, Pegasus) shows that Stevens closely resembled James in approaching life as a means to art. In a farfetched note entitled "James's 'The Awkward Age' and Pound's 'Mauberley'" (*N&Q* 17:49–50) Denis Donoghue contends that Ezra Pound, who obviously admired James, may have found his phrase "better tradition'" in *The Awkward Age*. In his *Peter Taylor* (TUSAS 168) Albert J. Griffith demonstrates the influence of James, especially in matters of technique, on Taylor, notably in his story "There." Richard Poirier in an amusing essay called "What Is English Studies, and If You Know What That Is, What Is English Literature?" (*PR* 37:41–58) boldly compares Herbert Marcuse and James for having similar "relevance," since, for both, "art and literature are essentially higher forms of life," and since both are "attached to historical or daily life by virtue of a provocative alienation, a challenge to the way things really are."

Drawing comparisons between James and British authors also engaged the critics. William F. Hall in "Caricature in Dickens and James" (*UTQ* 39:242–57) discusses simple caricatures of likenesses and relatively more subtle and complex caricatures of equivalence, in Charles Dickens and James. The first method stresses physical features; the second, distortion for the sake of unmasking essential character. Hall's abstruse essay deals with an important technique, somewhat neglected, at least by Jamesian critics. A glance at the index under "James" to *Critical Essays on George Eliot*, ed. Barbara Hardy (New York, Barnes and Noble), will lead interested readers to many brief passages showing points of comparison between Eliot and James. In *The Alien Protagonist of Ford Madox Ford* (Chapel Hill, Univ. of N.C. Press) H. Robert Huntley considers the influence of "the Jamesian international theme" on Ford's novel *An English Girl*.

Continental writers were related to James as well. Victor Terras's "Turgenev's Aesthetic and Western Realism" (*CL* 22:19–35) is of

tangential interest here because it "summarize[s] Turgenev's aesthetic ideas with a view to their application in his art, and confront[s]
them with the ideas of those of his Western contemporaries [includ-
ing James] with whom his name is most often associated." Raymond
Thorberg's "*Germaine*, James's *Notebooks*, and *The Wings of the
Dove*" (*CL* 22:254–64) is a superb, analytical source study which
covers more than its title can imply. It shows that James probably
wove elements from Edmond About's *Germaine* into *The Wings of
the Dove* and also into "Georgina's Reasons." Milly Theale derives
partly from Germaine; Kate Croy, from Madame Charmidy; Merton
Densher, from Don Diego; Sir Luke Strett, from Le Bris; and Susan
Stringham, from the Countess de Villanera. Plot elements and scenes
in *Germaine* are also echoed in *The Wings of the Dove*, and elements
in *The Portrait of a Lady* derive from *Germaine*. Jan W. Dietrichson's
"Henry James and Émile Zola" in *Americana Norvegica* (pp. 118–34)
is scholarly but obvious: it tediously documents "James's basically
ambivalent attitude to the work of Zola" and then shows that Zola's
influence on James "was *not* very important." Joseph Gerard Brennan
in a careful but pedantic essay called "Three Novels of Dépaysement"
(*CL* 22:223–36) proves the obvious thesis—that "Superstition or no,
much literature has been made round the notion that a man's being
taken out of his element, finding himself suddenly transported to
exotic soil, can lead to an important shift in his moral center of gravity"—by citing evidence from *L'Immoraliste* by André Gide, *Der
Zauberberg* by Thomas Mann, and James's *Ambassadors*. Wallace G.
Kay in a tightly packed little essay called "The Observer and the
Voyeur: Theories of Fiction in James and Robbe-Grillet" (*SoQ* 9:87–
91) points out that both writers use "fictive agents" to render impressions subjectively. Kay adds that James regards objects as existing
only to relate to people and tries to get beneath surface reality,
whereas Alain Robbe-Grillet "argues strongly for the independent
existence of things" and deals only with "the surface of things," which
have for him intrinsic attractiveness of the sort James denies.

iii. Criticism: General

The finest, most subtle book of the year on James is without any
doubt Viola Hopkins Winner's *Henry James and the Visual Arts*
(Charlottesville, Univ. Press of Va.). I stand in awe of its brilliance,

thoroughness, and unremitting grasp on the subject. The first four chapters are devoted to the development of James's aesthetic taste and to its leading principles. The next two deal with the part visual arts played in his conception of fiction and then in the techniques of his own fictional practice. The last two chapters handle his artistic characters and art connoisseurs. The book is graced with sixteen plates, competently related to the text. Mrs. Winner demonstrates that James saw with a painter's eye, was always devoted to pictorial art (mainly for its dramatic, anecdotal, and psychological elements), sketched and otherwise studied art, and later used studios and art life in his fiction. She discusses his familiarity with French and English art criticism; his awareness of the relation of art to both art life and the past, especially that associated with Roman Catholic institutions; and his definition of style, which includes conception, theme, treatment, and size. She then details the tension-building contrast in James between his delight in "the grand style" and his love of "the picturesque," both of which she superbly defines, and explains his preference for fused over multiple unity. Next she treats James's attitude toward Pre-Raphaelite aestheticism and his initial conservative distrust of Impressionism. Chapter 5 considers James's critical notions of technical parallels between painting and the novel. Mrs. Winner seems better when she turns to art devices and parallels in James's fictional practice. The last two chapters are tightly packed. One of them considers James's fictional artists. The final chapter contrasts those in James's fiction who love art and those connoisseurs who wrench it from its organic context to fill museums; in her thrilling treatment of *The Golden Bowl*, which she rightly reads as a rich tangle of all the major elements treated in her study, she is somewhat severe with Adam Verver.

In my view, Mrs. Winner is best when discussing the tension induced in James by his simultaneous love of the grand style and the picturesque; she is least effective when handling pictorialism in James's theory of the novel. Her footnotes are admirably thorough and reveal wide reading, not only in James and criticism of him but also in art history. She was fortunate in securing permission to quote on occasion from unpublished James family papers. Her index is slightly capricious and incomplete.

The other major book on James during the year also concerns his power to see. Peter Buitenhuis in *The Grasping Imagination: The*

American Writings of Henry James (Toronto, Univ. of Toronto Press) deals with James's ability to make literature out of a combination of visual observation of things about him and artistic schemata from his readings—and to a lesser extent from other art forms. Buitenhuis's book seems less impressive to me than Mrs. Winner's, probably because it deals with less than vintage James much of the time, it tediously overuses the words *schema* and *schemata* (from E. H. Gombrich's *Art and Illusion*), and it is uneven in quality.

Early in his book, Buitenhuis explains that his purpose is to refute Van Wyck Brooks and Maxwell Geismar, shows the pervasiveness of American elements in James, offers biographical information about young James, overstresses the importance of Prosper Mérimée's *Vénus d'Ille*, and goes over "the Hawthorne aspect." Only when it gets up to "Professor Fargo" and *Roderick Hudson* does *The Grasping Imagination* show its strength. By the time Buitenhuis reaches *The Europeans*, which he treats competently, his eclectic and uneven method becomes clear: he first presents relevant biographical facts, then indicates James's reading at about the time he was writing the work under scrutiny, and finally offers a personal critique of it—usually plot summary (often too extensive), then commentary on characters, themes, and techniques. Buitenhuis skimps on *Hawthorne* and *Washington Square*, after which he turns to *The Portrait of a Lady*, which he might legitimately have ignored entirely. He expertly handles "The Point of View," "Pandora," "A New England Winter," and especially "The Impressions of a Cousin"; but not until he gets to *The Bostonians* does he present truly superb criticism, particularly when he relates that novel to Hawthorne's *Blithedale Romance* and Alphonse Daudet's *L'Évangéliste*, and when he discusses James's picture of Boston, his naturalistic objectivity, and the tangle of his themes. In my view, the main value of Buitenhuis's disunified filler chapter on James's *Princess Casamassima* and his "American Letters" is that it offers proof (published for the first time, I believe) that James met Mark Twain, late in the summer of 1904. Like Mrs. Winner, Buitenhuis was fortunate in having permission to quote from unpublished James letters, more than a dozen of which he puts to enviable use in his book.

Unquestionably the best section of *The Grasping Imagination* concerns *The American Scene*. Buitenhuis offers a masterly presentation of its background, its structure, the resonance of its title, foreshortening and imagery in it, and fears for America expressed in it. Buitenhuis is incomparable again only when he takes up *The Ivory Tower*. His long chapter on it is the best yet in print, and he brilliantly shows that here James reversed his successful old formula to show the innocent European victimized by money-corrupted America; in addition, the critic discusses titular symbolism, manners, a few key images, and the contemporaneity of the old master's unremittingly "grasping imagination."

Lyall H. Powers gives us in *Henry James: An Introduction and Interpretation* (New York, Holt, Rinehart, and Winston) a fine general introduction to James. Powers begins by discussing the treatment of self-reliance and responsibility in James, then challenges us to respond favorably to James precisely because he is oblique like life and complex like all significant occurrences in life. A graceful biographical chapter shows the interrelationship of James's life and his works. The main part of Powers's little book concerns the fiction—its themes and some of its techniques. Toward the end Powers develops the thesis that James steadily believed and demonstrated that fiction is a fine art whose aim is to represent life faithfully.

In 1969 Ora Segal published *The Lucid Reflector: The Observer in Henry James's Fiction* (New Haven, Conn., Yale Univ. Press). In it, Mrs. Segal traces the evolution of the observer in more than a dozen important novels and tales by James, paying special attention to "Madame de Mauves," *The Portrait of a Lady*, "Lady Barbarina," "The Aspern Papers," "The Liar," *The Golden Bowl*, and a few stories of literary life. She notes the observer's shift from a subsidiary position to a central one: at first the Jamesian observer accurately mirrors the action; gradually, however, as he becomes more involved functionally, he analyzes more subjectively—and sometimes even meddles, pries, and tries to assume the role of savior of those he fancies are in distress. Mrs. Segal makes her method clear in the following definition of James's typical observer: "He is not omniscient, and his moral and epistemological perspectives are necessarily limited. This enables James to show his two main authorial activities—narration and interpretation—in the making, that is, to present them as complicated, groping processes of observation and evaluation. Narration thus ceases to be the expression of authoritative omniscience. Instead, the story generally progresses by means of a series of encounters between the observer and the protagonist, in the course of which the former gradually achieves a comprehensive view of the case." Mrs. Segal includes a bibliography subdivided to list items on seventeen fictional works by James, as well as a thorough index which is rendered more valuable through inclusion of many abstract concepts such as authorial withdrawal, choric commentator, center of consciousness, epistemological dilemma, irony, narrative distance, narrator, observer-protagonist relationship, and imagery.

Mention should be made here of a tiny "book" on an enormous subject. Kathleen Fitzpatrick's *Henry James and the Influence of Italy* (Sydney, Sydney Univ. Press, 1968) presents elementary biographical evidence that James loved Italy, and supports the truism by alluding to some of his fictional and nonfictional prose dealing with Italy and Italians. The essay suffers for not making the slightest use of the extensive and important previous scholarship on its subject.

In a chapter called "The Parting of the Ways" in his book *The English Novel from Dickens to Lawrence* (New York, Oxford Univ. Press, pp. 119–39), Raymond Williams describes James's works as moral presentations of deep human problems, in which "human speech in its intricacy, its particularity, its quality as a sequence, has never been better rendered," and in which, aesthetically, "the novel becomes its own subject." Williams briefly considers the split between James and H. G. Wells.

Articles, as well as books and chapters therein, also deal with general critical problems. Two essays concern money and businessmen. Alice Morgan's "Henry James: Money and Morality" (*TSLL* 12:75–92) pursues the "apparently necessary connection between renunciation of love, passion, or marriage, and certain financial attitudes." Typically, Americans are charitable and renunciatory, whereas Europeans operate on "the morality of computation" and want to get back the equivalent of what they spend. Miss Morgan suggests that to the end of his career James used money and other valuables as symbols of sexual passion. She attempts to cover too much ground, generalizes well, but cannot afford space to provide enough detailed evidence. Blair G. Kenney in "Henry James's Businessmen" (*CLQ* 9:48–58) begins with the statement that, given the frequency with which the businessman is made into a whipping boy by novelists, "It is surprising that only the most aesthetic, sensitive, perhaps effete of nineteenth-century novelists, Henry James, is able to see beyond the stereotype, and to portray for us that virile figure in all his variety,

in nobility as well as squalor." Mrs. Kenney then expresses the manifestly incorrect belief that James was "pleasantly intrigued by the
world of business"; in reality, he was terrified by it, voiced in *The
American Scene* his dismay at its growth, and avoided presenting it
directly in his fiction. Mrs. Kenney offers a number of inaccurate
opinions about James's businessmen, which fortunately she qualifies
later though only in part. She does present some valuable commentary on this character type as a "mixture of shrewdness and naivete."

A welcome contrast to all this commercialism in contained in
Eben Bass's stimulating "Henry James and the English Country
House" (*Markham Rev* 2,ii[4–10]), which knowledgeably considers
the etymological and symbolic overtones of the names of various
British country houses in James's fiction. Bass also discusses James's
attitudes toward life in such houses, which are sometimes dissolute,
occasionally romantic, and often overly concerned with social conventions. Ross Labrie in "Sirens of Life and Art in Henry James"
(*LaUR* 2[1969]:150–69) argues at great length the obvious point
that "For the artist in James's world, there would seem to be the
necessity to be attracted by the siren of life, and yet, like Ulysses
tied to the mast, detached enough to make room for the artist's specialized appraisal and treatment of those subjects which life offers."
Labrie's one valuable insight here is that in "The Lesson of the Master" Marian Fancourt so resembles Mrs. Henry St. George that writer
Paul Overt is professionally better for not marrying the girl. Labrie
reads "The Figure in the Carpet" reductively, in order to make that
complex story support his thesis; and he is inaccurate in his comments
on "Sir Dominick Ferrand," evidence from which does little in any
event to advance his argument.

Three general articles deal with aspects of style. In "A 'Shade of
a Special Sense': Henry James and the Art of Naming" (*AL* 42:203–
20) Joyce Tayloe Horrell considers the sources of James's fictional
names—in nature, myth, history, and connotative words. She argues
well that James shows an ever-increasing sophistication in choosing
apt names and in integrating their connotations with other fictive
elements, such as tone and characterization. Moving chronologically
through the fiction, Mrs. Horrell combines specific explications of
names with other insights into James's art. Strother B. Purdy in
"Henry James and the *Mot Juste*" (*WSinL* 6[1969]:118–25) takes "a
preliminary look at the *mot juste* as a linguistic phenomenon" and

then concludes after analyzing unconventional uses by James of the word *clever* that he fortunately was "a marked linguistic innovator" rather than a writer who regarded any *mot juste* "as a stylistic or aesthetic goal." This essay is brief but extremely illuminating. Barry Menikoff in "Punctuation and Point of View in the Late Style of Henry James" (*Style* 4:29–47) demonstrates that after 1900 James's punctuation "facilitate[s] his method of interior narration," with dashes and colons "functioning as loose ligatures that connect disparate statements" and encouraging "the reader to associate an unceasing series of thoughts, perceptions and ideas" as they go through a given character's mind. The conventional "subject-verb-object syntax" creates too much distance between character and reader. So James typically replaces it with "a sentence whose very structure simulates the process of the mind, the manner in which we apprehend or perceive an idea"; such a sentence "draws the reader to discover the revelation along with the character" and results in "an unexcelled degree of psychological realism."

E. R. Hagemann continues his examination of the reaction of *Life* magazine to James (see *ALS* 1968, pp. 86–87) with his sparkling " 'Unexpected light in shady places': Henry James and *Life*, 1883–1916" (*WHR* 24:241–50), where he discusses *Life*'s general gibes at James, its resentment of his expatriation, its comments on his style, its parodies, and its serious reviews of James's fiction.

James is incidentally mentioned in several works whose central concerns are not the novelist himself. Richard H. Rupp's interestingly focused *Celebration in Postwar American Fiction, 1945–1967* (Coral Gables, Fla., Univ. of Miami Press) alleges the impossibility of regarding James as an influence on fiction writers after World War II because "his concern for shades of awareness, individual and reciprocal, is intensely subjective. His esthetic method forced him away from the communal sharing and praise of life that underlie all celebrations." In "The 'Classic' American Writers and the Radicalized Classroom" (*CE* 31:565–70) James E. Miller, Jr., recommends "The Beast in the Jungle" and *What Maisie Knew*, for a start, to the now generation of readers demanding "relevance." Thomas Elliott Berry in *The Newspaper in the American Novel, 1900–1969* (Metuchen, N.J., Scarecrow) touches for background on *The Reverberator*, in which journalists invade the privacy of others, and on *The Wings of the Dove*, one of whose main characters is reporter Merton Densher.

(Berry's comments on James are marred by two inaccuracies: the title is not *The Reverberators*, nor is Densher seen in Vienna, but rather in Venice.) Charles P. Frank in *Edmund Wilson* (TUSAS 152) is curiously harsh toward his subject's imperfect but important essay, "The Ambiguity of Henry James" (see pp. 49–55). Frank likes Wilson's comments on James's post-*Golden Bowl* period but tries to rebuke the critic for vagueness in planning, carlessness, and "his biographical preoccupation." Giles B. Gunn's "Criticism as Repossession and Responsibility: F. O. Matthiessen and the Ideal Critic" (*AQ* 22 :629–48) includes deserved praise of Matthiessen's pioneering work on James.

iv. Criticism: Individual Novels

Some of the best criticism of the year is to be found in articles on individual novels. Especially commendable are studies by Sheldon W. Liebman, Taylor Stoehr, Alan W. Bellringer, Arnold Edelstein, and Philip M. Weinstein.

The American is discussed by Stanley Tick, who in "Henry James's *The American: Voyons*" (*SNNTS* 2:276–91) notes that its "principal theme is Seeing" and that *see* is "probably the most frequently used active verb" in it. Tick criticizes Christopher Newman "because he does not see adequately outside of himself," because he fails to see that he resembles his friend Tom Tristram, whose advice regarding Claire de Cintré he should have followed, because he does not see the value of Old World forms and ceremonies, and because even his bravery and decency are romantically obvious but really irrelevant.

Washington Square is treated by two writers. In a chapter called "Washington Square" in his book *The Polished Surface: Essays in the Literature of Worldliness* (New York, Knopf, 1969, pp. 233–45), Louis Kronenberger amid curious little curlicue phrases extols James's neglected little work as "conceivably . . . his best novel— which is not for a moment to say his greatest"—for its rough resemblance to Jane Austen's *Pride and Prejudice*, its "worldliness all compact," and its shapeliness, balance, and intensity. Kronenberger is especially incisive in analyzing Austin Sloper and discussing the element of love in his novel. William Kenney's "Doctor Sloper's Double in *Washington Square*" (*UR* 36:301–06) logically demonstrates that Sloper and Morris Townsend are so much alike that the younger man could be considered the physician's double. An intriguing corollary is the suggestion that Sloper's "intense reaction to Townsend may come in part from a transference of his own hatred of himself."

Three items concern *The Portrait of a Lady*. Sheldon W. Liebman's "The Light and the Dark: Character Design in *The Portrait of a Lady*" (*PLL* 6:163–79) is the most significant. Liebman considers the subordinate characters in terms of national origin, fictive role, and ability to shed light for Isabel Archer on her path and life. Liebman has especially good things to say about Ralph Touchett, who "occupies the middle ground" between suitor and confidante, and who is also half American and half European. In an elementary essay Mrs. N. Mukherji discusses "The Role of Pansy in *The Portrait of a Lady*" (*CalR* n.s.1:585–94). Pansy provides a contrast with Isabel Archer and Henrietta Stackpole, reflects her father Gilbert Osmond and expedites his marriage to Isabel, helps unify the novel, and helps motivate Isabel at the end. For *The Merrill Studies in "The Portrait of a Lady"* (Columbus, Ohio, Charles E. Merrill) Lyall H. Powers, the editor, provides a brief introduction dealing with James's high hopes for his big novel and with its themes. What follows are ten essays, all of which appeared earlier and some of which are now classics.

The Princess Casamassima was accorded only one essay, but it is one of the finest of its kind ever written. "Words and Deeds in *The Princess Casamassima*" (*ELH* 37:95–135) by Taylor Stoehr is a tough, tangled, enervating, but significant study relating the novel to the linguistic theory and active practice of anarchists. Stoehr deals with fictive victims of the differences between language and reality. He accuses James of confusing reportorial intensity with accuracy, makes use of Richard Henry Savage's *Anarchist* and Sir Lepel Henry Griffith's *Great Republic*, and then in detail shows sequential similarities in the characters and plots of Turgenev's *Virgin Soil* and James's novel. Finally Stoehr analyzes Hyacinth Robinson's vow (the anarchist's "ultimate speech-act"), which since "his newly developing character utterly depends on it" will doom him to a loss of awareness or to suicide; on the other hand, James knew that the artist who vows to see is delimited from a life of participation.

Of three essays on *The Tragic Muse* the best is Alan W. Bellringer's "*The Tragic Muse*: Objective Centre" (*JAmS* 4:73–89), which is a solid, thorough study of Miriam Rooth as the curiously objective center of the novel. She "functions symbolically . . . to represent the personal complications resulting from extreme passions for art." Bellringer discusses the contributions to this theme made by various other characters: Gabriel Nash flamboyantly interprets Miriam; Peter Sherringham attempts to raise her literary taste only to be laid low by his very success; Basil Dashwood stands for commercial ambition and consequent compromise; and Madame Voisin is "a social, not an intellectual, model for Miriam." Bellringer sums up the influence of these characters on the heroine thus: "By emphasizing her dependence on her associates and environment, James is . . . able to objectify her point of view. She becomes the objective centre." Bellringer closes with a look at the final chapter, which he says "has something of the quality of a Dickensian postscript." He handles best the ramifications of Peter's complex plea for Miriam's hand and James's superb account of the rejected suitor's misery. Related to Bellringer's study is Robert Falk's essay called *"The Tragic Muse*: Henry James's Loosest, Baggiest Monster?" in *Themes and Directions* (pp. 148–62). Falk undertakes "to discuss *The Tragic Muse* in terms of James's own comments [in its preface] on its form" and says at the outset that, "when analyzed through the perspective of James's own ideal of . . . thematic consistency and structural form," it cannot rightly be called loose and baggy. Miriam's story and Nick's story are both subsumed "under the larger theme of art-versus-worldliness" and fuse "into the larger fictive portrait of the actress-temperament." Miriam is pictorially central and is revealed "through the alternating consciousness" of Nick and Peter, who are both subordinate figures. As she rises professionally, Nick "recedes to his proper place as an amateur portraitist" and Peter must settle for Nick's sister, Biddy Dormer. Thus the pictorial arrangement is completed earlier than the dramatic climax, a fact which pained James but rightly does not bother Falk, who concludes by explaining why Miriam cannot become Nick's mistress and why James was wrong to apologize for Nick's lackluster. In my opinion, Falk is uniformly excellent (apart from proofreading) except when he unfairly downgrades Nick and suggests that his "heritage of upper-class British attitudes" vitiates his art aspirations (did such a heritage spoil those of Sir Joshua Reynolds, whom Falk cites?), when he blames Peter's rejection by Miriam on his being "condescending toward her art," and when he wrongly implies that Peter and Nick are equally subordinate to Miriam thematically, pictorially, and dramatically. John L. Kimmey in "*The Tragic Muse* and Its Forerunners" (*AL* 41:518–31) suggests that to understand this novel one must recognize that it is part of a single, sustained artistic burst which also produced *The Bostonians* and *The Princess Casamassima*. All three works are somewhat "similar . . . in theme, character, and structure." By the time he wrote *The Tragic Muse*, James had learned from his mistakes: "Where *The Bostonians* is overdone and static and *The Princess* too sprawling and unfocused, James's last long fiction of the 1880's reveals in every part control, economy, and proportion." Kimmey's essay is competent but workmanlike and a bit obvious throughout.

The Spoils of Poynton has evoked so many interpretations that Arnold Edelstein in " 'The Tangle of Life': Levels of Meaning in *The Spoils of Poynton*" (*HSL* 2:133–50) does us all a favor when he begins by mediating between Fleda Vetch's detractors and her supporters. He then argues that the novel, especially in "the climactic scene [in chapter 16] that occurs when Owen [Gereth] follows Fleda," is a skillful tangle of ambiguities—mainly concerning Fleda's "Secret," the bases of her fear of Owen, the sources of her possible shame, and her perhaps heroic but also perhaps escapist conduct. In his first section, Edelstein rather wildly theorizes that Owen's recognition of Fleda's secret love is symbolically a "defloration scene" and that her return to his mother represents not only fear of his "phallic threat" but also emotional regression. Next Edelstein explicates in "anal fantasy" terms "the dialectic of letting go and holding on [which] dominates the novel." He boasts of his admittedly mindstretching insight here, saying that "without recognition of the anal-fantasy level it is doubtful if a reader more than senses the nightmare world [of *The Spoils of Poynton*] . . . , since the surface level is so occupied with defense." Edelstein warns that the ideal reader should be simultaneously moved emotionally and challenged critically, opines curiously that he is "not advocating this kind or that kind of approach . . . nor a bland amalgam of approaches that masquerades as objectivity," criticizes all previous critical responses as "possible but not total," and suggests that our inability to "derive a unified experience" from reading this novel may be owing either to our reluctance to balance between "fantasy and defense" the way James himself could balance or to the novelist's lack of artistic sense in this instance. Edelstein gives us an outstanding essay flawed by psychological jargon, which may strike some as silly at times, and weakened by inconclusiveness at the close. Akio Namekata in "Some Notes on *The Spoils of Poynton*" (*SELit*[Eng. No.]19–35) takes the middle of the road as he conservatively summarizes and analyzes the four meetings between Fleda and Owen, in order to point out the quality of "her idealistic moral sense and sympathetic imagination," and concludes that she is what James says she is, "'successful,'" since the best way for a Jamesian character to protect both imagination and moral sense is to assume "the role of spectator in life." If Edelstein pays too much attention to Fleda's unconscious, Namekata pays too little.

The Sacred Fount drew forth one superb essay. It is Philip M. Weinstein's "The Exploitative and Protective Imagination: Unreliable Narration in *The Sacred Fount*," and it appears in *The Interpretation of Narrative: Theory and Practice*, ed. Morton W. Bloomfield, Harvard English Studies 1 (Cambridge, Mass., Harvard Univ. Press, pp. 189–209). Weinstein accepts and reinforces "the analogy between the narrator and the novelist," and argues that "the imagination is inevitably exploitative" but that it also "lovingly protects." The narrator's imagination does so through his not exposing others always; James's imagination does so by virtue of certain "formal techniques," such as restricted point of view, the stressing of surfaces, and the suggesting of depth through selective detail. In the second half of the essay Weinstein explores "the version of experience posited by the 'exquisite theory' of the sacred fount itself," explicates the imperfect titular metaphor, and relates its implications to James's attitudes toward sexual intimacy. Weinstein refuses to accord the novel unqualified praise, both because "the story of a story that fails to become clear makes, in the absence of other interests, a thin literary diet," and because "the vision of life posited by the sacred fount theory . . . is . . . more appalling than sublime" and led James on to envisage two men—John Marcher in "The Beast in the Jungle" and Lambert Strether in *The Ambassadors*—who imagined rather than realized life. Weinstein's essay is knotty, a little prolix, but significant.

Reynolds Price's introduction to a reprint of *The Wings of the Dove* (Columbus, Ohio, Charles E. Merrill) suggests that, remarkable though James's courage was for his attempting this novel, it partially fails because of his fear to handle sexual matters frankly, "for whatever reasons—his relations with Minny Temple, with his

brothers, his parents, whoever . . . ." Price wishes that James had told
the story more scenically and with more "visual effects," and identifies "a number of baffling omissions" in it. Price describes James as
resembling not Turgenev or Flaubert, who were both "lucid and
aware," but Franz Kafka, "as lurid and mad . . . as desperate . . . and
often as helpless" as James here. I should not imply that Price dis-
likes *The Wings of the Dove*, for he ranks it as second only to *The
Golden Bowl* in James's canon. Price's essay is dash-riddled, paren-
thesis-clouded, quirky, and precious, but also provocative.

Several essays concern *The Ambassadors*. Elsa Nettels's "*The
Ambassadors* and the Sense of the Past" (*MLQ* 31:220–35) is a sane
and mellow demonstration that in the decade before he wrote the
novel James increasingly sensed personal loss and dealt with the
vanished past not only in his fiction but also in his criticism. He was
aware that an old era was ending and a new one starting. Paradoxically, as Lambert Strether is launched into a new experience in
modern Paris, he remembers the past of France and his own irrecov-
erable youth. Madame de Vionnet's defeat by Chad Newsome dramatizes "the passing of the old order and the final, full emergence of
the new." Strether's predicament is melancholy, and yet there is "a
kind of health and vitality" in his responses. Kuno Schuhmann in
"Ethik und Ästhetik im Spätwerk von Henry James" (*JA* 15:77–87)
opposes the notion that James's later works have technical problems
and argues instead that because James came to live with the figures
of his own imagination, their problems were his own. Therefore,
ethical questions are presented in aesthetic terms: " 'consciousness'
and 'conscience' are synonyms." Schuhmann uses *The Ambassadors*
for evidence and suggests that the "aesthetic experience" Strether
has enables him to make "a moral decision." Reid Maynard in "The
Irony of Strether's Enlightenment" (*LHR* 11[1969]:33–44) asks
whether it is "not possible that James, out of his own inescapable
puritanic bias, created a protagonist [Strether] who does not become
quite so enlightened as either he or Strether would like to believe."
Maynard's question is better than his answer, which seems to ramble
a little: Strether remains essentially "Woollett-oriented," Maria
Gostrey seems partly another "Jamesian innocent who romanticizes
Europe," toward the end Madame de Vionnet grows aware that
Strether is "an idealist and a retreatist," and it is ironical that James

fancies Strether should implicitly claim that his "enlightened code, so recently acquired from his Parisian experience, . . . is superior to Madame de Vionnet's." Thomas J. Bontly in "The Moral Perspective of *The Ambassadors*" (*WSinL* 6[1969]:106–17) rightly assumes that for James there was always a "special affinity . . . between the intelligence of the novelist as he creates his 'picture of life' and the intelligence of the individual as he exercises his moral prerogative." Bontly then illustrates this assumption with a persuasive definition of Strether as a man who abandons the New England point of view, avoids the Parisian one, learns to see his own way, and "in the process . . . becomes[s] his own man." Bontly is especially admirable when discussing Madame de Vionnet in Notre Dame but is severe with Jim Pocock, whom he accuses of "crass lechery," and with Chad Newsome, whom he brands too easily, I think, as a "shallow, selfish little bourgeois" and as "immovable." Brief notice should be taken here of Leon Edel's suave little introduction to a reprint of *The Ambassadors* (London, Bodley Head, volume 8 of the Bodley Head James). Edel calls Strether's story "a lively modern comedy"; mentions elements of its style, form, tone, and point of view; defends its absence of detail; praises its message concerning the possibilities of increased awareness in one's older years; and contrasts types of Americans depicted in it.

v. Criticism: Individual Tales

Nine short stories by James were the subject of essays, and once again, as in former years, it is "The Turn of the Screw" which proved the most provocative.

Charles Feidelson, Jr., published "Art as Problem in 'The Figure in the Carpet' and 'The Madonna of the Future' " as an original essay in *Twentieth Century Interpretations of "The Turn of the Screw" and Other Tales,* ed. Jane P. Tompkins (Englewood Cliffs, N.J., Prentice-Hall). Using evidence from the two stories, Feidelson abstrusely and, in my opinion, quite unsatisfactorily considers the philosophical implications of art, which results from a consciousness of life, as containing naturalistically larger life within it, and the aesthetic problem of "a fatal flaw at the heart of all imaginative triumph."

Also disappointing is H. A. Bouraoui's "Henry James and the

French Mind: The International Theme in 'Madame de Mauves'"
(*Novel* 4:69–76), an essay which has a large title for a simple thesis.
The author properly, though not originally, criticizes James's central
intelligence, the American Longmore, for prejudice and romantic
naïveté. But then Bouraoui strangely suggests that Comte Richard
de Mauves might be judged as spiritually more faithful to his American wife Euphemia than she is to him, because he only sports a
physical mistress whereas Euphemia "has come close to committing
a *spiritual* infidelity by loving Longmore enough to give him up . . . ."
The essay does have a valuable touch: it contends that when old
Madame de Mauves tells her grand-daughter-in-law that Richard
will do her justice, the remark "is full of a terrible irony" because his
justice means suicide.

Leo Gurko in "The Missing Word in Henry James's 'Four Meetings'" (*SSF* 7:298–307) proposes three candidates—*happy, uncompleted,* and *alive*—for the word "deliberately omitted" in the opening
paragraph of the story. Each of the three words if used results in a
"perfectly rational and clear" interpretation, as is shown by Gurko,
who concludes by indicating his preference for *alive*, since that word
most sharply illuminates the narrator's character and also best takes
James's revisions into consideration.

In his *Studi e ricerche di letteratura americana* (Florence, La
Nuova Italia, 1968, pp. 173–81), Rolando Anzilotti includes a chapter
called "Un racconto italiano di Henry James: *Daisy Miller*," in which
he curiously regards Winterbourne as less a character than a "punto
di vista." Anzilotti takes up the characteristic "ambiguità" in the story
and asks the usual unanswerable questions raised by it. Interestingly,
he suggests that just as the full-length *Portrait of a Lady* follows
"Daisy Miller," which was only a study, so Ralph Touchett is a "personaggio derivato da Winterbourne." Anzilotti's contention that
Daisy may be interpreted as a symbol of America "giovane, fresca e
anticonformista" fighting against prejudices ironically represented
by Americans rather than Europeans is, frankly, a bromide in Jamesian criticism.

Philip L. Nicoloff's "At the Bottom of All Things in Henry James's
'Louisa Pallant'" (*SSF* 7:409–20) is the year's finest essay of explication on a single short story by James. Nicoloff begins by summarizing
the narrative according to the conventional reading, which he then

rejects as simplistic, given "major difficulties in accepting such a plot at face value." These difficulties include the discrepancy between Louisa's hysterical judgment of her daughter Linda and that girl's evident charm, the narrator's vacillating judgment, and the obscured tone of the tale at its close. Nicoloff sees the narrator as "the hidden protagonist of the story and the only truly relevant ethical figure," whose "outward passivity becomes the mask of an inward moral violence." Louisa tells him about her daughter's selfish ambition in order to impress him rather than to save his nephew, Archie Parker. The narrator responds in order to relieve "his habitual loneliness and boredom," and to assuage his sense of "unmanly stagnation." The climax comes when Louisa thus confirms his opinion of himself as a better man than the one she married; what follows is an uneasy retreat into passivity by the narrator, the sacrifice of Linda, and the narrator's awareness of his own hypocrisy.

Thomas M. Cranfill and Robert L. Clark, Jr., in "The Provocativeness of 'The Turn of the Screw'" (*TSLL* 12:93–100) document the popularity and challenge of the story, which has provoked editors, critics, poets, parodists, illustrators, dramatists, opera composers, and moviemakers. The authors commendably consider all forms of response to James's chiller except for study guides. Sidney E. Lind in " 'The Turn of the Screw': The Torment of Critics" (*CentR* 14: 225–40) begins with an opinionated survey of important previous scholarship and includes such rash generalizations as these: " 'The Turn of the Screw' is not a ghost story; it is a psychological study" and "the story illustrates James' literary imagination working on a level which precludes deep soundings and reverberations, so far as an understanding of the narrative is concerned." Even while Lind reminds us, as scores of critics have already done, that James called his celebrated tale a pot-boiler, a *jeu d'esprit*, a trap, and the like, Lind himself falls into a trap. Surely James's tale was not written to be any one thing, is not any one thing, and is as stimulating as it has been because its creator intended it to be legitimately read by a variety of people seeking and finding a variety of appeals. With this story least of all do we need dogmatic pronouncements. But Lind does valuably comment on James's relationship to psychological studies in his own time, and on his other psychologically oriented fiction which is similar to "The Turn of the Screw" in techniques, import, and character portrayal. Everett Zimmerman in "Literary Tradition and 'The Turn of the Screw'" (*SSF* 7:634–37) shows that the literary references in the story "create a sense of horror by providing a viewpoint too limited for [the governess to be able to deal with] succeeding events," whether those references are to Gothic literature or to eighteenth-century fiction featuring quixotic heroines. Thomas J. Bontly's essay called "James's General Vision of Evil in 'The Turn of the Screw'" (*SEL* 9[1969]:721–35) is ambitious, stimulating, and annoying. Bontly divides the critics into those who believe the ghosts are real and those who believe the governess is insane. He states simplistically that if the ghosts are hallucinations then evil is an illusion in this story but that if the apparitionist critics are correct then they are pretty much obliged to accept either a Manichean or a Puritan view of evil. Finally he argues that "the ghosts symbolize the origins of human fear in the adult's [specifically, the governess's] sense of sexual guilt"—which guilt the self-challenging governess passes on to innocent Miles and Flora. Bontly is suspicious of the governess's sanity but refuses to meet the arguments of critics on the other side. Worse, he praises James's skill at "sustaining two mutually exclusive interpretations of the events—a natural one and a supernatural one"—and yet ignores evidence supporting the logical conclusion of such praise, i.e., that there is evidence at every turn of the story which counters specific interpretations, including Bontly's. In short, Bontly argues persuasively but almost never irresistibly, and too often dogmatizes. Rolande Ballorain in " 'The Turn of the Screw': L'Adulte et l'enfante: Ou les deux regards" (*EA* 22[1969]:250–58) shows how central the tale is to an understanding of James's other fiction of the 1890s, much of which, Ballorain reports, deals with a sense of confinement, enigma, child-adult relations, surrogate parents, the proximity of love and death, and other "thèmes e rapports obsédants." C. Tournadre in his "Propositions pour une psychologie sociale de 'The Turn of the Screw'" (*EA* 22[1969]:259–69) develops the theory that "La situation [sociale] de la gouvernante comme celle de Miss Jessel est . . . ambigué et va se trouver à l'origine de frustrations constantes." One can interpret the story religiously, psychoanalytically, or socially, or in ways combining these three approaches; but the social interpretation—to the effect that the governess is hypersensitive to social considerations—has hitherto been somewhat neglected, says Tournadre.

In "Organic Unity in ' "Europe" ' " (*SAB* 35,iii:40–41) Pierre Han shows that the first sentence of " 'Europe' " starts a unifying rhetorical pattern which is elaborated later and completed surprisingly in the final sentence of the story.

"The Beast in the Jungle" constantly stimulates criticism. Peter J. Conn's "Seeing and Blindness in 'The Beast in the Jungle' " (*SSF* 7:472–75) shows that John Marcher tries to appropriate May Bartram and reductively possess her with his eyes for his own destructive use, but that since he is blind and lacks illumination he fails. The glaring eyes which he fears turn out to be his own: "Marcher and his Beast are not merely similar—they are one." Similar in approach and thesis is an essay by Ronald Beck called "James's 'Beast in the Jungle': Theme and Metaphor" (*Markham Rev* 2,ii:[17–20]). It is a subtle, overwrought demonstration that the beast metaphor organizes all thematic elements. Beck sees the beast as paradoxically both ignorance and tardy awareness, and regards unaccepted May and passive Marcher as the double object of the inept hunt. Beck is skillful when suggesting that the beast ironically strikes in every section of the story and not simply at the end, because it symbolizes Marcher's ignorance as well as the ultimate revelation of that ignorance. On the other hand, Elizabeth Hansot in "Imagination and Time in 'The Beast in the Jungle,' " an original essay in *Twentieth Century Interpretations of "The Turn of the Screw" and Other Tales* (pp. 88–94), is content to present the simple thesis that Marcher "declines to live in ordinary time," imagines instead that his future will be gloriously unique, but is caught in time all the same. Jane P. Tompkins in " 'The Beast in the Jungle': An Analysis of James's Late Style" (*MFS* 16: 185–91) presents a highly charged analysis of James's use of parenthetical statements, usually adverbial and often rhythmical, characteristic of his late style and illustrated here with evidence from "The Beast in the Jungle." By this technique, James suggests the simultaneity of exploration and didactic certainty, of diffidence and persuasiveness, in his characters. Miss Tompkins concludes in a brilliant sentence echoing some of the master's own efforts that in Marcher's story "The hard-won syntactical resolutions, delayed by frustrating qualifications, share, by virtue of their intensity and the sense they afford of welcome relief, the orgasmic nature of the story's conclusion." She then points to needed work, along this line, on other late novels and tales by James: "The moment of vision in James's fiction, like the closure of his sentences, comes late; the truth, in each case, is dearly bought." James L. Kraft in "A Perspective on 'The Beast in the Jungle'" (*LWU* 2[1969]:20–26) argues with delicate persuasiveness that Marcher and May, as symbiotic blind parasite and masochistic hostess respectively, "create all the life that is possible for them." Marcher needs someone to believe in his uniqueness; May's decision to watch passively with him "may be an unconscious defense to protect herself from fears of her ability to love in a more expressive relationship."

Leon Edel has reissued *Henry James: Stories of the Supernatural* (New York, Taplinger). It contains little that is new. In 1948 he published *The Ghostly Tales of Henry James* (New Brunswick, Rutgers Univ. Press), eighteen in number and some not very ghostly. In 1963 he reissued *The Ghostly Tales of Henry James* (New York, Grosset and Dunlap), keeping the ten most ghostly and including a new introduction. Realizing that the first title was inaccurate, Edel has altered it, and he has now reprinted the original eighteen eerie stories and provided still another general introduction (echoing parts of his 1948 one) and a set of partly new headnotes to the individual tales. One wonders why Edel should have felt it necessary to reissue this collection, since everything in it is available elsewhere; moreover, as he himself implies, much of the biographical material is contained in the first four volumes of his biography of James. Edel's best insight in his own seventy-odd pages here is his reiterated suggestion that in many of James's supernatural tales we have a continuing dramatization of the haunter haunted.

vi. Criticism: Specific Nonfictional Works

James's critical essays, travel writing, and plays have been neglected of late. Leon Edel does provide a brief introduction to a reprint of James's *Partial Portraits* (Ann Arbor, Univ. of Mich. Press), in which he explicates the title, explains how James saw the writer in the writing, touches on the stylistic grace of James's "literary portraiture," and especially extols his essay "The Art of Fiction" as "a veritable manifesto" and "the most significant statement ever made by a working novelist about his art." The introduction is marred by fulsome praise of James's undistinguished essay on Ralph Waldo Emerson, but Edel recovers when he cleverly suggests at the close that a portrait we get in *Partial Portraits* without James's intending to give it is one of James himself.

University of Pittsburgh

7. Faulkner

Michael Millgate

Although the thin listing under the first of my subheadings might suggest that bibliographical and textual work on Faulkner was at a standstill, such a conclusion would in fact be quite erroneous. At the United States Military Academy at West Point, for example, work is going ahead, in the Academic Computer Center, on the first titles of a Faulkner Concordance. By early 1971 the concordances to *The Hamlet* and the published poetry had already been completed, and although it did not seem feasible to publish these it was hoped that computer printout sheets suitable for binding could be deposited in selected university libraries. Obviously an ideal Faulkner concordance would need to be based upon ideal Faulkner texts, which seem still to be some distance away; the present undertaking, however, promises to be extremely useful, particularly for stylistic studies and as a major tool in the preparation of future scholarly editions.

i. Bibliography, Editions, and Manuscripts

The year produced only James B. Meriwether's *Merrill Checklist of William Faulkner* (Columbus, Ohio, Charles E. Merrill), a selective listing of Faulkner's own books and of books and articles about him, and two useful reprintings of Meriwether's "Notes on the Textual History of *The Sound and the Fury*"—a revised version in the Merrill Studies volume listed under *The Sound and the Fury*, below, and the earlier version in *Art and Error*. But see also the dissertations listed under *Sartoris* and *The Wild Palms*.

ii. Biography

The most substantial item to be recorded is Joseph L. Blotner's "William Faulkner: Committee Chairman," in *Themes and Directions*, pp. 200–19. This account of Faulkner's work as chairman of a writers' committee established under the auspices of President Eisenhower's People-to-People Program offers significant insights into Faulkner's attitudes, especially towards his responsibilities as a writer in the immediate aftermath of the Nobel Prize. Other biographical pieces are of minor importance. In "Bill's Friend Phil" (*JMiH* 32:135–45) O. B. Emerson gives a one-sided account of Phil Stone's relationship with Faulkner based on Stone's own statements; as the author acknowledges, the second half of the article is taken from his earlier essay, "Prophet Next Door" (see *ALS 1964*, p. 80). "The Picture of John and Brother Will" (*DeltaR* 7:12–14) is an anecdotal account by Faulkner's nephew of how Faulkner and his Brother John came to have their photograph taken together in the summer of 1949. And in "Faulkner in Massachusetts" (*NEG* 10,iii[1969]:37–42) Elizabeth Linscott, the widow of Robert N. Linscott, of Random House, recalls weekend visits by Faulkner to their farmhouse home in the foothills of the Berkshires.

Mention should also be made here of the book by Barbara Izard and Clara Hieronymus discussed with *Requiem for a Nun*, below, and of three other pieces which touch tangentially upon Faulkner biography. In "Colonel Falkner's Preface to *The Siege of Monterey*" (*NMW* 3:36–40) Hilton Anderson reprints in its entirety a statement (published as the preface to a volume of narrative verse) in which Faulkner's great-grandfather protests against the efforts of his enemies, "who are anything but few," to destroy his reputation by spreading false accounts of his killing of two men. In "A Deer Hunt in the Faulkner Country" (*MissQ* 23:315–20) Thomas L. McHaney quotes from a Ripley, Mississippi, newspaper of January 1935 an engagingly unsophisticated account of a recent deer hunt in the Coldwater-Tallahatchie River basin, where Faulkner himself hunted. Willard Pate's "Pilgrimage to Yoknapatawpha" (*Furman Magazine*, Winter 1969, pp. 6–13) does not pretend to be anything other than a personal reminiscence of a visit in 1966 to Oxford, Mississippi.

iii. Criticism: General

a. **Books.** Italian readers of Faulkner would appear to have been well served by Mario Materassi's *I romanzi di Faulkner* (Biblioteca di studi Americani, 17; Rome, Edizioni di Storia e Letteratura, 1968), even though it does not include *The Unvanquished* and *Go Down,*

Moses among Faulkner's novels. Of particular interest is an appended survey of Italian Faulkner criticism: Mario Praz, it transpires, was writing appreciatively of Faulkner as early as 1931. From a review by Virgil Nemoianu (*MissQ* 23:336–38) I gather that the long study in Rumanian by Sorin Alexandrescu, *William Faulkner* (Bucharest, Editura Pentru Literatură Universală, 1969), combines a general survey of Faulkner's career with an extended structuralist analysis of the Yoknapatawpha fiction, viewed as a single continuum.

Recent books in English are unimpressive. Although *William Faulkner: A Critical Essay*, a forty-eight-page pamphlet by Fr. Martin Jarrett-Kerr (Grand Rapids, Mich., William B. Eerdmans), is published in a series entitled Contemporary Writers in Christian Perspective, it does not greatly extend our understanding of Faulkner's theology and beliefs nor, indeed, of any other aspect of his work and personality. Again, despite occasional indications of an independent critical response, the commentaries on each of the novels and short stories offered by Walter K. Everett in *Faulkner's Art and Characters* (Woodbury, N.Y., Barron's Educational Series, 1969) remain little more than elaborated plot summaries; there is also a dictionary of characters and a badly out-dated bibliography.

b. **Articles and Dissertations.** In F. Garvin Davenport, Jr., *The Myth of Southern History: Historical Consciousness in Twentieth-Century Southern Literature* (Nashville, Vanderbilt Univ. Press), the long chapter on Faulkner (pp. 82–130) contains some valuable general reflections upon Faulkner's attitudes to history as seen in the context of contemporary historiography; it also comments sensibly upon *Absalom, Absalom!* as a "regional epic" with "a meaning which is national in implication." Faulkner's relationship to his region also provided the focus for Elmo Howell's pleasant but unimportant "William Faulkner's Mule: A Symbol of the Post-War South" (*KFR* 15[1969]:81–86) and for several review-articles prompted by Elizabeth M. Kerr's *Yoknapatawpha: Faulkner's "Little Postage Stamp of Native Soil"* (see *ALS* 1969, pp. 110–11). William T. Stafford spoke approvingly of the book in his brief comments in "Hemingway / Faulkner: Marlin and Catfish?" (*SoR* 6:1191–1200), but Hassell A. Simpson (*NMW* 3:43–47) criticized its basic unexamined assumption that Oxford "is" Jefferson, while Calvin Brown (*GaR* 23[1969]:

501–11) argued that its whole approach was vitiated by uncritical acceptance of standard stereotypes of the South. Most interestingly, Noel Polk (*MissQ* 23:323–35) moved from a rejection of Kerr's *Yoknapatawpha* on these and other grounds to a call for a study of Faulkner as a novelist writing *in* the South—and necessarily conditioned by it—but *about* universal human truths.

George Boswell's "The Legendary Background in Faulkner's Works" (*TFSB* 36,iii:53–63) lists instances of Faulkner's exploitation of legendary sources in the Bible, in Greek and medieval literature, and in local or even family history and tradition. The same author's "Notes on the Surnames of Faulkner's Characters" (*TFSB* 36,iii:64–66) is a brief, sketchy, and altogether casual piece of work. Also to be mentioned at this point are a number of dissertations on general topics: Brian M. Barbour, "Faulkner's Decline" (*DAI* 30:5436A–37A); Barbara N. Ewell, "To Move in Time: A Study of the Structure of Faulkner's *As I Lay Dying, Light in August,* and *Absalom, Absalom!*" (*DAI* 30:3940A); John H. Hafner, "William Faulkner's Narrators" (*DAI* 30:5445A); Tom M. Massey, "Faulkner's Females: The Thematic Function of Women in the Yoknapatawpha Cycle" (*DAI* 30:3468A); Frances W. Pate, "Names of Characters in Faulkner's Mississippi" (*DAI* 30[1969]:2036A–37A); and Myra J. Riskin, "Faulkner's South: Myth and History in the Novel" (*DAI* 30[1969]: 1148A–49A).

iv. Criticism: Special Studies

a. **Ideas, influences, intellectual background.** Of particular interest in 1970 were two articles on Faulkner's reading by the English critic M. Gidley, which contributed substantially to the mounting evidence of just how little of an "untutored" genius Faulkner actually was—though even Gidley greatly underestimates, it seems to me, the incidence of literary allusion in Faulkner's mature work. "Some Notes on Faulkner's Reading" (*JAmS* 4:91–102) is chiefly concerned to explore the possible influence on *Mosquitoes* of Aldous Huxley's *Chrome Yellow* and the essays by contemporary critics in *A Modern Book of Criticism,* edited by Ludwig Lewisohn, while "One Continuous Force: Notes on Faulkner's Extra-Literary Reading" (*MissQ* 23:299–314) considers other books to which Faulkner is known to

have had access, including Elie Faure's *History of Art,* James Harvey
Robinson's *The Mind in the Making,* and *The Education of Henry
Adams.* Also relevant here are the essays by Brooks and Yonce discussed with *Soldiers' Pay* and Blotner's article on *A Fable* (see be-
low). In "The Romantic Coordinates of American Literature" (*BuR*
18,ii:16–33) Jesse Bier argues, somewhat insubstantially, for Faulkner's general indebtedness to earlier American writers—Thoreau, Poe,
Hawthorne, James—while Peter L. Irvine's "Faulkner and Hardy"
(*ArQ* 26:357–65) insists that Thomas Hardy is "the writer whom
Faulkner most definitely resembles." Perhaps I may be allowed to
remark that this is a comparison I have myself explored in *Thomas
Hardy: His Career as a Novelist* (New York, Random House, 1971),
pp. 345–51.

In "Faulkner's Philosophy Again: A Reply to Michel Gresset"
(*MissQ* 23:64–66) Harry M. Campbell reasserts the view—first expressed in *William Faulkner: A Critical Appraisal,* which he wrote
in collaboration with Ruel E. Foster—that "a philosophy of cosmic
pessimism exists paradoxically in dramatic tension with Faulkner's
'lucid humanism.'" Two dissertations should also be mentioned:
George C. Bedell's "Kierkegaard and Faulkner: Modalities of Existence" (*DAI* 30:5056A–57A) and David D. McWilliams's "The Influence of William Faulkner on Michel Butor" (*DAI* 31:1282A–83A).

b. Language and style. Apart from a dissertation by Helen M.
Swink, "The Oral Tradition in Yoknapatawpha County" (*DAI* 30:
3920A), all the relevant studies deal with specific works and have
been listed accordingly. See, in particular, discussions of *The Sound
and the Fury* (especially Weber) and *Light in August.*

c. Race. In "Faulkner: Social Commitment and Artistic Temperament" (*SoR* 6:1075–92) Walter Taylor finds in Walter J. Slatoff's
theory of deliberate irresolution in Faulkner's fiction an attractive
analogy for the apparent inconsistencies in Faulkner's public statements about racial issues. The article's value is limited by questionable readings of Faulkner's statements and of novels like *Go Down,
Moses* and *Intruder in the Dust* and by the lack of any attempt to
assess the relative weight to be placed upon what Faulkner wrote for
publication and what he was quoted as saying in interviews—which
are themselves, of course, of varying reliability.

v. Individual Works to 1929

As Cleanth Brooks's first extended treatment of a non-Yoknapatawpha novel, "Faulkner's First Novel" (*SoR* 6:1056–74) is an important event in the Faulkner field. In addition to its critical perceptions, the article offers some useful identifications of Faulknerian literary allusions. In "Faulkner's 'Atthis' and 'Attis': Some Sources of Myth" (*MissQ* 23:289–98) Margaret Yonce very usefully explores the sources and functions of Faulkner's "Atthis" allusion in *Soldiers' Pay* and the possible relevance of the "Attis" myth to the presentation of Labove in *The Hamlet*.

Sartoris was the subject only of Lois Muehl's "Word Choice and Choice Words in Faulkner's *Sartoris*" (*LC* 35[1969]:58–63), which can safely be ignored, and of a dissertation by Stephen N. Dennis, "The Making of *Sartoris*: A Description and Discussion of the Manuscript and Composite Typescript of William Faulkner's Third Novel" (*DAI* 31:384A).

James B. Meriwether's *The Merrill Studies in "The Sound and the Fury"* (Columbus, Ohio, Charles E. Merrill) contains the full text of eight previously published essays (some of them revised by their authors) and of one essay not hitherto published. In the latter, "Caddy Compson's World" (pp. 89–101), Eileen Gregory sees Caddy in strongly positive terms; unhappily, in a "brutalized, secular world" Caddy is denied any opportunity to fulfill her natural feminine role. Among new essays published elsewhere pride of place should perhaps be given to Margaret Blanchard's exploration—in "The Rhetoric of Communion: Voice in *The Sound and the Fury*" (*AL* 42:555–65)— of the precise degree of privilege enjoyed by the fourth section narrator and of the relationship between the narrator's perspective, seen as largely coextensive with that of the intelligent reader, and his tone, which "maintains through style its own attitudes." Rhetorically, she maintains, the strategy is extremely effective: the narrator, having forced the reader into an intense participation in the first three sections, "establishes empathy in the fourth section by adopting his perspective and complimenting him by the way he speaks to him. Consequently the reader is much more ready to adopt, in turn, the narrator's tone, no matter how demanding its implications."

In "Quentin Compson's Universal Grief" (*ConL* 11:451–69) Mark Spilka examines what he sees as Quentin's search for timeless

values—especially "the certainties of the Southern past"—in the face
of modern "mechanistic principles" and his father's "reasoned view
of pointless life." James M. Mellard's *"The Sound and the Fury*:
Quentin Compson and Faulkner's 'Tragedy of Passion' " (*SNNTS*
2:61–75) presents Quentin as forced towards death by his desperate
need to escape from an existence in time, his role made tragic by the
destruction of his innocence and of his heroic capacity for passionate
idealism. In these and other respects, Mellard argues, the Quentin
section meets the requirement of the "tragedy of passion" archetype
as defined in Northrop Frye's *Fools of Time*. In another article, "Caliban as Prospero: Benjy and *The Sound and the Fury*" (*Novel* 3:233–
48), Mellard draws rather strained analogies with *The Tempest* as a
means of establishing that the Benjy section constitutes "a special
handling of the narrative archetype of romance." Suggestively, but
not in the end convincingly, Benjy is seen not only as a Caliban
figure—a "natural" innocent used in the tradition of pastoral satire as
a standard by which other characters can be measured—but also as a
kind of controlling Prospero.

A notable addition to the growing list of stylistic studies of *The
Sound and the Fury* is Robert Wilhelm Weber's monograph, *Die
Aussage der Form. Zur Textur und Struktur des Bewusstseinsromans.
Dargestellt an W. Faulkners "The Sound and the Fury"* (Heidelberg,
Carl Winter, 1969). Although no radically new reading of the novel is
advanced, the analysis of both the overall structure and the detailed
rhetorical, syntactic, and lexical texture is careful and full. L. Mof-
fitt Cecil's "A Rhetoric for Benjy" (*SLJ* 3,i:32–46) is a sensible if somewhat overextended analysis of Faulkner's success in so manipulating
the style of the Benjy section as to give some sense of Benjy himself
even while he fulfills his essential role of observer. In a more specialized study, "The Oral Quality of Rev. Shegog's Sermon in William
Faulkner's *The Sound and the Fury*" (*LWU* 2[1969]:73–88), Bruce
A. Rosenberg sets the sermon alongside actual recorded sermons of
black preachers in order to demonstrate that Faulkner has here "created one of the very few, and certainly the best, spontaneously composed oral sermons in fiction": it is, he maintains, superior even to
the sermons in *Moby-Dick* and *Invisible Man*.

Four other articles are of lesser importance. In "Jason Compson's
Paranoid Pseudocommunity" (*HSL* 2:151–56) Charles D. Peavy
adopts Norman Cameron's term for the conspiring "they" which the

paranoid sees as ranged against him as a way of describing Jason's hostility towards his family, his fellow-townsmen, and the world in general. George N. Dove's "Shadow and Paradox: Imagery in *The Sound and the Fury*" (*Essays*, pp. 89–95) offers one or two mildly interesting suggestions, and there are brief and apparently insubstantial references to *The Sound and the Fury* in Mircea Ivănescu, "Dostoievski și Faulkner" (*SXX* 12,iv[1969]:209–12) and John Logan, "Nota sobre el personaje balbuciente como héroe" (*Sur* no.332–23:148–54).

vi. Individual Works, 1930–1939

André Bleikasten's study of *As I Lay Dying*, 150 pages long, is included with François Pitavy's corresponding study of *Light in August* (see below) in an impressive double volume, *William Faulkner: "As I Lay Dying" [and] "Light in August"* (Paris, Armand Colin), edited by Michel Gresset. Gresset's introduction, organized around central problems in Faulkner criticism, is supplemented by a chronological table setting Faulkner's career in the context of contemporary political and literary events, a brief annotated bibliography of general Faulkner criticism, and a note on the texts of the two novels which properly stresses the importance of the 1964 Random House edition of *As I Lay Dying*; an appendix reproduces leaves from the manuscripts of the two novels. Bleikasten's critique is full and careful, and the volume as a whole—directed at the university student and incorporating numerous topics for discussion and further research—represents a kind of thoroughness and responsibility which Faulkner critics writing in English might well seek to emulate.

As I Lay Dying also provides the focus for an important article by Robert Hemenway, "Enigmas of Being in *As I Lay Dying*" (*MFS* 16:133–46). On the basis of a close, sustained analysis of Faulkner's conceptions of time and being as dramatized in the novel—notably but by no means exclusively in Darl's "is / was" reverie—Hemenway is able to argue that the Bundrens are both heroic *and* absurd, and that their essential triumph, in Faulkner's eyes, lies in their final emergence as "realists of the present," embodiments of the Faulknerian view that "one can only live in the present tense," that the past "cannot be permitted to determine present reality." In "Addie Bundren and the Design of *As I Lay Dying*" (*SoR* 6:1093–99) M. E. Bradford, noting that her family continue to speak of the dead Addie in the present tense, argues that Addie stands "between the reader and the fable" as the central, assembling auditor of the consciousnesses evoked in the various sections. The other three articles do not advance our understanding of the novel in any substantial way: John Ditsky, "Faulkner's Carousel: Point of View in *As I Lay Dying*" (*LauR* 10,i: 74–85); Richard B. Hauck, "The Comic Christ and the Modern Reader" (*CE* 31:498–506); Ora G. Williams, "The Theme of Endurance in *As I Lay Dying*" (*LaS* 9:100–04).

William Rossky argues quite effectively in "The Pattern of Nightmare in *Sanctuary*; or, Miss Reba's Dogs" (*MFS* 15:503–15) for the existence in the novel of a "technique of nightmare," a sequence of "dreamlike images and scenes" which create for the characters (especially Temple) and for the reader an experience of "impotent terror." Less convincing, if only because it is difficult to view the creatures so portentously, is his projection of Miss Reba's dogs, in their combination of viciousness and paralyzed fright, as paradigmatic of the novel as a whole.

The double volume which includes François Pitavy's study on *Light in August* has already been noticed above under *As I Lay Dying*. Like Bleikasten, Pitavy is thorough, perceptive, well-informed; particularly suggestive are his approaches to questions of setting and of style. For the English reader some impression of these approaches can be gained from the "free translation" of chapter 4, which constitutes the essay, "The Landscape in *Light in August*" (*MissQ* 23: 265–72)—it is essentially, Pitavy argues, an inner landscape, "the image of a state of mind."

Two articles published in Hebrew in *Hasifrut* are accessible to me only through their English summaries. Rina Litvin, "'William Faulkner's *Light in August*" (*Hasifrut* 1[1969]:589–98; summary 768), explores the relationship between the wagon wheel image, seen as a central symbol, and the presentation of the major characters, seen as roughly divided between those who take a dynamic view of reality and those for whom reality is static. Meir Sternberg's "The Compositional Principles of Faulkner's *Light in August* and the Poetics of the Modern Novel" (*Hasifrut* 2:498–537; summary 687–91) apparently follows an elaborately theoretical path to the conclusion that the fragmented structure of the novel is designed to deny the reader the conventional narrative and "mimetic" satisfactions of fiction and thus force him to focus on the significance of incorporated analogical patterns and on the rhythmic recurrence of particular objects (e.g., shoes) and motifs (e.g., that of "escape, pursuit and capture").

Criticism in English is represented by H. C. Nash's "Faulkner's 'Furniture Repairer and Dealer': Knitting Up *Light in August*" (*MFS* 16:529–31), an over-ingenious but lively and appreciative analysis of the novel's final episode, and by R. G. Collins's "The Game of Names: Characterization Device in *Light in August*" (*ER* 21,i:82–87), which makes a number of suggestions, some helpful, some strained, about the naming of the characters. Lester S. Golub rightly perceives some of the "Syntactic and Lexical Problems in Reading Faulkner" (*EJ* 59:490–96)—specifically, in reading *Light in August*—but fails to analyse them in an illuminating manner. There is also a dissertation: Alvin L. Gregg's "Style and Dialect in *Light in August* and Other Works by William Faulkner" (*DAI* 30:3009A).

Pylon provides the subject for only one article, "*Pylon*: The Ylimaf and New Valois," by W. T. Lhamon, Jr. (*WHR* 24:274–78). "Ylimaf" = "family" spelled backwards, and the article relates the favorable early reception of *Pylon* to its presentation of a fragmented, meaningless urban world in which all values are inverted.

A printing error in the title ("Canfield" for "Coldfield") obscures the subject of Cleanth Brooks's article, "The Poetry of Miss Rosa Canfield" (*Shenandoah* 21,iii:199–206), which offers a vigorous and effective defense—if such a defense is still necessary—of the rhetorical extravagance, rising at times to a kind of prose-poetry, of Miss Rosa's narrative. Lynn Gartrell Levins, in "The Four Narrative Perspectives in *Absalom, Absalom!*" (*PMLA* 85:35–47), categorizes that narrative as "Gothic mystery," Mr. Compson's as Greek tragedy, Quentin's as chivalric romance, and Shreve's as a form of tall tale. There are some interesting suggestions here, but the article as a whole breaks little new ground. In "Faulkner's Defeat of Time in *Absalom, Absalom!*" (*SoR* 6:1100–09) Ruth M. Vande Kieft sees all the varying perspectives of the novel—even including Shreve's—as segments of Faulkner's own total vision; she comments usefully on Faulkner's deliberate manipulation of these perspectives, on the importance of Charles Bon's letter as a tangible document from the past, and on the handling of time in the novel as a whole.

In *The Interpreted Design as a Structural Principle in American Prose* (New Haven, Conn., Yale Univ. Press, 1969), David L. Minter

takes *Absalom, Absalom!* (pp. 191–219) as a supreme example of his
book's subject—the kind of prose work which is organized around a
dramatized, dialectical interplay between "a man dedicated to realizing a grand design" and another man who attempts to interpret that
design and the reasons for its failure. Although his analysis is for the
most part along familiar lines, Minter concludes with valuable comments on dialectical elements in the structure of the novel and on the
"ordering" aspects of Quentin's and Shreve's roles as interpreters.
M. E. Bradford, in "Brother, Son, and Heir: The Structural Focus of
Faulkner's *Absalom, Absalom!*" (*SR* 78:76–98), argues that Charles
Bon is as destructive and inflexible as his father and "probably 'needs
killing' when Henry finally brings himself to do the deed." Quentin's
anguish, in this view, springs from his recognition of the implications
for his own situation—assumed to be identical with that of *The Sound
and the Fury*—of this spectacle of a young Southerner responsibly
discharging the role that is "his and his alone, the particular history
deposited on him as a Sutpen and as a keeper of the inviolable holies
of the communal body."

Two articles pursue interesting basic perceptions too hard and
too far: Leslie E. Angell, "The Umbilical Cord Symbol as Unifying
Theme and Pattern in *Absalom, Absalom!*" (*MSE* 1[1968]:106–10);
Nicholas M. Rinaldi, "Game Imagery in Faulkner's *Absalom, Absalom!*" (*ConnR* 4,i:73–79). In "The Historical Novel and the Southern Past: The Case of *Absalom, Absalom!*" (*SLJ* 2,ii:69–85), Hyatt
H. Waggoner insists upon—and quotes at some length—the view of
the novel which he put forward in *William Faulkner: From Jefferson
to the World* (1959).

Although Gorman Beauchamp's invocation of the Aeschylean
parallel—in *"The Unvanquished:* Faulkner's *Oresteia"* (*MissQ* 23:
273–77)—seems a somewhat extravagant critical gesture, it does
prove an effective method of stressing the nature of the moral development which occurs in "An Odor of Verbena." In "A Possible
Source in Ariosto for Drusilla" (*MissQ* 23:321–22) James E. Kibler,
Jr., points—too recondite1y, one suspects—to similarities between
Faulkner's Drusilla and the Drusilla who appears in canto 37 of
Orlando Furioso.

The one item on *The Wild Palms* to be recorded is Thomas L.
McHaney's dissertation, "William Faulkner's *The Wild Palms*: A
Textual and Critical Study" (*DAI* 30[1969]:2540A–41A).

vii. Individual Works, 1940–1949

The Faulkner chapter (pp. 85–120) in Edward Stone's *A Certain Morbidness: A View of American Literature* (Carbondale, So. Ill. Univ. Press, 1969) offers in part an analysis of the Labove episode in *The Hamlet* as a conscious variation upon Irving's "The Legend of Sleepy Hollow": an old ghost story, says Stone, is brought up-to-date "by shaping it along the new, shocking, psychosexual lines of the modern literary imagination." The article by Margaret Yonce, discussed with *Soldiers' Pay*, is also relevant here.

There is a dissertation on the Snopes trilogy as a whole—Irma A. Powell, "Man in His Struggle: Structure, Technique, and Theme in Faulkner's Snopes Trilogy" (*DAI* 31:1287A–88A)—and the dissertation by James Gray Watson, cited last year, has now become a book: *The Snopes Dilemma: Faulkner's Trilogy* (Coral Gables, Fla., Univ. of Miami Press). This is a conscientious, step by step study which follows the narrative faithfully and comments upon it sensibly but does not expand our understanding of the trilogy in any substantial way.

Richard P. Adams has a suggestive article, "Focus on William Faulkner's 'The Bear': Moses and the Wilderness," in *American Dreams*, pp. 129–35. He relates "The Bear"—seen, happily, within the context of *Go Down, Moses*—to antecedents in the Bible and in American literature and sees its central issue as Ike's failure to achieve maturity in either moral or sexual terms. There is also an intelligent and often perceptive study by Carol Clancey Harter, "The Winter of Isaac McCaslin: Revisions and Irony in Faulkner's 'Delta Autumn'" (*JML* 1:209–25). Arthur F. Kinney's "Faulkner and the Possibilities for Heroism" (*SoR* 6:1110–25), on the other hand, is hampered from the start by its arbitrary isolation of "The Old People," "The Bear," and "Delta Autumn" as a "trilogy" which "constitutes the fundamental portion of *Go Down Moses*." Not surprisingly, Kinney perceives very little of the full complexity and meaning of Ike's situation, examined here chiefly in terms of "Delta Autumn."

Clearly, *Go Down, Moses* still presents peculiar difficulties, and it is all the more useful to have articles such as "Ike's Gun and Too Many Novembers" (*MissQ* 23:279–87) in which Rosemary Stephens points to discrepancies in the detailed chronology of "The Bear." It seems safe, however, to pass over Elmo Howell's "Faulk-

ner's Elegy: An Approach to 'The Bear'" (*ArlQ* 2,iii:122–32), Ul-
rike Madeya's undiscriminating survey "Interpretationen zu William Faulkners 'The Bear': Das Bild des Helden und die Konstellation
der Charaktere" (*LWU* 3:45–60), V. R. N. Prasad's "The Pilgrim and
the Picaro: A Study of Faulkner's *The Bear* and *The Reivers*" (in
Indian Essays, pp. 209–21), and even, risking the loss of an occasional insight, Nadia Fusini's "La caccia all'orso di Faulkner" (*SA*
14[1968]:289–308).

Intruder in the Dust, though apparently one of Faulkner's simpler
works, has long eluded successful analysis, and it eludes Maxine
McCants's earnest attempt to grapple with its difficulties in "From
Humanity to Abstraction: Negro Characterization in *Intruder in the
Dust*" (*NMW* 2:91–104).

A very careful and helpful analysis of the title story of *Knight's
Gambit* is offered by Mary Montgomery Dunlap in "William Faulkner's 'Knight's Gambit' and Gavin Stevens" (*MissQ* 23:223–39). Her
treatment makes it clear that this largely ignored book needs to be
absorbed more integrally into our overall view of Faulkner's
achievement.

viii. Individual Works, 1950–1962

Requiem for a Nun, in its various stage versions, provides the subject
for *Requiem for a Nun: Onstage and Off* by Barbara Izard and Clara
Hieronymus (Nashville, Tenn., Aurora Publishers). This remarkable
book, a mixture of serious research and popular journalism, is full of
photographs and gossip and represents a contribution to theatrical
history rather than to Faulkner studies. At the same time, it does
contain important new information about the composition of the play
version and its relationship to the novel, as well as incidental glimpses
of Faulkner himself at various stages of his career.

In "Speaking of Books: Faulkner's *A Fable*" (*NYTBR* 25 May
[1969]:2,34,36,38–9), Joseph L. Blotner supplies important information about the sources, inception, and subsequent composition of the
novel. There are also valuable comments in Carl Ficken's "The Christ
Story in *A Fable*" (*MissQ* 23:251–64), which argues that criticism of
A Fable must free itself from too narrow an obsession with the Christ
images: these function positively (which is not necessarily to say
theologically), but they occupy only a minor place in the novel as a

whole and are by no means confined to the Corporal. An example of the kind of criticism Ficken has in mind is provided by Patrick Samway, S.J., in "War: A Faulknerian Commentary" (*ColQ* 18:370–78): this attempt to draw from *A Fable* a specific "message" about the nature of war founders upon the inadequacies in its reading of the novel itself—especially in its estimate of the role of the Marshal. There are two dissertations: Philip E. Pastore, "The Structure and Meaning of William Faulkner's *A Fable*" (*DAI* 31:397A–98A), and Elizabeth L. Hodges, "The Bible as Novel: A Comparative Study of Two Modernized Versions of Biblical Stories, Zola's *La faute de l'abbé Mouret* and Faulkner's *A Fable*" (*DAI* 30:5447A).

With regard to *The Town* and *The Mansion* see the discussions of the Snopes trilogy, above (p. 127). Under the editorial heading "Faulkner and His Sources" (*ConL* 11:310–12), Henry A. Pochmann contends that Joel A. Hunt might have looked to Mississippi oral tradition rather than to Rabelais for a likely source for the method by which Ratliff, in *The Mansion*, disposes of Senator Clarence Snopes (see *ALS* 1969, p.120); Hunt's rejoinder is also printed.

In "The Novel Faulkner Never Wrote: His *Golden Book* or *Doomsday Book*" (*AL* 42:93–96), James B. Meriwether clears up the confusion created by critics who have wrongly described *The Reivers* as Faulkner's "Golden" or "Doomsday" book. He shows that what Faulkner had in mind when he used these terms was something along the lines of the Compson "Appendix," perhaps incorporating certain aspects of the chronological organization of the *Portable Faulkner*. The article by V. R. N. Prasad (see above, p. 128) has better things to say about *The Reivers* than about "The Bear"; even so, it scarcely warrants consultation.

ix. The Stories

In the first part of his chapter on Faulkner in *A Certain Morbidness* (see above, p. 127). Edward Stone draws a suggestive though over-extended comparison between "A Rose for Emily" and George Washington Cable's "Jean-ah Poquelin," arguing that the distinction of Faulkner's story lies in its "domestication" of morbidity in "the American small town." The volume on "A Rose for Emily" in the Merrill Literary Casebook series (Columbus, Ohio, Charles E. Merrill) includes Cable's story, another by a young contemporary writer, and almost everything, good or bad, which has ever been written about "A Rose for Emily" itself. Since even the editor, M. Thomas Inge, acknowledges that the story is "quite atypical" of Faulkner's mature fiction, it seems a pity that the altogether excessive attention it has received in the past should be further endorsed by a collection which seems unlikely to enhance the reputation of Faulkner or of Faulkner criticism among the college students for whom it is intended. Too late for anthologization comes Helen E. Nebeker's over-ingenious "Emily's Rose of Love: Thematic Implications of Point of View in Faulkner's 'A Rose for Emily' " (*BRMMLA* 24:3–13).

Other stories, happily, do receive some attention. In "Faulkner's Heart's Darling in 'That Evening Sun' " (*SSF* 7:320–23) John Hermann makes some interesting points in the course of a slightly forced reading of the story as a whole, while in "Faulkner's 'Victory': The Plain People of Clydebank" (*MissQ* 23:241–49) Raleigh W. Smith, Jr., usefully stresses the dramatization of Faulkner's theme of the fatal sin of pride involved in the rejection of one's family traditions and roots. Smith also examines the function and meaning of "Crevasse" as the episode within "Victory" which Faulkner originally intended it to be. Suggestively, but a little extravagantly, Joy Rea ("Faulkner's 'Spotted Horses'," *HSL* 2:157–64) argues that the horses "are poetry" and links them with the buckskin pony in "Carcassonne" and with Pegasus.

Elmo Howell's "William Faulkner's General Forrest and the Uses of History" (*THQ* 29:287–94) begins interestingly enough by relating Faulkner's story, "My Grandmother Millard and General Bedford Forrest and the Battle of Harrykin Creek," to the actual career of General Forrest, but goes on to argue, somewhat preposterously, that Faulkner's abandonment of his "imaginative involvement with the history of his region" was responsible for "the senile maundering of the last two decades of his life." Another article by Howell, "William Faulkner's Chickasaw Legacy: A Note on 'Red Leaves' " (*ArQ* 26:293–303), offers little of substance; nor is there any need to consult the analysis of "Shingles for the Lord" in William V. Myres, "Faulkner's Parable of Poetic Justice" (*LaS* 8[1969]:224–30). *Twentieth Century Literature*, which published an ill-informed article on *Sanctuary* in 1969 (see *ALS 1969*, p. 116), has now published "Faulkner Draws the Long Bow," by Thomas W. Cooley, Jr. (16:268–77); the article has an interesting comment or two on *Mosquitoes* but its wider discussion of Faulkner's adaptation of the tall tale tradition is marred by lack of familiarity with the genesis of works like *The Hamlet* and by an apparent attempt to analyze "Afternoon of a Cow" without actually reading it first.

University College, University of Toronto

8. Hemingway and Fitzgerald

William White

The 1970 year's work in Ernest Hemingway and Scott Fitzgerald was, in many respects, just as good as the high year of 1969, though one would not think so on first looking at the *MLA International Bibliography*. The fifty-four MLA items under Hemingway seem to be a drop from eighty-four in 1969; but one entry, Matthew J. Bruccoli and C. E. Frazer Clark, Jr.'s *Fitzgerald / Hemingway Annual 1970*, actually contains eighteen articles and notes on Hemingway, and another special Hemingway issue of *Rendezvous* (5,ii) includes six articles. In addition to all these, there were a number of review articles, not cited in MLA, written by such major critics as Edmund Wilson, Malcolm Cowley, Irving Howe, and John W. Aldridge, among others, dealing with Hemingway's first posthumously published novel, *Islands in the Stream* (New York, Scribner's). Although there was an increase in the number of reported dissertations, and many, if not most, of the articles were of a high and serious calibre, there was no major book contribution of Hemingway scholarship, criticism, or biography. As for Fitzgerald, the *MLA Bibliography* has twenty-four entries, plus eighteen listed under the Bruccoli-Clark *FHA 1970*, an increase over the thirty-three citations of last year; if the level of Fitzgerald scholarship and criticism was varied and uneven, there was at least one substantial study, Milton R. Stern's *The Golden Moment: The Novels of F. Scott Fitzgerald* (Urbana, Univ. of Ill. Press), and as fine and full a biography of the novelist's wife, *Zelda* (New York, Harper and Row) by Nancy Milford, as we are likely to get for quite some time. It is interesting that both *Zelda* and Hemingway's *Islands in the Stream* were national best sellers for several weeks.

i. Bibliographies and Texts

Hemingway and Fitzgerald were each represented by a *Checklist* in the handy series of Charles E. Merrill Checklists (Columbus,

Ohio), the Hemingway selected list of 430 items compiled by William White, the Fitzgerald list of 371 items by Matthew J. Bruccoli. They contain material both by and about their subjects, with little or no annotation.

Audre Hanneman, author of *Ernest Hemingway: A Comprehensive Bibliography* (see *ALS 1966*, pp. 86–87), contributes the longest piece in *FHA 1970* (pp. 195–218): "Hanneman Addenda"—fifty omissions from her book (contributions to newspapers and periodicals, anthologies, book blurbs, books mentioning Hemingway, and articles on him), work by Hemingway published since 1965 (seventeen books and pamphlets, eleven items in books, newspapers, and periodicals, and four published facsimiles), and sixty-seven books significantly mentioning Hemingway since 1966. Omitted for reasons of space are translations, articles about Hemingway, and reviews of books by and about him. An important addition to Hemingway bibliography.

Two further contributions to Hemingway bibliography are the Russian book *Ernest Xeminguèj:Bio-bibliografičeskij* (Moscow, Kniga) and Jean M. Rogers and Gordon Stein's "Bibliographical Notes on Hemingway's *Men Without Women*" (*PBSA* 64:210–13), which identifies the first printing of the first edition (1927) by a perfect folio "3" on page three of the text and a book weight of approximately 15.8 ounces—other printings show considerable variation.

Despite its doubled size over 1969, the new *FHA 1970* did not include the expected yearly bibliographies of either Hemingway or Fitzgerald, similar to the useful lists in each issue of the old *Fitzgerald Newsletter*; there were however, a sketchy Fitzgerald and "general" checklist, and reviews of important books by and about the two novelists, reviews written with authority by Matthew J. Bruccoli, George Frazier, Cecil Eby, William H. Nolte, William Cagle, Pierre Kaufke, Sara Mayfield, and Arnold Gingrich.

Two short pieces by Fitzgerald, hitherto unrecorded, appear in *FHA 1970*: a fascinating letter to Hemingway about *The Sun Also Rises*, particularly the now-deleted first part, with comments on the letter by Philip Young and Charles W. Mann (pp. 1–13); Fitzgerald's poem, "Princeton Asleep" (pp. 14–15); six of his letters to the Menckens, without annotation (pp. 102–04); and Hemingway's only discovered contribution to *The Co-Operative Commonwealth* (Dec. 1920), "Will You Let These Kiddies Miss Santa Claus?" (pp. 105–07).

Ernest Hemingway, Cub Reporter: Kansas City Star Stories,

edited by Matthew J. Bruccoli (Pittsburgh, Univ. of Pittsburgh Press)
is a slight book, with a short preface by the editor; "With Hemingway Before *A Farewell to Arms*," by Theodore Brumback (from the
Kansas City *Star*, 6 Dec. 1936), who sailed to Europe with Hemingway in 1918; and twelve newspaper stories established by Bruccoli
(one by Charles Fenton) as Hemingway's. Several of them have
been reprinted before—in the Kansas City *Star* and *Esquire*—and
Hemingway enthusiasts will be glad to see them all within covers;
if they are by Hemingway, either written by him or phoned in to the
city desk, there is no doubt of their importance. But the evidence is
flimsy, and none were by-lined; Bruccoli himself cites negative evidence, even of one piece Hemingway sent to his father, who kept
the clipping and wrote on it, "Ernest's work entire colun [sic]." Now
and then a sentence or two, or very occasionally a stance or attitude
could be genuine early Hemingway; the subject matter certainly is
what we have come to associate with him, and as one knows from
his later work on the Toronto *Star*, the author was more interested in
color stories and character sketches than straight news reporting.
The writing is, however, good newspaper journalism of its time that
a competent reporter on the Kansas City *Star* would knock out, and
not necessarily distinguished prose.

Robert W. Lewis, Jr., and Max Westbrook, who have described
the manuscript of "The Snows of Kilimanjaro" (see *ALS 1967*, p.
107), now provide " 'The Snows of Kilimanjaro' Collated and Annotated" (*TQ* 13,ii:67–143). It is as detailed and careful a textual
study as one could wish (except for some misprints in the commentary), based on Hemingway's typescript with holograph revisions,
collated with the 1936 *Esquire* text, a 1949 *Esquire* reprint, the
text in *The Fifth Column and the First Forty-nine Stories* (New
York, Scribner's, 1938) and in the English edition (London, Cape,
1939). The two scholars say they have produced the "text closest to
the author's intention." No matter how Edmund Wilson or Ernest
Hemingway himself would react, this is the outstanding textual study
of a Hemingway story, short or long.

Two Fitzgerald studies of a textual nature appear in *FHA 1970*.
Jennifer E. Atkinson's "Fitzgerald's Marked Copy of *The Great Gatsby*" (pp. 28–33) notes forty-two revisions of four kinds: changes in
single words or phrases, additions of a word or sentence, omission of
a word or phrase, and the complete rewriting of a phrase or passage—

no wholesale alterations. Far more extensive is Colin S. Cass's "Fitz-gerald's Second Thoughts About 'May Day': A Collation and Study" (pp. 69–95), which deals with the 750 changes the author made in the short story between its publication in *Smart Set* (1920) and its appearance in *Tales of the Jazz Age* (1922), in which we get a close look at Fitzgerald's craftsmanship and watch him criticizing and improving his work, polishing and refining it.

The publication of *Islands in the Stream*, preceded by the appear-ance of "Bimini," the first part of the novel, in *Esquire* (74,iv:121–37, 190–202) was the Hemingway event-of-the-year. Despite the fanfare, selection by the Book-of-the-Month Club, heavy sales and the widest possible reviewing, its reception was mixed, as might well be ex-pected of an unfinished posthumous work. Long awaited after years of rumors of a "Land, Sea, and Air Novel," *Islands in the Stream* was prepared for publication by Charles Scribner, Jr., and Mary Heming-way, who corrected spelling and punctuation, made some cuts, but "added nothing to it." The result was a book worth publishing—most of those who wrote about the novel have agreed on that—though the story of Thomas Hudson, an artist with a considerable similarity to Hemingway, will win no literary awards. Of its three loosely con-nected parts, "Bimini," "Cuba," and "At Sea," the first and last pleased most reviewers, while the second section, even with the long and sometime amusing conversation with the big, warm-hearted prostitute, Honest Lil, was generally criticized. In *TLS* (16 Oct:1193–94) the reviewer says, "It is easy to make damaging criticisms of *Islands in the Stream*, yet it is, with all its weaknesses, the most inter-esting Hemingway novel to appear since *For Whom the Bell Tolls*." Though Geoffrey Wolff in *Newsweek* (12 Oct:118–20) found it "a very bad novel with a few bright moments," he said it "should be taken for what it is, a curiosity, an unfinished draft whose circum-stances are untidy and ambiguous." Jonathan Yardley, *New Republic* (10 Oct:25–26,30), was only a little less kind: "It provides no new keys to Hemingway's literary importance. Its narrative is competent (at narrative Hemingway was *never* incompetent), and it contains just enough flickering reminders of his wasted genius to make reading it a frustrating and saddening experience." In detailing the "pleasing and [also] disastrous things" in the book, Irving Howe, *Harper's* (Oct:120–25) nevertheless saw "Hemingway struggling desperately with both his need for some concluding wisdom—what, at the end of our journey, do we take the human enterprise to be?—and his habitual tough-guy swagger in all its sodden mindlessness." The smooth and accomplished writing, Howe says, is not enough, and Hemingway "knows it. Some element is wanting, call it idea or vision or coherence, some word that could make the world of his imagination come whole again"; and the terrible conclusion is that "an artist's, a man's search for moral growth can disable his performance, crippling him with the knowledge of what he doesn't know." Malcolm Cowley (*Atlantic*, Dec:105–08), delighted as he is to have the book in its present form, says something similar to Howe, but he puts it differently: Hemingway, handicapped by injuries and admirers, played a double life to the end ("the great man in public" and "standing alone at his worktable, humble and persistent, while he tried to summon back his early powers") yet found at the very end "he had been too deeply wounded to write even a single sentence after standing there all day." Virtually everyone saw some of Hemingway's finest qualities in *Islands* and few doubted the wisdom of publishing ("Mrs. Hemingway," wrote Edmund Wilson [*NY*:2 Jan 1971:59–62], is to be encouraged to publish further manuscripts") just as they said in their separate ways that between the "gold and the platitude" and the "triumph and disaster" Hemingway had lost the cause, the attitude the ideology—or whatever one wishes to call it—of his earlier writings. What was left was a skepticism turned into hopelessness, and as the best of the academic criticism, John W. Aldridge's discussion in *Saturday Review* (10 Oct:23–25,39) puts it: Hemingway no longer believes in anything, nothing motivates him except a vague sense of duty, life has no meaning, and he is ready to die "because he is tired to death of life. There is sadness in this but no real tragedy, because there is no sense of missed possibility, no conceivable alternative to dying." In both his book and his own life, there was only black emptiness, pain, despair.

ii. Memoirs and Biography

There was a distinct shortage of important biographical items on Hemingway published in 1970—ten items, six of them in *FHA 1970*. James Charters (who with Morrill Cody wrote *This Must Be the Place: Memoirs of Jimmie the Barman* [1937], to which Hemingway contributed an introduction) in "Pat and Duff: Some Memories"

(*ConnR* 3,ii:24–27), now talks about Pat Guthrie and Duff Twysden, who appear in *The Sun Also Rises* as Mike Campbell and Lady Brett Ashley. They were never in Charters's bar at the same time with Hemingway; he does not know their reaction if any to the novel; and he doubts the rumor that Clinton King, who later married Duff Twysden, ever knocked out Hemingway. In the same issue, Donald St. John has a long, informal and off-beat interview, "Leicester Hemingway, Chief of State" (*ConnR* 3,ii:5–19). The reason for Leicester's dislike of Carlos Baker and Mary Hemingway is not clear, but he comes through as a personality in his own right, and his comments on his brother are obviously of value, such as the remark that Ernest always needed a younger brother. "Father L. M. Dougherty Talks About Ernest Hemingway" (*Rendezvous* 5,ii:7–17) is made up of reminiscences of an old friend of Hemingway's who saw much of him at Sun Valley, Idaho, for nine years before 1950. Another article in this same special Hemingway issue is D. E. Wylder's "Hemingway's Satiric Vision—The High School Years" (*Rendezvous* 5,ii:29–35), more biographical than critical, though he does say that this high school writing shows "an attempt to see things as they really are and to present those things effectively."

Of the six items in *FHA 1970*, Fraser Drew's "April 8, 1955 with Hemingway: Unedited Notes on a Visit to Finca Vigía" (pp. 108–16) shows that the novelist could be kind to a professor. Drew sees him as "a very easy person to be with, slow-moving and slow-speaking, and with the gentle manner that sometimes characterizes the large man and the great man." Lawrence D. Stewart concludes in "Hemingway and the Autobiographies of Alice B. Toklas" (pp. 117–23) that it was she who so embodied all that Hemingway detested in the Gertrude Stein menage and work that he could not even speak her name. Hemingway's best man at his first marriage, William B. Smith, unfortunately writes that "I do not recall many details about the wedding," except that Smith was worried about the age gap but Hemingway was not ("A Wedding Up in Michigan," pp. 124–26). Bertram D. Sarason records a visit in December 1950 with Hemingway's second wife in Key West ("Pauline Hemingway: In Tranquility," pp. 127–35), less than a year before she died. She never wanted to give him up, "wanted to be considered young, wanted to remain youthful, pushed decades ahead the possibility of dying." The title of the article seems ironical. There is very little of Hemingway in Col. C. E.

Frazer Clark's "This Is the Way It Was on the *Chicago* and at the Front: 1917 War Letters" (pp. 153–69); the *Chicago* was the ship Hemingway went to Europe on in 1918, and this was the front the year before Hemingway got there. There is still less about the novelist in Winifred Healey's "When Ernest Hemingway's Mother Came to Call" (pp. 170–72)—"Mrs. Hemingway came over [Walloon Lake] in her rowboat to call on us and had to stay three days" because of the high wind, *her* three-day blow. Caresse Crosby's "The Last Time I Saw Hemingway" (p. 240) says almost nothing at all, only that it was in the Ritz bar in Paris before he became Papa Hemingway, he had a mustache but no beard—"I do not remember the year."

The one biographical piece on Fitzgerald in *FHA 1970*, Elizabeth Beckwith MacKie's "My Friend Scott Fitzgerald" (pp. 16–27), is by the "Fluff" Beckwith who inspired Fitzgerald's sonnet, "When Vanity Kissed Vanity." She begins her reminiscence, "I am unable to report (or boast) that during a long friendship with Scott Fitzgerald I ever slept with him," and goes on from there in an engaging tone.

Dr. Donald W. Goodwin, a psychiatrist of Washington University, in "The Alcoholism of F. Scott Fitzgerald," (*JAMA* 212:86–90), recites the facts of Fitzgerald's drinking at some length, and he then relates writing to drinking. "Fitzgerald," Dr. Goodwin says, "knew why he drank: it brought him closer to people and relieved his tortured sensitivity." Alcohol was a bridge over his shyness and fear of rejection, and it reduced the "sensory overload," Fitzgerald's need to register everything. "The puzzling thing about Fitzgerald was not *why* he drank, but why he drank as Poe did" ["as if he had to kill something inside himself, a worm that would not die"]; and the conclusion is that nothing "written by Fitzgerald or about him tells us" what was his worm or what he was trying to kill. "The origin of his alcoholism is as inscrutable as the mystery of his writing talent." At the end of his article Goodwin appends part of a letter which Fitzgerald sent in 1931 to an American woman psychiatrist. Fitzgerald describes a dream in which he is uninvited to a fashionable dance, feels deprived, and quarrels with his mother. The dream, he says, "became an ominous night mare."

Novelists' wives do not often come in for full-dress biographies, but Zelda was so much a part of both Scott's life and writings, and the two of them have prompted so much discussion, that a volume from her viewpoint was inevitable. Mrs. Nancy Milford's *Zelda, A*

Biography (New York, Harper and Row), based upon much new material, tells the whole sad story of the disastrous marriage, the bitter relationship, the marathon drinking, irresponsible private and public misbehavior, jealousies, and marital battles. Their need for each other and the damage they did to themselves through mutual instability reached its climax in Zelda's breakdown after ten years; yet the dismal and heartbreaking affair continued as she was in and out of institutions and Scott tried to do the one thing he could do well—write. Just as he had used her in *This Side of Paradise*, as Gloria Patch in *The Beautiful and Damned* and as Daisy Buchanan in *The Great Gatsby*, he used her as the mad Nicole Diver in *Tender Is the Night*. Zelda's death in the asylum is of course well known; yet to have it retold in the long and detailed, and almost unbearable, overview of a bound-to-be living hell can only give readers more insight into the life of Scott Fitzgerald and thus into his so heavily autobiographical fiction. Among the many reviews and commentaries, the majority of them favorable, Elizabeth Hardwick's "Caesar's Things" (*NYRB* 24Sept:3–6) is one of the best—for her the earlier tragic grandeur and glamor have been replaced by the heroism of Zelda's "efforts and the bitterness of her defeats. She was flawed and rich with liability, but we suddenly find ourselves discontent and more than a little resentful that this strange, valuable girl from Montgomery, Alabama, had to endure unnecessary rebuffs and discouragement—in a life where so much suffering was foreordained and beyond repair."

iii. Criticism

Whereas the Hemingway criticism ranges over almost the entire body of his work—novels, short stories, and nonfiction—the material on Fitzgerald is largely devoted to *The Great Gatsby* and *Tender Is the Night*. The exception to this is in dissertations: two of these are John A. Higgins's "F. Scott Fitzgerald as a Writer of Short Stories: A Critical Study of His Basic Motifs and Techniques," *DAI* 30(1969): 1169A–70A; and Ruth M. Prigozy's "The Stories and Essays of F. Scott Fitzgerald," *DAI* 30(1969):2544A–45A. The other reported dissertation, by Alan Margolies, is "The Impact of Theatre and Film on F. Scott Fitzgerald," *DAI* 30:3467A.

The seven Hemingway dissertations, largest number yet for a

single year, indicate his appeal to serious student researchers and to the academic community: Taylor Alderman, "Ernest Hemingway: Four Studies in the Competitive Motif" (*DAI* 31:380A); Lemuel B. Byrd, "Characterization in Ernest Hemingway's Fiction: 1925–1952, With a Dictionary of the Characters" (*DAI* 30:4444A); Richard C. Gebhardt, "Denial and Affirmation of Values in the Fiction of Ernest Hemingway" (*DAI* 31:1274A–75A); Robert W. Morrison, "The Short Stories of Ernest Hemingway: A Search for Love and Identity" (*DAI* 30:3018A–19A); Jon E. Nelson, "Religious Experience in the Fiction of Ernest Hemingway" (*DAI* 30:396A); John H. Raeburn, "Ernest Hemingway: The Writer as Object of Public Attention" (*DAI* 30:4462A); and Kenneth M. Rosen, "Ernest Hemingway: The Function of Violence" (*DAI* 30:5456A). Alderman and Rosen, both of whom took their degrees at the University of New Mexico, decided after a meeting at MLA in December to found a new journal, *Hemingway Notes*, first issues to appear in 1971.

Delbert E. Wylder's *Hemingway's Heroes* (Albuquerque, Univ. of N.Mex. Press, 1969), based on his dissertation reported last year, was received much too late for review in the 1969 *ALS*. Though drawing on previous research, Wylder in his own way treats each of Hemingway's seven novels (beginning with *The Torrents of Spring*) differently and separately. In the first, through Yogi Johnson and Scripps O'Neil, Hemingway parodies the sentimental hero; in the next three, Jake Barnes and Lieut. Frederic Henry and Harry Morgan are anti-heroes, wounded and guilt-ridden and self-destructive in this order; Robert Jordan he calls the mythic hero in the contemporary world; Colonel Cantwell is the tyrant hero; and Santiago "the sinning hero as saint." Although agreeing with earlier critics that *For Whom the Bell Tolls* marks a change in Hemingway, Mr. Wylder sees the change through Jordan and his relationship with Maria and thus man's need for others. Well reasoned and well written, *Hemingway's Heroes* is worth a place in Hemingway studies—though one may complain of undue regard for *Across the River and Into the Trees* (it "ranks with the best of Hemingway's works"—p. 198) and some loose definitions (for example, of the anti-hero).

Another Hemingway book is Jay Gellens's edition of *Twentieth Century Interpretations of "A Farewell to Arms": A Collection of Critical Essays* (Englewood Cliffs, N.J., Prentice-Hall). All of the essays, or parts of essays and chapters of books, have been published before. Some have been given new titles by the editor; Mr. Gellens's introduction is a useful one on the novel. The selections are good ones, but there are flaws. The Chronology of Important Dates is rather bad: the editor apparently does not know about *in our time* (1924) and *In Our Time* (1925); he fails to list *The Torrents of Spring, Winner Take Nothing, The Fifth Column* and the *First Forty-nine Stories*, and *A Moveable Feast*; he does list "The Dangerous Summer," which was never published as a book; and among other errors are the dates of Hemingway's divorce from Martha Gellhorn and marriage to Mary Welsh (not Walsh). The selected bibliography of five books and three articles is even worse: it cites A. E. Hotchner but not Carlos Baker's biography, or Audre Hanneman's bibliography. Another notable omission is the Ernest Hemingway number of *MFS* (14[1968]:255–369), which cites in its checklist seventy articles on *A Farewell to Arms*, important to anyone working on this novel.

The one 1970 article about *A Farewell to Arms* was a short one by a Japanese scholar, Tetsumaro Hayashi, "*A Farewell to Arms*: The Contest of Experience" (*KAL* 12:14–19). The same issue has a longer and more general piece, Keisuke Tanaka's "The Bipolar Construction in the Works of Ernest Hemingway" (*KAL* 12:32–44). Another foreign study, this one in French, Geneviève Hily's "Langage et communication: Un aspect inédit de la pensée de Hemingway" (*EA* 22[1969]:279–92) is easy to follow, deals with Hemingway's language, his interest in linguistics ("He was ... a bit of a linguist," she quotes Philip Young), style—mainly in the short stories. Miss Hily thus continues the few but excellent French contributions to Hemingway criticism. One more title, this time a book, now first reported though published in 1968, is Suzanne Bresard's *Empreintes: L'Analyse des écritures de Collette, Hemingway, Balzac, Musset* (Paris, Delachaux et Niestlé), more impressionist than analytical.[1]

It is Paul V. Anderson's view, in "Nick's Story in Hemingway's 'Big Two-Hearted River'" (*SSF* 7:564–72), that Nick, first lacking

---

1. Along with the scholarly interest in Hemingway abroad—and I have not cited, by any means, all of the publications—his popularity among European readers continues. A tour of bookshops shows that his works are available either in translation or in the British paperback series (Penguin Books), which has no less than thirteen titles in print. This is true even in such places as Brindisi in southern Italy, Dubrovnik and Split in Yugoslavia, and Herakleion on the island of Crete. In Athens Hemingway books can be bought in five languages.

self-confidence, begins—by performing tasks—to rehabilitate himself,
isolated from thought and action, he finally reaches the swamp, which
he cannot face now, but his own promise to return shows that the
setback is only temporary. Warren Bennett's "Character, Irony, and
Resolution in 'A Clean, Well-Lighted Place'" (*AL* 42:70–79), is a full
study of the short story, including a textual change; the story, he says,
is "charged with dramatic as well as verbal irony," as seen in the
young waiter's confidence which will dissolve into an impending
doom—he is "reality's dupe and victim" as he hurries to his own
undoing. According to Phillips G. and Rosemary R. Davies ("'A
Killer Who Would Shoot You for the Fun of It': A Possible Source
for Hemingway's 'The Killers,'" *IEY* 15:36–38), the story is based on
a real event: the murder of heavyweight boxer, "Bill" Brennan, by
Joseph Pioli and James Hughes, in Brennan's cafe, Broadway at 171st
Street, reported in the *New York American* and the *New York Times*
in June 1924, though the event has been transferred from a big city
to a small town and Andreson was not actually killed.

Marvin Fisher's "More Snow on Kilimanjaro" (*Americana Norvegica*, pp. 343–53) suggests the close relationship between Henry
James's "The Real Thing" and Hemingway's story, the various symbolic meanings of snow (such as "snow-job"), how Hemingway's
animals are "the real thing," and how the central problem in both
James and Hemingway "grows out of the interrelatedness of aesthetic
and moral issues." The younger writer "had learned the lesson of the
master." A brief note on the story (Jurgen K. A. Thomaneck, "Hemingway's Riddle of Kilimanjaro Once More," *SSF* 7:326–27) shows
that Hemingway got the symbol of the leopard at 5000 meters from
fact in A. E. Johann's *Gross ist Afrika* (Berlin, 1939), p. 316.

C. P. Heaton, in "Style in *The Old Man and the Sea*" (*Style* 4:11–
27), speaks with understanding and knowledge: "an organized presentation of factual data which tend to support the general opinion
that Hemingway's prose is *clear, forceful and direct*"; his language
flows and punctuation pauses are generally avoided; he "did what he
was trying to do; it was worth doing and he did it well." Another
piece on the Hemingway short novel, by Kenneth G. Johnston, "The
Star in Hemingway's *The Old Man and the Sea* (*AL* 42:388–91),
shows how the star Rigel in the constellation of Orion, to which
Hemingway refers, is important structurally and thematically: it
"lends a legendary aura to the exploits of the old fisherman," joins

our stars of the tale (Santiago, Manolin, DiMaggio, and the marlin), and suggests the unity of Santiago and his world, foreshowing the old man's penalty for "going out too far." A minor note on the novella, Samuel E. Longmire's "Hemingway's Praise of Dick Sisler in *The Old Man and the Sea*" (*AL* 42:96–98), deals with the son of the famous George Sisler; Dick was a two-day national hero in Cuban (winter) baseball (December 1945–February 1946): he was the first player to hit a ball out of Tropical Stadium and the next day he hit three home runs in one game, for which he got an honorary gold medal from the Cuban government. Reviewing recent books gives William T. Stafford, in "Hemingway / Faulkner: Marlin and Catfish?" (*SoR* 6:1191–1200), a chance to show differences in the two writers: "The Gulf Stream was Hemingway's domain, and fighting marlin, not catfish, was his game."

Regarding "Ernest Hemingway's Knowledge of German" (*JA* 15:221–32), Hans-Joachim Kann says that, despite the novelist's aversion to Germany as a political power, he learned a good deal about the written and spoken language during his stays in that country, Austria, and Switzerland, as seen in his works. Hemingway used German to create local color as well as a universe, and he "certainly had more than a negligible knowledge of the German language." "A Little Light on Hemingway's 'The Light of the World'" (*SSF* 7:465–67), by James J. Martine, cites similarities in Hemingway and Maupassant's "La maison tellier" and identifies the prizefighter in the story as Stanley Ketchel, not Steve Ketchel (but that had been done last year by Matthew J. Bruccoli, *FHA* 1969:125–29). A better article in the same issue, Paul C. Roger, Jr.'s "Levels of Irony in Hemingway's 'The Gambler, the Nun, and the Radio'" (*SSF* 7:439–49) shows how this story is "considerably bleaker and darker than 'A Clean, Well-Lighted Place,'" as the key to the story is the ironic viewpoint of the narrator, revealed through nuances of phrasing, emphasis, understatement, and in the selection and ordering of character, action, and episode. Another general study of a short story is Ramesh Srivastava's "Hemingway's 'Cat in the Rain': An Interpretation" (*LCrit* 9,ii:79–84), which sees in this tale of alienation and the fertility-wish of a barren American wife all the Freudian implications of her daydreams: "The maid brings her a big cat which is what should satisfy her—a compromise between her barrenness and realization of fecundity, actuality and day-dream." A further note on this short story in

a foreign periodical is Horst Kruse, "Hemingway's 'Cat in the Rain'
and Joyce's *Ulysses*" (*LWU* 3:28–30).

Julian Smith, an old Hemingway hand, contributes two articles
"Hemingway and the Things Left Out" (*JML* 1:169–82); and "More
Products of the Hemingway Industry" (*SSF* 7:638–46). The first one
deals with three stories, "In Another Country," "Now I Lay Me," and
"God Rest You Merry, Gentlemen," all built around something never
clearly expressed, in which "people feel something more than they
understand." The "products" of the second article are *By-Line: Ernest
Hemingway, The Fifth Column and Four Stories of the Spanish Civil
War*, Philip Young and Charles W. Mann's *Inventory*, Audre Hanneman's *Bibliography*, and Carlos Baker's *Life Story*.

The special Hemingway issue of *Rendezvous* (5, ii) includes six
articles: Philip Young, "Locked in the Vault with Hemingway" (pp.
1–5; reprinted from *NYTBR* 29 Sept 1968); Father L. M. Dougherty's
reminiscences, mentioned above (pp. 7–17); Robert W. Lewis, Jr.,
"Hemingway's Concept of Sport and 'Soldier's Home'" (pp. 19–27;
on the gap between a controlled, clean game and chaotic, dirty "real"
life—sport as therapy provides escape and the appearance of a meaningful pattern); D. E. Wylder, "Hemingway's Satiric Vision—The
High School Years" (pp. 29–35; also mentioned above); Jackson J.
Benson, "Patterns of Connection and Development in Hemingway's
In Our Time" (pp. 37–52; *In Our Time* is a unified and complex work
within its own covers as separate from *The First Forty-nine Stories*);
and Richard Etulain, "Ernest Hemingway and His Interpreters of
the 1960's" (pp. 53–70; on Marcelline Sanford, Leicester Hemingway, Montgomery, Callaghan, Kiley, Arnold, Baker, Killinger, Isa-
belle, Lewis, Joost, Stephens, DeFalco, Gurko, Wylder, and Benson).

Of all the Hemingway material in *FHA 1970*, there are two substantial critiques and four notes of minor value: the former pair are
William Goldhurst's "The Hyphenated Ham Sandwich of Ernest
Hemingway and J. D. Salinger: A Study in Literary Continuity," pp.
136–50; and Robert P. Mai's "Ernest Hemingway and Men Without
Women," pp. 173–86. Mr. Goldhurst traces the basic American run-
away boy (Huck Finn) through Hemingway (Nick Adams) to
Salinger (Seymour Glass): "a sensitive boy and young man who on
his journey through life encounters various evils in human experience." In other words, the influence of *In Our Time* on the younger
author. With the help of biographies by Hemingway's brother and

sister and Carlos Baker's *Life Story*, plus the Nick Adams stories and Robert Jordan's recollections, Robert Mai sees the "female domination" of the novelist's early life, the bitterness beneath narration, the "wound" in Hemingway and his fictional projections, and the imperative to test oneself (as seen in *The Old Man and the Sea*). Mr. Mai remarks in conclusion on "the sexual self-defensiveness that lay beneath [Hemingway's] bearishness and his courage."

The year's outstanding critical work on either Hemingway or Fitzgerald was Milton R. Stern's *The Golden Moment*, "a study that attempts to illuminate the fiction by trying to see it through Fitzgerald's personality [and] tries to bring together from one central perspective the portions of Fitzgerald's yearning imagination that were manifested in the novels" *This Side of Paradise, The Beautiful and Damned, The Great Gatsby,* and *Tender Is the Night.* Here's how Mr. Stern sums it up:

> *This Side of Paradise* is the imaginative expectation of the golden moment, and *The Great Gatsby* is the imagination working on the experience, already past, of having attained it. *The Beautiful and Damned* is the other side of the golden moment, the imagined expectation of defeat and failure, and *Tender Is the Night* is the imagination working on the experience, already past and still present, of having fallen in it. *This Side of Paradise* looks forward to *The Great Gatsby* as *The Beautiful and Damned* looks forward to *Tender Is the Night.* [p. 179]

Limiting himself to just the four novels, Stern defines his focus as "the national rather than the literary development of Fitzgerald's talent." Predominantly he considers *The Great Gatsby* and *Tender Is the Night;* he devotes twice as much space to these as to the other two novels. Fitzgerald's America is seen through three basic characters (two of them taken from himself): the completely romantic innocent, who believes in the American Dream; the moral commentator; and the "Golden Girl." The latter, based upon the feminine in Fitzgerald, is selfish, irresponsible, young, rich—yet having the "glittering, tawdry power and incomparable beauty of the U.S.A." that eventually betrays the adolescent innocent, leaving only the "golden moments" when we recall youthful hopes, the quest, and the expectation. In his views of Gatsby, Nick Carraway, Daisy, Dick and

Nicole Diver and others, Stern is extremely perceptive. One's reservations come from his silence on other of the fiction—and from the lack of a needed index.

Interest in Fitzgerald abroad comes nowhere near the foreign studies and notes on Hemingway, the MLA *Bibliography* reporting one book, and that two years old, Hans G. Schitter's *Die drei letzten Romane F. Scott Fitzgeralds: Untersuchungen zur Spiegelung von zeitgeschichtlichem und mythischem Bewusstsein im literarischen Kunstwerk* (Bonn, Bouvier, 1968); one article a year old, Marilia Bonincontro's "L'assolo di F. S. Fitzgerald (*Tender Is the Night*)," *PS* 5,i[1969]:18–23; and one chapter in Japanese, Tsutomu Hohki's "Fitzgerald and His Romantic World," *Kyoritsu Essays*, pp. 67–81.

E. C. Bufkin, in "A Pattern of Parallel and Double: The Function of Myrtle in *The Great Gatsby*" (*MFS* 15[1969]:517–24), is a little ingenious and labored: he sees Fitzgerald, influenced by Conrad and James, using a pattern "that makes Myrtle Wilson, through parallels, the double of Gatsby," and he finds in this vague and intricate device how "we can accurately align our vision of Gatsby; by which, without exaggeration, we can truly gauge and evaluate his greatness." Commenting on the same novel in a far more general way, Barry Gross, in "'Our Gatsby, Our Nick'" (*CentR* 14:331–40), says that Fitzgerald "wrote a love song to and a threnody for a time," the twenties, "back to all the dreams that had impossibly come true, ahead to all the nightmares that were surely to come." A readable essay, it shows Gatsby as the "hero we need to acknowledge and affirm, but the hero we dare not be"; Nick Carraway, "simultaneously repelled and enchanted by the inexhaustible variety of life, is the hero we can and must become." Somewhat between Mr. Bufkin and Mr. Gross is A. E. Elmore, ("Color and Cosmos in *The Great Gatsby*," *SR* 78:427–43), who discusses the novel as built around three major settings "which are depicted primarily in terms of light and color imagery and a fourth which, though somewhat less precise in its outlines and imagery, is of equal importance." These settings are East Egg, the valley of ashes, West Egg, and downtown New York, which take on a symbolic character as the imagery becomes more and more patterned, resonant and suggestive. And, Mr. Elmore concludes, "in an age of unbelief and vast carelessness, the romantic idealist like Gatsby is almost certain to be defeated before he reaches his particular goal"; but his enduring consolation, superseding tragedy and making it impossible, is that the "visionary pilgrim who is faithful to the end will find the journey itself sufficient victory." Three notes deal with *Gatsby*: Richard Johnson, in "The Eyes of Dr. T. J. Eckleburg Reexamined" (*AN&Q* 9:20–21), points out that Fitzgerald meant "eyeballs" instead of "retina" in the well-known passage; Horst H. Kruse, in " 'Gatsby' and 'Gadsby' " (*MFS* 15[1969]:539–41), suggests Mark Twain's *A Tramp Abroad* ("The Man Who Put Up at Gadsby") as a possible source for the name of the title character; and William T. Stafford, "Fitzgerald's *The Great Gatsby*, Chapter II, Paragraph 1" (*Expl* 28:item 57), sees the "ash heap" a double vision—a great rural midland with the possibly vast fruitful harvest, as well as "the crumbling, powdery, desolate valley of ashes it in fact is," a "fantastic farm" growing "ashes" instead of wheat.[2]

Although Tom C. Coleman III calls his article, "The Rise of Dr. Diver" (*Discourse* 13:226–38), his conclusion is that "We feel contempt and consequently reject as weak, childish, and unbelievable Dr. Diver; we accept and feel compassion for Dick Diver, the more or less innocent victim of false values, the romantic artist with too much lifetime left over after his life's work is completed." And thus Dick "must live with the haunting knowledge of his fatal error," his marriage to Nicole. Supplementing the Coleman approach is R. L. Samsell's "Won't You Come Home, Dick Diver?" (*FHA 1970*:34–42), in which the critic relates how he changed his view of the psychiatrist from a brave sort of fellow too good for his own good into one for whom Mr. Samsell felt pity, annoyance, and frustration; the change came about when he listened to the Talking Books' rendition of *Tender Is the Night* on eight records, which consumed twelve hours as transcribed by Alexander Scourby. Both using and quarreling with previous research, Keith Winter, in "Artistic Tensions: The Enigma of F. Scott Fitzgerald" (*RS* 37[1969]:285–97), treats the relationship (or confusion) between the author and his characters, also the "series of paired opposites which add moral complexity and social depth to his fiction," and Fitzgerald's ambivalent attitude toward these moral and social values, best seen by Mr. Winter in the novelist's feeling toward money. The critic's style is seen in these final remarks: "Fitzgerald selected and arranged his fiction in terms of basic dualities

2. Henry Dan Piper's *Fitzgerald's "The Great Gatsby": The Novel, the Critics, the Background* (New York, Scribner's) arrived too late for review. In the second printing many serious publisher's errors have been corrected.

because this was the habitual way he experienced life. As a result, there is a continual tension in his work. As an artist he was perpetually suspended over a gulf of ironic sensibility."

iv. Conclusion

Of the Fitzgerald articles and notes in *FHA 1970*, the fullest piece of criticism, "The Passion of F. Scott Fitzgerald," by R. W. Lid, pp. 43–59, says of *The Great Gatsby* that it succeeded because of the novelist's "personal passion": "Fitzgerald used his narrative art to curb and express this passion. In effect he manipulated the processes of his own heart, and in so doing enlarged the dimensions of narrative in twentieth century fiction." This is strong language; and whether or not we agree with Mr. Lid's long analysis to show that Fitzgerald "wrote out of himself, in effect put himself directly on paper, in a way that earlier writers cannot be said to," and for his generation "self-knowledge had become a human discovery," these comments do indicate how far Fitzgerald criticism has come and the high regard we now have for his writings.

As for Hemingway, his reputation is so well established, based on his short stories, *The Sun Also Rises*, and other fiction, that the publication of *Islands in the Stream*—unfinished at his death and obviously flawed—had little marked effect on the esteem in which he is held by readers and critics. The number of books, articles, notes, and reviews is testimony to that. Hemingway-watchers will of course be interested to see what happens as more of the unpublished material, which the Young and Mann *Inventory* describes, appears in print.

Wayne State University

Part II

9. Literature to 1800

J. A. Leo Lemay

Edward Taylor continues to be the most popular figure in early American literature (excluding the numerous nonliterary studies of Benjamin Franklin), even though there was some falling off from last year, due to the appearance in 1969 of a special issue of *Early American Literature* devoted to Taylor. Among the major works appearing in 1970 were Sacvan Bercovitch's monograph on the rhetoric of the jeremiad, Thomas Philbrick's book on Crèvecœur, Russel B. Nye's survey *American Literary History: 1607–1830*, and new volumes in the editions of Jonathan Edwards and Benjamin Franklin.

i. Edward Taylor

"The Rev. Mr. Edward Taylor's Bawdry," by Karl Keller (*NEQ* 43:382–406), shows "the extent to which Taylor's excremental view of life and erotic view of salvation are an important aspect of his Puritan faith." This well-written, perceptive and wide-ranging article places Taylor in the tradition of scatological writing ("part of world culture from the Bible and Augustine through Calvin, Luther, and Puritan theological discourse") before examining the bawdry. Another article by Keller, " 'The World Slickt Up In Types': Edward Taylor as a Version of Emerson" (*EAL* 5,i,pt.1:124–40), contrasts Taylor's typology with both Samuel Sewall's nationalistic message and Increase Mather's impersonal doctrinality. Taylor wittily uses "the mode's stock-in-trade of conceits, puns, jumps in logic, meiotic talk about man and hyperbolic talk about God, to express the joy with which he contemplated the hard matters of his faith, to make room for individuality within the closed system of thought that typology represented, and to probe the nature of reality." Taylor gives meaning to reality by constant christological typology. This brilliant, but too brief, essay is marred by its attempt to see Taylor as a type of Emerson. Such anachronistic readings of American literary

history, though fun and games for the creator, are usually synonymous with the logical fallacy *post hoc, ergo propter hoc*, as well as
the more insidious fallacy that willy-nilly lurks in the minds of the
author and the reader—the assumption of progress in literature,
which necessarily maligns the earlier writer.

The relationship between Taylor's poems and sermons is carefully
considered by Thomas M. Davis, "Edward Taylor's 'Occasional Meditations'" (*EAL* 5,iii:17–29)—but the materials hardly seem methodical enough to supply a logical answer from a rigorous analysis. Some
of the imponderables are stated by Donald E. Stanford in his note on
the composition of the meditations, *EAL* 5,ii:60–61. The important
role of the will in Taylor's faculty psychology is defined by William
J. Scheick, "A Viper's Nest, the Featherbed of Faith: Edward Taylor
on the Will" (*EAL* 5,ii:45–56). In another general essay, Robert E.
Reiter, "Poetry and Typology: Edward Taylor's *Preparatory Meditations*, Second Series, Numbers 1–30" (*EAL* 5,i,pt.1:111–23), points
out that this christological series contains typological meditations on
the personal types (nos. 1–14), on the traditional offices (nos. 14–16),
and on the ritual types of Christ (nos. 17–30).

Using the Renaissance Latin commentaries on the Bible, Judson
B. Allen shows how the logic of "Upon a Spider Catching a Fly" is
"neatly spiritual," and demonstrates that the images "which Taylor
uses come to him from centuries of an exegetical tradition raptly
attentive to the spiritual senses of things" ("Edward Taylor's Catholic
Wasp: Exegetical Convention in 'Upon a Spider Catching a Fly,'"
ELN 7:257–60). In two notes on individual poems, Kent Bales and
William J. Aull define the meaning of *overly* in Meditation I.6 (*EAL*
5,ii:57–58); and Dale Doepke suggests a reading for the difficult
lines 9–12 in "The Preface" (*EAL* 5,iii:80–82). Norman S. Grabo, in
"*God's Determinations*: Touching Taylor's Critics" (*SCN* 28:22–24),
demonstrates that no critic has yet dealt with this long poem "steadily
and whole" and argues that only personae—never Taylor's own voice
—are found in the poem.

ii. Puritanism, the Mathers, and their Contemporaries

The only major attempt in 1970 to focus upon Puritanism and literature was Sacvan Bercovitch's "Horologicals to Chronometricals:
The Rhetoric of the Jeremiad," in *LitM*, (pp. 1–124, of which "Ap-

pendix B: Bibliographical and Explanatory" occupies pp. 109–24, and notes, pp. 187–215). In "Jeremiah and the Two Covenants" (pp. 1–17), Bercovitch claims that the literal content (warnings to the people) in Puritan literature clashes with the prophetic form (the millenarian rhetoric). Beside overturning Perry Miller's contention of the American uniqueness of the jeremiad, he adds a new dimension to the reading of John Winthrop's Arbella sermon. In his second part, "The Blessings of Time and Eternity" (pp. 18–26), Bercovitch takes up the theory of church government and the right of the "saints" to participate in that government; in "Trial by Mercy and Justice" (pp. 26–38), he ingeniously argues—contrary to the usual interpretations—that the later seventeenth century Puritans became "more visionary with every major setback." The fourth and fifth parts trace the origin and growth of the legend of the heroic founders, examining various writings (especially Cotton Mather's *Magnalia*) and becoming almost sentimental in viewing Cotton Mather as the last Puritan (depriving Jonathan Edwards of this dubious distinction). The two final sections, treating the legacy of the jeremiad, are weak. The seventeenth-century American Puritan traditions may be the most important background for the thought of Jonathan Edwards (pp. 82–85), but they are not of great importance for such writers of the Revolutionary period as Philip Freneau, Joel Barlow, or even Jonathan Trumbull. Certainly the *translatio studii* motif (i.e., the "Rising Glory of America") as used by such writers owes more to Alexander Pope or to George Berkeley than to all the seventeenth-century American writers combined. The author's viewpoint is—to me—startling when he calls denigrators of the Great Awakening "forerunners of Plotinus Plinlimmon." And I am unconvinced that the discrepancy between the real and ideal in America stems in any important way from the dichotomy between form and content in the jeremiad. There is much to disagree with in this provocative monograph, but Bercovitch has given us much more to learn in one of the most important and original treatments of Puritan writers to appear in the last two decades.

A historian, Darrett B. Rutman, treats Puritanism in the context of the way of life of seventeenth-century England and America in *American Puritanism, Faith and Practice* (Philadelphia, Lippincott). Like many others, Rutman would have the reader believe that there was a core of standard Puritan beliefs about such matters as the con-

version process, but major differences existed among the leading
Puritan theologians. Michael McGiffert's "American Puritan Studies
in the 1960's" (*WMQ* 27:36–67), in surveying the ways in which
scholars have contradicted or enlarged Perry Miller's paradigm of
American Puritanism, particularly points out that recent studies disagree with Miller's monolithic structure, with his inadequate definition of Puritanism, with his stress of the rational rather than the
emotional (though this was, I think, a healthful antidote to the previous prevailing view), and with his understanding of typology. A
careful discrimination of the fundamental differences between John
Cotton and Thomas Shepard during the 1630s is the subject of Jesper
Rosenmeier's "New England's Perfection: The Image of Adam and
the Image of Christ in the Antinomian Crisis, 1634 to 1638" (*WMQ*
27:435–59), stressing that "the questions of the relationship of faith
to works and of the role of the Holy Spirit are subordinate to the
question of the nature of man's present and future renewal in God's
image." We need more studies like Rosenmeier's.

Because of its clear presentation of the variety of different answers to the problems of baptism and church membership among the
churches and ministers of seventeenth-century New England, Robert
G. Pope's *The Half-Way Covenant: Church Membership in Puritan
New England* (Princeton, N.J., Princeton University Press) is welcome. With some evidence, Pope argues that the period from 1675
to 1690 was an awakening rather than a declension in New England
Puritanism. Although King Philip's War, like all times of great stress
among a religious people, caused a temporary revival, yet surely the
movement of the people of New England in the late seventeenth
century was away from a religiously-centered society.

In a special issue of *EAL*, guest editor Sacvan Bercovitch wrote
that the contributors "have set out to show the significance of typology for American studies, to delineate the major fields of concern,
and to provide a fuller appreciation of the works and themes they
discuss" (*EAL* 5,i,pt.1:9). Thomas M. Davis, "The Exegetical Traditions of Puritan Typology" (*EAL* 5,i,pt.1:11–50), traces "the development of the principles of typological exegesis from the New
Testament through the early Greek and Latin Fathers to the works
of Tyndale, Luther, and Calvin, indicating the complexity of the
exegetical traditions which inform Puritan typology" (p. 12), correcting, along the way, Erich Auerbach (p. 21) and Perry Miller (pp. 11,

26–27). The last two paragraphs suggest the range of typology which "pervaded Puritan thought." Stephen Manning's "Typology and the Literary Critic" (*EAL* 5,i,pt.1:51–73), sets forth the complexities of typological interpretation. A special feature of this issue of *EAL* (5,i,pt.2) is Sacvan Bercovitch's "Selective Check-List on Typology," an annotated seventy-six-page listing of primary and secondary works. By a happy coincidence, the only book on the subject of typology and American literature, Ursula Brumm's *American Thought and Religious Typology* (New Brunswick, N.J., Rutgers Univ. Press) appeared in English this year. The German edition (1963) was widely and justly acclaimed as an important contribution.

The chronological, annotated bibliography of Anne Bradstreet by Ann Stanford has been reprinted from *EAL* (see *ALS 1968*, p. 121) in *BB* 27:34–37, with recent additions; I note, however, that such early nineteenth-century editors and critics of American poetry as Samuel Kettel and Rufus Wilmot Griswold are omitted. Robert Hutchinson's *Poems of Anne Bradstreet* (New York, Dover, [1969]) provides a sound text, a convenient arrangement of the poems, and good notes—all for an inexpensive price. Corrections from the manuscripts and from the 1678 errata leaf first found by Jeannine Hensley are incorporated into the John Harvard Ellis text of 1867. Anne Bradstreet's borrowings from and similarities to both Guillaume Du Bartas and Francis Quarles, as well as her use of the English poetic traditions of her own day, are discussed in Alessandra Contenti's "Anne Bradstreet, il petrarchismo e il 'Plain Style'" (*SA* 14 [1968]:7–27). Dorothea Kehler, "Anne Bradstreet and Spenser" (*AN&Q* 8:135), finds an echo of *The Faerie Queen* in Bradstreet's "Contemplations." The metrical differences between the earlier and later poetry are the subject of Rosemary M. Laughlin, "Anne Bradstreet: Poet in Search of Form" (*AL* 42:1–17). And Alvin H. Rosenfeld, "Anne Bradstreet's 'Contemplations': Patterns of Form and Meaning" (*NEQ* 43:79–96), like a number of earlier commentators, sees Bradstreet through the lenses of the English Romantic poets and senses a dichotomy between her religious and emotional attitudes.

When Michael Wigglesworth provided the "easiest room in hell" for unregenerate infants, he followed—not any theological doctrine—but the promptings of his own humanity: Gerhard T. Alexis, "Wigglesworth's 'Easiest Room,'" *NEQ* 42[1969]:573–83. O. M. Brack, Jr., argued that a poem attributed to Wigglesworth is probably not his

("Michael Wigglesworth and the Attribution of 'I Walk'd and Did a Little Molehill View,'" *SCN* 28:41–44); and Leo M. Kaiser called attention to the Latin errors in the original 1625 printing and in the 1791 reprinting of the Rev. William Morrell's *Nov-Anglia* ("On Morrell's *Nov-Anglia*," *SCN* 28:20). An aspect of promotion literature is treated by Richard P. Gildrie, "Francis Higginson's New World Vision" (*EIHC* 106:182–89), who examines the elements (especially natural abundance and—too sketchily—Puritanism) that constituted Higginson's vision of "our new paradise in New England," comparing Higginson's writings with John White's *Planters Plea*.

In an article based upon the mid-nineteenth-century publication of the journal of Richard Mather, B. Richard Burg narrates the Mather family founder's "Record of an Early Seventeenth Century Atlantic Crossing," *Husson Rev* 4:72–77. The better-known son, Increase, is one focal point in Mrs. Anne Kusener Nelsen, "King Philip's War and the Hubbard-Mather Rivalry" (*WMQ* 27:615–29), describing the rivalry between the Rev. William Hubbard and the Rev. Increase Mather as displayed in Hubbard's election sermon of 1676 and Mather's reply, and in their conflicting histories of King Philip's War.

Increase's still more famous son, Cotton, was the subject of four studies and an edition. Mukhtar Ali Isani, "Cotton Mather and the Orient" (*NEQ* 43:46–58), surveys Mather's knowledge of and writings about the Orient, providing identifications of his oriental references and of his books on the Near and Far East. Louis Weeks III in "Cotton Mather and the Quakers" (*QH* 59,i:24–33), traces Mather's change from rabid anti-Quaker to a provisional accommodation with at least the "finer sort" of Quakers, including William Penn; and William D. Andrews, "The Printed Funeral Sermons of Cotton Mather" (*EAL* 5,ii:24–44), argues that, for Mather, society is a macrocosm of his own family (and vice versa), and that the personal and social are simultaneously present in his thought. Mather's use of the American success story in biographies of William Phips and of Theophilus Eaton is noted by Sacvan Bercovitch (*ES* 51:40–43), who therefore names Mather the father of this motif; but the American Dream is found in most promotion tracts, sometimes with references to particular individuals—though Mather may be the first to use this as a paradigm of the American biography. Finally, George Harrison Orians, in an introduction to nine sermons by Mather, comments on sermons as news, on the pervasiveness and significance of the Deuteronomic formula in New England Puritan writing, and on Mather's attitude toward science and special providences: *Days of Humiliation: Times of Affliction and Disaster: Nine Sermons For Restoring Favor With an Angry God* (Gainesville, Fla., SF&R).

Roger Williams continues to be one of the most attractive Puritan writers. Henry Chupack, *Roger Williams* (TUSAS 157[1969]) examines the writings, analyzing their theology, purpose, effectiveness, and influence. Chupack evidently finished his manuscript in 1967, before he could take advantage of Edmund S. Morgan's work on the structure of Williams's thought (see *ALS 1967*, pp. 125–26) or Sacvan Bercovitch's important article, "Typology in Puritan New England: The Williams-Cotton Controversy Reassessed" (*AQ* 19[1967]:166–91). What I missed in Chupack's study was a discussion of Williams's comparative excellence as a writer. In "The Typological Argument for Religious Toleration: The Separatist Tradition and Roger Williams" (*EAL* 5,i,pt.1:74–110), Richard Reinitz examines the Renaissance, Continental, Reformation, and early English Separatists as a possible source for Williams's typological argument for religious freedom, finding that John Robinson "had laid the groundwork for an absolute, typological rejection of the kings of Judah and Israel as models for the religious powers of modern rulers." Williams's image of the American Indian as presented in *A Key Into the Language of America* is assessed by Donald M. Hines's "Odd Customs and Strange Ways, The American Indian *c.* 1640" (*WR* 7,ii:20–29). The work of another seventeenth-century Indian authority, Daniel Gookin, *Historical Collections of the Indians in New England* (Spencer, Mass., Towtaid), was reprinted from the Massachusetts Historical Society's *Collections* of 1792, edited with helpful notes and an index by Jeffrey H. Fiske, and with a map by Mary E. Brown which locates the Indian villages mentioned by Gookin. One hopes that Gookin's *Historical Account of the Doings and Sufferings of the Christian Indians* will also be edited (from the manuscript in the Newberry Library) and reprinted.

William Bradford's honesty in indicting Thomas Morton as a gunrunner is aspersed by Minor W. Major ("William Bradford Versus Thomas Morton," *EAL* 5,ii:1–13). Another Puritan historian, Edward Johnson, is examined by Edward J. Gallagher, who sets the *Wonder-Working Providence* in its historical context, examines the major metaphors of the book, and explains and justifies the "Soldier of Christ" metaphor ("An Overview of Edward Johnson's *Wonder-Working Providence*," *EAL* 5,iii:30–49). The persona, tone, and imagery of Ward's *Cobler* are examined by Robert D. Arner, who neither gives page references to the text nor relates Ward to the vital English "simple cobler" tradition ("*The Simple Cobler of Aggawam*: Nathaniel Ward and the Rhetoric of Satire," *EAL* 5,iii:3–16). Arner also, in "Plum Island Revisited: One Version of the Pastoral" (*SCN* 27[1969]:58–61), analyzes Samuel Sewall's concluding paragraph of *Phaenomena* as a particularly Puritan (and perhaps American) version of the pastoral; the biblical allusions, however, seem to me to be slighted. I might also note that Dorothy Brewster's brief, hagiographic biography of her Puritan ancestor *William Brewster of the Mayflower: Portrait of a Pilgrim* (New York, New York Univ. Press) contains no significant new information; and that Ward Allen, "Hooker and the Utopians" (*ES* 51:37–39), points out that Richard Hooker used Thomas More's *Utopia* in the fifth book of his *Laws of Ecclesiastical Polity* as part of his satirical reply to Puritan arguments.

iii. Smith to Byrd and Beyond

The new anthology, *Southern Writing, 1585–1920* (New York, Odyssey), edited by Richard Beale Davis, C. Hugh Holman, and Louis D. Rubin, Jr., contains, for the early period, one of the few real advances in anthology-making since the *Cyclopaedia* of Evert Duyckinck (1855) and the *Library of American Literature*, edited by Edmund Clarence Stedman and Ellen Mackay Hutchinson (1898). Over a dozen authors are included who have never before appeared in any anthology of early American literature; and Richard Beale Davis expertly provides biographical and bibliographical notes. A paper edition of John Rolfe's *A True Relation of the State of Virginia . . . 1616* (Charlottesville, Univ. Press of Va.) with an introduction by John Cook Wyllie, a biographical sketch of Rolfe by John Melville Jennings, and a detailed note on the manuscript by Francis L. Berkeley, Jr., presents this classic report in convenient form.

Following up her fascinating essay, "Ralph Wormeley: Anonymous Essayist" (*WMQ* 26[1969]:586–95), which demonstrated that Wormeley wrote *An Essay Upon the Government of the English Plantations on the Continent of America* (1701)—a copy of which was in John Locke's library—Virginia White Fitz has now shown that Micajah Perry was probably the author of *An Essay on Bulk Tobacco* (1692) and that Perry was evidently responsible for publishing Wormeley's *Essay* in 1701: "Micajah Perry, The Anonymous Author of 'An Essay on Bulk Tobacco' " (*VMHB* 78:436–41).

The various writings of William Byrd—verse, characters, sententiae, letters, diaries, and journals—are examined by Pierre Marambaud, "William Byrd of Westover: Cavalier, Diarist, and Chronicler" (*VMHB* 78:144–83), who makes full use of past scholarship and concludes that Byrd's "best claim to literary fame" is *The History of the Dividing Line*. A slightly later Virginian, who was also an extraordinarily polished man of letters, the Rev. William Dawson, is advanced as the author of "The Latin Epitaph of Sir John Randolph," by Leo M. Kaiser (*VMHB* 78:199–201), who edits the epitaph, noting the classical allusions. Replying to a number of scholars who have denied the existence of intellectuals in the colonial South, Richard Beale Davis, in "The Intellectual Golden Age in the Colonial Chesapeake Bay Country" (*VMHB* 78:131–41), convincingly maintains that "from about 1720 to 1789, there is in actuality a strong expression of discriminating and widely-held taste in the arts, as high a proportion of literate and well-educated men as existed anywhere in the colonies, frequent written and oral discourses on religious doctrine and application, a creativity in belles-lettres, and a dynamic and reasoned political expression springing from scores of thoughtful and sophisticated minds."

Edward H. Cohen, "The 'Second Edition' of *The Sot-weed Factor*" (*AL* 42:289–303), rehashes the evidence for a second edition of Ebenezer Cooke's *Sot-Weed Factor*; carefully examines the muniments of the Taylor family of Calvert County, Maryland, for a possible relationship between Cooke and the Taylors; and incidentally mentions in footnote 22 (from some mysterious "unpublished papers of the Cooke family") that Cooke "was born in the early months of 1667." Thomas Cradock's interesting sermon on the irregularities of some of the Maryland clergy (in effect, a plea for a bishop in America or at least a commissary to supervise the clergy) has been edited, with an introduction, by David Curtis Skaggs (*WMQ* 27:630–53). Volume 2 of *The Papers of Henry Laurens* (Columbia, Univ. of S.C. Press) contains little more than the business correspondence of Laurens, because practically the only surviving manuscript for this period (1755–1758) is a letterbook of Laurens's business firm; but later volumes will contain the interesting bellestristic writing of this cosmopolitan Carolinian.

As readers of Boswell's biography will recall, Dr. Samuel Johnson immediately recognized the name and reputation of Arthur Lee. But this Virginian's prolific writings have remained largely unknown until now. The first full attempt to detail the propagandist achievement of Lee is A. R. Riggs, "Arthur Lee, a Radical Virginian in London, 1768–1776" (*VMHB* 78:268–80). Contrary to Riggs, Lee was not "the most experienced essayist and pamphleteer the American patriots had" (pp. 268–69—how could Franklin be overlooked!), yet by writing over 170 essays (including his well-known "Junius Americanus" series), Lee established himself among the best American propagandists.

The Papers of George Mason (3 vols., Chapel Hill, Univ. of N.C. Press), edited by Robert A. Rutland, contain all of Mason's extant writings (regrettably few for his first forty years), including his protest, at the time of the Stamp Act, against the English arrogance toward America; the interesting letter of "Atticus," published May 11, 1769—with a fine discussion of the authorship; and those writings for which he is famous, the Virginia Declaration of Rights, 1776, and the constitution of Virginia, 1776. With a full index, a map of Mason's area of the Potomac, an eighty-page "Biographical-Geographical Glossary," and a brief genealogical chart, this is a valuable collection. Just as Rutland's edition of Mason's papers replaces the "letters" part of the nineteenth-century "life and letters" biography of Mason by Kate Mason Rowland (1892), so too Thomas O'Brien Hanley's biography, *Charles Carroll of Carrollton: The Making of a Revolutionary Gentleman* (Washington, D.C., Catholic Univ. of America) supersedes the early life in Rowland's *The Life and Correspondence of Charles Carroll* (1898). Unfortunately, Rowland's remains the fullest biography of Mason and her selection of Carroll's letters remains the most complete edition. Hanley's biography carries Carroll's career up to the Revolution, and much of the book, happily, is devoted to Carroll's education, intellectual growth, and to his literary pursuits. Containing valuable information about the literary milieu of Pre-Revolutionary Maryland, this enjoyable biography whets the appetite for a complete edition of the correspondence of Carroll— whom Hanley demonstrates to be an intellectual and man of letters.

iv. Franklin and the Enlightenment

Volume 14 of *The Papers of Benjamin Franklin* (New Haven, Conn., Yale Univ. Press) marks the last volume of this great edition to appear under the general editorship of Leonard W. Labaree. This volume, devoted to Franklin's papers for the year 1767, contains six pieces of his periodical journalism and numerous fascinating letters: a letter to Henry Home, Lord Kames, on American politics; a philosophical and bantering letter to his sister Jane Mecom on the usefulness of enemies; a poem and a humorous letter on the birthday of Mary Stevenson; a letter to his wife Deborah on their expenses; one to Rudolph Erick Raspe (better known as Baron Munchausen) on the possibility of a job in America; another to George Croghan, frontiersman and Indian expert, on the mastodon fossils; to Joseph Galloway on English politics affecting America; to Mary Stevenson on reason and on the benefits of travelling; another to his sister Jane on his past writings ("I could as easily make a Collection for you of all the past Parings of my Nails"); and to his son William Franklin relating a political anecdote between George Onslow and George Grenville (which, like numerous other passages from his private letters, was widely reprinted in the contemporary newspapers); and innumerable others—some profound, many witty, and all interesting.

Melvin H. Buxbaum has written two articles dealing with the relations between Franklin and Provost William Smith. In "Benjamin Franklin and William Smith: Their School and Their Dispute" (*HMPEC* 39:361–82), Buxbaum over-states Franklin's "enmity" to the College of Philadelphia and ignores the fact that political differences between Franklin and Smith were the basis and major thrust of their disagreement. The other article, "Franklin Looks for a Rector: 'Poor Richard's' Hostility to Presbyterians" (*JPH* 48:176–88), reads into Franklin's satires of religion and his dealing with individuals a particular antipathy to Congregationalists and Presbyterians, claiming that he especially liked liberal Anglicans. The truth is that Franklin satirized, at one time or another, all religions, and included among his good friends Presbyterians and Congregationalists, as well as Anglicans. In a study of Franklin's economic views, V. Dennis Golladay, "The Evolution of Benjamin Franklin's Theory of Value" (*PH* 37:40–52), argues that Franklin's seeming change of position between 1729 and 1768 "was actually no more than a natural modification of his ideas due to the smooth integration of two long-standing concepts on the labour theory of value and the importance of agriculture," resulting from his acceptance of physiocratic economics, to which he was exposed by his travels in France in 1767 and by his subsequent correspondence with such physiocrats as Du Pont de Nemours.

C. William Miller, whose exhaustive study of Franklin's printing is about to appear, has sketched Franklin's road to financial security: "Benjamin Franklin's Way to Wealth," *PBSA* 63 [1969]:231–46. The only new literary essay to appear on Benjamin Franklin is James A. Sappenfield's "The *Autobiography* of Benjamin Franklin: The Structure of Success," *WSinL* 6[1969]:90–99, where the character sketches of the first part of the *Autobiography* are examined as the basis for the dramatic structure of the theme of the American Dream.

"The Social Thought of James Logan," Franklin's older contemporary, is examined (*WMQ* 27:68–89) by Roy L. Lokken, overstating, I believe, Logan's "great significance" on Franklin's intellectual development and failing in its attempt to link the Quaker intellectual's social thought with "the America of Thomas Jefferson." Logan's metaphysical treatise "The Duties of Man Deduced from Nature" (which was still "lost" when Lokken wrote this essay) has just turned up in a large group of valuable manuscripts given to the Pennsylvania Historical Society. This new Logan material—including his later letter-books—should (in conjunction with Edwin Wolf II's forthcoming study of his library) finally enable students to judge the extraordinary intellectual achievement of William Penn's secretary.

In "Deism in Philadelphia During the Age of Franklin" (*PH* 37: 217–36), Harold E. Taussig surveys "the religious ideas of the forty-eight members of the American Philosophical Society as of January 26, 1768." He concludes that "deism did not crystalize as a religion in the beliefs of most educated Philadelphians" but that it "tended to highlight certain emphases in the Christianity of those who came under its influence." Henry F. May's "The Problem of the American Enlightenment" (*NLH* 1:201–14) defines the American Enlightenment in European terms, dividing American thought into the period of English, of French, and of Scotch influence. May calls Jefferson "our only real philosophe." This progress report on May's book on the subject suggests that May is studying, not the American Enlightenment (which would have to deal with—to name only Virginians of the prerevolutionary Period—such figures as Ralph Wormeley, James

Blair, William Byrd of Westover, Robert Beverley, Sir John Randolph, John Mercer, Richard Bland and Robert Bolling), but the American reflections of various European influences; it is like writing a study of the French Enlightenment which would view the philosophes only in terms of foreign influences. The political genius of the early eighteenth-century Americans is an almost unexplored subject. The writings and speeches of those creators of the American political system should be examined by literary historians—but few have been. One of the few speeches to survive from any colonial legislature has just been edited by Anthony Nicolosi: "Colonial Particularism and Political Rights: Jacob Spicer II on Aid to Virginia, 1754" (*NJH* 88:69–88), which deserves attention as an example of political oratory and of provincial patriotism.

David H. Dickason has followed up his edition of William Williams's *Mr. Penrose: The Journal of Penrose, Seaman* (see *ALS 1969*, pp. 145–46) with a biography, *William Williams, Novelist and Painter of Colonial America, 1727–1791* (Bloomington, Ind. Univ. Press) and with the publication of Benjamin West's complete letter of October 10, 1810, on Williams (*Winterthur Portfolio* 6:127–34). Dickason's fascinating detective work on the biography of the elusive Williams is one more proof of the need for fundamental research into the culture of colonial America. Regrettably little information has turned up on Williams's thirty American years (1747 to c. 1776), but Dickason has written a critical study of the novel *Mr. Penrose* as well as a fine appreciation of the paintings of Williams. The survey of the genre of fictional shipwrecks and maroonings is brief; Dickason minimizes Williams's debt to previous writers such as Woodes Rogers and Daniel Defoe; and Defoe scholars may well doubt, as I do, that *Penrose* is "a more aesthetic and satisfying literary creation than Crusoe" (p. 111).

v. Edwards and the Great Awakening

Volume 3 of *The Works of Jonathan Edwards, Original Sin* (New Haven, Conn., Yale Univ. Press), edited by Clyde A. Holbrook, continues the strengths and weaknesses of its predecessors. The editor contributes an important, monograph-length introduction (101 pages) presenting the eighteenth-century context in which the book was produced; a section on "Edward's Life and Literary Sources," in which Holbrook comments on the influence of the American Indians on Edwards's view of the nature of man (pp. 25–26); a long section on the argument of the book; an important consideration of Edwards's sources, including John Locke and Francis Hutcheson—though, surprisingly, no reference is made to Leon Howard's edition of Edwards's *Notes on the Mind,* which is the best consideration of the extent and significance of Locke's influence; a section on the manuscripts and text; and a notice of the reputation of *Original Sin.* This carefully annotated, fully indexed volume is now the standard edition of Edwards's work. Its weakness is that the text itself is an unhappy mixture of modernization, carelessness, and faulty theory. It is ridiculous to think that by modernizing the text, the edition will have more readers. All that is accomplished is to cast doubt upon the textual authority of this book for the theologians, historians, philosophers, literary scholars, and students who will be its users.

After examining the structure of Edwards's spiritual autobiography (and finding four repetitive cycles or "seasonings of awakenings" in it), Norman S. Grabo, "Jonathan Edwards' *Personal Narrative:* Dynamic Stasis" (*LWU* 2[1969]:141–48), concludes that the *Personal Narrative* conflictingly achieves a "pure stasis" through an organic form, thus "by its essentially circular and self-contained formal structure" betraying the evangelical cause and escaping from life, history, and reality—a wild thesis, but a valuable examination of the structure. Two articles appeared on Edwards's minatory sermons. Willis J. Buckingham ("Stylistic Artistry in the Sermons of Jonathan Edwards," *PLL* 6:136–51) examines Edwards's prose style, particularly his rhythm and texture, and notices in detail the Enfield sermon (pp. 145–50); while James C. Cowan anatomizes the structure, rhetoric, and imagery of "The Future Punishment of the Wicked Unavoidable and Intolerable," (*SCB* 29[1969]:119–22).

Paul J. Nagy, "Jonathan Edwards and the Metaphysics of Consent" (*Person* 51:434–46), argues that Edwards's idea of "consent to being" is the cornerstone of his philosophic system. And Ellwood Johnson, in "Individualism and the Puritan Imagination" (*AQ* 22:230–37), finds six versions of individualism evolving from Edwards's psychology, ignoring the obvious influence of democratic institutions and impulses as well as the general current of history. Mason I. Lowance, Jr., "Images or Shadows of Divine Things: The Typology of Jonathan Edwards," *EAL* 5,i,pt.1:141–81, points out that Edwards's typological approach is conservative (i.e., that the Old Testament is historically true and grounded in fact as well as specifically fore-shadowing events in the New Testament) when applied to Scripture; but that he also used and justified the allegorical reading of types as "a fit method of instruction" because of man's "natural delight in the imaginative arts, in painting, poetry, fables, metaphorical language, and dramatic performances" (p. 150). Lowance notes that Edwards's "Typology of nature is significantly medieval rather than Puritan" (p. 157). Edwards's shift from the Ramistic logic advocated by his Yale teachers to the newer Port Royal logic is examined by Leon Howard ("The Creative Imagination of a College Rebel: Jonathan Edwards' Undergraduate Writings," *EAL* 5,iii:50–56), who demonstrates the influence of this basic way of thinking in Edwards's *Notes on the Mind*, particularly where Edwards applies the Port Royal logic to John Locke's writings.

An interesting collection concerning Edwards's comparative modernity is John Opie, ed., *Jonathan Edwards and the Enlightenment* (Lexington, Mass., D. C. Heath, 1969), which centers on the quarrel that scholars have carried on concerning Edwards's intellectual relationship to the thinkers of his day. The presentation of selections from Locke and Francis Hutcheson, with comparable passages from Edwards's own writings, provides Opie's own answer—and evidence—to the question, though his dogmatic assertion that Edwards "was the most acute American analyst of the achievements of the Enlightenment, far surpassing the perceptiveness of Franklin, Mayhew, Paine, and even Jefferson, in science, psychology, and philosophy," is obviously based upon an inadequate knowledge of Franklin and other unmentioned colonial Americans. Frank C. Shuffelton shows that, in editing Thomas Hooker's *Poor Doubting Christian*, Thomas Prince changed the text in order to provide an authoritative precedent for the emotional preaching of the Great Awakening (*EAL* 5,iii:68–75).

A surprising but welcome publishing development is the appearance of five readers concerning religion in the mid-eighteenth century. David S. Lovejoy, in *Religious Enthusiasm and the Great Awakening* (Englewood Cliffs, N.J., Prentice-Hall, [1969]) has interesting selections, especially Gilbert Tennent's public letter of February 12, 1742, regretting his own and others' enthusiastic excesses; but Lovejoy omits Tennent's earlier sermon (representing the position against which he was reacting), *The Danger of an Uncon-*

verted Ministry (1740). Richard L. Bushman's *The Great Awakening: Documents on the Revival of Religion, 1740–1745* (New York, Atheneum), has a clear organization, and like several of the other editions, makes use of contemporary newspapers. J. M. Bumsted, *The Great Awakening: The Beginnings of Evangelical Pietism in America* (Waltham, Mass., Blaisdell) has more snippets than the others, and is thus less useful for literary students. Darrett B. Rutman, *The Great Awakening: Event and Exegesis* (New York, John Wiley) inspires doubts of his accuracy by twice mis-dating the first document 1742 rather than 1724; but has a valuable collection of recent scholarship as well as sources. A different focus is found in Peter N. Carroll's *Religion and the Coming of the American Revolution* (Waltham, Mass., Ginn-Blaisdell), which begins with the legacy of the Great Awakening and focuses on the role of religion and of individual ministers in the Revolution. Unfortunately, this collection, too, tends to snippets. Still the best collection by far is Alan Heimert and Perry Miller, eds. *The Great Awakening: Documents Illustrating the Causes and Its Consequences* (see *ALS 1967*, p. 121), which includes several complete sermons, an extensive introduction, and material from the minor controversies.

vi. The Revolutionary and Early National Periods

Bernard Bailyn, in "Religion and Revolution: Three Biographical Studies," *PAH* 4:83–169, characterizes Andrew Eliot, Jonathan Mayhew, and Stephen Johnson. According to Bailyn, who specifically disagrees with Alan Heimert's evaluation of Eliot, this minister emerged as a conservative not because of his intellectual position, but because of an indecisive, hesitant, and timorous personality. Bailyn's view of New England election sermons as "Puritan New England's 'mirror-of-the-prince' literature" (p. 95) is an especially revealing lens through which to study this genre. He prints Jonathan Mayhew's "Memorandum" (pp. 140–43) of the radical sermon of August 25, 1765, which was popularly supposed to be responsible for the sacking of Thomas Hutchinson's house the following day, and examines the tension between the "political antiauthoritarianism and social stability that is the essence of the libertarian creed" (p. 111). The third minister, Stephen Johnson of Lyme, Connecticut, is the only one not familiar to literary scholars, but Bailyn shows that Johnson wrote the six anonymous newspaper essays (here reprinted) in the *New London Gazette*, September 6–November 1, 1765, which first refuted the doctrine of Parliament's sovereignty over America. Literary qualities of the political essay (and sermon) in the American Revolution are analyzed under such rubrics as "The Poetry of Invective" (with interesting observations on the American humorous traditions), "The Poetry of Axioms," "Argumentation and Demonstration," "Form of Dramatization," and "Persona and Mask" by Martin Christadler, "Politische Diskussion und literarische Form in der amerikanishen Literatur der Revolutionszeit" (*JA* 13[1968]:13–33).

Thomas Philbrick's *St. John de Crèvecoeur* (TUSAS 154) is the first critical book on this major early American writer. The biographical sketch, emphasizing Crèvecœur's various changes of names, his travels, and his adoption of different countries, is presented by Philbrick as a symbol of his shifting literary personae. The heart of the book is the discussion of *The Letters from an American Farmer* (1782). Chapter 2, which examines the ideas of the *Letters*, represents a great advance over the opinions of some former critics who did not think the book reflected any learning. Philbrick here makes good use of Howard C. Rice's French study in 1932 of Crèvecœur. (I wish that a revised English version of this were available.) But Crèvecœur's profound synthesis of Enlightenment ideas, his balancing of Enlightenment theory against American actuality, and his familiar use of English Enlightenment sources—remain unappreciated. Chapter 3, on the literary art of the *Letters*, is not so thorough an examination of the persona, the over-all structure, or the parables as it might be; but Philbrick is excellent on the tone, diction, forms, and symbols, and superb on the imagery. His comments on other writings, especially on the genres of "A Snow Storm" (which he compares to James Thomson's anecdotal sketches in *The Seasons*, pp. 128–30) and of the *Journey in Northern Pennsylvania and the State of New York* (which he compares to a symbolic dream-journey, pp. 150–56) are extremely valuable. Philbrick's book demonstrates and documents the suggestive literary insights of William Hazlitt and D. H. Lawrence—Crèvecœur is a classic of American literature.

Jack Babuscio, "Crèvecoeur in Charles Town: The Negro in the Cage" (*JHS* 2:283–86), is too brief to do Crèvecœur justice and lacks insight into his literary art. James C. Mohr, "Calculated Disillusionment: Crèvecoeur's *Letters* Reconsidered" (*SAQ* 69:354–63), argues that *Letters of an American Farmer* defines the American culture as dynamic process, in which man persists in the ideals of peace and order and progress, though he knows the falsity of the hopes of ever fulfilling these ideas. Mohr's argument that Crèvecœur does not only present an idyllic view of America is certainly correct; but his argument that the real thesis grows out of the form of the book (in the last chapter, "Farmer James" supposedly recognizes that social ideals exist only in illusion and deliberately chooses to continue the illusion) is unconvincing.

The poet of the American Revolution, Philip Freneau, is still comparatively unknown as a prose writer. Philip Marsh's *Freneau's Published Prose: A Bibliography* (Metuchen, N.J., Scarecrow) lists 1145 items of Freneau's prose, published for the most part in scattered periodicals. No doubt Marsh has some false attributions (especially among those dubious entries marked with an asterisk), but this is by far the most complete bibliography of the prose of this important writer. Freneau's "The American Village" is shown by William L. Andrews to be a nationalistic and philosophic reply to the issues raised in Oliver Goldsmith's "The Deserted Village," ("Goldsmith and Freneau in 'The American Village,'" *EAL* 5,ii:14–23). Freneau's political poems of the 1790s are discussed, with generous quotations but little new information, by Edward K. Eckert ("Philip Freneau: New Jersey's Poet as Propagandist," *NJH* 88:25–42).

The works of Jupiter Hammon (1711–*post* 1790), an early American Negro poet, have been published in a useful edition by Stanley Austin Ransom, Jr., *America's First Negro Poet: The Complete Works of Jupiter Hammon of Long Island* (Port Washington, N.Y., Kennikat), containing also Oscar Wegelin's "Biographical Sketch" of Hammon (1915) and Vernon Loggins's "Critical Analysis" (1959). The claim of primacy is open to question, for Lucy Terry's ballad on the Deerfield, Massachusetts, raid of 25 August 1746 is earlier than any of Hammon's known works; but Hammon may well be the first published American Negro poet; and, since he was older than Lucy Terry (c. 1730–1821), he may have written earlier poetry. Robert C. Kuncio has turned up four hitherto unknown manuscript poems by Phillis Wheatley, and a manuscript of one poem that differs considerably from the published version: "Some Unpublished Poems of Phillis Wheatley" (*NEQ* 43:287–97). "The Earliest-Published Poem of Phillis Wheatley" is identified and reprinted by Carl Bridenbaugh from the *Newport Mercury* of 21 December 1767 (*NEQ* 42[1969]: 583–84). In "Matilda's 'On Reading the Poems of Phillis Wheatley, the African Poetess'" (*EAL* 5,iii:57–67) Eugene L. Huddleston uses a discussion of this poem as an occasion to examine the works of the pseudonymous "Matilda," a New York poet of the 1780s and 1790s.

What Moses Coit Tyler dubbed the "Prison Literature" of the American Revolution has been generally ignored (except for Israel Potter's *Life and Remarkable Adventures*) since Tyler wrote. *A Narrative of Colonel Ethan Allen's Captivity* (1779) is examined by John Ditsky ("The Yankee Insolence of Ethan Allen," *CRAS* 1:32–38) for its nationalistic American posture and for Allen's attitude toward the Canadians. The primary author of *Reason the Only Oracle of Man* (sometimes still attributed solely to Ethan Allen), Dr. Thomas Young, is the subject of a sketch by David Freeman Hawke, who follows the career of this peripatetic radical, who was a poet and essayist, as well as an infamous freethinker: "Dr. Thomas Young— 'Eternal Fisher in Troubled Waters'" (*NYHSQ* 54:7–29).

The Connecticut Wits continue to interest readers. Kathryn and Philip Whitford examine "Timothy Dwight's Place in Eighteenth-Century American Science" (*PAPS* 114:60–71), comparing him to Thomas Jefferson and pointing out his interest in geology, agriculture, ecology, meteorology, and climate, and his influence on Benjamin Silliman. The first collected edition of *The Works of Joel Barlow*, (2 vols., SF&R) has been published, with an introduction by William K. Bottorff and Arthur K. Ford. This reprints all the separately published writings for which Barlow is best known, including both *The Vision of Columbus* (1787) and its later, much revised expansion, *The Columbiad* (1825). One of my favorite bits of Barlow's prose, the introduction to his translation of Brissot de Warville's *New Travels in the United States* (with its early—1792—attack on the English travellers who write about America) is omitted. The brief introduction is sound, but colonialists will chafe at being told that the Connecticut Wits "composed the first literary 'school' in American literature." This ignores Provost William Smith's group of Philadelphia poets of the 1760s; Dr. Alexander Hamilton's Tuesday Club wits of the 1740s–50s; Mather Byles's circle in the 1730s; the *New England Courant* wits in the 1720s; Samuel Sewall's circle *c.* 1700; and others. Barlow's 1788 diary, kept in France and England, is examined for what it reveals about his nationalism and esthetics by Kenneth R.

Ball ("American Nationalism and Esthetics in Joel Barlow's Unpublished 'Diary—1788,'" *TSL* 15:49–60).

Nearly a thousand pages in length, *The Poetry of the Minor Connecticut Wits* (SF&R), edited with an introduction by Benjamin Franklin V, contains the collaborative *The Echo*, and the poetry of Richard Alsop, Elihu Hubbard Smith, Lemuel Hopkins, and Theodore Dwight. In the introduction, Franklin suggests that the minor wits fulfilled the myth of the American cultural lag because they were writing poetry in the neoclassic style while the English were producing the *Lyrical Ballads* (p. xii), but of course the overwhelming mass of English poetry during the entire romantic period was—like the overwhelming mass of American poetry—neoclassic in style. Franklin calls attention to the neglected artist and writer, Elkanah Tisdale.

Lewis Leary writes an appreciation of "Samuel Low: New York's First Poet" (*BNYPL* 74:468–80), characterizing his *Winter Display'd* (1784) as the "first long poem to attempt a picture, other than political, of life in the United States." Leary also identifies "The First Published Poem of Thomas Paine of Boston [i.e., Robert Treat Paine, Jr.]: A Note on the Generation Gap in 1786" (*NEQ* 43:130–34). The discovery of a unique copy of Isaac Campbell's *A Rational Enquiry into the Origin, Foundation, Nature and End of Civil Government* (1787?), has prompted James F. and Jean H. Vivian to examine the life and thought of "The Reverend Isaac Campbell: An Anti-Lockian Whig," *HMPEC* 39:71–89. In discussing the thought of a better-known minister, M. L. Bradbury, "Samuel Stanhope Smith: Princeton's Accommodation to Reason" (*JPH* 48:189–202), demonstrates how Smith's attempt to reconcile the common sense philosophy of John Witherspoon with Calvinism led to his being suspected of Arminianism.

The views (all seem typical of his day) of James Elliot, as found in his *Poetical and Miscellaneous Works* (1798), on the Western Reserve, on the frontier, the Indian, the frontiersman, and the "Future Glory of America," are examined by Eugene L. Huddleston, "James Elliot and 'The Garden of North America': A New Englander's Impressions of the Old Northwest" (*NOQ* 42:64–73). Noah Webster is revealed as the author of a group of essays in the *Connecticut Courant*, 1783–1784, by Bonnie Bromberger, who also calls attention to Webster's annotations disclosing other authorships (including John

Trumbull): "Noah Webster's Notes on his Early Political Essays in the *Connecticut Courant*" (*BNYPL* 74:338–42). Robert M. Dell and Charles A. Huguenin show that the woodcut, supposedly of New York's John Street Theater, has no connection with that theater, but is evidently "a British juveniles' playhouse, improvised probably at the end of a hall or dormitory" ("Vermont's Royall Tyler in New York's John Street Theatre: A Theatrical Hoax Exploded," *VH* 38: 103–12). In an article dealing in part with the influence of Laurence Sterne and with the vogue of travel literature, Donald Davie writes an appreciation of John Ledyard, for whom travelling became "the epistemological landscape through which one seeks for knowledge and self-knowledge": "John Ledyard: The American Traveler and his Sentimental Journeys" (*ECS* 4:57–70). Leo M. Kaiser examines the classical training and interests of John Quincy Adams, and prints a critical, annotated edition of his translation of the "Thirteenth Satire of Juvenal" ("John Quincy Adams and His Translation of Juvenal 13," *PAPS* 114:272–93).

Except for *Modern Chivalry*, the writings of Hugh Henry Brackenridge are unfamiliar and unobtainable. Daniel Marder has attempted to remedy this with *A Hugh Henry Brackenridge Reader, 1770–1815* (Pittsburgh, Univ. of Pittsburgh Press), containing selections from the *United States Magazine*, the *Pittsburg Gazette*, his collection *Gazette Publications*, and other sources. "The Trial of Mamachtaga," the story of an Indian who while drunk attacked a group of white men and killed two, is recounted by Brackenridge with superb consciousness both of the clash of cultures involved and of "the force of opinion, from education, on the human mind" (p. 361). I wish that Brackenridge's plays and his narratives of Indian captivity and fighting were reprinted, rather than the excerpts from the conveniently available *Modern Chivalry*. W. Benjamin Kennedy argues that the Whiskey Rebellion made Brackenridge a more cautious and temperate democrat—and one with more respect for the "popular fervor" ("Hugh Henry Brackenridge: Thoughts and Acts of a Moderate Democrat," *WGCR* 2,ii[1969]:26–38).

In the second volume of *Arthur Mervyn*, Charles Brockden Brown experimented with "the techniques of multiple perspective and the device of the unreliable," in order to bring out both the symbolic meanings of the tale and the oedipal tendencies of the hero, according to Patrick Brancaccio: ("Studied Ambiguities: *Arthur Mervyn* and the Problem of the Unreliable Narrator," *AL* 42:18–27). Suggesting that the novel echoes Franklin's *Autobiography*, James H. Justus ("Arthur Mervyn, American," *AL* 42:304–24) sees *Arthur Mervyn* as an examination of the commercial society of America and of the "success story" of the selfish and deluded Mervyn. In a general view of Brown's fiction as a mirror of the author's troubled relation to the American experience, Max F. Schulz, "Brockden Brown: An Early Casualty of the American Experience" (*A-A* 2[1968]:81–90), particularly examines Edgar Huntley's fight with the Indians as Brown's attempt to assess the meaning of the history of Indian-white relations in America.

vii. Books, Bibliography, Libraries

With the appearance of Clifford K. Shipton and James E. Mooney's *National Index of American Imprints Through 1800: The Short Title Evans* (2 vols.; [Worcester, Mass.] American Antiquarian Society and Barre Publishers, 1969), we have at last a convenient guide to the books, pamphlets, and many of the broadsides published in America to 1801. With small, but easily legible, print, and with three columns to a page, these two volumes ("incorporating all of the tens of thousands of bibliographical corrections of the Evans entries") print all the target cards preceding the reproduction of the items in the Early American Imprint series. The *National Index* is the most useful single bibliography of Americana now existing. Not without contradictions and weaknesses, and particularly frustrating to use without the companion chronological Evans, it is nevertheless such a useful bibliography that to dwell on its shortcomings is blatant ingratitude, as well as blindness to the function (an index to the Early American Imprint microcards) for which it was designed.

Roger P. Bristol's *Supplement to Charles Evans' American Bibliography* (Charlottesville, Univ. Press of Va.) lists an additional 11,262 items. Bristol helpfully gives the American Imprint series microprint number of his items. A number of important items listed by Bristol are not in the *National Index*, and I hope that at periodic intervals, additions to the Evans microprints (and guides to the additions, supplementing the *National Index*) will be issued by the American Antiquarian Society. As Roger E. Stoddard points out, Oscar Wegelin's *Early American Poetry* (1930) was a "heroic achieve-

nent," but since 1930 numerous additional books, pamphlets and
specially broadsides have come to light. Stoddard's *A Catalogue of
Books and Pamphlets Unrecorded in Oscar Wegelin's "Early Ameri-
an Poetry"* (Providence, R.I., Friends of the Library of Brown Univ.,
1969]), which lists 262 items, is the first step toward a new and com-
lete bibliography. Stoddard's listings are fuller than Wegelin's and
nclude cross-references to Evans and other standard bibliographies
nd to at least one location. Since this is meant as a companion to
Wegelin (and is not the ultimate replacement of Wegelin which
toddard will do), the arrangement is alphabetical.

The two final parts of J. A. Leo Lemay's "A Calendar of American
Poetry in the Colonial Newspapers and Magazines and in the Major
English Magazines Through 1765" appeared in *PAAS* 80:71–222;353–
69. The Calendar chronologically lists all the American poems (and
hose which previous scholars have thought were native, even when
uch are now identified as reprintings of English poems) published
n the American periodicals to 1766. At the end, there is a first line
ndex; a name, pseudonym and title index; a subject and genre index;
nd a periodical index. Hitherto unknown poems by Mather Byles,
oseph Green, John Maylem, James Sterling, Dr. Adam Thomson,
nd Robert Bolling—among others—turn up in the calendar; and early
rintings of known poems by Thomas Godfrey, Nathaniel Evans, Pro-
ost William Smith, and Francis Hopkinson—among others—are also
ocated.

The Botetourt Bibliographical Society, founded to issue annual
ublications describing eighteenth century Virginia libraries, pub-
shed *The Henly-Horrocks Inventory*, edited by Fraser Neiman (Wil-
amsburg, Botetourt Bibliographical Society and the Earl Gregg
wem Library, [1968]), which contains the list drawn up by Samuel
enley (the translator of William Beckford's *Vathek*) of books
ought by William and Mary College from the library of its former
resident, James Horrocks. More substantial is John Gwilym Jones,
*Goronwy Owen's Virginian Adventure: His Life, Poetry, and Literary
Opinions, With a Translation of His Virginian Letters* (Williamsburg,
otetourt Bibliographical Society, [1969]). Owen, generally regarded
s the best Welsh poet of the eighteenth century, spent his last years
n Virginia. This pamphlet concludes with a listing of the few identi-
able books from his library.

Hannah D. French continues her studies of early American book-

binders with an article on "Caleb Buglass, Binder of the Proposed
Book of Common Prayer, Philadelphia, 1786," *Winterthur Portfolio*
6:15–32. In "An Annotated Check List of Puritan Sermons Published
in America before 1700" (*BNYPL* 74:286–337), Robert M. Benton
gives the biblical text, the doctrine, reasons, and uses; comments
upon Ramistic influence as well as upon such literary devices as
dialogue and extended metaphor; and also gives the genre of the
sermon. The popularity and influence of "Laurence Sterne in America" before 1807 are briefly discussed by Martin Roth (*BNYPL* 74:428–
36), who notes Sterne's influence on William Dunlap, Francis Hopkinson, and Joseph Dennie. The early career of Asbury Dickins, first
publisher of the *Port Folio*, is traced by Peter J. Parker from his
initial success to his London imprisonment ("Asbury Dickins, Book-
seller, 1798–1801, or, The Brief Career of a Careless Youth," *PMHB*
94:464–83). Finally, Charles Mann reports finding *The Life and
Adventures of Simon Crea McMahon* (1790), "A Hitherto Unseen
Virginia Imprint: An Explanatory Note" (*Serif* 7,i:32–33).

viii. General and Miscellaneous Studies

The first separately published literary history of early America since
the appearance of Moses Coit Tyler's ground-breaking and magis-
terial work of a century ago is Russel B. Nye's *American Literary
History, 1607–1830* (New York, Knopf). Among the many excellent
parts of Nye's book are the discussion of meditations (pp. 35–36), the
presentation of folklore, witchcraft, the Indian, and Indian captivities
(pp. 46–55), the changing sermon style of the eighteenth century
(p. 74), the account of Cotton Mather (pp. 76–79), the analysis of
Crèvecœur's "Letter III" (pp. 154–59), and the appreciation of "Narratives of War and Prison" (pp. 161–63). There are also, however,
numerous errors of fact and occasional bloopers. Although it may be
unfair to quibble about proportions, it is surprising to find that Edward Taylor has only two pages—one of which consists entirely of
quotation. The work cannot be compared with Tyler's, for Nye's is in
part based upon secondary scholarship. Neither is it as sound and
judicious as the relevant chapters in Robert E. Spiller's *Literary
History of America* or as Kenneth B. Murdock's survey in Arthur
Hobson Quinn's *Literature of the American People*. Nye does, however, have strengths that no one else possesses who has surveyed the

literature of early America—mainly related to his special expertise in the history of American culture.

The role of the Negro in early American fiction, particularly in Tabitha Tenney's *Female Quixotism* (1801) is examined by Paola Cabibbo, "Il Negro come personaggio" (*SA* 14[1968]:29–39). The typical colonial attitude toward the Indian is reversed by Wilbur R. Jacobs, who presents all colonial Indians as angels and all colonial whites as devils—"British Colonial Attitudes and Policies Toward the Indian in the American Colonies," in *Attitudes of Colonial Powers Toward the American Indian*, edited by Howard Peckham and Charles Gibson (Salt Lake City, Univ. of Utah Press, 1969), pp. 81–106. And a long study, "The American Image of Ireland: A Study of Its Early Phases," is presented by Owen Dudley Edwards (*PAH* 4:197–282), who especially examines the view of the Irish held by John Dickinson, Samuel Adams, John Adams, and Benjamin Franklin. I am disappointed, however, not to find any mention of the humorous uses of the Irishman in the colonial eighteenth century (by Benjamin Franklin and Joseph Green, among others) and not to find any reference to that American novelist and kleptomaniac, Thomas Atwood Digges, who tried to foment revolution in Ireland.

Some characteristics of the early American lyric are discussed by N. Christoph de Nagy, who begins with Philip Freneau and mainly considers James G. Percival: "Tendenzen in der frühen amerikanischen Lyrik," *Festschrift Rudolf Stamm* (Bern, Francke, 1969), pp. 267–76. In one of the strangest articles (premised on the notion that Puritans were "solemn and humorless") of the year, we are told that Yankee humor derives from the Puritan plain style and Puritan reticence and that it "appeared as a compensation for declining faith": Chard Powers Smith, "Plain Humor: New England Style" (*NEQ* 43:465–72).

The first sketch in volume 15 of that indispensable tool for the intellectual history of New England, Clifford K. Shipton's *Biographical Sketches of Those Who Attended Harvard . . . 1761–1763* (Boston, Massachusetts Historical Society), is of the testy Nathaniel Ames, Jr., physician, diarist, jokester, lover of the theater, poet, and the preeminent almanac maker of the revolutionary and early national periods. His literary classmates of 1761 include William Emerson, builder of the Old Manse, minister of Concord, patriot, and grandfather of Ralph Waldo Emerson; Peter Oliver, Tory historian of the Revolution; Stephen Sewall, poet, Hebraicist, and drunk; Samuel West, essayist and anecdotalist; and Samuel Williams, historian, scientific writer, editor, rascal, and essayist. Other important literary figures characterized in this volume include Jeremy Belknap, poet, historian, satirist, novelist, essayist, biographer, hymnist, and collector of books and manuscripts; Governor James Sullivan, prolific newspaper essayist, versifier, and historian; and Josiah Quincy, Jr., political essayist and diarist. Although Shipton supplies full documentation in the footnotes, I lament the absence of the bibliographies of the writers, which adorned all of Shipton's previous volumes in this superb series.

Finally, an indispensable book for all students of colonial intellectual history and for those literary scholars interested in the colonial naturalist-writers is Raymond Phineas Stearns, *Science in the British Colonies of America* (Urbana, Univ. of Illinois Press). Among the numerous authors who figure importantly in this masterful study are John Winthrop, Jr., John Josselyn, Increase Mather, Cotton Mather, Benjamin Colman, Isaac Greenwood, Dr. William Douglass, Dr. John Mitchell, Cadwallader Colden, John Bartram, Dr. Alexander Garden, Professor John Winthrop, and, of course, the great Benjamin Franklin.

University of California, Los Angeles

10. Nineteenth-Century Fiction

M. Thomas Inge

In sheer quantity, the amount of scholarship published in 1970 on nineteenth-century fiction exclusive of Hawthorne, Melville, Twain, and James is nearly twice that produced in 1969. The most significant activity was the publication of authoritative texts in CEAA-approved editions and numerous reprints of standard works either in facsimile or corrected editions. Since trustworthy texts must precede sound criticism, this is as it should be. The criticism itself, unfortunately, is not so impressive; much of it is repetitive and uninspired. As usual, Irving, Cooper, Howells, and Crane continue to receive the most attention, while several minor figures—such as Kate Chopin, Julian Hawthorne, and George Lippard—have suddenly become the subjects of elucidating and even definitive critical treatments. In general, nineteenth-century fiction continues to hold a large appeal for modern scholarly inquiry.

i. General Topics

The most important single critical volume to be considered in this chapter is Harold H. Kolb's excellent exercise in critical definition, *The Illusion of Life: American Realism as a Literary Form* (Charlottesville, Univ. Press of Va.). Kolb evaluates and finds wanting most of the attempts by literary critics and historians to define realism, and he derives a new definition by concentrating on "only one kind of realism, that which was practiced most significantly by three Americans—James, Twain, and Howells—in the mid-1880's." He discovers identifying characteristics in four areas: philosophy, subject matter, morality, and style, and proceeds to discuss them separately in lean, lucid prose. While many critics predictably will disagree with his conclusions, to this writer they are eminently sensible and apply to a broader spectrum of realistic writing than the select works from which they are derived. In addition, many of his statements provide provocative topics for class discussions devoted to American literary realism. It is one of the most useful critical volumes to appear in years.

Although it focuses specifically on three writers beyond the concern of this chapter, *Naturalistic Triptych: The Fictive and the Real in Zola, Mann, and Dreiser* by Haskell M. Block (New York, Random House) provides a concise summary of the meaning of literary naturalism in its first fifteen pages. One of the most influential and seminal studies of nineteenth-century literature to appear in this century, Henry Nash Smith's *Virgin Land: The American West as Symbol and Myth*, has been reprinted in its "Twentieth Anniversary Reissue" (Cambridge, Mass., Harvard Univ. Press) with a brief new preface which answers several criticisms of the book with a refreshing degree of humility.

The University Press of Kentucky has issued eight reprints in "The Novel as American Social History" series under the general editorship of Richard Lowitt: *The Sky Pilot* by Ralph Connor (pseudonym of Charles William Gordon), introduction by Robin W. Winks; *Maggie* by Stephen Crane, introduction by Philip D. Jordan; *The Clansman* by Thomas Dixon, Jr., introduction by Thomas D. Clark; *The Circuit Rider* by Edward Eggleston, introduction by Holman Hamilton; *Jimmie Higgins* by Upton Sinclair, introduction by David A. Shannon; *Hagar's Hoard* by George Kibbe Turner, introduction by John Duffy; *A Certain Rich Man* by William Allen White, introduction by John D. Hicks; *The Turn of the Balance* by Brand Whitlock, introduction by Allan Nevins. All these novels deal with social tensions and problems in America during the decades from the 1870s to the 1920s, and their introductions focus almost entirely on the historical content of the novels to the exclusion of commentary about their literary value (which in most instances is indeed slight). Only the introductions by Clark and Nevins are distinctive in their scholarship and critical acumen, and in the case of *Maggie* too much attention is paid to prostitution and other social problems with which the novel deals only inferentially. For the most part, a great many opportunities have been lost here for making judgements of an interdisciplinary nature about the relations between history and literature, but a valuable service has been rendered by making these novels available once more (except for *Maggie*, which has been reprinted entirely too often for the need).

The University of North Carolina Press rounded out its "Southern

Literary Classics Series," for which C. Hugh Holman and Louis D. Rubin, Jr., serve as general editors, with five additional reprints of nineteenth-century works: *The Knights of the Golden Horseshoe* by William Alexander Caruthers, introduction by Curtis Carroll Davis; *The Planter's Northern Bride* by Caroline Lee Hentz, introduction by Rhoda Coleman Ellison; *The Valley of Shenandoah* by George Tucker, introduction by Donald R. Noble, Jr.; *The Partisan Leader* by Nathaniel Beverley Tucker, introduction by C. Hugh Holman; and *Letters of the British Spy* by William Wirt, introduction by Richard Beale Davis. Unlike most of the contributors to the University Press of Kentucky series, the authors of the introductions to these reprints have admirably provided essays which are informative combinations of biography, history, and literary criticism. They not only summarize available scholarship but constitute in themselves important appreciations and critiques of these little known Southern classics. Textual scholars will also appreciate the bibliographical and textual notes provided on the editions reprinted, information generally missing in most reprints.

One of the largely untapped sources of information about nineteenth-century fiction is that of the numerous magazines and periodicals where all the major and many minor writers first saw their work in print. Extensive studies of the relationships between periodical writing and novel writing, and between editors and authors will ultimately be needed before we can see the fiction in its fullest cultural context, but in the meantime indices and general essays on the journals, their contents, and their editorial policies should be supplied. One effort in this direction, at least for the Southern journals, is the competent series of essays appearing in the *Southern Literary Journal*, of which three installments have appeared: Robert D. Jacobs, "Campaign for a Southern Literature: *The Southern Literary Messenger*" (2,i[1969]: 66–98); Rayburn S. Moore, " 'A Distinctly Southern Magazine': The *Southern Bivouac*" (2,ii:51–65); and Richard J. Calhoun, "The Ante-bellum Literary Twilight: *Russel's Magazine*" (3,i:89–110). A similar but brief history of the first quarterly of literary importance published in Georgia in 1860 is Lawrence Huff's "Joseph Addison Turner and His Quarterly, the *Plantation*" (*GHQ* 54:493–506). John G. L. Dowgray's "Literature and History: *Harper's Magazine*," in *Literature and History*, edited by I. E. Cadenhead, Jr. (UTMS 9), outlines the publishing history of

Harper's from 1850 to 1900 and relates its contents to contemporary literature, history, and cultural forces. Interesting information is also found in Robert Stinson, "McClure's Road to *McClure's*: How Revolutionary Were 1890s Magazines?" (*JQ* 47:256–62). The manner in which one particular journal's contents could influence American literature in general is described in generous detail in Richard Hauck's "The Dickens Controversy in the *Spirit of the Times*" (*PMLA* 85:278–83). In examining editor William T. Porter's use of Charles Dickens's writing in the columns of the *Spirit*, Hauck shows how Porter helped contribute to the shape of early comic realism in America.

In one provocative general essay, "The Machine in the Anglo-American Garden" (*CentR* 14:201–12), Nicolaus C. Mills questions Leo Marx's explanation of the uniqueness of American literature and the special character of the novel in *The Machine in the Garden* (1964) by a comparison of English and American literature of the nineteenth century. Mills finds that concern over the impact of technology on social and cultural mores had its counterpart in British literature and thus was not a uniquely American phenomenon. Two complementary studies reaching the same valid conclusion are Jan Cohn's "The Negro Character in Northern Magazine Fiction of the 1860's" (*NEQ* 43:572–92) and David W. Levy's "Racial Stereotypes in Antislavery Fiction" (*Phylon* 31:265–79). Cohn examines black stereotypes in the antislavery fiction of Harriet Beecher Stowe, Louisa May Alcott, and John W. DeForest among others to conclude that "If, as one supposes, popular literature reflects the attitudes of the popular audience, then the North remained complacently racist, if nobly abolitionist, throughout its decade of independent examination of the black character in fiction." Levy found the same true of the writings of E. D. E. N. Southworth, William Wells Brown, Lydia Maria Child, and numerous little-known novelists.

Among general dissertations of interest are Victor Joseph Contoski, "The Southern Aristocratic Lover: Symbol of National Unity, 1865–1885" (*DAI* 30:3903A–04A); Leo Augustus Weigant, "The Manners Tradition and Regional Fiction in Nineteenth-Century Fiction" (*DAI* 31:2406A); Charles Taylor Pridgeon, Jr., "Insanity in American Fiction from Charles Brockden Brown to Oliver Wendell Holmes" (*DAI* 31:1766A–67A); and Robert Franklin Marler, "The American Tale and Short Story, 1850–1861" (*DAI* 31:1764A).

ii. Irving, Cooper, and Their Contemporaries

Irving scholars will surely welcome volume 3 of the *Journals and Notebooks* for 1819–1827 in the CEAA-approved *Complete Works of Washington Irving* (Madison, Univ. of Wis. Press). Editor Walter A. Reichart has exercised great skill, thoroughness, and judgment in preparing these unpublished materials for scholarly use, materials of considerable interest because of what they reveal about the period when Irving had the admiration and respect of both Europe and America because of *The Sketch Book* and *Bracebridge Hall*. Another volume issued this year is Irving's sectarian interpretation of the life of Mohamet and the growth of Islam, *Mohamet and His Successors*, edited with the same skill and care as the above volume by Henry A. Pochmann and E. N. Feltskog. Issue no. 3 of *CEAAN* contains brief but relevant technical notes on textual problems encountered by the editors of the works of Irving, Cooper, and Howells.

Rolando Anzilotti's *Studi e ricerche di letteratura americana* (Florence, La Nuovo Italia, 1968), includes three chapters on Irving's relations to and reputation in Italy, a bibliography of Italian criticism and translations, and a collection of nineteen unpublished letters to J. C. L. de Sismondi dated from 1827 to 1842 by the early female novelist Catharine Maria Sedgwick. Joan D. Berbrich, in *Three Voices from Paumanok: The Influence of Long Island on James Fenimore Cooper, William Cullen Bryant, and Walt Whitman* (Port Washington, N.Y., Ira J. Friedman, 1969), gathers the superficial evidence for Cooper's use of the inhabitants, history, culture, and lore of Long Island in his fiction.

David Durant's "Aeolism in *Knickerbocker's A History of New York*" (*AL* 41:493–506) is a perceptive description of the unifying factor in Irving's satiric work, the "treatment of Aeolism—the inflation of empty subjects into false importance through idle words." This makes the narrator intentionally complex: "The Aeolistic narrator is a historian whose work involves, as an allegory, a satiric attack on political Aeolism and includes, as a casebook of bombast, a similar attack on Aeolistic historians. He is, as well, a creative writer ill-disguised as historian and a fictional character large in his own right." Most of the other articles on Irving add only brief footnotes to our knowledge. M. A. Weatherspoon's "1815–1819: Prelude to Irving's *Sketch Book*" (*AL* 41:566–71) is a biographical note about how a young lady, Serena Livingston, contributed to Irving's despondent mood during his years in England (1815–1819). Ben H. McClary, in "A Bracebridge-Hall Christmas for Van Buren" (*ELN* 8: 18–22), publishes a letter from Irving to the Rev. Cornelius H. Reaston Rodes of December 5, 1831, and suggests that his home near Chesterfield might also have provided a suggestion or model for Bracebridge Hall in *The Sketch Book*. Donald R. Noble notes an obscene pun on the name "Peter" Stuveysant in Irving's *History* in "Washington Irving's 'Peter' Pun" (*AN&Q* 8:103–04) and Kenneth T. Reed summarizes Irving's typically ambivalent attitude toward women as reflected in his fiction in "'Oh These Women! These Women!': Irving's Shrews and Coquettes" (*AN&Q* 8:147–50). Two promising dissertations were completed this year: Richard Holton Cracroft, in "The American West of Washington Irving: The Quest for a National Tradition" (*DAI* 31:1221A), describes Irving's temporary transition from a creator of comic mythology to a romantic historian when he returned to the states in 1832 and was impressed by the promise of the West for Jacksonian democracy, while Adele Gillespie Jenney's "The Irvingesque Story in the United States, 1820–1860" (*DAI* 31:1760A–61A) is a more technical study of the distinctive characteristics of the Irving short story and an evaluation of the impact of his example upon 3400 stories published in the four decades.

Cooper scholars appear to have been especially prolific this year and demonstrated marked tendencies to clarify and deepen our understanding of his thought and to defend the integrity of his artistry. John P. McWilliams, "Cooper and the Conservative Democrat" (*AQ* 22:665–77), undertakes a fresh and revealing assessment of Cooper's nonfictional work *The American Democrat* to show that "Cooper's tract is not so much an exposition of political convictions as it is an attempt to thrash out certain ideological dilemmas that, by 1838, were threatening to upset those political convictions." Thus, it should not be viewed, as it often is, as Cooper's definitive statement of political belief. In "James Fenimore Cooper and the City" (*NYH* 51: 287–305), Thomas Bender traces his changing attitudes toward urban life (1838–1851) from hostility to accomodation through his observation of the decline of the landed gentry and the rise of the urban merchant elite in the maintenance of social stability. Bender not only corrects the common assumption that Cooper remained a

Jeffersonian agrarian throughout his life but also provides an interesting chapter in the history of American urbanization.

A study of the function of diction in Cooper is Alan F. Sandy's "The Voices of Cooper's *The Deerslayer*" (*ESQ* 60:5–9). In a convincing discussion which adds a degree of respect for his reputation as an artist, Sandy finds that "all of Cooper's novels deserve to be read with awareness of the complicated relationships among levels of diction, but *The Deerslayer* makes the most formal and thematic use of these relationships." A complementary analysis of words and style is Thomas L. Philbrick's "Language and Meaning in Cooper's *The Water Witch*" (*ESQ* 60:10–16): in the speeches of Tom Tiller and Alderman Van Beverout, "Cooper extends a technique which he adopted early in his literary career, the assignment to a character of a distinctive diction and a habitual mode of metaphorical reference." A formalistic reading of *The Pioneers* which unsuccessfully attempts to discover a "composite order" in the novel's disparate and incongruous elements is Gerry Brenner's "Cooper's 'Composite Order': *The Pioneers* as Structured Art" (*SNNTS* 2:264–75). Marilyn G. Rose discovers a "Time Discrepancy in 'Last of the Mohicans'" (*AN&Q* 8:72–73) between the facts of the Fort William Henry massacre and Cooper's artistic use of them.

"Cooper's Use of Proverbs in the Anti-Rent Novels" by Florence Healy French (*NYFQ* 20:42–49) locates 206 proverbs in the 1840s trilogy—*Satanstoe, The Chainbearer*, and *The Redskins*—and argues with insufficient detail or support that Cooper drew from the oral tradition rather than the literary and used proverbs to support his Jeffersonian political philosophy. Max I. Baym and Percy Matenko in "The Odyssey of *The Water-Witch* and a Susan Fenimore Cooper Letter" (*NYH* 51:33–41) publish an 1886 letter by Cooper's daughter which provides interesting but unessential information on the Cooper family and the composition of *The Water-Witch* (1831). In two valuable review essays, both James H. Pickering in "Fenimore Cooper in Our Time" (*NYH* 51:545–55) and Donald A. Ringe in "James Fenimore Cooper: An American Democrat" (*PLL* 6:420–31) agree that James Franklin Beard's edition of *The Letters and Journals* (1960–1968) is a turning point in the history of Cooper scholarship because of Beard's scrupulous editing and the rich biographical material he makes available. In a general study of "Prison and Society in

Nineteenth-Century American Fiction" (*WHR* 24:325–31), Nicolaus C. Mills notes that the modern practice of describing American society in terms of prison and imprisonment has its roots in the past century's fiction: "In the work of Cooper, Hawthorne, Melville, and Twain it is not merely the oppressive institutions but the very structure of American society that in one form or another is imprisoning."

Dissertation writers trod heavily on Cooper's trail with four completed, the titles of which are mostly self-explanatory: Donald Charles Irving, "James Fenimore Cooper's Alternatives to the Leatherstocking Hero in the Frontier Romances" (*DAI* 30:4947A–48A); James Richard Lindroth, "The Comic Perspective of James Fenimore Cooper" (*DAI* 31:1234A); Orm Harald Overland, "James Fenimore Cooper's *The Prairie*: The Making and Meaning of an American Classic" (*DAI* 31:1285A); and Sarah Latimer Marshall, "The Concept of History in Cooper's Fiction" (*DAI* 31:2885A). Also relevant is Annette Kolodny, "The Pastoral Tradition in American Writing, 1590–1850" (*DAI* 31:731A), which pays some attention to Cooper and Simms.

While critical interest in William Gilmore Simms and Harriet Beecher Stowe continues, the amount of scholarship decreased since last year. The most important essay is Joseph V. Ridgely's "Simms's Concept of Style in the Historical Romance" (*ESQ* 60:16–23). Without apologizing for Simms's rapid and sometimes careless mode of composition, Ridgely analyzes his style for its unique qualities and examines Simms's own theoretical statements, the influences on his work, and the variations between his style and the styles of his contemporaries. This is a dependable and intelligent summary. In "Leonard Voltmeier's 'Invictus': Vol. One of the *Centennial Simms*" (*SLJ* 2:135–47), Mary Ann Wimsatt successfully achieves a discriminating reassessment of Simms through a review of *Voltmeier* (see *ALS 1969*, p. 169). While she finds this novel derivative of his early romances, "the pictures of frontier life and the use of symbolic detail transcend the uninventive plot and the stilted (or melodramatic) characters to provide some nourishment for the persevering reader." Benjamin Lease publishes a letter to author John Neal about his contributions to *The Magnolia*, edited by Simms, in "William Gilmore Simms, A New Letter" (*GHQ* 54:427–30); and Miriam Jones Shillingsburg has provided the critical apparatus for "An Edition of William Gilmore Simms's *The Cub of the Panther*" (*DAI* 31:402A–03A), a novel published only in serial form in 1869.

A discussion of the problems encountered by George L. Aiken in transposing Harriet Beecher Stowe's *Uncle Tom's Cabin* to the nineteenth-century stage and the effect the limitations of the stage had on it is found in David Grimsted's thorough "*Uncle Tom* from Page to Stage: Limitations of Nineteenth-Century Drama" (*QJS* 56:235–44). Peter R. Allen's "Lord Macaulay's Gift to Harriet Beecher Stowe" (*N&Q* 17:23–24) is an inconsequential note on Macaulay's unfavorable reaction to Mrs. Stowe. The purpose of Theodore Richard Hovet's dissertation, "Harriet Beecher Stowe's Holiness Crusade Against Slavery" (*DAI* 31:2919A), is to show that "Mrs. Stowe's moral response to slavery was shaped by liberal and popular theological doctrines created by the evangelical movement in the 1840's, that these doctrines controlled the themes and techniques of her antislavery fiction, and that they explain her response to national events during the slavery crisis."

Several generally neglected writers underwent important reevaluations this season. Gerald E. Gerber's "James Kirke Paulding and the Image of the Machine" (*AQ* 22:736–41) adds a chapter to *The Machine in the Garden* by Leo Marx by examining the image of the "machine" in the pre-1830 writings of Paulding, who used it as a metaphor for the condition of man and as a composite sign of the times a year before Thomas Carlyle called the century "the Age of Machinery." Michael Davitt Bell, "History and Romance Convention in Catharine Sedgwick's *Hope Leslie*" (*AQ* 22:213–21), rescues for our attention an often forgotten novelist who before 1850 was one of America's most popular female writers. Arthur Wrobel, in " 'Romantic Realism': Nathaniel Beverley Tucker" (*AL* 42:325–35), develops the idea that Tucker's fiction of the 1830s "adapted the realistic formulas popularized by Sir Walter Scott and attempted to incorporate verisimilitude to human nature, setting, manners, speech, and customs in a plot that invited comparison to historical or well-known events." His failure exemplifies why truly realistic writing was postponed. Nancy Esther James's dissertation, "Realism in Romance: A Critical Study of the Short Stories of Edward Everett Hale" (*DAI* 31:1802A) evaluates the short fiction of the seldom-discussed author of "The Man Without a Country."

iii. Local Color, Humor, and Popular Fiction

While none of the local color writers are receiving editorial attention
under the auspices of the CEAA, since there are so many major
writers to process first, a few of their important works are being reprinted or issued in textbook editions. Under the general editorship
of Nathalia Wright, the "Tennesseana Editions" series was inaugu-
rated with a facsimile reprint of an 1884 edition of Mary Noailles
Murfree's collection of short stories *In the Tennessee Mountains*
(Knoxville, Univ. of Tenn. Press). The appreciative introduction by
Nathalia Wright is one of the best critical statements on Miss Murfree's skills as a local colorist and dialectician in print. A facsimile
reprint of an 1864 edition of William Wells Brown's 1853 novel
Clotelle; or, The President's Daughter, designated the first American
Negro novel, appears in a volume prefaced by a thorough 200-page
biography by J. Noel Heermance entitled *William Wells Brown and
Clotelle: A Portrait of the Artist in the First Negro Novel* (Hamden,
Conn., Archon Books, 1969). An excellent textbook selection and
edition of *The Awakening and Other Stories* by Kate Chopin has
been prepared by Lewis Leary (New York, Holt, Rinehart and
Winston). Included are one novel, twenty stories, and an introduction in which Leary assesses this fine writer's accomplishment.

An interesting general essay is "Southern Local Color and the
Black Man" (*SoR* 6:1011–30) by Louis D. Rubin, Jr. Following out
the idea that "if we look at the way that representative Southern
writers have depicted Negroes, we will be able, in part at least, to
gain insight into the progress of race relations and ideas of race in
the South," Rubin examines with brief elucidating commentary
fiction by Simms, Thomas Nelson Page, Joel Chandler Harris, George
W. Cable, and Twain. He finds that gradually the writer overcame
the traditional view of the black as not fully human, except that
"however vivid the human characterizations they created, however
free they may have been from the limitations of their time and place,
none of the nineteenth-century Southern novelists could consistently
view the situation of the Negro from the viewpoint of the Negro;
they could not recognize in his circumstance a full and sustaining
metaphor of their own." A general dissertation by Ronald L. Lycette,
"Diminishing Circumferences: Feminine Responses in Fiction to
New England Decline" (*DAI* 31:1764A), considers cultural decline

in New England and the development of the grotesque in the fiction
of Stowe, Rose Terry Cook, Helen Hunt Jackson, Elizabeth Stuart
Phelps, Sarah Pratt McLean, Sarah Orne Jewett, Mary W. Freeman,
and Alice Brown.

The recently inspired Kate Chopin revival seems to be in full
bloom. In addition to his fine edition of Chopin mentioned above,
Lewis Leary has published "Kate Chopin, Liberationist?" (*SLJ* 3,i:
138–44). Although Mrs. Chopin was not necessarily a full-fledged cru-
sader for women's rights as recently portrayed by her admirers, he
says, she is significant because, except for Jewett and James, "there
was no writer of short fiction in the late nineteenth century who
played with equal virtuosity and with such a variety of characters
over so wide a range. . . ." John R. May, in "Local Color in *The Awakening*" (*SoR* 6:1031–40), takes a new stance by noting that the environment of Mrs. Chopin's novel has a strong influence on Edna
Pontellier and by arguing that "the novel is not simply about a woman's awakening need for sexual satisfaction that her marriage cannot
provide; sexuality in the novel represents a more universal human
longing for freedom, and the frustration that Edna experiences is a
poignant statement about the agony of human limitations." Robert
D. Arner's "Kate Chopin's Realism: 'At the Cadian Ball' and 'The
Storm'" (*Markham Rev* 2,ii:1–4) measures her progress away from
slick local color sentimentalism toward genuine realism by comparing
an early story with a later unpublished sequel to it and thereby adds
a measure of artistic stature to this most unconventional writer. Two
most helpful bibliographic tools are Per Seyersted's essay review of
scholarship, "Kate Chopin (1851–1904)" (*ALR* 3:153–59), and Richard H. Potter's thorough and briefly annotated checklist of 125 books,
articles, reviews, dissertations, and theses, "Kate Chopin and Her
Critics: An Annotated Checklist" (*MHSB* 26:306–17).

A good many other regional writers continue to receive brief if
not always distinguished attention. As a part of his general study of
the influence of George Eliot on American realists of the seventies
and eighties, Jack H. Wilson's "Eggleston's Indebtedness to George
Eliot in *Roxy*" (*AL* 42:38–49) finds that Edward Eggleston borrowed extensively from *Romola* and *Middlemarch* and under this
influence wrote a serious study of character degeneration rather than
a piece of local color. Patrick David Morrow has collected all of Bret
Harte's major literary criticism in "The Literary Criticism of Bret

Harte: A Critical, Annotated Edition" (*DAI* 30:4996A–97A), and the same author has prepared an essay review of research and criticism, "Bret Harte (1836–1902)" (*ALR* 3:167–77). Joseph J. Egan takes issue with those critics who feel that Cable's worth lies in the social criticism implicit in his fiction by providing a balanced appraisal of the craftsmanship and mythic dimensions of one story in " 'Jean-Ah Poquelin': George Washington Cable as Social Critic and Mythic Artist" (*Markham Rev* 2,iii:6–7). In addition to Nathalia Wright's introduction to Mary Noailles Murfree's *In the Tennessee Mountains* mentioned above, there is a highly flattering tribute, "Local Color and Literary Artistry: Mary Noailles Murfree's *In the Tennessee Mountains*" (*SLJ* 3:154–63), in which Harry R. Warfel asserts that she was more concerned with the artistic manipulation of literary technique than with merely the photographing of places and people. A superficial summary of Miss Murfree's life, which contributes nothing new in biographical or critical insight, is Dennis Loyd's "Tennessee's Mystery Woman Novelist" (*THQ* 29:272–77).

In an admirable piece of careful research, "Attempt and Failure: Thomas Nelson Page as Playwright" (*SLJ* 3:72–82), Harriet R. Holman chronicles Page's unsuccessful attempts at drama to justify her point that he was a man of wider and more cosmopolitan interests than his reputation as a Southern local colorist suggests. Miss Holman has also edited "The Kentucky Journal of Thomas Nelson Page" (*RKHS* 68:1–16), a selection of extracts about his visits to Kentucky from an 1891 journal, and three other related collections of materials: *On the Nile, 1901* and *North African Journal, 1912*, two diaries by Page, and *John Fox and Tom Page, As They Were*, letters exchanged between the writers (all published by Field Research Projects, Coconut Grove, Miami, Florida). Lyle Glazier's "The Uncle Remus Stories: Two Portraits of American Negroes" (*JGE* 22:71–79) contrasts the views of the black as reflected in the white man's narrative framework of Joel Chandler Harris's tales and the animal fables told by Uncle Remus based on African folklore. James Milton Highsmith, "The Forms of Burlesque in *The Devil's Dictionary*" (*SNL* 7:115–27), examines with clear critical insight Ambrose Bierce's experiments in forms of burlesque in his devilishly delightful definitions and makes a strong case for calling attention to them as a high contribution to American letters, and Lawrence I. Berkove sensibly summarizes "the depth of his serious and purposeful thoughts about war" in "Arms and the Man: Ambrose Bierce's Response to War" (*MichA* 1[1969]:21–30). A balanced and sensitive appraisal of a man who fits uncertainly into American literature is found in Arthur E. Kunst's *Lafcadio Hearn* (New York, Twayne, 1969). Focusing on the poetic and imaginative side of Hearn, Kunst discusses his travel sketches, folklore, Gothic tales, and impressionistic pieces from his early days in Cincinnati and New Orleans to his final days in Japan and clarifies admirably the nature of Hearn's small but impressive accomplishment. Robert F. Coyne finds in "Lafcadio Hearn's Criticism of English Literature" (*DAI* 30:4940A) that despite their simplicity, Hearn's lectures gathered in *A History of English Literature* made a contribution to Japanese understanding of western literature. Although William E. Farrison in *William Wells Brown, Author and Reformer* (Chicago, Ill., Univ. of Chicago Press, 1969) is more concerned with his life and career as a reformer, he does summarize the facts and contents of the black author's literary output in this thoroughly researched and scholarly biography.

In the area of nineteenth-century humor, an early classic critical anthology of 1929, *Some American Humorists* by Napier Wilt, has been reprinted (New York, Johnson Reprint Corp.) with a full, original forty-page introduction by Martin Roth. Roth's essay is a fresh and perceptive reassessment of the critical importance of the humorists represented in Wilt's anthology. An important foreign anthology not noticed here before is Claudio Gorlier's *Gli umoristi della frontiera* (Vicenza, Neri Pozza Editore, 1967), an extensive collection of over 600 pages of selections from the works of Seba Smith, Thomas Chandler Haliburton, David Crockett, A. B. Longstreet, J. G. Baldwin, J. J. Hooper, T. B. Thorpe, George W. Harris, David Ross Locke, Joel Chandler Harris, Bill Nye, Artemus Ward, Finley Peter Dunne, Bret Harte, Mark Twain, and over twenty other lesser-known or anonymous writers in the frontier school. While the very thought of translating Sut Lovingood's east Tennessee dialect or Uncle Remus's slave speech into Italian is a fearful prospect, Gorlier (who knows Southern literature, culture, and speech more thoroughly than any Italian scholar) has brought it off with great skill. In addition he has prefaced the book with a fifty-one-page concise and intelligent critical introduction, thirty-six biographical notes on the humorists, and a full bibliography. James C. Austin's *Bill Arp* (New York, TUSAS, 1969) is the third of his biographical-critical volumes on American humorists for the Twayne series. Like the others it is a carefully researched and balanced treatment, in this case with special emphasis on Charles Henry Smith's "thoughts on Southern history, his use of American English, and his recording of Georgia folklore." Winston Smith's "*Simon Suggs* and the Satiric Tradition" is a contribution to *Essays in Honor of Richebourg Gaillard McWilliams*, edited by Howard Creed (*Birmingham-Southern College Bulletin* 63,ii:49–56). Drawing on his extensive knowledge of Johnson Jones Hooper's classic of frontier humor, Smith places *Some Adventures of Captain Simon Suggs* in the picaresque tradition and makes informative comparisons with *Don Quixote, Lazarillo de Tomes, Gil Blas, Modern Chivalry*, and *A Tale of a Tub*. A new edition of a standard biographical study of the first of the humorists of the old Southwest is John Donald Wade's *Augustus Baldwin Longstreet: A Study of the Development of Culture in the South* (Athens, Univ. of Ga. Press, 1969). M. Thomas Inge, editor, has corrected the typographical errors in the original 1924 text, added a bibliography of Wade's writings from 1922 to 1962, and contributed an introductory essay outlining Wade's full contribution to modern Southern letters.

George Washington Harris, the best of the Southwestern humorists, and his notorious creation Sut Lovingood continue to spark critical interest. In tune with what recent commentators have been saying, Elmo Howell asserts in fine style in "Timon in Tennessee: The Moral Fervor of George Washington Harris" (*GaR* 24:311–19) that Sut Lovingood is not the immoral representative of Southern perversion that Edmund Wilson and Kenneth S. Lynn saw in him but rather an aggressive agent against those who fail to measure up to his ideals of good behavior: "Like Gulliver among the Houyhnhnms, he is inspired by the principle of right reason in human kind and can never be satisfied again among the Yahoo kind." Ormonde Plater tackles a rich subject in "Narrative Folklore in the Works of George Washington Harris" (*DAI* 30:4461A) and the success with which he handles it is indicated in "Before Sut: Folklore in the Early Works of George Washington Harris" (*SFQ* 34:104–15), an accurate study of folk motifs and other elements of folklore in Harris's apprenticeship sporting epistles and sketches of 1843–1847. Of related interest is

George R. Ellison, "William Tappan Thompson and the *Southern Miscellany, 1842–1844*" (*MissQ* 23:155–74), an analysis of one Southern journal for its humorous literary content. Ellison's prize find, reprinted here, is a hitherto unknown "Georgia Scene" by Augustus Baldwin Longstreet. The study of American popular culture, from colonial times to the present, has been given an impressive boost through Russel B. Nye's intelligent and comprehensive survey *The Unembarrassed Muse: The Popular Arts in America* (New York, Dial Press). Relevant here are his chapters on popular nineteenth-century fiction, especially the widely read dime novels. In a specific study of this form of entertainment, "Literature as History: The Dime Novel as an Historian's Tool" (pp. 9–20) in *Literature and History*, edited by I. E. Cadenhead, (UTMS 9), as his title indicates, William A. Settle, Jr., finds that subliterary fiction contains extremely useful data for the historian, although much of what he says is derivative. Frederick R. Lapides, "John Beauchamp Jones: A Southern View of the Abolitionists" (*JRUL* 33:63–73), describes and summarizes a popular novel by an undistinguished Baltimore author, *Border Way* by John Beauchamp Jones (1859; republished in 1861 as *Secession, Coercion, and Civil War: The Story of 1861*), interesting for its use of a dream vision of the coming Civil War and its anti-abolitionist but pro-Union sentiment. George Lippard appears to be a popular novelist who is undergoing a minor revival. He is resurrected in typical Fiedler-style, in Leslie Fiedler's "The Male Novel" (*PR* 37:74–89), as author of a scandalous socialist novel of 1844, *The Quaker City; or, The Monks of Monk Hall.* Only Norman Mailer's *An American Dream* is close to what Lippard was doing, says Fiedler: a subpornographic popular novel for males. A more sedate and scholarly summary of Lippard's career is found in "The Chapter of Perfection: A Neglected Influence on George Lippard" by Carsten E. Seecamp (*PMHB* 94:192–212), who focuses on the influence of historical circumstances at Wissahickon Creek, near Germantown, Pennsylvania, on Lippard's socialistic theories (especially the religious fraternity of German mystics known as the Chapter of Perfection). A comprehensive critical biography of Lippard as "a representative American giving expression to widely held social, political, religious, and literary principles" has been attempted by Emilio De Grazia, "The

Life and Works of George Lippard" (*DAI* 31:741A). Leslie Fiedler
has also edited an edition of Lippard's *The Monks of Monk Hall*
(New York, Odyssey Press).

iv. Howells, Realism, and Post-Civil War Fiction

As one Howells critic noted during the season here under review,
"For some ten or fifteen years now a portion, at least, of the scholarly
and critical world has hovered on the edge of a 'Howells Revival'
that has never come about. Indeed, although we teeter constantly on
the brink, we seem also to be as secure from precipitous fall as we
were in the days when Gertrude Atherton, C. H. Grattan, and Sinclair
Lewis described the Dean as Old Nobodaddy himself." One has but
to add to this accurate statement that the Howells criticism for 1970,
though plentiful in quantity, is of such a generally mundane quality
that it isn't likely to inspire much reading of his novels, much less
generate a Howells revival. Should a revival occur, however, we will
at least be prepared for it with dependable, authoritative texts,
which continue to appear in the CEAA-approved *Selected Edition
of W. D. Howells* (Bloomington, Ind. Univ. Press). The two recent
volumes are: Volume 17, *"The Shadow of a Dream" and "An Imperative Duty"*, introduction and notes by Martha Banta, text established by Martha Banta, Ronald Gottesman, and David J. Nordloh,
and Volume 20, *The Son of Royal Langbrith*, introduction and notes
by David Burrows, text established by David Burrows, Ronald
Gottesman, and David J. Nordloh. With the editorial apparatus kept
to a concise but useful minimum, these are among the most attractive
and readable volumes appearing under the auspices of the CEAA.
Destined for the Indiana edition is David J. Nordloh's "A Critical
Edition of W. D. Howells' *Years of My Youth*" (*DAI* 30:4997A),
with a text established according to CEAA standards.

The only book-length study devoted to Howells to appear in 1970
is James L. Dean's *Howells' Travels Toward Art* (Albuquerque,
Univ. of New Mex. Press), a specialized critique in that it focuses
solely on the nine volumes of travel writing produced by Howells
from *Venetian Life* (1866) through *Familiar Spanish Travels* (1913).
With critical sensitivity and skill, Dean traces Howells's developing
techniques and proves him to be "an uncommonly good writer of
travel literature, for it is his unique talent to find new adventure in

old places, to discover the extraordinary in the ordinary, and to impart to the common and incidental the luster of art. . . . Howells does more than practice the craft of travel writing; he demonstrates that he knows much about the theory underlying his practice. By considering such matters as vision, role of the narrator, function of irony and humor, appropriate style, and use of art and history in a travel account, he convincingly shows his awareness of the necessities of his craft and the value of travel literature as a means of revelation and discovery." This study is as conclusive or definitive an account of the subject as we are likely to have, but while Dean clearly confirms Howells's considerable accomplishment in travel literature, it is doubtful that the books discussed will experience a revival among general readers.

Modern Fiction Studies devoted its autumn issue to a "William Dean Howells Special Number." Only two of the seven original essays are particularly distinctive: Joseph H. Gardner's "Howells: The 'Realist' as Dickensian" (*MFS* 16:323–43) and Sanford E. Marovitz's "Howells and the Ghetto: 'The Mystery of Misery' " (345–62). Gardner notes an interesting paradox: "To Howells, Dickens was a novelist who, by all rights, ought to be bad, but who turned out to be one of the major, one of the great figures of our literature. To us, Howells ought to be good, but in fact, novel by novel, his works turn out to be deeply disappointing." Gardner's examination of this paradox, by way of a detailed discussion of the relationships between the writers, is elucidating. Marovitz questions the profundity of Howells's presumed awakening to social responsibility during the eighteen-eighties: "His desire to identify with the 'struggling mass' and support social advancement in a rapidly urbanizing America were implacably checked by his more worldly ambition to dwell comfortably in good society." The evidence Marovitz marshalls is fairly convincing that Howells's commitment to social problems was "as ephemeral as his sensitivity for the poor and the Jews was shallow." Each of the remaining essays has its point, though specialized and seldom innovative: James W. Tuttleton's "Howells and the Manners of the Good Heart" (271–87), Charles L. Campbell's "Realism and the Romance of Real Life: Multiple Fictional Worlds in Howells' Novels" (289–302), Jerome Klinkowitz's "Ethic and Aesthetic: The Basil and Isabel March Stories of William Dean Howells" (303–22), Marion W. Cumpiano's "Howells' Bridge: A Study of the

Artistry of *Indian Summer*" (363–82), and Tom H. Towers's "'The Only Life We've Got': Myth and Morality in *The Kentons*" (383–94). The usual *MFS* checklist of criticism, this one by Maurice Beebe, complements the issue and is an excellent supplement to the annotated bibliography by James P. Woodress and Stanley P. Anderson published as a special issue of *ALR* in 1969.

The best of the other general essays on Howells is "William Dean Howells: Reverie and the Nonsymbolic Aesthetic" by William C. Fischer, Jr. (*NCF* 25:1–30), a subtle, extensive analysis of Howells's use of the reverie convention and how "certain kinds of psychic energy and moral value associated with the reverie ambiguously converge to produce a particular aesthetic perspective, one that tends to limit both his conception of artistic truth and the literary style by which that truth can be represented." Not easily summarized, this essay repays a careful reading. Arthur Boardman, in "Howellsian Sex" (*SNNTS* 2,i:52–60), reaches the fairly obvious conclusion that Howells "associates animal sex with the lower levels of society in his fiction . . . [and] tends to think of sex in connection with the high levels of society as something else, namely ideal love." His second conclusion, that this tendency is a contradiction of his own critical theories, needs qualification and further support which does justice to Howells's qualifications offered in *Criticism and Fiction*. Clare R. Goldfarb, "William Dean Howells' *The Minister's Charge*: A Study of Psychological Perception" (*Markham Rev* 2,i[1969]:1–4), affirms that Howells could and did deal with the psychology of sex, and along with his recently developed social consciousness in *The Minister's Charge*, he also demonstrated an awareness of sexual motivation behind his characters' behavior. While a little heavy on the Freudian line of interpretation, a reasonable case is made out for Howells's realistic perception of sexuality. In "The Transcendental Phase of William Dean Howells" (*ESQ* 57[1969]:57–61), Marilyn Baldwin gathers evidence for the influence of the Swedenborgian mysticism of Howells's youth on the social philosophy of the mature man. A revealing comparative analysis of a personal and literary relationship is Berit S. Johns's "William Dean Howells and Bjørnstjerne Bjørnson" (*Americana Norvegica* 2[1968]:94–117), which discusses the evidence for Bjørnson's influence on Howells's theories of realism and fiction. We need more such studies which remind us that the republic of letters is universal. James Woodress, in "An Interview with Howells" (*ALR* 3:71–75), reprints an interview from the *New York Sun* of February 6, 1898, in which Howells indicates his preference for the term "naturalism" to describe what he previously called "realism" and predicts that the development beyond naturalism is psychological fiction.

Francis Albert Berces asks, in "Mimesis, Morality and *The Rise of Silas Lapham*" (*AQ* 22:190–202), whether a "realistic" novel can be forcefully moral without distorting its historical elements or injuring the quality of its realism, according to Howells's aim. He explores the question by measuring Howells's mimetic and moral principles against those concepts found in Plato's *Republic* and Aristotle's *Poetics*, using *The Rise of Silas Lapham* as an example, an exercise which throws useful light on Howells as an artist and that novel in particular. While *April Hopes* (1888) has generally been consigned to oblivion by critics, Howells noted in 1896 that it was the first novel he wrote with the distinct consciousness that he was writing as a realist. In order to discover what he meant by this, Kermit Vanderbilt, in "The Conscious Realism of Howells' *April Hopes*" (*ALR* 3:53–66), compares the novel with the theoretical statements he was making in *Harper's* "Editor's Study" columns as he wrote it and finds that the novel dramatizes and reinforces his esthetic ideas—an elucidating piece of criticism. Kenneth Andersen's "Mark Twain, W. D. Howells, and Henry James: Three Agnostics in Search of Salvation" (*MTJ* 15:13–16) contains a debatable explication of *A Hazard of New Fortunes* as reflective of Howells's agnosticism and pragmatic faith that salvation is achieved only in this world through a higher awareness of man's responsibility to his society. In a minor note, "The *Medea* Howells Saw" (*AL* 42:83–89), Gerard M. Sweeney provides evidence that the production of *Medea* which was observed by Howells in 1875 and inspired *A Modern Instance* was a romantic German melodrama written by the Austrian, Franz Grillparzer, rather than Euripides' classical play.

Four dissertations completed this year maintain the high degree of interest among graduate students in Howells: Harvey M. Sessler, "Concept and Craft: Sources of Ambiguity in Howells' Novels" (*DAI* 30:3476A); Joseph Hogue Gardner, "Dickens in America: Mark Twain, Howells, James, and Norris" (*DAI* 30:4409A–10A); James Edward Woodard, "Pragmatism and Pragmaticism in James and Howells" (*DAI* 31:408A); and James William Taylor, "The Swedenborgianism of W. D. Howells" (*DAI* 31:735A–36A). David J. Nord-loh's "Eating Off the Same Plates: First Editions of W. D. Howells in Great Britain" (*Serif* 7,i:28–30) is a bibliographical note on the pub-lication of British editions of Howells's novels to secure copyright protection abroad and the significance of such data to the bibliog-rapher. Rudolf and Clara M. Kirk provide in the "Kirk-Howells Col-lection" (*LC* 35[1969]:67–74) a description of books, manuscripts, photostats, and other materials by and about Howells given by the authors in 1963 to the University of Pennsylvania's Van Pelt Library.

The most intriguing literary biography published this year in the area of nineteenth-century fiction is Maurice Bassan's *Hawthorne's Son: The Life and Literary Career of Julian Hawthorne* (Columbus, Ohio State Univ. Press). For a man who in his day was compared favorably with George Eliot, Henry James, and Howells, the total eclipse of the reputation of this son of a giant is indeed strange. In explaining his decline, Bassan says with admirable candor that Haw-thorne "was a fascinating but shallow man, and his works reflect more of the shallowness than of the fascination. . . . Yet, surprisingly, there are quite genuine if rare treasures scattered here and there in the work of the younger Hawthorne, treasures that ought to be recov-ered unapologetically." Bassan examines the influence of the father on the son's literary theories, analyzes Julian Hawthorne's works (his fiction appeared between 1873 and 1911, including twenty-six novels and six collections of stories), and identifies those writings worth serious attention. Perhaps the freshness of the material contributes to the pleasure with which one reads this book, but much credit be-longs to the author who has woven his careful research into such a readable and sensible narrative. Julian Hawthorne has clearly re-ceived his due.

Minor American Novelists, edited by Charles Alva Hoyt (Car-bondale, So. Ill. Univ. Press) includes chapters on DeForest and Chesnutt. "John William DeForest's 'Great American Novel'" by E. R. Hagemann notes DeForest's little-successful effort to produce a series of novels describing the social, economic, and political his-tory of the United States, a point which does nothing particularly to enhance his reputation. Robert M. Farnsworth provides, in "Charles Chesnutt and the Color Line," a contemporary review of his achieve-ment and finds what is already quite clear, that in his best and most biting work Chesnutt challenged the prejudices of the dominantly

white reading audience. In his well-known pattern of literary rediscovery, Edmund Wilson undertook the assessments of two late
nineteenth-century novelists in his pleasantly readable *New Yorker*
style: "Two Neglected American Novelists: I—Henry B. Fuller: The
Art of Making It Flat" (*NY* 46[May 23]:112–16,120–22,125–27,131–
32,134,137–39) and "Two Neglected American Novelists: II—Harold
Frederic, the Expanding Upstater" (*NY* 46[June 6]:112–14,117–19,
123–26,129–34). Like the faithful graduate student, Wilson summarizes the available scholarship (with his usual barbed asides for
academics), provides plot summaries for the seldom read novels,
and adds spice by paying unnecessary attention to his subjects' sex
lives—Fuller's discreet homosexuality and Frederic's excessive hetero-
sexuality. His point seems to be that both authors deserve attention
for their skilled use of local background (Chicago for Fuller and
upstate New York for Frederic) and their membership in "a kind of
underground of real social critics and conscientious artists." Yet Wilson adds little that is new or important to our appreciation of these,
indeed, worthy writers whose work deserves modern scrutiny. Contending that Frederic's first novel has been misinterpreted, Richard
VanDerBeets objects to previous views that the novel is centrally political or a work of comic realism ("Harold Frederic and Comic Realism: The 'Drama Proper' of *Seth's Brother's Wife*," *AL* 39[1968]:553–
60). The novel itself and the unpublished dramatic version, *Seth*,
refute such views and show it to be a strong indictment of rural life
and the Agrarian Myth. Darrel Abel's "Expatriation and Realism in
American Fiction in the 1880's: Henry Blake Fuller" (*ALR* 3:245–57)
is the first publication of an 1886 essay by Fuller on the state and
prospects of American literary realism. Edward Magdol, in "A Note
of Authenticity: Eliab Hill and Nimbus Ware in *Bricks Without
Straw*" (*AQ* 22:907–11), finds historical prototypes for characters in
Albion W. Tourgée's novel, which he asserted was drawn from life.

   In addition to the articles already mentioned elsewhere, *American
Literary Realism* published its annual bumper crop of checklists,
essay reviews of scholarship, and notes on such figures as David
Graham Phillips, Harris Merton Lyon, Zona Gale, Ridgely Torrence,
Harold Frederic, John William DeForest, Richard Harding Davis,
Abraham Cahan, and Robert Herrick. One of the little pleasures of
this fine journal is its sense of humor, as conveyed through cartoons
and other materials reprinted from nineteenth-century periodicals.

v. Stephen Crane

The University of Virginia edition of *The Works of Stephen Crane* (Charlottesville, Univ. Press of Va.), under the editorship of Fredson Bowers, continues the excellent beginning it made last year with the publication of two further volumes of CEAA-approved texts: volume 5, *Tales of Adventure*, introduction by J. C. Levenson, and volume 6, *Tales of War*, introduction by James B. Colvert. The excellent introductions by Levenson and Colvert, which are informative blends of biography and criticism and in themselves represent important contributions to Crane scholarship, and the patient and thorough textual introductions by Bowers, all contribute to a most intelligent and fruitful scholarly endeavor. No book length studies devoted to Crane appeared this year, except for Joseph Katz's *Stephen Crane: The Blue Hotel* (Columbus, Ohio, Charles E. Merrill Literary Casebook series), a thorough and useful collection of critical comment on this popular story. *Essays in Honor of Esmond Linworth Morilla*, edited by Thomas Austin Kirby and William John Olive (Baton Rouge, La. State Univ. Press), includes "The Principal Source of Stephen Crane's *Red Badge of Courage*" by Alexander R. Tamke, who zealously pursues parallels in an earlier suggested source for Crane's novel, Joseph Kirkland's *Captain of Company K*, although what this should mean in our appreciation of *The Red Badge* remains unstated.

Carrying the suggestion that Crane's work draws heavily on Christian symbolism almost to the edge of absurdity, Daniel Knapp's "Son of Thunder: Stephen Crane and the Fourth Evangelist" (*NCF* 24[1969]:253–91) is a verbose, heavily detailed brief drawn up to prove that "The Blue Hotel," "The Monster," *Maggie*, and *George's Mother* are probably based directly and consciously on the New Testament, especially the gospel of John. The parallels Knapp discovers are indeed curiously striking, yet all the evidence is finally circumstantial and, if there at all, deeply buried—matters which Knapp willingly acknowledges. Most readers, however, will find it difficult to believe that Crane composed with his Bible before him opened to the Book of John, or how to account for his esthetic purpose of so doing. One is led to envision an incongruous scene late one evening in the Crane household in England as Cora complains, "For

God's sake, Steve. Put that damn Bible down and come to bed!"
While admitting to the validity of the current trend to perceive the
parody and sure-handed irony in Crane's work, W. M. Frohock in
"The Red Badge and the Limits of Irony" (*SoR* 6:137–48) asserts
that there is yet much in his work that such analyses do not account
for. *The Red Badge of Courage* in particular, he notes, "supports the
case that Crane's genius shows itself fully as much in his knowing
when not to parody and when to leave stereotypes and clichés intact."
Henry Fleming is examined as an example of the American version of
the bucolic swain in an essay worthy of careful consideration.

A reexamination of the question of how French impressionist
painting influenced Crane's work is found in "Stephen Crane and
Impressionism" (*NCF* 24:292–302) by Rodney O. Rogers, who suggests that his strongest link with impressionism is through his sense
of the nature of reality, and that he adopted the world view upon
which impressionism as a style depended. Toby Fulwiler's "The
Death of the Handsome Sailor: A Study of *Billy Budd* and *The Red
Badge of Courage*" (*ArQ* 26:101–12) is a comparison of two novels,
written within four years of each other, which attempts to explain
"why Melville remains forever linked to the romantic past while
Crane strikes out toward the existential future," but the comments
remain at a superficial level. Suggesting the ultimate impossibility
of satisfactorily teaching one of Crane's best stories, John T. Frederick's "The Fifth Man in 'The Open Boat'" (*CEA* 30,viii[1968]:1,
12–14) notes ways to approach it through style, sensory experience,
and point of view, and concludes that finally it is "an intense paradigm of the human situation as a whole." Richard A. Davison,
"Crane's 'Blue Hotel' Revisited: The Illusion of Fate" (*MFS* 15
[1969]:537–39), adds a gloss to the question of free will and fatalism
in Crane's story by observing that he creates the illusion of a deterministic world in which the characters stupidly abrogate their
freedom of choice. A fine explication of a Whilomville tale—"Making
an Orator"—"which examines with sharpness and high originality
the familiar nineteenth-century theme of the victimized child," has
been provided by George Monteiro: "With Proper Words (or Without Them) the Soldier Dies: Stephen Crane's 'Making an Orator'"
(*Cithara* 9,ii:64–72). Marston LaFrance, "Crane, Zola, and the Hot
Ploughshares" (*ELN* 7:285–87), locates one of Crane's metaphors

in *The Red Badge* in a variety of possible English sources, rather than as thought in the John Stirling translation of Zola's *L'Assomoir*.

The three dissertations completed should prove important: James Milton Ewing, "Figurative Language in the Prose of Stephen Crane" (*DAI* 30:4941A–42A), studies the role of figurative language in Crane's style, a quality Ewing feels distinguishes his work from other Naturalistic writing; Ellen A. R. Brown, "The Uneasy Balance: A Study of Polarity in the Work of Stephen Crane" (*DAI* 31:1220A), attempts "to demonstrate that Stephen Crane's most effective short fiction is the offspring of the critical tension between two impulses: one demanding responsibility to truth, grows from Crane's respect for experience and trust of factual details; the other asserting freedom in art, arises from his affirmation of individual vision and belief in the value of imagination"; Richard Morris Weatherford, "The Growth of Stephen Crane's Literary Reputation" (*DAI* 31:2893A) traces critical reactions to Crane's work and the unsteady growth of his reputation to the present.

A special Stephen Crane issue of *Serif* (6,iv[Dec. 1969]) contains three essays contributing useful biographical data on his relationships with several contemporaries: "Stephen Crane and Willa Cather" by Bernice Slote (3–15); "Stephen Crane and Joseph Conrad" by Austin M. Fox (16–20); and "Stephen Crane and the Harold Frederics" by Lillian B. Gilkes (21–48). Also, George Monteiro provides a note on "*The Illustrated American* and Stephen Crane's Contemporary Reputation" (49–54). In "Stephen Crane and the Biographical Fallacy: The Cora Influence" (*MFS* 16:441–61), Lillian Gilkes makes out a good case for considering biographical data in understanding an artist's works and for perceiving in Crane's writing during the London years the influence of his wife Cora, but Miss Gilkes finally pushes too many points to a specious and tenuous degree until finally one is compelled to ask—what difference does it make? She is rightly oversensitive to the mythic and symbolic interpretations imposed on Crane, yet her approach contributes little more elucidation to the finally important matter, the work of art itself. As the title indicates, Miss Gilkes's "Stephen Crane's Burial Place: Some Inconsequential Ghost Laying" (*Serif* 7,ii:7–11) provides inconsequential data about mistaken assumptions regarding Crane's burial spot. It turns out he is buried in the same cemetery with Mary Mapes Dodge, editor of *St. Nicholas* and author of *Hans Brinker*, a fact over which Miss

Gilkes expresses excessive dismay (does highbrow disdain for popular culture extend even beyond the grave?). In "Stallman's Crane" (*CEA* 31,viii[1969]:8–9), Thomas A. Gullason finds that R. W. Stallman's biography *Stephen Crane* (see *ALS 1968*, pp. 152–53) loses a sense of the man in the accumulation of minutiae, contains numerous factual errors, and displays little critical acumen. The retort by Stallman and counter-retort by Gullason in a later issue (*CEA* 32,ix:11–13) represent a kind of public backbiting which does little credit to the profession of scholarship. "The *Thoth* Annual Bibliography of Stephen Crane Scholarship" by Imogen Forster (*Thoth* 10,ii[1969]: 25–27) lists forty-eight items published from 1967 to 1969, and volume 4 of the *Stephen Crane Newsletter* (Fall 1969–Summer 1970), edited by Joseph Katz, published mostly valuable source and analogue notes, unpublished biographical and bibliographical data, letters, and checklists of recent criticism.

vi. Naturalism and the Late Nineteenth Century

Unfortunately, the works of Frank Norris are not being issued in authoritatively edited texts yet, so we must be satisfied with the occasional reprints. Some newly published material, forty-four student themes written by Norris at Harvard in 1894–1895 in Professor Lewis E. Gates's class in composition, is collected in James D. Hart's *A Novelist in the Making* (Cambridge, Mass., Harvard Univ. Press), along with reprints of his early novels *Blix* and *Vandover and the Brute*. Hart has provided a full introduction, incorporating the biographical facts of Norris's early years, an outline of the way in which he drew on his themes for his fiction, and an appreciation of the two novels. His scholarship is thorough, but textual editors will not approve of his silent correction of errors in the text of the novels, and there is an odd repetition of sentences on pages 18 and 20 (perhaps a typographical error) of the introduction. *Studies in "The Octopus"*, compiled by Richard Davison (Columbus, Ohio, Charles E. Merrill, 1969), is a useful collection of materials (three letters, nine reviews, and fourteen critical essays) on that novel. Otis B. Wheeler also examines *The Octopus* (see pp. 346–49) in a general essay, "The Sacramental View of Love in the Nineteenth and Twentieth Centuries" in *Essays in Honor of Esmond Linworth Morilla*, edited by Thomas A. Kirby and William J. Olive (Baton Rouge, La. State Univ.

Press). Although Norris rejected Victorian literary values, Wheeler says, when sexuality is approached as mystery in the novel, it takes on religious overtones, as was the case in Victorian literature. John S. Hill, "The Influence of Cesare Lombroso on Frank Norris's Early Fiction" (*AL* 42:89–91), notes parallels between the Italian physician's theory of criminal types and Norris's fiction, and James B. Stronks, "John Kendrick Bangs Criticizes Norris's Borrowings in *Blix*" (*AL* 42:380–86), takes note of an unnoticed 1899 essay by Bangs which satirically took Norris to task for his method as a novelist, especially his plagiarizing of material from the newspapers and "Sherlock Holmes" for *Blix*. A dissertation by Francis Ralph Ginanni deals with the "Impressionistic Techniques of Frank Norris" (*DAI* 31:2343A), and John S. Hill's *Merrill Checklist of Frank Norris* (Columbus, Ohio, Charles E. Merrill) is a useful selective compilation, including contemporaneous reviews of the novels.

Warren French asks "What Shall We Do About Hamlin Garland?" (*ALR* 3:283–89) and responds with a negative stance toward those who have demanded greater appreciation for and study of Garland: "Garland strikes me as one of those comparatively rare figures in literary history whose name has not endured because of his work, but whose works . . . have endured because of his personal activities." French believes that Garland is to American literature what William Jennings Bryan is to American politics—a master of "Me-Tooism" who takes bold stands against already discredited practices. Just in case French is wrong, Jackson R. Bryer and Eugene Harding make an excellent beginning on a two-part annotated checklist, "Hamlin Garland (1860–1940): A Bibliography of Secondary Comment" (*ALR* 3:290–387). Jane Frances Early establishes a reading text for an unpublished drama of 1909 vintage in "An Edition of Hamlin Garland's 'Miller of Boscobel'" (*DAI* 30:2964A), and Gertrude Sugioka Fujii's purpose in "The Veritism of Hamlin Garland" (*DAI* 31:2914A) is "to delineate the principal elements of veritism, identify its influences, and show its relationship to Garland's work and to the development of literary criticism."

As was the case last year, this survey concludes with mention of a discussion of the late nineteenth-century populist reformer and sometime novelist from Minnesota, Ignatius Donnelly—"Alliance and Antipathy: Ignatius Donnelly's Ambivalent Vision in *Doctor Huguet*" by John S. Patterson (*AQ* 22:824–45). Although the anti-semitism of

Donnelly has been the subject of spirited commentary lately, little attention has been paid to his novel *Doctor Huguet* (1891), written to counter anti-Negro prejudice and contribute to the formation of a political alliance between poor whites and blacks. Patterson finds, however, an ambivalence in Donnelly's attitude: "Donnelly consciously sought to encourage his readers to rise above prejudice, to see beyond the color of the skin, to have a proper regard for the human spirit, yet time and again his efforts are marred by his theoretical preconceptions, by his fundamental assumptions about the superiority of whiteness, by his deeply rooted antipathy to blackness." Donnelly isn't easy to read, but this intriguing critique makes him almost interesting once more.

Virginia Commonwealth University

11. Poe and Nineteenth-Century Poetry

Patrick F. Quinn

By way of preface to this chapter last year I remarked on the imbalance between the large amount of space needed for a review of work on Poe and the modest amount needed to discuss work done on the other writers who are bracketed in this chapter with him. I mentioned also the primacy of interest that Poe's fiction continues to have, and I made note of the increased attention given *Eureka*. One important change I am aware of this year is that *Eureka* is not so markedly in the ascendant. What has come to the fore in a major way is a view of Poe that stresses his achievement—hitherto overlooked or misunderstood or undervalued—in the areas of comedy, satire, and irony. This seems to me the one important new development in Poe studies. As for those other writers, some of them still considered classic, with whom this chapter is customarily concerned, the evidence continues to suggest that interest in them is not strong.

i. Poe

a. General studies. A lacuna of long standing in the Minnesota series has been filled by the publication of Roger Asselineau's *Edgar Allan Poe* (UMPAW 89). Although his name as a critic and scholar is most immediately associated with Whitman, Asselineau is at home in the various branches of American literature, and the work of Poe, not unexpectedly, has been a major interest for him. The first published indication of this was his edition of a bilingual *Choix de contes* in 1958, with an introductory essay of over one hundred pages. In the years since then Asselineau has introduced French readers to three other volumes of Poe's tales; and now we have, in effect, one more introduction, this time in English and intended primarily for an

American audience. Aside from differences in language and format the message remains unchanged: a fear of death, a fear of engulfment by nothingness, is what most of Poe's tales are about; and the intensity with which this feeling is conveyed is proof of the author's own experience of it. Not hoaxes or mere literary exercises, the tales of imagination are the emanations of unconscious cravings rather than the products of conscious effort. The Usher archetype dominated the Dupin within Edgar Poe. Through what amount to "veiled confessions" he attempted to make us "share his dreams and through the rational reveal the irrational to us." What Poe accomplished or tried to accomplish in his comic and satiric stories, in his theory and practice of literary criticism, in *Eureka*—Asselineau gives these matters the status only of sub-topics, nor is the poetry given much attention. What fascinates Asselineau is the submerged presence of the Poe psyche as it may be discerned in certain of the tales. This is his recurring thematic chord. Why, for instance, is there such a close family resemblance among Poe's more memorable protagonists? This happens, Asselineau believes, because Poe, whether he wanted to or not, took "the story of his own life as a starting point, a rather empty story on the whole, since he had mostly lived in his dreams, inspired by his neuroses and obsessed by the image of his dead mother." Here, especially in the last phrase, is a residue of the virtually unqualified endorsement that Asselineau at great length gave in his *Choix de contes* volume to the psychoanalytical theories of Marie Bonaparte. That excrescence is not present in this new monograph, but what I do regret missing is an inquiry into Poe's diction and style along the perceptive lines in which Asselineau discussed these matters in his 1958 essay.

What contribution has been made or can be made by psychoanalysis (taking the term broadly) to our understanding of what Poe wrote remains pretty much an open question. Promising to be only partially helpful, since the text is in Japanese, is an item I find listed in the current bibliography: Ichigure Ushida, "A Review of Psychological Studies on Edgar Allan Poe, 1860–1967" (*Kyoritsu Essays*, pp. 120–39). Not helpful at all, I regret to say, is the brief chapter (pp. 43–63) in Arthur Lerner's *Psychoanalytically Oriented Criticism of Three American Poets: Poe, Whitman, and Aiken* (Rutherford, N.J., Fairleigh Dickinson Univ. Press). The depth of the discussion may be gauged from this representative sentence: "Poe's early life with women and even his later relations with women were filled with a good deal of tragedy and unhappiness of all kinds."

Quite a different kind of discussion, trenchant and thorough, is that of the Swiss critic Roger Forclaz in "Edgar Poe et la psychanalyse" (*RLV* 36:272–88, 375–89). He begins by summarizing the conclusions reached by Marie Bonaparte in her *Edgar Poe: Étude psychanalytique* (1933) and proposes four areas for inquiry: the legitimacy of a Freudian interpretation of a literary work, the factual basis of the interpretations made by Mme Bonaparte, her explanation of Poe's personality and its psychological origins, and, in general, the validity of her mode of literary interpretation. In all four areas the findings prove to be decidedly negative. No suspense is aroused, however, for early in the inquiry Forclaz makes plain his irritated distaste for Freudian theory, which he characterizes as a form of scientism, mechanistic and reductive. Obviously, he implies, no good can come out of it. To demonstrate this he puts the work of Mme Bonaparte under close examination. For him she is preeminently *la psychanalyste*, if not *la psychanalyse* itself. Everyone who has formed some acquaintance with her work and has found himself variously disconcerted, bemused, and put off by it will initially at least sympathize with Forclaz's position. He deplores the way in which she ignores or dismisses evidence recalcitrant to her premises. He finds her twisting facts, converting hypotheses into facts, arriving at multiple and incompatible conclusions. What is centrally amiss, he decides, is that the analyst can "prove" just about anything, since symbols function as wild cards and these are the only cards the analyst cares to play. Forclaz's conclusion is that psychoanalytic inquiry à la Bonaparte does not provide a key to either Poe or his work, for in the end it presents only a grab bag of different interpretations, contradictory theories, and varying explanations of one and the same thing. Here is perhaps a symptom of a weakness in Forclaz similar to one for which he indicts Mme Bonaparte: a taste for the simplistic. That is, he seems to find psychoanalysis offensive primarily because of the great role it attributes to the unconscious, the irrational. Forclaz is foursquare on the side of "the laws of logic," the canons of commonsense. Why, he asks, should lurid symbols be construed out of motifs that appear in Poe's writings not as the expression of his private deliria but which are instead, as copious source studies demonstrate, the result of his extensive reading? Or again, in the instance of "Hans Pfaall," why bother with psychoanalytic guesses when we have from Poe himself an explanation both of the origins of this story and of its burlesque aspect? But literary critics, as well as psychoanalysts, would have little to do if the principle implicit here were to become generally established. Excessively polemical, the Forclaz essay tries to demolish *any* claim on serious attention that *Edgar Poe* may be thought to have. I prefer the appraisal made by G. R. Thompson: "Bonaparte's book, for all its faults, is strangely provocative and insightful."

Thompson makes this remark in an extensive bibliographical essay at the end of his anthology *Great Short Works of Edgar Allan Poe* (New York, Harper and Row). His judgment is worth notice for it comes from a scholar who, as the introduction to this anthology shows, admires Poe as a highly conscious artist who was in control of his work at every point. The conventional and by no means implausible theory that duality is the key to Poe is put aside by Thompson. He proposes instead a unitary key, irony: "Almost everything that Poe wrote is qualified by . . . a prevailing *irony* in which the artist presents us with slyly insinuated mockery of both ourselves as readers and himself as writer. The view of art (and life) informing both the tales and the poems, and to an extent the criticism, is that of skeptical dissembler and hoaxer, who complexly, ambivalently, and ironically explores the fads of the Romantic Age." In support of this thesis Thompson asserts that the literary movement associated primarily with the work of Hoffmann, Tieck, and the Schlegels—Romantic Irony—was Poe's basic intellectual and artistic milieu. Of interest to this school were investigations into psychology and the occult. Poe also shared with these German writers a pessimistic feeling about human ability to break through the web of illusion that was existence itself. In response to this feeling they developed a liberating theory of the "darkly comic," which would enable perception and expression "of the element of Absurdity in the mysterious contrarieties of the Universe." In sharper focus the Thompson thesis is this:

> The whole of Poe's Gothic fiction can be read not only as an ambivalent parody of the world of Gothic horror tales, but also as an extended grotesquerie of the human condition. Nothing quite works out for his heroes, even though they some-times make superhuman efforts, and even though they are oc-

casionally rescued from their predicaments. . . . The universe
created in Poe's fiction is one in which the human mind tries
vainly to perceive order and meaning. The universe is deceptive. . . . In its deceptiveness, the universe of Poe's Gothic
fiction seems not so much malevolent as mocking or "perverse."
The universe is much like a gigantic hoax that God has played
on man. Thus, the hoaxlike irony of Poe's technique has its
parallel in the dramatic world in which his characters move.
[p. 37]

Irony, ambivalence, tough-mindedness, the absurd—these are chief
among the interests and values that Thompson discerns in Poe, and
it is in these terms that he reviews his work. Surprisingly, some of the
poems looked at by Thompson lend themselves quite well to this
approach. But if one were asked to collect evidence that Poe liked to
spoof his readers would one not begin at the beginning, with some
examples of Poe's aesthetic theorizing? Such as: "In the whole composition there should be no word written of which the tendency, direct
or indirect, is not to the pre-established design." Thompson accepts
this at face value, and he taxes our credulity by affirming that Poe
observed this principle in all the sixty-eight tales he wrote. Although
Thompson's introduction is a long one he does not have space to
develop that point, or to sustain another large affirmation, viz., that
Poe is "one of the great ironists of world literature." But a thesis as
complex and implicative as Thompson's requires book-length treatment. Meantime, another sampling of it may be found in his "Poe's
'Flawed' Gothic: Absurdist Techniques in 'Metzengerstein' and the
Courier Satires" (*ESQ* 60Sup.:38–58)[1] and in his shorter, more
incisive article, "Unity, Death, and Nothingness—Poe's 'Romantic
Skepticism'" (*PMLA* 85:297–300). *Eureka* is the principal text examined. Together with some of the tales of exploration, which are
glanced at in passing, Poe's final work leads Thompson to conclude
that Poe's major theme is the *possibility* that the terms "ultimate"
and "nothing" are interchangeable.

   That Poe's first efforts in fiction were in the areas of comic and
satiric writing—burlesques, parodies, and hoaxes—that he continued
to experiment with these genres throughout his career are consider-

   [1] This supplement to *ESQ* 60, edited by Richard P. Benton, is available in
book form: *New Approaches to Poe: A Symposium* (Hartford, Conn., Transcendental Books).

ations emphasized by Claude Richard in "Les Contes du Folio Club et la vocation humoristique d'Edgar Allan Poe" (pp. 79–96), Richard's contribution to the collection of essays he has edited, *Configuration critique de Edgar Allan Poe* (*RLM*, no. 193–98 [1969]). More thoroughly than anyone else, Richard has followed up on the suggestion made in 1931 by James Southall Wilson that a parodic intention is to be found in some of Poe's tales, and that this intention might be clarified by the documents in which Poe mapped out his plans for a volume of seventeen tales "of a bizarre and generally whimsical character." Richard surveys the pertinent evidence in Poe's letters and elsewhere, and then, on a mere inferential basis, he tries to show that these Folio Club tales were designed as *pastiches* of the tastes and mannerisms of certain contemporary writers. "King Pest," for instance, is the tale told by that club member who is benighted enough to admire the moralistic fiction of Disraeli. The presence of a similar gimmick, Richard maintains, is demonstrable in each of the tales. As for what he calls Poe's "vocation humoristique," several suggestions are made. Poe admired Sterne, but he was not a humorist in the Sterne manner, nor is he like Dickens or Thackeray. His kinship is rather with the Pope of the *Dunciad*: both are agitated by the same kind of anger, and, as Richard puts it, in underlining the parallel, "les sots qui se pressent autour du nouveau trône de Dullness sont les romanciers britanniques et leurs plats imitateurs américains." Poe's brand of humor in the Folio Club tales has a serious purpose, for he uses it as an instrument of literary criticism to indicate his reservations about some of the ruling conventions in contemporary writing. Richard concludes that Poe should not be seen, on the basis of these tales, as a heavy-handed humorist, a merely inept entertainer, but rather as a demanding critic, an artist who can govern the special effects he wants in what amounts to a denunciation of the decadence of the creative imagination.

Poe's plans for the Folio Club enterprise are summarized at the outset of a wide-ranging article by Robert Regan, "Hawthorne's 'Plagiary'; Poe's Duplicity" (*NCF* 25:281–98). Regan believes, as do Thompson and Richard, that the aspect of Poe revealed by those plans deserves careful study. "It has been widely assumed," Regan says, "that Poe gave up his Folio Club antics at an early date, but I can find no evidence to support such an assumption." The particular bit of antic behavior which Regan investigates is Poe's allegation, in his May 1842, review of *Twice-Told Tales*, that there are in "Howe's Masquerade" some details stolen from "William Wilson." Poe in fact had no case at all—the dates of publication render his charge baseless —as he himself must have known. And yet in the same issue of *Graham's* in which he made this charge he, as editor, published his "The Mask of the Red Death: A Fantasy," in which story there are several striking parallels with "Howe's Masquerade" and with the three other "Legends of the Province House." In his explanation of this curious behavior Regan decides, after a devious but cogent train of speculation, that Poe was *testing* his readers, defying them to discover that the really culpable plagiarist, given the evidence in front of them, was not Hawthorne but his accuser. Hence Regan sees Poe's forte as duplicity rather than irony, in this definition of the terms: "The intention of the writer who employs irony is that the reader shall, perhaps after momentary difficulties, decipher his code; the intention of the writer who employs duplicity is that his code baffle as many readers as possible." Is the truly alert reader of Poe, then, engaged in a form of cryptanalysis? Regan thinks so. But a difference is that Poe's plain text retains multiple meanings. There are various valid ways of reading "The Masque of the Red Death," for instance. But bascially it is, Regan believes, "an exercise of wit, a colossal spoof," the serious elements in it existing "in splendid concert" with the element of parody.

What, by the way, was Poe's real opinion of Hawthorne? Why in his first comments, in 1842, did he extol Hawthorne's originality and then in 1847 deny that he was original in any way? In "Poe et Hawthorne" (*EA* 32[1969]:351–61), Claude Richard looks into these two questions. He reminds us of Poe's generally negative attitude towards allegory and didacticism, and shows that Poe's positive response to Hawthorne in 1842 was not a statement of personal opinion but an echoing of the way Hawthorne was being praised in publications that hewed to the line of the Democratic party. But in 1847, following his break with the Young America group, Poe reversed himself, turning against the Democrats and their man, Hawthorne. The whole affair, then, as Richard reconstructs it, was essentially extra-literary in character; and one regrettable consequence of this is that Poe's comments "sur l'art de son plus grand contemporain ne puissent pas nous aider à mieux pénétrer les complexités de ses propres créations."

One way of dealing with some of those complexities is proposed by Alice Chandler in " 'The Visionary Race': Poe's Attitude Towards his Dreamers" (*ESQ* 60Sup.:73–81). Her major point is that Poe, as his career continued, revised his opinion about imagination and illusion. What he wrote before the 1840s "increasingly criticizes the destructiveness of a dualistic universe in which the ideal can only be achieved through the destruction of the real," as in "MS. Found in a Bottle" and "Berenice." But Poe's later work, his detective stories and, especially, "The Domain of Arnheim," imply his vision of a monistic world, in which art is both creative and redemptive. In "Arnheim" the portrait of Ellison culminates this development: a man in control of his actions and under no compulsion to escape through dreams, he is not doomed to the madness-and-death punishment visited on Poe's earlier visionaries. Presumably the shift took place as Poe's metaphysical and cosmological notions altered in the 1840s. Poe came to see matter and spirit not as disjunct but continuous; and, as if by corollary, the Poe protagonist becomes enabled to move from reality to dream without having to experience a breakthrough or breakdown.

There is a somewhat similar orientation in Sheldon W. Liebman's "Poe's Tales and his Theory of the Poetic Experience" (*SSF* 7:582–96). Liebman suggests that some of the more interesting stories may be read as if they were aesthetic allegories, reflecting what Poe believed to be the two major events of the poetic experience, the pursuit of beauty and knowledge, and the making of a poem. The pattern seems to be (a) failure of the pursuit, followed by (b) poetic creation, an equally futile effort to realize the unattainable Ultimate. This movement from "imagination" to "construction" is circular only. Having written his poem the poet finds that it only arouses the sense of the beautiful all over again. The mysterious and beautiful woman (who is Imagination in this theory) "comes back from her tomb, the murderer confesses his crime of self-destruction, and the poet is compelled to begin another quest." I gather that Liebman's theory is akin to Wilbur's in that the fictional action is interpreted as an allegory of dream-experience within the poet's mind. Hence the stories are created works about the work of literary creation, specifically the writing of poems.

As if having the Chandler and Liebman articles in mind, Robert Shulman remarks that "the most interesting Poe criticism of the last decade has established that Poe's aesthetic and cosmology are central to an understanding of his fiction and poetry" ("Poe and the Powers of the Mind," *ELH* 37:245–62). But instead of continuing this line of inquiry Shulman elects to return to the much traversed terrain of the psychological revelations that are conveyed by Poe's fiction. He points out the difference between these two orientations: Poe's aesthetic and cosmological thorizing is all rather lofty and abstract, providing no account of "what the tarn, the abyss, and the dark, hidden chambers in his fiction suggest—that realm associated, not with supernal Beauty, but with conflict, chaos, hostility, and fear, the depths his power comes from, much as Poe would like it otherwise and prettier." And this creative power of his is most strikingly manifested in his representations, at once precise and suggestive, of irrational and destructive forces, of turbulent states of mind and feeling. In "The Masque of the Red Death," for instance, Poe's concern is not with the *morality* of isolation, as Hawthorne's would be; Poe is picturing how irrationality works. In "Hop-Frog" we have Poe's insights into a complex of experiences he was intimately acquainted with: the destructive powers of hostility, drink, thwarted creativity. Hop-Frog is Poe's portrait of the alienated artist who was himself. Shulman moves on to other tales, notably "A Descent into the Maelström" and "The Black Cat," with further precise and suggestive commentary.

An article concerned not with subject matter or themes but with the medium through which these are handled is Donald B. Stauffer's "Poe's Views on the Nature and Function of Style" (*ESQ* 60Sup.:23–30). The views as described prove to be rather superficial. Uncharacteristically, Poe was not interested in defining his critical terms. Thus he uses the words *manner, tone, style* sometimes as synonyms and sometimes not. The best that Stauffer can do with *style*, then, is to say that by it Poe meant something like "artistic use of the resources of language." His own style as a writer of fiction reveals an increasing commitment to rational values; and this is evidence, Stauffer hypothesizes, of how he "tried to impose an order and unity upon an existence and a universe which confronted him unceasingly with the threat of disintegration."

One of Poe's ways of responding to that threat was to fall back on the fantasy of the Edenic Garden. This is the dominant motif in "The Landscape Garden," "The Domain of Arnheim," and "Landor's Cottage," a curious pictorial trio examined by Jeffrey A. Hess in "Sources and Aesthetics of Poe's Landscape Fiction" (*AQ* 22:177–89). The sources Hess brings to light are two works by the landscape architect

Andrew Jackson Downing and, especially in regard to "Arnheim," Thomas Cole's paintings in his series "The Voyage of Life" and Cole's own commentary on that work. Poe appears to have studied both. What the three pieces imply about Poe's aesthetic theory, Hess concludes, is consistent with what Poe said more directly elsewhere: artistic perfection, as in the ideal landscape garden, can only be briefly and indeterminately glimpsed.

b. **Fiction and poetry.** If present trends continue it seems possible that *Arthur Gordon Pym* will one day rival "Usher" in the amount of attention given it. Of the several new essays that have appeared the briefest and least innovative is David M. LaGuardia's "Poe, *Pym*, and Initiation" (*ESQ* 60sup.:82–84). The focus is on the initiation theme as seen in the context of "Rip van Winkle" and *The Rime of the Ancient Mariner*. In her "Deceit and Violence: Motifs in *The Narrative of Arthur Gordon Pym* (*EJ* 59:206–13), Josie P. Campbell tends to overestimate the originality of her principal contribution, the emphasis she gives in her reading to the two motifs named. Their importance has been noticed before. But other of her observations are new and worth attention, especially those concerned with the way details in the prologue relate to details that are found later. Everything in the first half of *Pym*, she says, is made symbolic in the second half. In general, her essay argues that there are parallels of a meaningful kind among the episodes of the story, and it seeks in this way to diminish the force of the Cecil-Ridgely-Haverstick-Moss contention that *Pym* is a collection of narrative splinters. Problems, and some possible answers to them, involved in the preparation of an annotated edition of this work are discussed by J. V. Ridgely in "The Continuing Puzzle of *Arthur Gordon Pym*: Some Notes and Queries" (*PN* 3:5–6). Of most interest and difficulty is the problem of deciding what Poe was up to when he "quoted" Tsalalian words and phrases. Is this, Ridgely asks, a problem for the student of comparative linguistics or of cryptography, or is *hoax* the simple answer? A Tsalalian word is made the most of in Evelyn J. Hinz's lively and original essay " 'Tekeli-li': *The Narrative of Arthur Gordon Pym* as Satire" (*Genre* 3:379–99). This essay touches on a number of interesting considerations, but its main contention is that the story should be read for what it successfully is, a Menippean satire, and not a bungled effort at a well-made novel. What Poe does over and over again is to defeat the expectations of both Pym and the reader. Reversals of one kind and another keep recurring. The salient instance of this is that we start with the obviously archetypal situation of the young-man-on-a-journey, and we expect a development of the latent initiation theme, culminating in maturation and return. But Pym's voyage takes him instead "into milky waters and white, outstretched arms; instead of the final vision [we find] a veil; instead of awakening, drowsiness; instead of conclusion or catharsis, an abrupt *cul-de-sac*." There is plenty of movement in the story, but no progress. This, however, is the way Menippean satire (as per Frye) behaves. *Pym* is also typical of this genre in being a fragmented, episodic work, its story clumsily and very digressively told. The character of Pym is also handled satirically. Everything that happens to him calls into question the values of civilization, but he remains attached to his cliché responses, impervious to the implications of what he sees and what he says. The strange cry of the Tsalalians, "Tekeli-li, Tekeli-li," suggests primarily the warning that David deciphered at Belshazzar's feast. (Thus Poe, Miss Hinz observes, makes God a cryptographer.) The Tsalalian cry is an expression of fear or horror of whiteness, the ambiguous nature of which disturbed Poe as it did Melville. Once the satirical dimension of the work is perceived it becomes clear that the point of Pym's diatribe against the black Tsalalians—"the most barbarous, subtle, and bloodthirsty wretches that ever contaminated the face of the earth"—is to tell us something about Pym himself. In short, the racist undercurrent which some critics have noticed in the story proceeds from the narrator rather than the author.

That Poe could deal satirically with his preoccupation with the grotesque and the bizarre is made clear by "How to Write a Blackwood Article" and its companion-piece, "A Predicament." Joseph R. McElrath starts from this premise in "Poe's Conscious Prose Technique" (*NEMLA-N* 2:38–43). Despite the large promise of his title, however, he is content to make just this one point: a pair of stylistic devices spoofingly recommended in the two silly tales are employed by Poe with evident seriousness in "The Tell-Tale Heart" and "The Black Cat."

In an article written some years ago emphasizing the dramatic quality of Poe's tales, James W. Gargano demonstrated that the storytelling "I" is not be to casually equated with the story-telling author. The Hinz essay on *Pym* shows in what new light Poe can be read if that distinction is respected. But respect for it does not insure triumphs of explication. Joseph M. Garrison, Jr., for instance, in "The Irony of 'Ligeia'" (*ESQ* 60Sup.:13–17), begins his discussion by stipulating that the narrator and his dramatic situation should be seen as *données*, quite apart from Poe and his personal problems. Well and good; but the next steps seem increasingly misdirected. The narrator is writing in order to communicate with himself, hoping to reach an understanding of his obsession with Ligeia. However, hobbled by deficient self-knowledge, he is unsuccessful in this. He claims he loved Ligeia passionately, for herself, wanted her to live, and so on. Poe wants us to see through this claim and see that the man is a highly cerebral type who, without realizing it, reveals himself as unable to see that his method and assumptions are inappropriate to the quest he is on. In this reading "Ligeia" is an account of an unsuccessful epistemological inquiry. In the same Poe symposium (pp. 18–22) James W. Gargano writes more convincingly about "William Wilson," the tale in which Poe most nearly succeeded in abiding by his excessively severe requirement that every detail count. Gargano shows how the structure of the story and its symbols of light, mirror, and masks develop its psychological theme. The defining fact about Wilson is that he cannot accept himself; instead he declares war "on a potential ally and sure source of strength." Although Gargano does not use the term, what Jung meant by "the shadow" could not be better defined.

Another story about the phenomenon of psychic duality is the subject of John W. Canario's "The Dream in 'The Tell-Tale Heart'" (*ELN* 7:194–97). There are a few original observations in this essay, but for the most part it rehearses familiar considerations: the old man in the story is the alter ego of the narrator, and the relationship between the two is a classic instance of a hate / love standoff.

A different kind of story is the subject of H. Allen Greer's "Poe's 'Hans Pfaall' and the Political Scene" (*ESQ* 60Sup.:67–73). In this story Poe is having his little joke at the expense of science fiction. Presumably the dullest of Poe's readers will see this point. But only the elect among them could, without Greer's help, discover that Poe is making a covert attack on Andrew Jackson and his followers.

Whatever the major interest may be in "Hans Pfaall," no one would think of nominating it as Poe's greatest story. That eminence, according to Francis J. Henninger, belongs to "The Cask of Amontillado." In "The Bouquet of Poe's Amontillado" (*SAB* 35,ii:35–40) Henninger surveys some of the other important tales, looking particularly at what he considers the Poe hallmark: logical development leading to a surprising, unpredictable ending. He finds this pattern worked out with such consummate skill in "Amontillado" that he appraises it, one of the last stories Poe wrote, as his best; and he sees in it evidence that Poe matured in the practice of his craft during his relatively brief career.

Of the poems of Poe "To Helen" (1831) is the one currently drawing most, if not exclusive, attention. For readers interested in aural values and with the patience to follow a delicate and deliberate inquiry there is John B. Lord's "Two Phonological Analyses of Poe's 'To Helen'" (*Lang&S* 3:147–58). Of more general interest, though perhaps making too much of the connotations the name Helen *might* have, is a note by J. M. Pemberton, "Poe's 'To Helen': Functional Wordplay and a Possible Source" (*PN* 3:6–7). A more extensive set of thoughtful and imaginative observations, based firmly on the diction, rhythm, and syntax of the poem, is to be found in Arthur Schwartz, "The Transport: A Matter of Time and Space" (*CEA* 31,iii[1968]:14–15). Nonetheless, and in spite of the fact that nothing is said about the poem's meter and its rhymes, I would place at the top of the list the very careful explication which the poem receives in Alice Moser Claudel's "Poe as Voyager in 'To Helen'" (*ESQ* 60Sup.:33–37).

c. Sources. Poe understood originality as essentially the ability to find new ways of combining. His own work, when screened, proves to be original in this sense (among others); and there seems no end to the task of tracing out in what Poe wrote the combinations and permutations of details that he had picked up in the vast amount of material he read. Probably the most productive scholar in this area is Burton R. Pollin. Since 1965, when his name first appeared in the Poe section of the *MLA Bibliography*, he has published an extraordinary number of articles in elucidation of overlooked aspects of Poe's life and writings. His *Discoveries in Poe* (Notre Dame, Ind., Univ. of Notre Dame Press) brings together twelve of the more substantial of these articles. One of their distinctive features is that they each sort out a complex of interrelationships. Accordingly, the "discoveries" come in clusters. In "Poe's Iron Pen," for example, the initial question concerns "Sir Launcelot Canning," whose "Mad Trist" appears as an interior tale within the last section of "Usher." But Poe used the same fictitious name as a pseudonym for his own when, in 1843, he drew up a prospectus for the "Stylus," the magazine he hoped to establish and edit. What connection can be made between the two citations? Pollin's elaborately worked out answer proves to be an account of the growth and definition of Poe's ambition to preside, in the role of an influential editor, over American literary culture.

It has long been agreed that Poe's acquaintance with Jane Porter's romance, *Sir Edward Seaward's Narrative of His Shipwreck* (London, 1831), is reflected in "MS. Found in a Bottle." That the same work was in the back of Poe's mind while he was writing another of his sea stories is persuasively shown by Randel Helms in "Another Source for Poe's *Arthur Gordon Pym* (*AL* 41:572–75). The myriad musty pages of *Blackwood's* continue to be scrutinized for what they might reveal about the ways in which Poe's mind and imagination were influenced. Daniel E. Lees, in "An Early Model for Poe's 'The Raven'" (*PLL* 6:92–95), invites attention to an issue of *Blackwood's* containing a long, unsigned doggerel narrative entitled "The Owl." Intrinsically a wretched piece of work, it has some interest because of its thematic, metrical, and linguistic resemblances to Poe's poem. Resemblances of a much more intriguing kind are pointed out and discussed by David K. Jeffrey in "The Johnsonian Influence: *Rasselas* and Poe's 'The Domain of Arnheim'" (*PN* 3:26–29). Specifically, the resemblances are between two sublime retreats, Arnheim and the "happy valley" in Amhara, similar both physically and symbolically: both are associated with death.

d. **Biography.** The year's most important contribution in this area is a book by Sidney P. Moss, *Poe's Major Crisis: His Libel Suit and New York's Literary World* (Durham, N.C., Duke Univ. Press). Its thesis is that the nearly total eclipse of Poe's reputation in the last three years of life was owing to the antagonism aroused by publication of his "Literati" series, the first installment of which came out in May, 1846, and drew an immediate counterattack from Lewis Gaylord Clark. A later consequence was Poe's libel suit, a legal but not a financial success for him, against Thomas Dunn English. Moss's display of the evidence demonstrates that the major result of the affair was total defeat for Poe. Not only was he ostracized socially,

he was "almost literally starved out of the profession. The poverty
and persecution he suffered . . . led to his being found semiconscious
on a street in Baltimore and to his death on 7 October 1849." The
book is a documentary history of the whole sad business. Some additional light on it is provided by James B. Reece in "A Reexamination
of a Poe Date: Mrs. Ellet's Letters" (*AL* 42:158–63). Although his
was probably the better cause in the Ellet controversy, public opinion
went against him, and Poe was deplored as someone who had im-
peached the integrity of an innocent woman. Since this affair took
place early in 1846, Reece infers, Poe was a marked man even before
his "Literati" venture, with its unhappy consequences, was begun.
C. Merton Babcock in an article eccentrically entitled "The Wizards
of Baltimore: Poe and Mencken" (*TQ* 13,iii:110–15) reviews the
earlier "Autography" series, in which Poe, in the guise of a graphol-
ogist, made comments about his literary contemporaries. At first play-
ful in mood, this autographical hoax took on a caustic tone when Poe
dealt with the more important writers of the day. And what is the
relevance of Mencken's name? That Poe's hoax was taken as serious
work—it was published as such in book form in 1926—is the kind of
evidence of gullibility that Mencken loved to collect. Poe's relationship to the *Boston Notion*, a literary weekly of which Griswold was for
a while editor, is discussed, with his customary command of biographical and bibliographical minutiae, by Burton R. Pollin in "Poe and the
Boston Notion" (*ELN* 8:23–28).

e. **Miscellaneous.**   Of chief interest under this heading is Jacques
Barzun's entertaining article "A Note on the Inadequacy of Poe as a
Proof-reader and of his Editors as French Scholars" (*RR* 61:23–26).
In the first paragraph of "The Purloined Letter" there is mention of
Rue Dunôt, of the Rue Morgue, and of Marie Rogêt. This is spurious
French, Barzun tells us: the circumflex accents are *de trop*, and Poe
should have called his famous street the Rue de la Morgue. Worse
than this (and here Poe's editors are called to task) allusion is made
later in the story to four authors whose names have been let stand as
Rochefoucault, La Bougive, Machiavelli, and Campanella. By the
first of these Poe no doubt meant LaRochefoucauld. The careless
misspelling here is hardly a serious blunder. But who is La Bougive?
In the forty-one editions and reprints checked by Barzun, this name,
unquestioned, almost invariably appears. The name is meaningless,

however, being no more than a garbled printing of La Bruyère. (Barzun mentions that in the text Mabbott was preparing for his Harvard
edition the two names are correctly spelled, as they are, I notice, in
the standard French and Italian translations, both of which also de-
lete the offending circumflexes.) But it seems that errors in proofreading are unavoidable where Poe is concerned. In each of the first
two volumes of *ALS* his middle name is misspelled in the index, and
even Barzun succumbs to the fatality: as proof that Poe knew how
to spell the name of La Bruyère he points to its appearance in "The
Man in [*sic*] the Crowd."

   "The Man of the Crowd" is written from the point of view of the
unnamed narrator who participates in the action. How many such
narrators, all told, are there in Poe's fiction? To answer this question
and others like it one now need merely repair to the inventory of
characters compiled by Robert L. Gale in *Plots and Characters in the
Fiction and Poetry of Edgar Allan Poe* (Hamden, Conn., Archon
Books) and look under *Narrator*. In reducing the tales—and the
poems!—to laconic paraphrase Gale does better than one would have
thought possible. His book is an interesting one to page through, but
its importance as a reference work is not immediately evident.

   Probably of more interest to Baudelaire scholars than to readers
of Poe is Melvin Zimmerman's note on "Baudelaire's Early Conception
of Poe's Fate" (*RLC* 44:117–20). His point is that Baudelaire's metaphysical poem, "L'Irrémédiable," not only echoes several motifs found
in the fiction of Poe but is in its totality an emblematic representation
of how the French poet saw Poe: less the victim of an indifferent or
hostile milieu than of a *"Providence diabolique."* How Whitman responded to the work of Poe is sketched by way of context in Joseph
DeFalco's article "Whitman's Changes in 'Out of the Cradle' and
Poe's 'The Raven'" (*WWR* 16:22–27). This is not the first time the
two poems have been juxtaposed. DeFalco's purpose in his reexamination is to show how Whitman's revision of his poem for the fourth
edition of *Leaves of Grass* deployed echoes from "The Raven" in a
deliberate way "to put to rest once again the themes of the 'old poetry'
that he so much despised."

   Of rather tangential interest is Joan Delaney's "Poe's 'The Gold
Bug' in Russia: A Note on First Impressions" (*AL* 42:375–80). In
1847 Poe appeared for the first time in Russian translation, albeit the
text used for the purpose was an 1845 French translation of "The

Gold Bug." First impressions are lasting. This continues to be the
story by which Poe is best known in the Soviet Union.

A lecture I gave in Baltimore on the topic "Poe and France: The
Last Twenty Years" has been published as a pamphlet by the Edgar
Allan Poe Society and the Enoch Pratt Free Library of Baltimore.

ii. Longfellow, Whittier, Lanier, Riley, and Others

Under the editorship of J. Chesley Mathews, the *Emerson Society
Quarterly*, no. 58, is made up of papers on Longfellow. Biographical
interest is strong among the contributors to this symposium, as ev-
idenced by Carl L. Johnson's "Longfellow's Studies in France" (pp.
40–48) and by Richard Harwell's "Librarian Longfellow" (pp. 63–
69). In "Voices of Longfellow: *Kavanagh* as Autobiography" (pp.
3–14) Steven Allaback judges *Kavanagh* an artistic failure, but he
analyzes it as an important biographical document in his essay on
that book. One aspect of Longfellow's intellectual life is the subject
of "The Importance of Time in Longfellow's Works" (pp. 14–22), by
Phyllis Franklin. Another aspect is treated by Robert S. Ward in what
seemed to me the most interesting item in the collection, "The Influence of Vico upon Longfellow" (pp. 57–62). Ward shows that, although Longfellow's knowledge of Viconian theory was probably
second-hand, he did grasp its essentials, and its impact on him is
discernible in several of his most famous poems, especially in the
Christus trilogy.

In an article on "Mrs. Clemm and Henry Wadsworth Longfellow"
(*HLB* 18:32–42), Steven Allaback prints and comments on fifteen
letters that Poe's mother-in-law wrote to Longfellow between the
years 1850 and 1866. The patience and generosity of Longfellow are
indirectly revealed as the letters continue, but they are certainly
more memorable for the pathetic human interest they have. All the
letters request small favors, such as a small loan, an autographed
copy of a volume of Longfellow's poems, and, in one touching instance, some simple grammatical advice: "Will you please reply to
this," Mrs. Clemm writes at one point, "and tell me which is the most
correct way, 'Mary and *me* went, or, Mary and I went'."

A recurrent theme in American writing, especially the writing of
New Englanders, is the hostility of the natural environment. In Sidney Poger's " 'Snow-Bound' and Social Responsibility" (*ATQ* 1[1969]:

85–87) this theme is declared central to Whittier's poem. Whittier, it is argued, is concerned with the human group and not just the family. The feeling of nostalgia, which has been emphasized in discussions of the poem, is less important than the question of man's place in nature and the social responsibilities man must have.

Nature was the cause, and his affirmative response to it the subject, of much of the poetry of Ellery Channing. But he could not shake his diction loose from trite and bookish conventions. He agreed in theory with the "best impulses" of the Transcendentalists. As a poet he simply lacked edge, originality, or in one word, talent. This is the verdict of Robert W. Hudspeth in "Ellery Channing's Paradoxical Muse" (*ESQ* 57[1969]:34–40).

A convenient way of getting to know Sidney Lanier and his work is provided by Charles R. Anderson's anthology of Lanier's *Poems and Letters* (Baltimore, Md., Johns Hopkins Press, 1969). The notes are reprinted intact from the centennial edition that Anderson principally edited. His introduction repeats the essentials of what he wrote when he introduced volume 1 of that edition, published in 1945. It seems a pity that Anderson did not add a postscript commenting on how other scholars and critics have addressed themselves to the case of Lanier during the intervening years. A recent example of such commentary is an essay by Elmer A. Havens, "Lanier's Critical Theory" (*ESQ* 55[1969]:83–89). The upshot of this discussion is that Lanier in his thinking about literature took so moralistic a line that he had no critical theory worthy of the name.

Peter Revell's *James Whitcomb Riley* (TUSAS 159) is a serious effort, never condescending in tone, to deal with a poet who reached the height of his powers in such an item as "Little Orphant Annie." Revell concedes right off that literary criticism is irrelevant. Riley, he says, wrote nothing of lasting interest. Most of his work, judged by even the most unexacting standards, is simply bad. So the real challenge is to discover why Riley in his day was so immensely popular. Eventually, after a fair and full survey of Riley's output, Revell reverts to this question and proposes a disappointingly predictable answer, i.e., Riley pictured an image of happy small-town life in midwestern America that the reading public of the late nineteenth century wanted to believe in.

The poetry of Paul Hamilton Hayne is discussed in an even-handed way by Rayburn S. Moore in "Hayne the Poet: A New Look"

(*SCR* 2[1969]:4–13). Following the death of Simms in 1870, Hayne was generally recognized as the representative Southern poet and man of letters. But after his own death, in 1886, his reputation faded fast. In taking his new look at Hayne, Moore on the one hand calls him "the most substantial Southern poet of the nineteenth century," a poet who could, on occasion, "be as musical as Poe, as eloquent as Timrod, and as lush as Lanier." On the other hand he was, Moore recognizes, a minor bard at the end of an exhausted poetic tradition.

Primarily of antiquarian interest is Robert Mehlman's article "The Poems of Thomas Kennedy of Maryland" (*JRUL* 33[1969]:9–19). Kennedy (1776–1830) published two volumes of verse, on personal and political themes, in 1817. Mehlman writes with warmth about instances of the man's democratic activism. But Kennedy's poems? The tepid conclusion is that they "are not so poorly wrought as to make them worthless."

Some Ohio poets of Kennedy's generation are discussed by David D. Anderson in "Ohio's Pioneer Poets" (*NOQ* 42[1969]:9–18). No case is made on their behalf for belated national recognition. They are identified as early romantics, their verse is characterized as respectable, and it is suggested that what they wrote should be of interest to Ohioans with a sense of history. What I found of main interest in Anderson's article was not its central concern—the genuine "pioneer poetry" written in early nineteenth-century Ohio—but a preliminary and contextual matter, Twain's satire on pioneer poetry via the character and verse of Emmeline Grangerford.

Wellesley College

12. Fiction: 1900 to the 1930s

Warren French

This year's gathering, except for Max Westbrook's book on Walter Van Tilburg Clark, may be characterized as lightweight. Much is being written about the fiction of the first four decades of this century, but few critics are venturing beneath the generally realistic surface of this fiction. The multiplication of "newsletters" dealing with single writers makes especially necessary the separation of superficial gossip from challenging criticism.

i. General Studies

Has new critical method made us incapable of significant studies of a wide range of fiction? This question comes up in view of the continued absence of any overview of American fiction from 1900 to 1939 to supplement Kazin's, Geismar's, and Beach's now dated studies. Two recent general works exemplify the two kinds of misguided effort encountered increasingly.

Thomas Elliott Berry's *The Newspaper in the American Novel, 1900–1969* (Metuchen, N.J., Scarecrow) is based on the premise that "because the novelist's interpretations of institutions exert a strong impact on conclusions held by society, the interpretations of the American newspapers by American novelists merit a careful examination." But the examination is superficial. Because the important novelists have not written at any length about newspapers, Berry is obliged to deal principally with obscure works. One would think that the author might have had some qualms about his undertaking when he felt it necessary to observe that Faulkner "like most other major writers of his time, does not deal with the American newspaper, because it does not fall within his sphere of interest."

Bernard Sherman's *The Invention of the Jew: Jewish-American Education Novels* (*1916–1964*) (New York, Thomas Yoseloff, 1969) is a much richer book that struggles with the problem of trying to identify a distinctly Jewish-American novel and concentrates finally

on dealing with those *Bildungsromane* that concern the education of
a young man whose experiences essentially reproduce those of American Jewry as a whole. Sherman discusses at length Abraham Cahan's
The Rise of David Levinsky, Samuel Ornitz's *Haunch, Paunch, and
Jowl*, Lester Cohen's *Aaron Traum* and Eliah Tobenheim's *Witte
Arrives* as examples of "first generation" work. He chooses well and
carries the examination through another two generations but the
book lacks any central focus. Sherman jumps from one topic to
another and arrives at no conclusions. Like some other recent writers, he seems simply to be printing a series of painstakingly collected notes from which a book might eventually be fashioned; his
own work would be much more useful in the form of annotated
bibliography.

Small wonder then that by far the most useful general work
dealing with the fiction of this period is Landon C. Burns's "A
Cross-Reference Index of Short Fiction and Author-Title Listings"
of the currently available anthology of short stories, which makes
up the entire contents of the first issue of volume 7 of *Studies in Short
Fiction*, an enormously useful guide to busy instructors trying to
choose the most suitable text from the current welter of short story
anthologies.

Special mention must also be made of David Madden's *American
Dreams, American Nightmares*, which, while not pretending to be
comprehensive, gives a much better overview of American achievement in fiction from 1900 to 1940 than presumably more inclusive
studies. The separate essays will be discussed in connection with
the authors concerned; but here let me call attention to a key statement in Madden's introduction: "if serious fiction has, in the main,
been an indictment of American society for its failure to translate
the Dream into reality, or for its obstinate pursuit of the wrong
dreams, popular culture has been the multifaceted medium of American sunlit daydreams" (p. xxv). This is one of the clearest and most
satisfactory distinctions to be found between categories of works
often confused by fuzzy thinkers.

ii. The Inheritors of the Genteel Tradition

With each passing year, Willa Cather receives more affectionate attention than any other twentieth-century novelist except possibly

Thomas Wolfe. In large measure Miss Cather's reputation has been sustained by the self-effacing labors of Virginia Faulkner of the University of Nebraska Press, who explains in the publisher's foreword to the most impressive recent addition to the Cather library the rationale behind the project of preserving the apprentice writings. *The World and the Parish: Willa Cather's Articles and Reviews, 1893–1902*, edited by William M. Curtin (Lincoln, Univ. of Nebr. Press) is an admirable companion to Bernice Slote's *The Kingdom of Art: Willa Cather's First Principles and Critical Statements, 1893–1896* (see *ALS 1967*, p. 171). The two handsome volumes reproduce the previously uncollected material from Nebraska and Pittsburgh newspapers. The foreword calls attention to the quantity, range, and unusual quality of the material. These very characteristics make it impossible to summarize this work in a survey of this kind, except to suggest its importance in understanding the relationship between a developing artist and a period of rapid change.

One of the things that this book and others in the series make possible is a study like James Woodress's *Willa Cather, Her Life and Art* (New York, Pegasus), which—the author modestly explains—corrects some of the errors in E. K. Brown's *Willa Cather, A Critical Biography* (1953) and is intended to serve until "someone will be able to write the definitive biography." Woodress's straightforward, tasteful, dignified book, which places Miss Cather squarely in "the tradition of American romanticism" (p. 159), tells us, however, all that we genuinely need to know to understand the woman behind the works. Indeed the book should have been titled "Her Life *in* Art," for Woodress is especially thorough and sympathetic in revealing the ways in which Willa Cather transformed people and scenes from her life into her fictions.

The choice of Woodress as the author of this unassuming but invaluable companion to the impressive collections of Miss Cather's early writings and the paperback editions of her novels that are at last beginning to appear is especially happy because he represents the same tradition of reserve and painstaking craftsmanship that she does. He wisely avoids efforts to psychoanalyze his subject or to lose sight of the distinctly individual qualities of her work in a mythopoetic analysis; yet he provides a stable foundation for such potentially valuable efforts in an enthusiastic study that makes lively reading.

One somewhat surprising matter that Woodress emphasizes—
Willa Cather's condescending distaste for William Dean Howells—
raises problems about classifying her as an inheritor of the "genteel
tradition" that Howells epitomized. Sargent Bush, Jr.'s "*Shadows on
the Rock* and Willa Cather's View of the Past" (*QQ* 76[1969]:269–85)
argues, however, that this novel is "traditional" in T. S. Eliot's positive sense, because the author "does not typically mourn the loss of
the past, though she regrets our loss of its vitality, but rather insists
upon the need of our memory of the past to put it to constructive use
for the present and future."

Two other writers stress an affirmative quality in Willa Cather's
work. J. M. Ferguson, Jr.'s " 'Vague Outlines': Willa Cather's Enchanted Bluffs" (*WR* 7,i:61–64)—perhaps generalizing too much
about the writer's position on the basis of a single work—points out
that she shares with Eliot "a preference for the past to the present,"
but whereas his wasteland is completely arid, there is in hers a spring
that is "a haven for all who seek a religious or spiritually meaningful
life." Sister Lucy Schneider, C.S.J., in "Cather's Land-Philosophy in
Death Comes for the Archbishop" (*Renascence*, 22:78–86), analyzes
yet another Cather novel, and goes beyond Ferguson's view by
arguing that in this novel Willa Cather suggested that "a real awareness of the rhythm and pattern of life should, ideally, transcend created essence and lead to the divine" and then provided an example
of such transcendence through the characters' reaction to the Southwestern desert land.

The more traditionally humanistic quality of Willa Cather's work
is stressed in Bernice Slote's "Willa Cather as a Regional Writer," the
lead article in a special issue of the *Kansas Quarterly* (2,ii:7–15)
devoted to regional writing. Although Miss Slote discusses in detail
the novelist's use of Nebraska materials, the article begins with the
assertion that "in one sense Willa Cather was not at all a regional
writer" and ends with the explanation that her prairie novels "have
the same melancholy and nostalgia, the simplified lines, the elemental
core we find in folk songs and tales," so that they "might well be read
as folk literature with timeless appeal."

Two other distinguished women novelists often linked with Willa
Cather have received less attention lately, though both Ellen Glasgow and Edith Wharton have been the subject of recent dissertations.

Only two rather slender articles provide overviews of Mrs. Wharton's career. Hilton Anderson's "Edith Wharton as Fictional Heroine" (*SAQ* 69:118–23) examines the way in which the traits of her American expatriate characters enable us better to understand the frustrations she felt in her relationships with Edward Wharton and Walter Berry; and Margaret B. McDowell's "Edith Wharton's Ghost Stories" (*Criticism* 12:133–52) surveys these works to argue that while Mrs. Wharton's achievement does not equal Hawthorne's and James's, she felt as they did that "all readers maintain atavistically a preoccupation with, or fear of, the supernatural and reveal states of mind inherited from an earlier phase of race-culture."

Only a juvenile work, Mrs. Wharton's generally neglected first novel, has been accorded detailed analysis recently; in "Convention and Prediction in Edith Wharton's *Fast and Loose*" (*AL* 42:50–69), Viola H. Winner maintains that though the novelist herself later parodied the work, "it anticipates her larger fiction" by showing her "to have been imbued in traditional culture and the manners novel" sufficiently well to have both accepted and questioned "the conventions of literary sentimentalism."

While what might best be labeled "Easterns," by genteel male writers about the Atlantic seaboard cities, have received little attention, the study of "Westerns" in the Owen Wister manner—which must also be viewed as products of the genteel tradition, since they deal with the effort to "civilize" (perhaps "feminize") the Wild West —has flourished.

James Gould Cozzens, however, does continue to attract attention. Edward Krickel's "Cozzens and Saroyan: A Look at Two Reputations" (*GaR* 24:281–96) provides only a crotchety, conservative review of two recent novels, but James D. Boulger's "Puritan Allegory in Four Modern Novels" (*Thought* 14[1969]:413–32) is a pontifical attempt to demonstrate that *By Love Possessed*, Edwin O'Connor's *The Last Hurrah*, Ellison's *Invisible Man*, and Bellow's *Herzog* all try to dramatize the Puritan patterns of election, vocation by trial, and glorification that still hold great power in the United States. Colin S. Cass's "Two Stylistic Analyses of the Narrative Prose in Cozzens' *By Love Possessed*" (*Style* 4:213–38) is a heavy-handed analysis of sample "descriptive" and "disquisitive" paragraphs, leading to the conclusion that the need to create a narrator who could be "a convincing exponent of the reasonableness" that Cozzens believes in "helped to determine the narrative manner."

Turning to the genteel "Western," one finds founding-father Wister the subject of only one note—L. Moody Simms, Jr.'s *"Lady Baltimore*: Owen Wister and the Southern Race Question" (*Serif* 7;ii:23–26)—that shows the way in which the novelist's conservatism is revealed by his feeling that the Fifteenth Amendment to the Constitution was "a sweeping folly" and that "something between slavery and equality" would have to be worked out in the South. More comprehensive treatment is given a neglected contemporary in Delbert Wylder's *Emerson Hough* (SWS 19[1969]), which concentrates on those two of Hough's novels that are not based on the popular romantic formula of a conflict between lovers. Wylder pleads for more attention to *John Rawn* (1912), "a Dreiser-like attack on American materialism" and especially to *Heart's Desire* (1905), which shows the novelist's ambivalent reactions to the merits of East and West through a mock-heroic treatment of the disappearance of a primitive but contented Western community under pressure from the missionaries of Eastern culture.

Few other recent writings about Western authors come so sharply to grips with the fundamental issues underlying East-West conflict. Frank Gruber's *Zane Grey, A Biography* (New York, World) is a journalistic tribute by a fellow popular writer who has been granted access to family papers. Richard Skillman and Jerry C. Hoke's "The Portrait of the New Mexican in the Fiction of Eugene Rhodes" (*WR* 6,i[1969]:26–36)—handsomely illustrated with photographs of the ghost town of Eagle—makes the point that this most sophisticated of cowboy-writers observed the persecution of New Mexican ranchers "fighting almost hopeless odds against the forces of both Nature and the Establishment" with regret at the changes occurring, but without bitterness. John R. Milton's "The Land as Form in Frank Waters and William Eastlake" (*KanQ* 2,ii:104–09) concludes that, despite formal differences between the writers' works, they share the view that "man's meaning comes out of the earth, and if his relationship to the earth is a receptive and intuitive one he finds hope and contentment" in it.

John Barsness takes a less conventional view of the Western writer's situation in "Creativity through Hatred—with a Few Thoughts on the Western Novel" (*WR* 6,ii[1969]:12–17). Starting from Wil-

liam Faulkner's statement that you have to hate your country to write
well about it, Barsness argues that Western writers have been too
much in love with assumed superiority of the past over the present
and the incomparable character of Western men to produce a major
literary work. John Cawelti's "Prolegomena to the Western" (*WAL*
4:259–71) supports this view by arguing that the popular Western
"is not primarily a set of characters, events and settings, but a set of
rules or formulas for shaping many different kinds of material into a
certain pattern of experience," essentially "one in which society demands the destruction of much that is valuable in the individual
self."

Gradually critics are discovering how much the small body of
works by Walter Van Tilburg Clark departs from these formulae.
Edward H. Cohen's "Clark's 'The Portable Phonograph' " (*Expl.* 28:
item 69) identifies Debussy's "Sirènes" as the nocturne referred to in
the story, because it fuses sea imagery as life-giving energy with
music "to represent all that remains of value to man in a post-
holocaust world." Kenneth Andersen explores more general qualities
of Clark's work in two articles: "Form in Walter Van Tilburg Clark's
The Ox-Bow Incident" (*WR* 6,i[1969]:19–25) discusses the use of
structural devices of light and sound and the role of nature imagery
in shaping the novel into a voyage both through time and into the
soul; "Character Portrayal in *The Ox-Bow Incident*" (*WAL* 4:287–
98) argues that Clark uses the abstract character types of the classic
American romance of Melville and Hawthorne.

The striking exception to the general superficiality of recent criticism of early twentieth-century American fiction, however, is Max
Westbrook's *Walter Van Tilburg Clark* (TUSAS 155), a discussion of
the unconscious and "sacrality" (defined as "the belief that concrete
acts, here and now, can recreate the primordial energy and meaning
of the relevant cosmic or original act") as "the established modes of
thought" most consistently held to by Clark. Consciously departing
from the general pattern of the Twayne series, Westbrook produces
a thoughtful, original thesis that makes much greater demands on the
reader than many intensely specialized studies published by university presses and provides also greater rewards. Very briefly, Westbrook starts from the premise that because Clark has been read in the
preconceived context of the "Western" writer (as explained by John
Cawelti), he has been misread, because Clark has faced more cou-

rageously than most writers the "irony of democracy"—that "if the ultimate authority for ethics is the vote of individual men, the ultimate meaning of our history cannot be greater than man's ability in creation," so that it becomes man's paradoxical obligation "to unify his sacred self and his historical self" (p. 13).

After establishing Clark's credentials for this difficult task ("his family heritage is not the ranch . . . but a vital type of the academic," p. 24), Westbrook maintains that the problem in reading Clark is that "a writer who believes in sacrality takes an approach to actuality which is disturbing and confusing to the expectations of readers accustomed to the art of a profane world view," so that the reader must "heighten his sensibility" to read the novelist well (p. 53).

Against this background, Westbrook analyzes *The Ox-Bow Incident* not as "a plea for legal procedure," but the tragedy of self-mutilated man, "alienated from the saving grace of archetypal reality" (p. 67). He then discusses the less successful *The City of the Trembling Leaves* as an account of Clark's sacred man becoming domesticated "without surrendering his fundamental dedication to primal reality" (p. 90), and finally presents *The Track of the Cat* as the account of the development of the capacity "to see the sacred as a presence" in everyday life, without separating one's self from the mundane and falling into "the sacred doom of ecstasy" (p. 110).

Westbrook does not succeed—any more than he admits Clark does himself—in explaining clearly every step of this complicated argument that demands the same kind of heightened sensibility in the reader that Westbrook maintains Clark's novels do. He convincingly concludes, however, that "the bifurcation of the conscious self from the unconscious self and not the corruption of the frontier . . . is the central concern of Walter Clark" and argues eloquently that "Clark's explorations into the 'unspeakable' may well represent one version of the only hope we have" (p. 138).

iii. "The Redskins"—Ungenteel Voices of Protest

Exactly what differentiates the "palefaces" of the genteel tradition from their "redskin" attackers (to borrow Philip Rahv's term) is the lack (to borrow one of Westbrook's terms) of any conscious or disciplined "sacrality" in the latter (just as the former has suffered "the absolute loss of a fundamental dedication to primal reality"). Louis

Auchincloss—who has recently become one of the principal perpetu-
ators of the genteel tradition—makes us aware of the difference between the two groups in his introduction to a facsimile of the first
impression of the first edition of Dreiser's *Sister Carrie* (Columbus,
Ohio, Charles E. Merrill). After calling the novel "a perfect deter-
minist work of fiction," in which "Dreiser imbues his principal characters with much of his own attachment to life," so that he manages
to entertain us even while he "appalls" us, Auchincloss goes on to
object to what he considers an altered concept of Carrie near the end
of the book, when this hitherto rather "inert" figure is revealed as "a
dreamer." Criticism could hardly better illustrate the "gap" between
the legalistic and the intuitive minds that Westbrook argues Clark
feels must be reconciled if the American dream is not to become a
permanent nightmare.

Despite the value of Auchincloss's introduction, those teaching
Sister Carrie may find more useful another new edition by Donald
Pizer (New York, Norton), which prints along with the text a considerable amount of background material and criticism. Included is
an excerpt from the editor's "The Problem of Philosophy in the Novel"
(*BuR* 18:53–62), one of the more noteworthy recent articles, in
which material from *Sister Carrie* is used to illustrate the point that
philosophical ideas in fiction "are often inadequate guides to the interpretation of the novel in which they appear." Pizer finds that
Carrie's two illicit relationships rather than being immoral as Dreiser
suggests in chapter 8 are moral, "since they contribute to Carrie's
'spiritual' development."

The most considerable addition to Dreiser scholarship as the
centenary of his birth in 1871 neared was Ellen Moers's *The Two
Dreisers* (New York, Viking, 1969), an elegant example of the art
of bookmaking that is often unserved by scholarly publications. The
book is, regrettably, more satisfying to look at than to read. The
author turns out to share Dreiser's own penchant for "verifiable facts,"
so that the book is an aimless compilation of Dreiserana, loosely
grouped around his two "masterworks," *Sister Carrie* and *An American Tragedy*. Mrs. Moers's preoccupation with "family" indicates a
talent better suited to genealogical study than criticism. Certainly
the questionableness of such a generalization as "journalism, even
more than naturalism, seems to have changed the shape of the American novel for good in the 1890s" (p. 21) and suggests the reasons for

her difficulty in finding a thesis to unify her study, beyond an effort to adorn Dreiser with a previously unsuspected respectability by asserting that being "a genteel author" meant "the culmination of all Dreiser's ambitions" (p. 170). Perhaps the book will win new readers among those who, like Mrs. Moers, were previously suspicious of Dreiser's "coarse-minded and ill-spoken" characters; but the study of fiction is not advanced by peremptory declarations that Dreiser—or any other single novelist studied in isolation—is "perhaps the greatest of Americans" (p. ix).

Two other new Dreiser books are of little critical account, though one—Ruth E. Kennell's *Dreiser and the Soviet Union (1927–1945): A First-Hand Chronicle* (New York, International Publishers, 1969)— is a valuable source book that makes available a diary that Dreiser's secretary kept for her employer during a seventy-two-day tour of the Soviet Union, along with an appended collection of documents reflecting the long-range influence of the tour. Haskell M. Block's *Naturalistic Triptych: The Fictive and the Real in Zola, Mann, and Dreiser* (New York, Random House) simply rehashes, however, the history of *An American Tragedy* and concludes that the novel is "not a reproduction of literal reality," but a heightening and an intensification of our understanding of reality that transcends the documentary foundations that stirred Dreiser's imagination.

More provocative than such recent reconsiderations of already much discussed novels is Richard B. Hovey and Ruth S. Ralph's "Dreiser's *The Genius*: Motivation and Structure" (*HSL* 2:169–83), a "preliminary" Freudian critique of a usually lightly regarded work that meant a great deal to its author. After closely analyzing protagonist Witla's "psychosexual conflicts," which the authors see as his pursuing the pleasure principle as steadily as he can while at the same time trying to gain acceptance by a matriarchal superego, they conclude that the novel deals with dogged honesty with the practical problem of how the artist, "in the unavoidably narcissistic absorption in his own dream" and his struggle to give it form, will be able also to "meet the necessities of the flesh and survive in the everyday world."

Anticipating the Dreiser centennial conference in Terre Haute, August 17–18, 1971, Indiana State University launched in the spring, 1970, a semiannual *Dreiser Newsletter*, which has so far consisted principally of news notes, interviews with W. A. Swanberg and Ellen Moers, reviews, and bibliography. Richard Lehan's "Assessing Dreiser" (1,ii:1–3) makes large claims for the novelist on the basis that his novels "cannot be judged solely on matters of form and structure," because "every work uses a pattern of experience that is extrinsic to the work itself, and . . . every literary judgment is in part a response to that pattern of experience."

The three-year-old *Jack London Newsletter*, on the other hand, is carrying substantial critical studies of its subject. The most comprehensive of these is "Jack London's Socialism" (*JLN* 3:73–81), a chapter of Sakae Fujiwara's dissertation, which argues that despite London's sympathy for the misery of the working class, he could not accept the socialist state, because he felt that with equality, "the average strength of each generation would begin to diminish."

A principal aim of the *Newsletter* appears to be the reclamation of London from socialism, if not for Christianity, at least for traditional humanism. Edwin B. Erbentraut's "The Intellectual Undertow in *Martin Eden*" (*JLN* 3:12–24) maintains, for example, that although London called the novel a socialist's attack on extreme individualism, it shows that the author preferred a compassionate individualism to either socialism or extreme individualism. Martin Eden is made to appear almost a parallel to Christ. Erbentraut also pleads in "The Symbolic Triad in London's *The Little Lady of the Big House*" (*JLN* 3:82–89) for this generally ill-received novel on the strength of the "exuberance" of the presentation and "the shining symbolism." Stephen T. Dhondt's " 'There Is a Good-Time Coming': Jack London's Spirit of Proletarian Revolt" (*JLN* 3:25–34) also claims that although "The Apostate" is a bitter attack on the bourgeoisie, it does not end on a hopeless note, but expresses a hope for proletarian education.

Earle Labor also blasts old stereotypes through close reading in " 'To the Man on the Trail': Jack London's Christmas Carol" (*JLN* 3:90–94), discovering that in the novelist's "Northland Code," "contrary to the usual naturalistic prescription, the true guide for *human* conduct, even in the savage wilderness, is not an eat-or-be-eaten Darwinian ethic, but a situational ethic predicted upon joyous, selfless love of man for fellow man." Labor has additionally provided a revised introduction for five of the Northland stories collected in *Great Short Works of Jack London* (New York, Harper and Row), discussing the thematic development through the stories and concluding that it is the "symbolic presentation of landscape as deity—not beneficent but inviolable, stark, and above all, Absolute—which imparts to the Northland saga its philosophic integrity as well as its mythic force." In another account of Northland stories, "The Role of 'Local Color' in Jack London's Alaskan Wilderness Tales" (*WR* 6,ii[1969]: 51–56), John Nichol discusses "To Build a Fire" as an example of the way London redirected "the local color tradition from genteel superficiality to the tough and vivid re-creation of the universal in particular experiences."

Two contrasting articles stress the slicker side of London's work. Earl Wilcox's " '*Le Milieu, Le Moment, La Race*': Literary Naturalism in Jack London's *White Fang*" (*JLN* 3:42–55) describes the story as a highwater point in London's blatant use of evolutionary concepts that shows his intentness upon creating popular adventure stories buttressed by thin philosophizing rather than arguing in any systematic way for the philosophy. James R. Giles's "Some Notes on the Red-Blooded Reading of Kipling by Jack London and Frank Norris" (*JLN* 3:56–62) finds that the Americans differ from Kipling in that they do not treat other races with the respect he did and they praise violence as an end in itself, whereas he did not.

Two of the most important recent articles about London deal with the last days of his life. James I. McClintock's "Jack London's Use of Carl Jung's *Psychology of the Unconscious*" (*AL* 42:336–47) discusses a group of short stories that London wrote during the last year of his life, which derived their "scientific authority" from his reading of Beatrice M. Hinkle's 1916 edition of Jung's book. McClintock finds that "while the mature Alaskan stories dramatized the tragedy of youthful, energetic protagonists testing their vitality against the brutal forces of nature only to be drawn catastrophically toward the demonic, the irrational, and death-dealing," these last few stories "dramatize the pathos of aging and disillusioned, even cynical, men awaiting death." Alfred S. Shivers's "Jack London: Not a Suicide" (*DR* 49:43–57) presents a highly technical argument against Irving Stone's implication in *Sailor on Horseback* that London committed suicide and in support of the story that he died of uremic poisoning, as recorded on his death certificate.

The recent flurry of interest in B. Traven seems to be dying down. Neville Braybrooke's "The Hero Without a Name" (*QQ* 76[1969]: 312–18) is a generally rambling plot summary of *Death-Ship*, which argues that in all Traven's fiction, but particularly in this novel, the author fights "the dictatorial power which money invests in one man over another." John M. Warner's "Tragic Vision in B. Traven's 'The Night Visitor'" (*SSF* 7:377–84) argues against Jack Durant's conclusion that Traven does not see the human condition as tragic by pointing out the portrayal in "The Night Visitor" of the tragic dimension of reason, which isolates man from existential reality and creates for him a world of dread and anxiety.

Interest in Abraham Cahan, on the other hand, continues to grow. Cushing Strout's "Personality and Cultural History in the Novel: Two American Examples" (*NLH* 1:423–38) uses *The Rise of David Levinsky* (along with Henry Adams's *Esther*) to illustrate that "the narrative method of certain authors whose imagined chronicles, drawn directly from experience, dramatize in their lives the sort of intellectual, cultural, and psychological interplay" that Erik Erikson describes as characterizing an identity crisis. Cahan's novel, Strout maintains, modulates our understanding of the cultural strain involved in the movement of Russian Jews to America "in a way that dramatization can achieve better than any sociological generalization." Jules Chametzky considers the same novel in "Focus on Abraham Cahan's *The Rise of David Levinsky*: Boats Against the Current" (*American Dreams*, pp. 87–93) and finds it "a haunting, suggestive, and . . . finally, prophetic book" about "the spiritual malaise that seems to be at the heart" of the present rather affluent American Jewish community, which—like Levinsky—has purchased success at the expense of "inner spirit."

iv. The Iconoclasts

Although one might suspect that their work was becoming dated, the writers who rattled American complacency just after World War I continue to attract admirers, especially abroad.

Most of the foreign tributes to Sherwood Anderson are difficult to locate, but are probably typified by Mikhail Landor's "Skola Servuda Andersona" [The School of Sherwood Anderson] (*VLit* 13,xii[1969]: 141–72), which was translated into German by Wilfried Braumann as "Die Schule Sherwood Andersons" (*KuL* 18:841–55, 961–75). Landor discusses Anderson's influence on Faulkner, Wolfe, and Hemingway and concludes that this "school" surprisingly combines the unexplored with the well-known, the normal with the grotesque in order to provide both a liberating force for those locked up in tragic situations and a clue to the mature political awakening of those whose growth is thwarted by champions of capitalism.

More specifically insightful is Alves Pires's "O cinema na litera-tura: John Dos Passos" [The film in literature] (*Brotéria* 87[1968]: 74–87), the work of a Brazilian scholar who rapidly surveys Dos Passos's varied work, commenting upon traditional and modern in-fluences upon it, especially those of expressionist films like Paul Strand's *Mannahatta* (1921) and Fritz Lang's *Metropolis* (1926). Also concerned about Dos Passos's relationship to tradition, Arnold Goldman in "Dos Passos and His U.S.A." (*NLH* 1:471–83) explains *U.S.A.* as a mock-heroic parody that forms part of an epic tradition that goes back to colonial days, but that reverses the assumptions of the earlier epics and instead of heralding the triumph of the United States, discovers its foundations to be built on sand. Charles T. Lud-ington, Jr.'s "The Neglected Satires of John Dos Passos" (*SNL* 7:127–36) examines similar elements in the novelist's work and argues that if the major novels are treated as satirical chronicles, "they have a value few critics have been willing to accord them."

Major attention continues to be accorded James Branch Cabell through Julius Rothman's *The Cabellian* and also through a journal called *Kalki: Studies in James Branch Cabell*. Most of each of the semiannual issues of *The Cabellian* consists of biographical material and collectors' notes, but the reexamination of Cabell's works con-tinues in articles like Emmons Welch's "*Beyond Life* and *Jurgen*: The Demiurge" (2:48–53), which explains that to understand *Jurgen* it is necessary to understand Cabell's concept of "the demiurge"— "man's impulse to be 'as he ought to be,'" "to conceive noble illusions and then to act on them, thereby bringing the reality a little closer to the illusion." Gerard P. Meyer's "Young Jurgen: A Comedy of Deri-sion" (3:16–21) reprints from *The Morningside* (August 1929), a Columbia College literary magazine, *The Banals* of Tacitus Minus, a mythical Latin source of *Jurgen*. G. N. Gabbard's "Deems Taylor's Musical Version of *Jurgen*" (3:12–15) is an enlightening account of a 1925 tone poem that quickly disappeared from the repertoire.

Two novels besides *Jurgen* are discussed: one in Desmond Tar-rant's "Cabell's *Hamlet Had an Uncle* and Shakespeare's *Hamlet*" (3:10–11); the other in Penn Dameron's "Inside Book Two of James Branch Cabell's *The Silver Stallion*" (3:22–23). Tarrant points out that in Cabell's story Hamlet's uncle survives, whereas Hamlet is destroyed "because of his sentimentality or feelings about honour." Dameron explains that "the rationale of the Cult of the Redeemer is that it removes the followers from the reality of the future." Edgar E. MacDonald considers the broader subject of "The Influence of Provençal Poetry on James Branch Cabell" (3:1–6), tracing the inspiration for "Cabell's basic three-part philosophical structure for his epic romance, the chivalric, the gallant, and the poetic attitudes toward life" to his knowledge of Provençal poetry. Elsewhere, MacDonald in "Cabell's Richmond Trial" (*SLJ* 3:47–71) painstakingly sets straight the record concerning two early scandals involving Cabell and their influence in shaping his early novels, *Cords of Vanity* and *The Rivet in Grandfather's Neck*.

The *Sinclair Lewis Newsletter* also continues to be a principal source of information about its author. Robert L. Coard's "*Arrowsmith* and These Damn Profs" (2,i:6–8) reports that the criticism of higher education in the novel differs from that today, because Lewis's questioning is that of a "loner," not a peer group. Marion S. Sargent's "The Babbitt-Lapham Connection" (2,i:8–9) traces parallel "rises and falls" in Lewis's and Howells's novels, but argues that Babbitt's relapse at the end shows the complete difference in tone between the two. Editor James Lindquist's "*World So Wide* and Sinclair Lewis's Rewritten Life" (2,i:12–14) advances the theory that Lewis's generally ignored last novel provided him the chance "to rewrite his own life, giving it the ending he wished for," by having the protagonist return to his early love. In a more comprehensive study of Lewis elsewhere, "Sinclair Lewis's Sociological Imagination" (*AL* 42:348–62), Stephen Conroy argues that the major novels of Lewis's greatest decade are "the working out in dramatic form" of sociological insights that anticipate the formulations of David Riesman in *The Lonely Crowd* about the responses of the individual to the surrounding culture—adjustment, anomie, autonomy. James C. Austin's "Sinclair Lewis and Western Humor" (*American Dreams*, pp. 94–105) finds in Lewis's work "an ambivalence, a reaction against itself, even in the end a kind of self-torture" that is characteristic of the humor of the northern West and Midwest.

Iconoclasm is a demanding trade; many marginal figures lacked the strength to survive the masochistic tendencies that Austin describes. One of the most colorful yet pathetic of these receives his due at last in Jack B. Moore's *Maxwell Bodenheim* (TUSAS 156), which provides a model for treating one likely to be remembered for his behavior rather than his creations. Moore describes Bodenheim's childhood as "a disaster he never recovered from" with the result that "he seems never to have possessed the equipment psychologically necessary to live with even minimal security in the ordinary confines of society" (p. 14). "Although Bodenheim wrote twelve novels between 1923 and 1934," Moore reminds us, "he was never very seriously considered as a novelist," because "reviewers generally found his books clumsy, tasteless, and too subjective" (p. 33). "At their worst," Moore writes of novels like Bodenheim's first, *Blackguard*, they seem "tracts designed for revenge" (p. 74). Moore also singles out a convincing cause for Bodenheim's failure, "the journalism [he] wrote for the *Chicago Literary Times* was of high order. . . . If Bodenheim had been temperamentally suited to maintain the pace of disciplined journalism, he clearly would have had the talent to succeed"; but, "setting his goals impossibly high, he could only find failure" (pp. 90–92).

The Harlem Renaissance of the 1920s is the subject of the November 1970 issue of *Black World* (20,i). Many of the articles, like Arna Bontemps's "The Black Renaissance of the 20's" (pp. 5–18) are largely reminiscences of the period, with special attention to important figures like Marcus Garvey; but George E. Kent's "The Soulful Way of Claude McKay" (pp. 37–50) and Clifford Mason's "Jean Toomer's Black Authenticity" (pp. 70–76) specifically evaluate literary achievements. Kent finds that McKay's work "represents a *strategic*, rather than a *radical*, dissociation of sensibility" from that provided by contemporary American culture, although this dissociation made possible the radical one of later writers. Mason extravagantly praises Toomer's insistence in *Cane* that "the reality and salvation" of all blacks lie in the embodiment of African existence. In a somewhat more detached analysis of the novel in an earlier issue of the retitled magazine, Darwin Turner finds in "Jean Toomer's *Cane*" (*NegroD* 18,iii:54–61) that the book marks the transition of the lyricist into philosopher. The first two sections, Turner explains, present a contrast "between a natural response to sexual drive and a self-conscious frustrating inability to realize oneself"; then the third section, "Kabnis," "represents the twentieth-century educated Northern Negro searching for his identity" and being unable to mate with "the sensual Negro female," because he is "intellectual rather than physical."

Benjamin McKeever's "*Cane* as Blues" (*NALF* 4:61–63) differently interprets the book as an "oracular" attempt to bear witness to the idea that "the Negro is not an apprentice to equality but a journeyman in suffering." Donald G. Ackley's "Theme and Vision in Jean Toomer's *Cane*" (*SBL* 1,ii:45–65) reads the first section of the book as "primarily an effort to catch the parting soul of slavery and pour it into song"; the second, as clarifying the "vague specter" of the dominant but dead white society that "haunted the early stories," and "Kabnis" as a dramatic presentation of the major themes of the earlier sections. None of these articles offers as satisfying an interpretation of this still puzzling work as Todd Lieber's "Design and Movement in *Cane*" (see *ALS 1969*, p. 212).

A single magazine issue presents two sharply contrasting attitudes toward J. W. Johnson's major novel. Robert E. Fleming's "Contemporary Themes in Johnson's *Autobiography of an Ex-Coloured Man*" (*NALF* 4:120–24) finds that the treatment of the themes of namelessness, black self-hatred, the important place of the mother in black family life, and the relationship of blacks to white liberals makes the book still meaningful and relevant "for the reader who wishes to understand the traditions that underlie the twentieth-century black novel." Clarence A. Amann, to the contrary, reports in "Three Negro Classics: An Estimate" (*NALF* 4:113–19) that he finds it "difficult" to discover much to recommend this "shabby and superficial" work.

v. The Expatriates

The recent falling of Henry Miller into the hands of scholars may not benefit his reputation. Michael J. Hoffman maintains in "Yesterday's Rebel" (*WHR* 24:271–74) that Miller has lived a legend rather than a life and has not been just a writer of risqué books, but a symbol of "how to defy a Puritanically repressive society." Recently, however, Hoffman continues, Miller has become so acceptable that there has been an effort to make him academically respectable, "seeing him as the builder of a little corner of the modern sensibility," while his work fails to stimulate the interest it once did.

A ponderous example of the effort that Hoffman characterizes is Jane A. Nelson's *Form and Image in the Fiction of Henry Miller* (Detroit, Wayne State Univ. Press), a study—drawing largely on Jungian psychology—of archetypal patterns in Miller's work. The aim of the book is described in a chapter entitled, "Ne te quaesiveris extra," which explains that Miller has succeeded in dramatizing stages in the process of a human lifetime as Jung described them: "in *Cancer*, for example, the confrontation of the unconscious symbolized as the Archetypal Feminine in its elementary form; in *Capricorn*, the emergence of Mara as the anima figure" (p. 111). The author credits Miller with a utopian vision that "sees a world in which an unknowable and unknown self can flourish—a self whose nature can be described only in symbols and which is only partly accessible to consciousness" (p. 114). This vision results in the theoretical and intellectual interests of the work lying not in the personal self of Henry Miller, but in "a transpersonal self whose nature is explored and experienced by a fictional Henry Miller" (p. 118).

This approach leads Mrs. Nelson to such questionable assertions as one that "Miller's male figures are essentially symbols in an allegory, even when they correspond more closely to mimetic reality than obviously iconographical figures" (p. 150) and that "the detail with which coitus is described by Miller functions magically. (Readers who consider such details 'realistic' demonstrate that they have failed to recognize the essentially symbolic and allegorical nature of Miller's work)" (p. 167).

The merits and shortcomings of an approach like Mrs. Nelson's are the subject of Paul R. Jackson's "Henry Miller's Literary Pregnancies" (*L&P* 19:35–49), which argues

> There seems little doubt that, under the influence of Rank, Jung, Erich Gutkind, D. H. Lawrence and a host of others, Miller did fashion out of the broken shards of his experience, a personal legend of fulfillment and life. . . . Yet, unless one values form at the expense of all other literary values, the myth seems peculiarly unsatisfying. It involves the most pretentious side of Miller. . . . And it tends to submerge the most genuinely American humor of much of the most vital writ-

ing. . . . More important it does not sufficiently account for the violence of Miller's attitudes—especially those involving women. [pp. 39–40]

"Comic vengeance," Jackson concludes, is as staple a part of Miller's work

> as his Christ-like emergence from Brooklyn. And most comic of all is the dramatized admission . . . that if he was returning to the womb as cultural example and mythic man, he was also returning as ill-used son and husband, turning against those female birds of prey their own creative-destructive weapons. [p. 46]

Mrs. Nelson's humorless, disembodied approach was also pre-empted by José Arthur Rios's "O outro lado de Henry Miller" [The Other Side of Henry Miller] (*Comentário* 10[1968]:299–304), in which the Brazilian critic also argues that Miller utilizes the obscene as a device that will make stand out in sharp relief the great cosmic forces to which art is the gateway and also as an allegory of death and a secret exorcism of all that which is mechanical, obsolescent, and dead.

In another article, "The Balconies of Henry Miller" (*UR* 36 [1969]:155–60, 221–25), Paul R. Jackson looks again with disfavor on the increasing religiosity that some critics seem to admire in Miller's work. Jackson considers "Miller's transformation from comic revolutionary to contented saint" to be accompanied by an increasing pretentiousness. Alan Trachtenberg agrees and finds in " 'History on the Side': Henry Miller's American Dream" (*American Dreams*, pp. 137–48) that "the excitement in Miller's early work is its authentic emotion of release, its unhindered explorations of the suppressed fringes of middle-class fantasies, where respectability fades into criminality," "an act of aggression against all confining values," in which the principal literary method is caricature.

From a totally different standpoint Al Katz examines "The *Tropic of Cancer* Trials: The Problem of Relevant Moral and Artistic Controversy" (*Midway* 9,iv[1969]:99–125) and observes that the eight trials studied in detail "provide a unique opportunity to investigate the actual operation of the constitutional test of obscenity established by Roth vs. U.S." He finds that the real issue in the trials was respectability—"the depictions must be made illegal to prevent [perverse sexuality] from becoming respectable," so that the censors were correct in finding Miller's book dangerous since it provided "an alternative vision of existence" for those seeking one.

As Miller's reputation begins to vaporize, his long-time friend Anaïs Nin moves more and more into the foreground as the real nerve center of the Paris expatriate group of the 1930s. Régis Durand theorizes in "Anaïs Nin et le 'langage des nerfs' " (*LanM* 64:289–96) that the source of her creative power is a "nervousness" generated by the tensions of fluctuating between the two poles of rigorously different forms of activity—natural, represented by Henry Miller, and pure fiction, represented by Antonin Artaud. This "nervousness" accounts for the way in which her work encompasses but transcends Miller's.

Richard R. Centing and Benjamin Franklin V show the shift by entitling the newsletter dealing with the expatriate group *Under the Sign of Pisces: Anaïs Nin and her Circle*. The first four quarterly issues are largely devoted to interviews with Miss Nin, news items about her and her associates, and book reviews; but Centing's "Anna Kavan's Shout of Red" (1,iii:1–8), which discusses the cosmopolite author Helen Edmonds (who wrote under the pseudonyms of Helen Ferguson and Anna Kavan), and the unsigned tribute, "Caresse Crosby: 1892–1970" (1,ii:1–4) shows the interest of the journal in calling attention to neglected members of the Nin circle.

Miss Nin, like Miller, is receiving some of her most substantial treatments in Latin-American journals. Wayne McEvilly's "Dos rostros de la muerte [Two faces of death] en *Seduccion del minotauro* de Anais Nin" (*Sur*, Nos. 322–23, pp. 233–47) compares this difficult novel to a sonata in three movements and explains that like all of Miss Nin's fiction it awakens in us echoes at times of familiar phantasms, of problems that we have confronted and solved after long effort, including some of those still not fully perceptible, whose scope eludes us even though at the same time we foresee them clearly.

vi. The Cosmogonists—Porter, Steinbeck, West, Wilder, Wolfe

Katherine Anne Porter continues the darling of the explicators, with her short stories, especially "Flowering Judas," receiving far more attention than *Ship of Fools*. The role of her Mexican experience in her work has been a focus of recent attention. William L. Nance's "Katherine Anne Porter and Mexico" (*SWR* 55:143–53) argues that in Mexico Miss Porter found an atmosphere of "living arts" and "a temper of rebellion" that made the country a symbol of her desire for literary and personal independence. Colin Partridge's "'My Familiar Country': An Image of Mexico in the Work of Katherine Anne Porter" (*SSF* 7:597–614) similarly finds "the experience of Mexico was a central formative influence on her life and art." Partridge illustrates the progression in her writings about Mexico from "adventure" into meaningful "experience" that was to become the basis for many of her stories that trace a similar progression from "a sense of betrayal" to "a reversal of values in the individual who undergoes the betrayal." David Madden's "The Charged Image in Katherine Anne Porter's 'Flowering Judas'" (*SSF* 7:277–89) explains the way in which the author, by spoking all the other images in the story from the potent central hub of the waiting figure of Braggioni and then creating an interplay between these images, appropriately renders Laura's state of mind as "self-delusion producing paralysis of will."

Turning to the stories grouped under the title "The Old Order," Jan Pinkerton maintains in "Katherine Anne Porter's Portrayal of Black Resentment" (*UR* 36:315–17) that while these stories are usually considered attempts to understand the interrelationship of the author's past and present worlds, she also gives glimpses in them of "the apparently docile black's recognition of his long-standing injustices and of his desire for compensation."

Two new books about John Steinbeck stress the post-World-War-II fiction, especially *East of Eden*, and make extensive use of the philosophical speculations in *The Log from "The Sea of Cortez."* Lester Jay Marks's *Thematic Design in the Novels of John Steinbeck* (The Hague, Mouton, 1969) discusses "a system of ideas . . . beneath the surface diversities of Steinbeck's work that reside in three recurrent thematic patterns"—man's nature as a religious creature who must "create a godhead to satisfy his personal need," a biological view of man as a "group animal" with a will and intelligence separate from those of the individuals composing it, and "the non-teleological concept that man lives without knowledge of the cause of his existence," yet is spurred in a search for values by the very mystery of his life. Marks finds *East of Eden* the apex of a consistent development of these themes through all of Steinbeck's works. John Clark Pratt's briefer *John Steinbeck, A Critical Essay* (CWCP) discusses the novelist's use of Christian elements in "syncretic allegories," which discard the traditional one-to-one ratio of allegory while attempting to utilize the suggestive power of the genre. Pratt deliberately avoids evaluating either the artistic merits of the novels or Steinbeck's attitude towards religious questions. Richard O'Connor's *John Steinbeck* (New York, McGraw-Hill) is a biography for teenagers by a prolific journalist.

The *Steinbeck Quarterly* continues its series of comparative articles. Andreas K. Poulakidas's "Steinbeck, Kazantzakis, and Socialism" (3:62–72) finds that "Steinbeck's view of socialism is localized, narrowed down to the needs of the suffering Americans, whereas Kazantzakis conceives socialism as a movement with . . . a more universal setting." Sanford E. Marovitz's "John Steinbeck and Adlai Stevenson: The Shattered Image of America" (3:51–62) traces affectionately the two men's parallel efforts to project "America's golden image to the world."

Critical attention is shifting from *The Grapes of Wrath* to *Tortilla Flat* and the post-war novels. *The Grapes of Wrath* has been inspected recently only in Harold F. Delisle's "Style and Idea in Steinbeck's 'The Turtle'" (*Style* 4:145–57), an exhaustive analysis of the famous third chapter, demonstrating how this "miniature short story" describes a movement that "parallels in tempo and mood a life cycle from birth to death," aimed at affirming "the indomitability of the urge to life" and "the circularity of the pattern."

James Justus's "The Transient World of *Tortilla Flat*" (WR 7,i: 55–60) discusses Steinbeck's summoning up a dream, "a golden world which invites our participation." Raising the question of the validity of *paisano* values as essential to determining "the worth or triviality of Steinbeck's creation," Justus denies as an oversimplification the common charge that the characters "cloak unacceptable modes of action by socially acceptable and praiseworthy ones," because he finds that the *paisanos* are usually "unhampered by consistency" and "allow their intense and primitive vitality (true emotion)" to operate successfully within "a workable, ritualized, and stable system of conduct (necessary and decent emotion)." Howard Levant takes a less favorable view of the novel in "*Tortilla Flat*: The Shape of John Steinbeck's Career" (*PMLA* 85:1087–95), speculating that the novel's popularity may have strengthened its author's "weakness for a predetermined structure," which may have obscured a defect in the structure of the novel and have ultimately had the sinister effect of leading to "an extreme simplification of the whole relationship between structure and materials" in some of Steinbeck's later work.

Richard Astro's "Steinbeck's Post-War Trilogy: A Return to Nature and the Natural Man" (*TCL* 16:109–22) groups *Cannery Row*, *The Pearl*, and *The Wayward Bus* as Steinbeck's last novels to express "his traditional view of nature and the natural world," in which "nature assumes an active role in directing the course of human existence." Lawrence William Jones's "'A Little Play in Your Head': Parable Form in John Steinbeck's Post-War fiction" (*Genre* 3:55–63) begins with these three novels and also examines the later ones as examples of Steinbeck's turning to the "parable mode" in a continuing effort to find "the best medium for his vision." James A. Hamby makes a close study of just one of these novels in "Steinbeck's *The Pearl*: Tradition and Innovation" (*WR* 7,ii:65–66), arguing that the theme of the novel is that "Kino's *method* of change must be at fault," since he attempts an impossible departure from his traditional culture in "a single, swift alteration."

Donald E. Houghton's dubious reading of a popular short story in "'Westering' in 'The Leader of the People'" (see *ALS 1969*, p. 217) is answered directly by Robert E. Morsberger's "In Defense of 'Westering'" (*WAL* 5:143–46) and indirectly by Philip J. West's "Steinbeck's 'The Leader of the People': A Crisis in Style" (*WAL* 5:137–41). Morsberger explains that "westering" was the crucial experience for the grandfather's generation, so that the old man's trying to explain it to his grandson "is not a digression that should be cut but the basis of the generation gap" that has since been dramatized in a series of movies. West sees the grandfather's statement as "elegiac" and argues that Steinbeck concludes the cycle with this story because it correlates "the decline of the frontier, the decline of the heroic quality in all the characters of the story, and the end of Grandfather's role as epic singer."

Every year must witness, it seems, the appearance of a bulky, "standard" biography. The year brought us Jay Martin's *Nathanael West, The Art of His Life* (New York: Farrar, Straus and Giroux), written with the aid of a hoard of family documents. The value of the material is unquestionable; but perhaps Martin's achievement can be no better summed up than it was by Irving Howe (*NYTBR* 12 June:1,40), who, after observing that the study is "always meticulous, responsible, and affectionate," concludes: "We are given large amounts of information but no persuasive image; we learn everything that West did but do not see clearly who he was. Scrupulous scholar that he is, Mr. Martin lacks those stylistic skills that enable a biographer to create the illusion of character." Perhaps in preparing the five drafts of the book he speaks of in the preface, Martin lost sight of the forest because of the trees. It should be much more satisfactory to present the kind of material he was working with in a form like Jay Leyda's *The Melville Log* (1951), so that it could be drawn upon by scholars elaborating a thesis. The kind of clue that Martin might have followed up to give his study direction is provided, for example, by one recent dissertation provocative enough to warrant violating the general exclusion of as yet unpublished material from this already overburdened account, John M. Brand's "Fiction as Decreation: The Novels of Nathanael West" (*DAI* 30:3449A), which speculates that what West wrote and the way he wrote it served to confirm "his worst fears about human nature and destiny."

From Germany—where Thornton Wilder is much admired—comes one of the most perceptive analyses so far of his art, Liselotte Mickel's "Thornton Wilder und der amerikanische Optimismus" (*FH* 24[1969]:875–82), which explains that what Wilder sought was not an economic turning point in the United States, but the importance of human existence. This quest puts him into the tradition of American optimism, which he himself sees as a typical American quality. *The Eighth Day*, the article maintains, especially exemplifies his respectful amazement before the inexhaustible possibilities of life, so that one may regard this many-layered novel as a contribution toward American self-understanding.

Wilder's most recent novel is explored from several viewpoints in *Literature and Religion: Thornton Wilder's "The Eighth Day"*, papers collected for MLA Seminar 4 and edited by Paul Schlueter (Evansville, Ind., Univ. of Evansville—each article separately paginated). Edward E. Erickson's "The Figure in the Tapestry: The Religious Vision of Thornton Wilder's *The Eighth Day*" finds Wilder the one major modern author to answer Father William F. Lynch's call in *Christ and Apollo* for "the "affirmation of time and the concrete." In "Some: An Examination of the Religious Tenets of Thornton Wilder's *The Eighth Day*," Dalma Brunauer finds that "the central problem" for the Christian reader of the novel is "the nature of providence" as it operates in the novel.

Dennis Loyd's "God Is Alive and Well in Wilder" soundly points out that while the novel is filled "with thoughts of faith, acts of hope, and moments of love," it is difficult to call its influence Christian "if one means by that term the usual Catholic or Protestant conceptions." Steve J. Van Der Weele's somewhat labored "Hotels, Boarding Houses, and Homes: The Mystique of the Family in Wilder's Novel *The Eighth Day*," after exploring the thorough analysis of familial relationships in the novel, reaches the conclusion that "Wilder seems to be implying that marriage and families can be justified on a purely natural basis, and without the sanction of the institutions of religion and the state." Warren French's "Christianity as Metaphor in *The Eighth Day*" argues that "the central problem of the Christian approaching this book . . . is to achieve the detachment necessary to appreciate that his own passionate convictions may serve simply as the framework for another's artistic enterprise," because "what Wilder is saying is that—questions of belief aside—what the Christian Bible communicates to us is a metaphor of archetypal experience that orders the chaos of the universe."

One of the most ambitious publications of the year is *The Notebooks of Thomas Wolfe* (2 vols.; Chapel Hill, Univ. of N.C. Press), edited by Richard S. Kennedy and Paschall Reeves. The editors believe that "the notebooks and supplementary materials give us as close a look as possible at the creative process that transformed Wolfe's experience into fiction," for they see his compulsive notetaking as his own research method into "the multiplicity and diversity of American life." Despite the prodigious effort involved in transcribing and judiciously pruning Wolfe's staggering number of memoranda to himself, one must question whether formal book publication is a justifiable mode of making this material of specialized interest available. One would think that carefully prepared facsimiles of the notebooks themselves would best serve scholarly purposes.

Another analysis of Wolfe's manuscript legacy, Francis E. Skipp's "*Of Time and the River*: The Final Editing" (*PBSA* 64:313–22) asserts that Maxwell Perkins made "the most drastic cuts in the typescript by eliminating more than seven hundred lines of Thomas

Wolfe's lyrical prose," in which Wolfe "had expressed his most deeply felt insights and certainties." Otherwise Perkins eliminated banal and irrelevant material that Wolfe should have cut out himself.

Turning to analyses of Wolfe's output, we find Martin Wank's "Thomas Wolfe: Two More Decades of Criticism" (*SAQ* 69:244–56) surveying the notably increased amount of writing about the novelist since Elizabeth Nowell's biography appeared in 1960. In the same magazine, Leslie T. Field's "Thomas Wolfe and the Kicking Season Again" (*SAQ* 69:464–72) takes yet another look at some of this criticism and attacks it as unwarrantedly derogatory while arguing that the most serious and sensitive critics have been concerned with Wolfe's work not as formless autobiography but as the record of his "discovery of America." The kind of criticism Fields approves is found in Thomas E. Boyle's "Frederick Jackson Turner and Thomas Wolfe: The Frontier as History and as Literature" (*WAL* 4:273–85), which contrasts Turner, who "unable to reconcile . . . mythic assumptions and historical realities" remained optimistic by clinging to his ideals, "at the expense of ignoring experience," with Wolfe, who "confronted fully, openly and honestly the disparity between assumption and experience" and developed "an operational set of beliefs grounded in the living facts of ordinary existence." Long-time Wolfe student C. Hugh Holman, however, finds that Wolfe is really very much like the Turner that Boyle describes. After observing at the beginning of "Focus on Thomas Wolfe's *You Can't Go Home Again*: Agrarian Dream and Industrial Nightmare" (*American Dreams*, pp. 149–57) that this novel is "a fictional record of the conflict of the American Dream with a capitalistic society and the descent of that Dream into nightmare," Holman concludes that the essential theme of the book is "not the triumph but the betrayal of the Dream" and that some powerful positive rhetorical assertions are not supported by "convincing dramatic actions," so that one is left with the realization that "knowing and feeling about the nature of his native land were at variance in Wolfe."

An ambitious Wolfe study that has hitherto been overlooked is Hans Helmcke's *Die Familie im Romanwerk von Thomas Wolfe* (Heidleberg, Carl Winter, 1967), which is discussed at length and with great expertise in a review by Daniel L. Delakas (*AL* 42:257–59). Delakas reports that "what purports to be a dissertation on the theme of family life is in reality a study of the theme of death in

Wolfe's novels," which arrives at the conclusion that "while in both cycles of [Wolfe's] novels solutions are sought primarily in a real here-and-now area of life, also in the historic past, they are really found—unnoticed in large measure by the author—in a symbolic, other-worldly area of life and in the future."

vii. The Tough Guys and Others of the 30s

Charles A. Reich observes in his best-selling *The Greening of America* (New York, Random House) that so far as the deep ills of industrialized, urban America are concerned, "the remarkable novels of Raymond Chandler, James M. Cain, and Dashiell Hammett come closer to the truth than almost anything else in literature or social sciences" (p. 46); yet few critics except David Madden have so far given these novelists serious attention.

Madden caps his long studies of Cain (see *ALS 1967*, p. 188) with *James M. Cain* (TUSAS 171), which incorporates material from "James M. Cain's *The Postman Always Rings Twice* and Albert Camus's *L'Etranger*" (*PLL* 6:407–19), commenting on the former work as a possible model for the latter. Rather than discuss Cain's novels chronologically, Madden first describes Cain's place among the "hard-boiled" writers and his life in relation to his time and his writing. Madden then looks at each of the novels in the light of concepts central to Cain's writing, such as "the love-rack and wish-come-true" theme, analyzes Cain's characters, explores possible influences on his work, and discusses the way in which Cain's novels exemplify the concept of the "pure novel" (a work that contains no teaching or journalism, only what is absolutely part of the drama). Madden closes with a statement of the reasons for studying "tough" fiction that closely parallels Reich's:

> with a special vision unimpaired by ideology, [the tough writer's] manner of dealing with the universals of sex, money, and violence presents a somewhat expressionistic picture of American society and culture in the 1930's and 1940's and provides insights into the American-Dream-turned-nightmare and into the all-American-boy-turned-tough guy. [p. 165]

Two studies testify to the increasing seriousness with which detective-story writer Raymond Chandler is being regarded. Robert

H. Miller's "The Publication of Raymond Chandler's *The Long Goodbye*" (*PBSA* 63[1969]:279–90) studies revisions in the stages of the text; and Frederic Jameson's "On Raymond Chandler" (*SoR* 6:624–50) argues that Chandler's novels "have not one form, but two," an objective, rigid, external detective story and a more personal, subjective story peopled with recurrent characters through whom the social world is interpreted. Jameson thinks that Chandler's works have the intellectual effect of dramatizing American decadence by showing how all the energy and activity wasted on the long dead strips away the bustling activity of the present and makes us feel "the presence of graves beneath the bright sunlight."

Bernard McCormick's "A John O'Hara Geography" (*JML* 1:151–68) reprints from the *Philadelphia Magazine* (Nov. 1969) an illustrated account of the relationship between O'Hara's fictional Gibbsville and Pottsville, Pennsylvania, where O'Hara worked as a newspaperman. Jonathan Williams's *Edward Dahlberg, A Tribute* (New York, David Lewis) is exactly that. A reprinting of *Tri-Quarterly* 19 (Fall 1970), it consists principally of reminiscences and photographic and poetic tributes. Most of the critical articles are revisions of ones that appeared earlier elsewhere; but Eric Mottram's "Ishmael in America" (pp. 10–24) argues freshly that the one classical myth that Dahlberg totally rejects is "the greatest of all . . . the myth of Prometheus, on which the humanistic Romantic liberals of the nineteenth century centered their rejection of reactionary authoritarianism." "Before Prometheus," Mottram opines, "Ishmael seeks stability in the mother." Dahlberg's own "A Letter to *Prose*" (1:69–80) actually proves to be two cryptic putdowns of some of the many contemporaries to incur his displeasure.

The most discussed of the "tough guy–proletarian" writers continues to be Richard Wright, who has been the subject of two additional books and two more special magazine issues.

Russell C. Brignano's *Richard Wright: An Introduction to the Man and His Works* (Pittsburgh, Univ. of Pittsburgh Press) is directed by the generalization that "despite Wright's personal agony and outrage stemming from the very fact of his black skin color in a white-dominated Western culture, his fundamental belief was that inhumanity could be abolished if man would heed his reason" (p. xii). Particularly intriguing is Brignano's thesis that Wright's late and often scorned novel, *The Outsider*, is proof not of his existentialism "but of his rejection of existentialism," inspired by his contention "that man's reason could discover a way out of a history of injustices and irrationalities" (pp. 163–64).

John A. Williams's *The Most Native of Sons: A Biography of Richard Wright* (Garden City, N.Y., Doubleday) is an account for young people of Wright's struggles and achievements by a younger black novelist of considerable reputation. The oversimplified approach of the book is indicated by the debatable conclusion that had Wright "been a white writer there is no doubt that he would have gained his honors earlier on" (p. 135). To attribute Wright's problems solely to racism is to ignore the plight of *all* really serious, sensitive artists in the United States.

Several articles in the special December 1968 Richard Wright issue of *Negro Digest* (18,ii) come closer to suggesting the complexity of Wright's problems. Addison Gayle, Jr.'s "Richard Wright: Beyond Nihilism" (pp. 4–10) considers Wright the "last black writer to admonish men to listen," because he saw "the possibilities of transcendence in the Bigger Thomases of the nation, and he warned America that a nation incapable of putting its ideals into practice would produce Cross Damons [*The Outsider*], seeking their manhood through a nihilistic attempt to negate the very structure of democracy itself." James A. Emanuel's "Fever and Feeling" (pp. 16–24) explores a variety of image patterns in *Native Son*—especially the use of wall-and-curtain images to dramatize the black American's experience, especially his sense of isolation. Cecil Brown's "Richard Wright's Complexes and Black Writing Today" (pp. 45–50, 78–82) maintains that the tragedy of Wright's life was that he had to exile himself, "because his definition of 'Negro life' was too narrow, too confining, too puny, and too dependent on White Society."

The more recent Richard Wright issue of *Studies in Black Literature* (1,iii) is much thinner critically, being composed principally of poems by and about Wright and impressions of him from Simone de Beauvoir and Dorothy Padmore. Editor Raman K. Singh's "Wright's Tragic Vision in *The Outsider*" (pp. 23–27) labors parallels with *Oedipus Rex* and *Hamlet* to attempt to prove that what may be "the only American tragic novel written in the last two decades" deals with a secular concept of "original sin"—that man is doomed because he is born. Michel Fabre's "The Poetry of Richard Wright" (pp. 10–22) traces the change from the brutal revolutionary works of the 30s to the intimately symbolic haiku of the 50s to illustrate Wright's often overlooked "sense of the universal harmony." In an earlier issue of the journal, Kenneth T. Reed's "*Native Son*: An American *Crime and Punishment*" (*SBL* 1,ii:33–34) points out parallels that may suggest Wright's recognition of the potential of Dostoevsky's model for treating the American scene.

Wright's "The Man Who Lived Underground" is deservedly attracting increasing attention. Shirley Meyer's "The Identity of 'The Man Who Lived Underground'" (*NALF* 4:52–55) finds that the story is not a social protest like *Native Son,* but an existential work that "carries the universal message that the acceptance of one's responsibility in an absurd world can result in self-realization," a point made also by Ronald Ridenour's "'The Man Who Lived Underground': A Critique" (*Phylon* 31:54–57). William Goede's "On Lower Frequencies: The Buried Men in Wright and Ellison" (*MFS* 15 [1969]:483–501) argues that while many critics consider Wright's story the chief source for Ellison's *Invisible Man,* the difference between the principal characters of the two works is that "nothing has happened in any significant way" to Wright's hero, "and he is finally killed"; whereas Ellison's "endures, and, if we can believe him, is on his way back to us, a man of wisdom and hope."

Other regional writers besides Willa Cather receive attention in the special Spring 1970 issue of *Kansas Quarterly* (2,ii). Ruel E. Foster's "Jesse Stuart's W-Hollow—Microcosm of the Appalachians" (pp. 66–73) finds that Stuart's charm resides in his "being able to catch in his work the feel of the *last* period of isolate mountain life before it was run over by the juggernaut of twentieth-century technology." Samuel Irving Bellman's "Marjorie Kinnan Rawlings, A Solitary Sojourner in the Florida Backwoods" (pp. 78–87) identifies "the central fact" of her life and career as "her geographical primitivism,' her abandonment of an urban, Northern or Midwestern mode of existence . . . for the north Florida woods." Deriding the neglect of *The Winds of Spring* (1940), Joel M. Jones argues in "To Feel the Heartland's Pulse: The Writing of Walter Havighurst" (pp. 88–96) that although other interpreters of the Midwest have "approached their region in a similar dual capacity as novelist and historian," few have "demonstrated a comparable competence and craftsmanship in both capacities."

Indiana University–Purdue University at Indianapolis

13. Fiction: The 1930s to the Present

James H. Justus

Predictions of critical activity centering on contemporary American fiction continue to be risky. Last year's interest in both I. B. Singer and Thomas Berger failed to sustain itself; the once-languishing Salinger industry is flourishing again; work on Mailer dropped sharply in 1970; and while Bellow, Warren, Nabokov, and O'Connor continue to get their usual attention, Ellison and Malamud are subjects of more articles than at any time in the past. Judging from dissertations recently completed, we may see further shifts in fashion. Five dissertations on Agee were reported, followed by Bellow (four), Mailer, Wright Morris, O'Connor, Welty, and John Hawkes (two each), and Malamud, Nabokov, James Purdy, Kurt Vonnegut, Warren, and Salinger (one each). Four doctoral studies were more comprehensive—two on writers of the 1950s and 1960s, one on the Catholic novel, and one on postwar Southern fiction; one additional dissertation is a comparative study of Styron and Heller.

i. General Studies

Richard H. Rupp's *Celebration in Postwar American Fiction, 1945–1967* (Coral Gables, Fla., Univ. of Miami Press) gathers together ten somewhat arbitrarily chosen writers linked in their attitudes toward adequate forms which reveal the "sense of the possibilities for a full life in modern America." As Rupp defines it, *celebration* is the expression of tradition—in feasts, weddings, songs, funerals, parties, even riots—which illustrates man's encounter with reality. Despite its shagginess, the book makes a few valuable points about contemporary fiction, and the relevant subjects will be listed below.

Overlooked until now is James Hall's *The Lunatic Giant in the Drawing Room: The British and American Novel Since 1930* (Bloomington, Ind. Univ. Press, 1968). Though it contains a comprehensive segment ("From Faulkner to Salinger"), the book concentrates on the second-generation novelists and their responses to the "reconstitution" of the hero, located in the idea of the mind "as a set of forces, with possibly definable speed and direction," which has replaced the notion of mind as fluid consciousness. Hall discusses the varied ways in which these writers' personae are seen as representative forces colliding in conflicts that eventuate in modest resolutions; the techniques of theatricality are means for expressing energy, and their forms for seeking direction tend toward allegory. *The Lunatic Giant*, despite its unhappy title, is a sophisticated overview of the psychological shifts in narrative art in this century, quite apart from the specific readings of Warren, Bellow, Iris Murdoch, Graham Greene, and Elizabeth Bowen.

Kafka is the "spiritual pioneer" of the fictional territory explored by our novelists of the last two decades, says Helen Weinberg in *The New Novel in America: The Kafkan Mode in Contemporary Fiction* (Ithaca, N.Y., Cornell Univ. Press). Though she defines and illustrates the absurdist novel as a type and its origins in Kafka, Weinberg's larger interest is the activist novel, a "post-absurd" type which disavows the destructive terms of the absurd world. The activist hero, also Kafkan, "chooses to sustain his alienation in order to assert his own subjective truth and to seek for himself a wonderful, improbable, transcendent self" which refuses to participate in a competitive world. Weinberg's subject, along with many of her conclusions on particular authors, coincides with any number of studies in the past decade, but her sensitivity to Kafka's fictions and their influence on authors of Bellow's generation makes *The New Novel* more convincing than some of her predecessors who have been obsessed with the ideological-theoretical backgrounds in existentialism.

Another influence study is Lewis A. Lawson's "Kierkegaard and the Modern American Novel" (*Essays*, pp. 111–25), which suggests that postwar interest in the Dane accounts for both a new fictional method for the analysis and development of character and a new structure for "the achievement of narrative progression." Unfortunately, Lawson is skimpy with examples of the latter, though he shows how Kierkegaardian themes influence portraiture in Styron, Salinger, McCullers, and Walker Percy.

Louis D. Rubin, Jr., makes the point in "Southern Literature: A

Piedmont Art" (*MissQ* 23:1–16) that a substantial number of Southern writers have been "upcountry" rather than Tidewater, both in
birth and in their subjects, a point implicitly corroborated in a symposium on *The Writer and His Tradition*, edited by Robert Drake,
with Cleanth Brooks, James Dickey, and Reynolds Price as participants (Knoxville, Univ. of Tenn. Press, 1969). The actual topics
range widely, including the detailed changes in the South from the
Depression years to the late 1960s, but the participants generally
agree that the native country, the art, and the "*rootedness* of the
culture" (as Dickey phrases it) remain. Price sees similarities between Jewish and Southern writers in their "assumptions about religion" and "intense family life." Brooks cites the need for reassessing
the Nashville Agrarians, who were "misunderstood" and who themselves "misunderstood the situation in many ways." One of the bo-
nuses in this interesting pamphlet is Dickey's anecdote of a canoe
trip in North Georgia and his encounter with a bootlegger, the obvious germ for *Deliverance*; readers will quickly note, however, that
the point of the story—filial trust and respect—bears little resemblance
to the hokey lust of the fictional episode.

In "Choice: Ironic Alternatives in the World of the Contemporary American Novel" (*American Dreams*, pp. 175–87), Alvin Greenberg explores three major ways in which man asserts his will in a
world seen as irresistibly predetermined. Though it is always ironic,
man's choice can be an opening up of possibilities through the alternatives of conformity, destruction, and withdrawal. With *Invisible
Man* as his central text, Greenberg uses works by Bellow, Heller,
West, and others to support his argument.

In a substantial generic study, "The Shrinking Garden and New
Exits: The Comic-Satiric Novel in the Twentieth Century" (*KanQ*
1,iii[1969]:5–16), Robert M. Davis sees the practice of contemporary
absurdist comedy and satire as evolving from the novelists of ideas
(Norman Douglas, Aldous Huxley) through what he calls the "ex-
ternalist" writers (Ronald Firbank, Evelyn Waugh). Despite the
work of Barth, Heller, and others, this most recent stage can claim no
obvious masters. Characters are not only volitionless, but they are
also denied the escapism common to their literary ancestors; for the
reader, increased awareness prevents even the "refuges of detachment, irresponsibility, contempt."

The late Olga W. Vickery, in "The Inferno of the Moderns"

(*Shaken Realist*, pp. 147–64), sees the *Inferno* as a "controlling metaphor of the human condition"; for the modern imagination the world is a "displaced existential projection" of Dante's world, especially in such writers as John Hawkes, LeRoi Jones, and Ken Kesey. Nathan A. Scott, Jr.'s subject in "The 'Conscience' of the New Literature" (*Shaken Realist*, pp. 251–83) is the convergence of the theological and literary imaginations in the avant-garde novelists (mostly Continental, though there are hit-and-run insights on Barth, Thomas Pynchon, James Purdy, and others). In his own grand style, Scott finds distinguishing characteristics of contemporary fiction to be a reluctance to write in the grand style and a refusal to compete with reality, traits which describe somewhat older literatures as well.

Although Gene Kellogg's "The Catholic Novel in Convergence" (*Thought* 45:265–96) says nothing new about either J. F. Powers or Flannery O'Connor, the definitions and historical survey will be useful for those interested in the Catholic novel as a subgenre.

ii. Flannery O'Connor

Josephine Hendin's version of O'Connor will doubtless irritate many, but *The World of Flannery O'Connor* (Bloomington, Ind. Univ. Press) is the first effort to place this writer in a tradition dominated by neither region nor religion. The fiction is not a "monologue on redemption," says Hendin; the "very act of writing was itself a redemptive process for her." For Hendin, O'Connor's great strength springs from the "silent and remote rage that erupts from the quiet surface of her stories," a surface which shows the transitional nature of O'Connor. She moves from older forms of allegory and symbolism, which describe a traditional universe of significance, toward the "newer objectivism," which denies a meaningful universe in an art of stripped-down concreteness. Though she is surely right in her judgment that O'Connor is "most convincing when most literal and least convincing when consciously symbolic," her energetic attempt to make her an American Robbe-Grillet is finally unpersuasive. The conviction that life offers "no spirit, mind, soul, or any transcendent quality" in O'Connor's fiction may be a perverse reading, but it is also corrective, one that may well stimulate future studies that are more balanced and varied than those we have yet seen.

Leonard Casper, in "The Unspeakable Peacock: Apocalypse in

Flannery O'Connor" (*Shaken Realist,* pp. 287–99), believes that O'Connor's pervasive theme of death is free of morbidity because of her attention to "transfiguration," the "apocalyptic vision of possibility" after death. Although Casper cites dozens of stories to illustrate O'Connor's "delight in eschatology," his interpretations verge on literalism, showing little regard for the author's dramatic moments, her wit and irony, or her vision beyond a modest habit of prophecy. In contrast, William L. Nance's "Flannery O'Connor: The Trouble with Being a Prophet" (*UR* 36[1969]:101–08) is a perceptive discussion of what disturbs some readers, the recurring moment of "forced illumination" in the stories. Nance says that her "superior knowledge" (her gift as a Christian as well as that of a writer) accounts for such "forcing." He sees only "The Artificial Nigger," with its "appropriate action to contain and illuminate" its redemptive experience, untouched by gratuitous effects.

Frederick Asals contributes a superb essay on "Flannery O'Connor's 'The Lame Shall Enter First'" (*MissQ* 23:103–20). Believing that too much emphasis has been placed on the author's violence, melodrama, and grotesquerie, Asals contends that the depth, richness, and subtlety which we associate with the best modern fiction are to be found in close attention to O'Connor's language. In an integrated reading of this longest of the stories, Asals relates scenes of eating, and traces connections of food and digestive imagery to biblical allusions to shepherds and sheep. In "Flannery O'Connor's *Wise Blood*: 'Unparalleled Prosperity' and Spiritual Chaos" (*MissQ* 23:121–33), Daniel F. Littlefield, Jr., somewhat mechanically uses the author's grotesque effects as dramatic indicators of her belief in the "distortion of spiritual purpose" in America caused by affluence.

Richard H. Rupp, in "Flannery O'Connor: A Hidden Celebration" (*Celebration,* pp. 77–98), finds a lot of phony rituals and false ceremonies in "The Enduring Chill," but he seems to confuse O'Connor's "literal, banal style" with her literal, banal characters. One insight—that the typical story is built on "sacramental action"—tends to grow into criticism by assertion, as he sees the best stories revealing "the priesthood of the laity" in a "sacred celebration in the secular world." Moreover, too many of Rupp's discoveries are asserted in a tasteless rhetoric of Al Capp vintage ("the biblical, rural, real South, scoring victories against these New Yankees at Agnostic Station, Joyce Junction, and Vedanta Hollow").

Patricia Dinneen Maida's " 'Convergence' in Flannery O'Connor's 'Everything That Rises Must Converge' " (*SSF* 7:549–55) is a murky gloss of Teilhard's influence, but the christic energy, the message of "power and shocking clarity" which comes to the protagonist results apparently in nothing more than "potential" personal fulfillment and public usefulness to "a society in need of reform." The same story and five others are discussed by John R. May in "The Pruning Word: Flannery O'Connor's Judgment of Intellectuals" (*SHR* 4:325–38), a study of the "dramatic structures of judgment" which reveal O'Connor's unambiguous rejection of salvation through education.

O'Connor's revisions are the subject of two essays. Concentrating on idiom, point of view, and symbolism, Roy R. Male gives a fine account of "The Two Versions of 'The Displaced Person' " (*SSF* 7:450–57), a comparison of the 1954 periodical story with the revised version a year later. Stuart L. Burns continues his study of the textual relationship of *Wise Blood* and the relevant stories preceding it (see *ALS 1969*, p. 234) in "The Evolution of *Wise Blood*" (*MFS* 16:147–62). In her apparent shift from dual protagonists of psychosexual motivations to a single religiously dominated protagonist "surrounded by a quintuplet of alter-egos," O'Connor alters the story and theme as well as characters. Though the manuscript of *Wise Blood* is not yet available, Burns's judicious conclusion about certain structural and thematic confusions in the novel seems justified.

In a confused, rambling study, "O'Connor's Religious Viewpoint in *The Violent Bear It Away*" (*Renascence* 22:108–12), Francis J. Smith thinks that the second novel is a kind of *Everyman* drama, though he is reluctant to practice "literary legerdemain" that would turn backwoods idiots into allegorical figures. Finally, Louise Hardeman Abbot contributes an amusing and touching reminiscence, "Remembering Flannery O'Connor" (*SLJ* 2,ii:3–25), which is marred only by an arty and overwritten account of the author's funeral.

iii. Saul Bellow

A few years ago Melvin J. Friedman observed that William Styron has never been the "favorite of the Establishment that Saul Bellow" has been, and if it suggests a response of total enthusiasm, the remark is accurate. John J. Clayton began his study by claiming that "Saul

Bellow is America's most important living novelist" (see *ALS 1968*, p. 214). In *Saul Bellow's Fiction* (Carbondale, So. Ill. Univ. Press, 1969), Irving Malin is only slightly less immodest: "Saul Bellow is probably the most important living American novelist." A nononsense book in plodding prose, it reflects its author's high opinion of his subject, in this case a Bellow more interested in "metaphysical" questions than in "mere craftsmanship." Malin's own prose, studded with rhetorical questions and careless superlatives, shows little regard for critical diction. Admitting that Bellow is subtle in the use of images, Malin says they are " 'natural,' archetypal, and carefully chosen," the kind of imagery which presumably transcends technical skill. This newest book on Bellow is best in its exploration of father-son relationships, the kinds of "serious play" throughout the fiction, and the varying treatments of the dualities of experience.

Bellow's novels are the most impressive in recent times in dramatizing "the endless losing race to make cultural formulations fit experience," says James Hall (*Lunatic Giant*, pp. 127–80). Emphasizing not their passivity but the "high energy" they put into even "following other people's leads," Hall sees Bellow's heroes as "problem-solvers rather than illustrators of dilemma and are full of surprise and anger when 'natural' solutions fail to work." The Bellovian hero as claustrophobic sufferer may still be the dominant view, but Hall's version is refreshing.

In *The New Novel* (pp. 29–107), Helen Weinberg sees Bellow and Kafka linked in their storytelling impulses and strategies, their uses of a "felt metaphysicality functioning as symbolic meaning," and their distrust of ideology. Out of Kafka (and Hasidic spokesmen) comes Bellow's pervasive theme as well as his method: "Exploration of the varietal forms of self." Just as his vision "affirms the possibility of new forms for human life," so the novel becomes for him "a form of inquiry."

Ronald L. Lycette, in "Saul Bellow and the American Naturalists" (*Discourse* 13:435–49), isolates Bellow's stress on an urban milieu, his awareness of "deterministic necessities," and his appraisal of "what it means to be 'less than human' " as continuities with the naturalistic tradition. Bellow's heroes may indeed be caught in the tensions "between the emptiness of the self in quest of itself and the terror of the external 'demons' of naturalistic reality," but Lycette's account gives only a slight nod to the fact that internal "demons" are a part of the "naturalistic reality" too—the kind of biological necessity dramatized in *McTeague*.

iv. Bernard Malamud and J. D. Salinger

Naresh Guha's "Notes on the Importance of Jewish-American Literature" (*Indian Essays*, pp. 247–59) is mostly a factual survey of the progress of Jewish intellectuals, but there is a brief discussion of Bellow's Augie March (a modern Wandering Jew in search of his identity) and Malamud's Frank Alpine of *The Assistant* (an "American Stephen Dedalus in search of his father in the Jew").

In "Bernard Malamud: A Party of One" (*Celebration*, pp. 165–88), Richard H. Rupp finds that the basic form of celebration in Malamud is the ritual lament; unlike Bellow, who accepts the "pluralism" of the present, Malamud "probes the past for the guilt that gives his Jews their primary identity." In "There Are Jews Everywhere" (*Judaism* 19:283–94), Oscar B. Goodman discusses Malamud's use of Jewishness as an "encompassing image in which concrete human experience transcends abstract ideals" in the short stories and *The Fixer*.

Helen Weinberg (*The New Novel*, pp. 165–85) finds more of Kafka's K. in Malamud's Levin of *A New Life* than most readers are likely to see, but her comments on this "*schlemiel*-as-activist" are nevertheless interesting. She also briefly considers *The Natural* and *The Assistant*, along with works by Philip Roth and Herbert Gold, in a discussion of "The School of Saul Bellow."

Both David J. Burrows and Max F. Schulz attempt to see a dimension of *A New Life* that is not normally found in the "academic novel." In "The American Past in Malamud's *A New Life*" (*Private Dealings*, pp. 86–94), Burrows suggests both the serious and ironic uses of classic American authors in Levin's career, as well as the fusion of the European immigrant image with that of the covered-wagon pioneer in the shaping of Levin as "the new man in the new world." And although his heady plans for a new life go awry, Levin chooses responsibility for Pauline because not to do so would be to repeat another series of false starts and escapes. Schulz, however, sees Levin as an explicit moral failure. "Malamud's *A New Life*: The New Wasteland of the Fifties" (*WR* 6,i[1969]:37–44) is one of the better readings of that novel; Schulz stresses the reluctance and ethical timidity of this "sacrificial victim and saviour." Malamud uses Eliot's example with vegetation myths to comment on the American psyche in the uninvolved 1950s.

In "Malamud's Trial: *The Fixer* and the Critics" (*WHR* 24:1–12), Gerald Hoag reassesses the author's most ambitious novel, clarifying its place in a long line of suffering heroes and the context of the times. The key to myth in *The Fixer* is not allusion (to Hosea, for example) but the skill that "raises a neutral anecdote to cosmic exemplum in the natural course of tale-telling." Charles E. May explicates the metaphor of bread loaves in "The Bread of Tears: Malamud's 'The Loan'" (*SSF* 7:652–54), and John S. Hill's "Malamud's 'The Lady of the Lake': A Lesson in Rejection" (*UR* 36[1969]:149–50) is a brief reading of one story about the high cost of denying one's past and heritage.

Alternately chatty and pedantic, "The Hyphenated Ham Sandwich of Ernest Hemingway and J. D. Salinger: A Study in Literary Continuity" (*FHA* 1970:136–50) is William Goldhurst's recapitulation of Nick Adams in "the Salinger hero," a composite made up of Seymour Glass, Holden Caulfield, and some unnamed narrators. By conflating many Salinger narratives, Goldhurst is able to conflate still further: "From a Huck-Finn-like childhood, to a Nick Adams youth, to a Seymour Glass conclusion, the Hemingway biography reflects, encompasses, and dramatizes a cycle covering almost one hundred years of American experience, lending to it a fascinating and fatal air of inevitability."

Mohamed Sethom is considerably less sympathetic with both the American experience seen in Salinger's works and the nature of the Salinger hero. "La société dans l'œuvre de J. D. Salinger" (*EA* 22[1969]:270–78) summarizes critical attitudes common enough earlier: the Salinger hero is an Ishmael by definition, and the society which contains him is a vast network of pariahs, martyrs, and prophets.

Holden rejects society "under the sign of sexuality," says James M. Cox, who discusses him along with characters by Mark Twain and Ring Lardner in "Toward Vernacular Humor" (*VQR* 46:311–30). What saves Holden from the fate of the "good bad boy who grows up" is his swearing, a protective and instinctive means of self-expression which insulates him from adolescent sexuality.

David J. Burrows, in "Allie and Phoebe: Death and Love in J. D.

Salinger's *The Catcher in the Rye*" (*Private Dealings*, pp. 106–14),
isolates a few important scenes to show how his sister's love comes
to offer Holden an alternative to those moments of dread (envisioned
by images of falling) of a world of change and death (represented by
his brother's death). Luther S. Luedtke makes two points in "J. D.
Salinger and Robert Burns: *The Catcher in the Rye*" (*MFS* 16:198–
201): that Holden's admission of error about *meet* and *catch* in
Burns's song comes from the "balanced perspective of his post-
Christmas rest" and that Holden, not Phoebe, is the "Jenny" who
undergoes initiation into the "world of the rye."

The Kafkan mode, ostensibly Helen Weinberg's subject in *The
New Novel*, is pretty much lost in her discussion of Salinger (pp.
141–64), which becomes a spirited defense of the mystical openness
of form in the later work. Most of the "crafted" stories are slight and
ephemeral, says Weinberg; only two of *Nine Stories* are informed by
"a mystical vision of madness which provides the way to fullness of
being otherwise unavailable in modern life," and Holden's "closed,
prestructured" character is a product of Salinger as "overzealous
craftsman." This emergent vision of the potential of the spiritual self
(which is nevertheless out of reach because of existential facts of
life) triumphs in "Seymour: An Introduction" in which Salinger fully
takes his risks with form.

"Bunnies and Cobras: Zen Enlightenment in Salinger" (*Discourse*
13:98–106) is the least of three pieces this year by Bernice and Sanford Goldstein. The goal of enlightenment, which follows the blending of the real and unreal (and various dichotomies not always spelled
out), means action and achievement for Salinger, not contemplation
as in his Eastern counterparts. "Zen and *Nine Stories*" (*Renascence*
22:171–82), though plagued by fuzziness (implicit perhaps in the
subject), makes useful distinctions among those stories whose protagonists reach a *satori* of one kind or another. But the Goldsteins
have written perhaps the best piece yet on Salinger's most exasperat-
ing story with " 'Seymour: An Introduction'—Writing as Discovery"
(*SSF* 7:248–56). Concentrating on the two epigraphs by Kafka and
Kierkegaard, they see the entire story as a narrative process taking
place "in its most Zen-like immediacy before our very eyes," and
with the emphasis on the process rather than the product of creation,
the story is really Buddy's, "his battle with himself and the changing
nature of his act of creation."

Richard H. Rupp, on the contrary, sees "Seymour" as "out-and-out hagiography," self-destructive because it is mere exhortation. In "J. D. Salinger: A Solitary Liturgy" (*Celebration*, pp. 113–31), Rupp, however, admires *The Catcher in the Rye*, neatly defining and defending Holden's sacerdotal role. He sees "Teddy" as a kind of turning point for Salinger, after which there is a radical evasion of those realities of evil which are admitted and grappled with in the earlier fiction.

v. James Baldwin and Ralph Ellison

Griffith T. Pugh has edited "Three Negro Novelists: Protest and Anti-Protest—A Symposium" (*SHR* 4:17–50), which includes, in addition to a reprinted essay on Richard Wright, Charles T. Ludington, Jr.'s "Protest and Anti-Protest: Ralph Ellison" (pp. 31–39) and Fred L. Standley's "James Baldwin: The Artist as Incorrigible Disturber of the Peace" (pp. 18–30). The first, with biography, history, and criticism all competing for attention, contains nothing new. The second is a defense of Baldwin against the attacks by Saunders Redding and others, who see and use the novel as a sociological instrument. Standley observes that the protagonists, all sensitive rebel-victims, are assaulted by their urban milieu, but that Baldwin makes them responsible for their destiny, however crushing the forces against them. His suggestion that these fictional characteristics account for the ambiguous judgments of Baldwin's contemporaries is dubious; certainly much distaste for Baldwin stems directly from the author's repudiation of political activism, one of the topics in John Hall's "An Interview with James Baldwin" (*TransR* 37/38:5–14). Standley's version of Baldwin's protagonists is corroborated in a minor item, Sam Bluefarb's "James Baldwin's 'Previous Condition': A Problem of Identification" (*NALF* 3[1969]:26–29).

Unlike that of most black novelists, Baldwin's imagery of chaos, impending doom, and catastrophe is religious, says John R. May in "Images of Apocalypse in the Black Novel" (*Renascence* 23:31–45). Wright, Ellison, and LeRoi Jones typically use secular analogues for such specific religious expectations as "the last loosening of Satan," the Judgment, and the New Heaven.

Baldwin's first novel, with community worship at its center, is "full-throated celebration," and the succeeding novels all show the search for a "secular equivalent," argues Richard H. Rupp in "James Baldwin: The Search for Celebration" (*Celebration*, pp. 133–49). What is envisioned in the essays—a community based on love, freedom, and an achieved individual and social identity—becomes "holy fantasy" in the fiction. A less sanguine view of Baldwin's first novel is found in Michel Fabre's "Pères et fils dans *Go Tell It on the Mountain*, de James Baldwin" (*EA* 23:47–61).

Using *protest* in its largest sense, Thomas A. Vogler argues in his fine "*Invisible Man*: Somebody's Protest Novel" (*IowaR* 1,ii:64–82) that the black hero is not the conventional "outsider" who serves to define weakness in the social structure; he is also a writer—and both the black and the writer are part of the society, functioning by the very virtue of that connection. "The final test of the mastery of illusion and reality, and the discovery of an identity, is the ability to *tell* it," says Vogler, and Ellison enters the mainstream of modern art through his fusion of the problems of his black protagonist with those of the writer. Vogler also investigates the intricate use of puns, name origins, caricatures, popular lore, and images which expand into symbolic acts.

Vogler and Nancy M. Tischler clash in "An Ellison Controversy" (*ConL* 11:130–35), occasioned by Tischler's "Negro Literature and Classic Form" (*ConL* 10[1969]:352–65), an intelligent study of stereotypes within a generic framework which focuses largely on *Invisible Man* and Styron's *Nat Turner*. Since Vogler believes that seeing Ellison's novel as comedy is a view *of* the novel which is included *in* the novel, he is not likely to agree with Richard H. Rupp's claim that *Invisible Man* is "probably the major festive novel" in the postwar era. Not one to emphasize the absurd hero caught in existential impasses, Rupp in "Ralph Ellison: A Riotous Feast of the Self" (*Celebration*, pp. 151–64) comes out strongly for this novel as an "elaborate musical and verbal joke, celebrating love, sacrifice, and self-knowledge as our ultimate resources against the vicissitudes of life."

Stewart Rodnon's "Ralph Ellison's *Invisible Man*: Six Tentative Approaches" (*CLAJ* 12[1969]:244–56) contains some useful pedagogical suggestions, one of which is picked up by Lawrence J. Clipper ("Folkloric and Mythic Elements in *Invisible Man*," *CLAJ* 13: 229–41), who develops it according to Lord Raglan's formula and Vladimir Propp's morphology of the folktale. Clipper's essay is one of several in the special Ralph Ellison number of *CLAJ* (13,iii), and perhaps the most provocative is Eleanor R. Wilner's "The Invisible Black Thread: Identity and Nonentity in *Invisible Man*" (pp. 242–57), which suggests two concurrent structures in the novel and two "figures"—an "ambiguous clown figure whose emergence as hero plays off against the narrator's emergence as fool."

George E. Kent takes an approach similar to Clipper's in "Ralph Ellison and Afro-American Folk and Cultural Tradition" (pp. 265–76), but the result is more diffuse. Archie D. Sanders argues that the novel is cast in a Homeric mold in "Odysseus in Black: An Analysis of the Structure of *Invisible Man*" (pp. 217–28); Phyllis R. Klotman, in "The Running Man as Metaphor in Ellison's *Invisible Man*" (pp. 277–88), sees the novel as a culmination of a tradition which begins with Natty Bumppo, of the man in flight from the values of the dominant culture; and Lloyd W. Brown shows, in "Ralph Ellison's Exhorters: The Role of Rhetoric in *Invisible Man*" (pp. 289–303), that a part of the narrator's education is in learning that all kinds of rhetoric "owe their validity to the exhorter's capacity and willingness to see life in human rather than schematic terms."

Grosvenor E. Powell attempts too much in "Role and Identity in Ralph Ellison's *Invisible Man*" (*Private Dealings*, pp. 95–105). He explores Ellison's place in the relationship "between social structure and the various ways of conceiving reality in literature." Stendhal's Julien Sorel becomes a pertinent antecedent to Ellison's protagonist. Powell also isolates and describes the several kinds of prose which appear in the novel. Like William J. Schafer (see *ALS 1968*, p. 223), Allen Guttmann sees Ellison's narrator acting out the stages of Negro history in America. In "Focus on Ralph Ellison's *Invisible Man*: American Nightmare" (*American Dreams*, pp. 188–96), Guttman sees our recent history, confirming the novel as a prophetic book, transforming an unironic affirmative conclusion into a nightmarish denial of its "small measure of optimism."

"Ralph Ellison: Novelist as Brown Skinned Aristocrat" (*Shenandoah* 20,iv[1969]:56–77), an intelligent, appreciative sketch by Richard Kostelanetz, stresses the novelist's musical experience, but it also defines Ellison's "aristocratic style of commitment," which Kostelanetz says is the avoidance of politics, even the literary variety. The late William T. Fontaine devotes part of his essay, "The Negro Continuum from Dominant Wish to Collective Act" (*AForum* 3,iv/4,i

[1968]:63–96), to what he considers the explicit exposure of communism in Ellison's Harlem scenes.

vi. Norman Mailer and I. B. Singer

The most important essay on Mailer this year is Tony Tanner's "On the Parapet: A Study of the Novels of Norman Mailer" (*CritQ* 12: 153–76). Throughout his career, argues Tanner, Mailer has unflaggingly converted "environmental pressures into lexical gestures"; his conscious effort at a "binary reduction" of life (postulating extreme alternatives, such as love-hate, victory-defeat) begins as early as 1957 as an attempt to dissipate the vagueness of "the enemy." Tanner has pertinent observations on *An American Dream* (connecting Rojack's balancing act on the parapet to Mailer's style), and his discussion of the frantic, manic voice of *Why Are We in Vietnam?* is original and persuasive.

Though she chooses *The Deer Park* as Mailer's "finest novelistic achievement," Helen Weinberg (*The New Novel*, pp. 108–40) strikes fire only when she turns to *An American Dream*, the culmination of Mailer's conception of man as the battler for his own total freedom. She suggests that Rojack operates on the political and social level as superhero (unchanging, typal), while he is what she calls the post-absurdist, activist hero (changing, searching, learning) on the personal and metaphysical level of narrative. J. Normand also stresses two different levels in Rojack, perhaps the most interesting segment of "L'Homme mystifié: Les héros de Bellow, Albee, Styron et Mailer" (*EA* 22[1969]:370–85). The various complex contradictions and ambiguities in Rojack stem fundamentally from his fertile androgynous duality, which Normand terms the fusion of "anima" and "animus."

The new oracular criticism of Ihab Hassan—an extension of Lawrence, Fiedler, Robbe-Grillet, Sontag, and others—is desultorily applied to one of Mailer's more interesting works in "Focus on Norman Mailer's *Why Are We in Vietnam?*" (*American Dreams*, pp. 197–203). Though such mannered exercises can open up astonishing depths in an author, as we know from Charles Olson's 1947 book on Melville, Hassan's seems mostly self-reflexive. Despite its uppercasing of Important Substantives, its sententiae smacking of the thoughts of both Gibran and Mao, its marvellous mingling of delphic paradoxes, orphic rhapsodies, and cthonian chants, Hassan's is a modest piece which even Mailer can do without.

There are some important omissions in B. A. Sokoloff's *A Bibliography of Norman Mailer* (Folcroft, Pa., Folcroft Press), which nevertheless includes many marginal items. This casually compiled checklist seems to incorporate works through 1968, though a few 1969 items also appear. Joe Flaherty has written his personal account of Mailer as politician in *Managing Mailer* (New York, Coward-McCann).

Ben Siegel's *Isaac Bashevis Singer* (UMPAW 86) is a warmly appreciative estimate of the Yiddish author, whose characters constitute "the most varied and coherent cavalcade of Jewish life in modern fiction." Especially alert to Singer's attitudes toward psychic phenomena and the occult, Siegel sees the fiction falling into two major modes: narratives embodying the demonic and supernatural, and the more direct, realistic tales. *The Family Moskat*, of the latter mode, has been undervalued, says Siegel, while *Satan in Goray*, his "miracle-and-cabala narrative indebted to Yiddish gothics," has been overpraised. *The Slave*, with its precise imagery and lyrical prose rhythms, is Singer's most effective fiction. This pamphlet happily devotes considerable space to the short stories, often ignored in critical surveys. George Salomon's "In a Glass Darkly: The Morality of the Mirror in E. T. A. Hoffmann and I. B. Singer" (SSF 7:625–33) is a comparative study of the evolving significance of the mirror as an artistic device which carries the admonition to "look away from the self into the hearts of men."

Unnoted here until now is Irving H. Buchen's *Isaac Bashevis Singer and the Eternal Past* (New York, New York Univ. Press, 1968), perhaps the best introduction to Singer yet written for non-Yiddish readers. Both sensitive and scholarly, Buchen's book includes two chapters on *The Family Moskat* (which reveals how Singer's "religious and demonic concerns are inevitably involved in history"), and one chapter each on *Satan in Goray, The Magician of Lublin, The Slave, The Manor*, and the shorter fiction. These are flanked by an account of the biography (approved by Singer himself) and a masterful little essay on "The Aesthetics of the Eternal Past," Buchen's attempt to isolate Singer's unique vision which allows a trafficking with the dead. Buchen relies heavily on "biblical extension" and revelation as well as the covert myths behind secular utopianism. In the past, with the *shtetl* as pivot, Singer finds "biblical and mystical proximity."

vii. Vladimir Nabokov

The Winter number of *Tri-Quarterly* (vol. 17), guest-edited by Alfred Appel, Jr., is a handsome collection of brief tributes (in prose and poetry), reminiscences, notes on translations, and a clutch of critical essays in honor of Nabokov's seventieth birthday. Only some of the contributions can be noted here, but this volume should be added to L. S. Dembo's anthology, *Nabokov: The Man and His Work* (see *ALS 1967*, p. 200 and *ALS 1969*, p. 237), as indispensable sources for future Nabokov studies. Appel's collection, however, even more than Dembo's, is a stunning confirmation of the fact that Nabokov, like Joyce a few years ago, seems to inspire the kind of criticism which he least needs—unstructured appreciations in prose that is purple, allusive, cute. Some, like Nina Berberova's "The Mechanics of *Pale Fire*" (pp. 147–59), bravely investigate the lucid intricacies of Nabokov's idioms in tortured, unidiomatic prose; and even one of the best—Peter Lubin's "Kickshaws and Motley" (pp. 187–208)— collapses from a competitive mimesis in which the critic seems determined to out-Nabokov Nabokov. (In a gloss on his critics in a supplement, Nabokov suggests that Lubin's parody-interview is "a little more exquisitely iridized" than his actual ones.)

One of the least "iridized" essays is Robert Alter's "*Invitation to a Beheading*: Nabokov and the Art of Politics" (pp. 41–59), a good defense of the anti-realist method. Both the theme and the mechanics are united in an aesthetic critique of totalitarianism; the novel affirms the "tough persistence of humanity in a world that is progressively more brutal and more subtle in its attempts to take us away from ourselves."

George Steiner ("Extraterritorial," pp. 119–27) argues that a "poly-linguistic matrix" is the determining fact of Nabokov's life and art. He sees most of the canon as a meditation in several genres on the "nature of human language." A bit thin is Stanley Edgar Hyman's "The Handle: *Invitation to a Beheading* and *Bend Sinister*" (pp. 60–71)—both novels have as their common theme "the vulgarity of power." Dabney Stuart, in "*Laughter in the Dark*: Dimensions of

Parody" (pp. 72–95), discusses the cinematic modes governing the form of this work and explores ways in which "perceptual constructions," both fictive and actual, are parodies; the idea that man lives in a " 'factual' reality is the most disturbing parody of all."

Simon Karlinsky, in "Nabokov and Chekhov: The Lesser Russian Tradition" (pp. 7–16), compares the reaction to these two writers from the defenders of the "humanitarian" tradition. "On Sirin" (pp. 96–101) is a sketch by Vladislav Khodasevich, one of Nabokov's champions among the Russian émigrés of the 1930s. Two of the more engaging personal pieces are Morris Bishop's "Nabokov at Cornell" (pp. 234–39) and Julian Moynahan's "*Lolita* and Related Memories" (pp. 247–52). Jeffrey Leonard contributes a piece on *Ada* ("In Place of Lost Time," pp. 136–46); Barbara Heldt Monter writes on the short stories ("Spring in Fialta': The Choice That Mimics Chance," pp. 128–35); and Appel's own rich "Backgrounds of *Lolita*" (pp. 17–40) with some changes becomes the introduction to *The Annotated "Lolita"* (New York, McGraw-Hill).

The only other significant item, and one which complements Steiner's essay, is Geoffrey Wagner's "Vladimir Nabokov and the Redemption of Reality" (*CimR* 10:16–23), a graceful discussion of a career which has been one long flirtation with language; Nabokov's basic technique is described as a "type of acrostic which is a mirror image of the whole wisdom of words."

viii. Robert Penn Warren and William Styron

Perhaps the most important essay on Warren this year is "*All the King's Men* and the Shadow of William James" (*SoR* 6:920–34) by Cushing Strout, who argues that the novel is not a protest against pragmatism (as exemplified in Stark's demagoguery) but a "dramatic exploration" of major Jamesian themes—the place of the hero in history, the struggle of free will and determinism, the mediating role of truth in relation to experience, the moral conversion of the "self."

Allen Shepherd's "Robert Penn Warren as a Philosophical Novelist" (*WHR* 24:157–68) is a broader study covering familiar ground, but it is a good summary. Shepherd rightly points out that our interest in Warren lies not in the originality of his ideas but in the sense of their evolution in changing contexts of his fiction, and he is fine as he describes the varied dimensions of the "dialogic life of the self" in the fiction. Shepherd also offers an interesting study of parallels and precursors in "Robert Penn Warren's 'Prime Leaf' as Prototype of *Night Rider*" (*SSF* 7:469–71). Most valuable is his observation that in transforming the novella to novel Warren shifted his protagonist's hard immovability to vacillating passivity.

Like Roger Sale some years ago, Jerome Meckier, in "Burden's Complaint: The Disintegrated Personality as Theme and Style in Warren's *All the King's Men* (*SNNTS* 2:7–21), uses the "terrible division" of the age as a crux which suggests schizoid tendencies not only in many of the characters but also in the theories and styles of Burden.

In his discussion of Warren (*Lunatic Giant*, pp. 81–110), James Hall also concentrates on the crucial conflicts in *All the King's Men* ("spontaneity and technique," "distrust for the use of mind divorced from the integrity of anger"). Of all his contemporaries, Warren most successfully activates the imagination to "the testing of hopes" and becomes a true shock novelist, not because of his violence-drenched plots or "embarrassed sexuality" but because of his "focus on the tender, murderous imagination of the twentieth century suddenly authorized to practice control upon events."

Christopher G. Katope convincingly uses Warren's essay on *The Rime of the Ancient Mariner* for explicating important imagery in the novel he was writing at the same time. "Robert Penn Warren's *All the King's Men*: A Novel of 'Pure Imagination'" (*TSLL* 12:493–510) suggests that the sun and glaring light, associated with the "reflective faculty" of Coleridge, function as death symbols in the novel; the moon, linked with the imagination, functions as a value-creating agent.

The once-fashionable rage for Sartre lies behind most of Walter Sullivan's strictures in "The Historical Novelist and the Existential Peril: Robert Penn Warren's *Band of Angels*" (*SLJ* 2,ii:104–16). Amantha's agony of identity is anachronistic, says Sullivan, because Warren indulges in "the errors of the present," and "the one thing above all else that our secular, scientific culture should have taught us is that we are always wrong." Most readers would see the problems of this novel to be more technical than ideological.

Richard B. Sale conducts "An Interview in New Haven with Robert Penn Warren" (*SNNTS* 2:325–54)—one of the most valuable of such transcripts now available for what it reveals about the author's craftsmanship as well as his opinions on other writers. In the course of it Warren repudiates the notion that *The Mill on the Floss* strongly influenced *Flood*, the subject of Russell M. Goldfarb's two-part essay, "Robert P. Warren's Tollivers and George Eliot's Tollivers" (*UR* 36:209–13, 275–79). Although he sees *Flood* as "an act of literary criticism"—"The Incest Motif in *The Mill on the Floss*"—Goldfarb seems disappointed that "neither novel explores, much less exploits, the perversity of incest."

Although most interest in Styron continues to focus on *Nat Turner*, Renate Wiemann contributes a substantial German study of the first novel, "William Styron: *Lie Down in Darkness*" (*NS* 19: 321–32). While most critics are content to speak of the pervasive Faulknerian flavor of the work, Wiemann draws specific parallels, but, more importantly, places *Lie Down in Darkness* in a larger literary context in which the corruption of innocence appears as a central theme.

Henry Irving Tragle, in "Styron and His Sources" (*MR* 11:134–53), contends that much factual information on Nat Turner and his times was available to Styron, and that ignorance or suppression accounts for his fictional distortion of characters other than Turner. Most of the punch in J. Mitchell Morse's essay on *Nat Turner* appears in his title: "Social Relevance, Literary Judgment, and the New Right: Or, the Inadvertent Confessions of William Styron" (*CE* 30 [1969]:605–16). Though the novel may be a satisfactory subject for classes in sociology and political science, says Morse, its bad writing removes it from serious consideration by students of literature.

General infelicity of style is also the subject of Roy A. Swanson's "William Styron's Clown Show," one of two new essays included in *William Styron's "The Confessions of Nat Turner": A Critical Handbook*, edited by Melvin J. Friedman and Irving Malin (Belmont, Calif., Wadsworth). In his jaunty polemic (pp. 149–64), Swanson characterizes Styron as a "seedy impresario" who "mistakes his clown show for existentialist high tragedy and grand endeavor." The other new essay in this handbook is Karl Malkoff's "William Styron's *Divine Comedy*" (pp. 164–75), which, though mistitled, is a fine explication of the major theme—the tensions between "freedom and necessity, master and slave, father and child." "William Styron: A Bibliography" by Jackson R. Bryer and Marc Newman (pp. 258–80) supplements and updates previous checklists, and to be welcomed is an important interview (from 1967) by R. W. B. Lewis and C. Vann Woodward, "Slavery in the First Person: Interview with William Styron" (pp. 51–58), previously available only in a hard-to-find journal.

Two pieces explore religious aspects of *Nat Turner*. In "Religious Implications in *The Confessions of Nat Turner*" (*CimR* 12:57–66), William J. Swanson sees Margaret Whitehead transformed from a corporeal Desdemona to a spiritual Beatrice; both Dante and Nat Turner are brought to ultimate felicity by a "mediatrix who embodies the principle of supernatural love." The philosophy of the book derives more from the "remonstrations of the Old Testament prophets" than from New Testament teachings. Donald K. Pickens agrees, in "Uncle Tom Becomes Nat Turner: A Commentary on Two American Heroes" (*NALF* 3[1969]:45–48). As "God's men," both heroes are committed to that theology which stresses living in this world "but keeping soul apart and pure for the judgment day." Potentially rich, Pickens's essay suffers from a lack of firm development.

ix. Eudora Welty and Carson McCullers

Substantial scholarship appears in two pieces on Welty's revisions by W. U. McDonald, Jr. Some critics have charged Welty with being unconcerned with social injustice, but "Welty's 'Social Consciousness': Revisions of 'The Whistle'" (*MFS* 16:193–98) is a detailed account of her artistic representation of the evils of sharecropping. "Eudora Welty's Revisions of 'A Piece of News'" (*SSF* 7:232–47) concludes that Welty's revisions go beyond the stylistic and that some of her most distinctive traits emerge late in composition.

A special Welty number of *Shenandoah* (20,iii[1969]) is comprised of brief tributes by several hands and several longer studies varying in usefulness. Joyce Carol Oates ("The Art of Eudora Welty," pp. 54–57) admires the bizarre combination of "feminine nonsense" (talk of food, intricate relationships) and the "seams of the world, through which a murderous light shines." A few biographical details emerge in Diarmuid Russell's "First Work," (pp. 16–19), a succinct and factual account of the difficulties Welty encountered in getting her stories published in book form, and "Eudora Welty's Jackson" (pp. 8–15) is Nash K. Burger's light reminiscence of his school days with Welty.

In "The Onlooker, Smiling: An Early Reading of *The Optimist's Daughter*" (pp. 58–73), Reynolds Price praises the "stripped iron efficiency" of Welty's language in her recent work, a style which differs markedly from the imagistic impressionism of the earlier fiction. In one of the best discussions of *The Bride of the Innisfallen*, Alun R. Jones, in "A Frail Travelling Coincidence: Three Later Stories of Eudora Welty" (pp. 40–53), explores the interrelated motif of the journey and the themes of homesickness and exile.

In Ashley Brown's reading of *The Robber Bridegroom*, "Eudora Welty and the Mythos of Summer" (pp. 29–35), Welty's Natchez Trace is informed by Grimm and perhaps Apuleius. Brown's distinctions between her Southern stories (told in rich vernacular) and her romances (permeated by rich mythic resonances in the Isak Dinesen manner) are valuable. Using the polarities of country and city, Robert B. Heilman, in "Salesmen's Deaths: Documentary and Myth" (pp. 20–28), gives a fine close reading of "The Death of a Traveling Salesman," Welty's first printed story, with pertinent contrasts with Arthur Miller's *Death of a Salesman*.

Concentrating on *Delta Wedding*, Elmo Howell finds the ultimate worth of Welty in "the rare delicacy of her portraiture," a talent comparing favorably with Jane Austen's, in "Eudora Welty's Comedy of Manners" (*SAQ* 69:469–79). Through the complicated genealogy of the Fairchilds and their seemingly trivial chatter, Welty posits the values on which a civilized order is based. Richard H. Rupp's interest is similar in "Eudora Welty: A Continual Feast" (*Celebration*, pp. 59–75), which offers perhaps no original readings, but Welty's lyricism works well for Rupp, who crystallizes those fictional moments which celebrate "wonder at being."

Alice Hamilton finds strange variants of Neoplatonism in "Loneliness and Alienation: The Life and Work of Carson McCullers" (*DR* 50:215–29). Though the central subject is the nature of "radiance" in its various forms—the offering of love to another, the act of artistic creation—the essay is mostly a catch-all, with a strangely misplaced biographical sketch, much plot summary, and no evident concern that other critics have treated many of these topics before.

Lawrence Graver's *Carson McCullers* (UMPAW 84) is a dispassionate, often unsympathetic, estimate in which *The Member of the Wedding* assumes first place in the canon because of its clarity of motive and act and the vivacity of its narrative rhythms. McCullers's work, says Graver, shows a continuing conflict between her "nearer and her further vision, between her desire to document the world and a desire to give it evocative poetic significance." In an essay nearly as long as Graver's pamphlet, Francesco Gozzi emphasizes the author's tradition of the grotesque as derived from and defined by Sherwood Anderson. "La narrativa di Carson McCullers" (*SA* 14[1968]:339–76) illustrates some of the common themes (the mystery of communication between people who are themselves unresolved antinomies, the private obsessive truths which tend toward further alienation) and concludes that their manipulation reveals a limited sensibility which finally insures McCullers's place among the second-rank.

x. Joseph Heller and John Barth

Doug Gaukroger, in "Time Structure in *Catch-22*" (*Crit* 12,ii:70–85), disputes a contention that Yossarian and Milo coexist in two different time structures (psychological and chronological) and that Heller's "structural absurdity" enforces the "absurdity of character and event in the novel." Gaukroger argues, with some precision, that chronological paradoxes are rare (and appends a summary of events to support his thesis). In " 'What Difference Does It Make?': Logic in *Catch-22*" (*DR* 50:488–95), W. K. Thomas comes to the not very surprising conclusion that Heller uses faulty logic for "a number of different purposes"—to amuse, to force us to look at ideas in a new light, and to show up the irrationality that lies behind many of our acts.

Two critics see a religious sensibility as the linchpin to Heller's novel. For Victor J. Milne in "Heller's 'Bologniad': A Theological Perspective on *Catch-22* (*Crit* 12,ii:50–69), the mock-epic form explains the digressive structure as well as the author's moral vision. Milne compares the theological flavor of the final chapter to Dietrich Bonhoeffer's teachings: exploitation and submission to it are the two great sins, which Heller expresses in political-economic terms. If, for Milne, Yossarian is a kind of modern Christian plunged into the indifferent "pre-Christian universe of the primary epic," for Eric Solomon he is an ineffective scapegoat-rebel (sometimes an anti-Christ, sometimes an Everyman) trapped "in a mad world of the seven deadly sins." In his survey, "From *Christ in Flanders* to *Catch-22*: An Approach to War Fiction" (*TSLL* 11[1969]:851–66), Solomon argues for a religious base as a defining characteristic in all serious war novels.

Barth's fictive reality is the subject of two complementary essays. Jean E. Kennard's interest in "John Barth: Imitations of Imitations" (*Mosaic* 3,ii:116–31) is the theoretical connections between Barth's essay on "The Literature of Exhaustion" and his later fiction. With the premise that all meaning is subjective and therefore "false," both *The Sot-Weed Factor* and *Giles Goat-Boy* are imitations of novels which use parody and illusion to stimulate a sense of the absurd in the reader. In "Barth and the Representation of Life" (*Criticism* 12:51–67), Daniel Majdiak focuses on *The End of the Road*; both the theme of nihilism (characters realizing their unreality) and its techniques are carried by parody, which in calling attention to itself tends to "transform normative 'reality' into fictive vision."

John W. Tilton's thesis in "*Giles Goat-Boy*: An Interpretation" (*BuR* 18,i:92–119) is that psychic fragmentation, a common trait in Barth's work, is most successfully developed in the mythopoeic treatment of the various hero myths in the novel.

xi. Others

a. John Updike. No one knows Updike's work better than Alice and Kenneth Hamilton, and in *The Elements of John Updike* (Grand Rapids, Mich., Eerdmans) they offer a treasury of information—biographical details, influences (Robert Benchley and Karl Barth), aesthetic patterns, and themes. Despite chaotic organization and its cheerful mingling of the trivial and the profound, *Elements* is a more valuable book than is indicated by its preface, which promises us Updike in "an outline of his thought" in various genres.

The Hamiltons probe Updike's language for puns and other wordplay, trace the various versions of the story which becomes *Rabbit, Run* (and point out Updike's use of the church calendar for its time sequences), and give a substantial interpretation of *Couples*. Their argument against those who charge Updike with superficiality is religious: his theme is the smallness of earthly things set against the radiance of eternity; no event "can be trivial in a universe ordered by truth and justice."

The Hamiltons also offer "Theme and Technique in John Updike's *Midpoint*" (*Mosaic* 4,i:79–106), a study of the author's first long poem, particularly his allusions and narrative and thematic links with the fiction. R. W. Reising counters Arthur Mizener's interpretation of one short story in "Updike's 'A Sense of Shelter'" (*SSF* 7:651–52).

Ceremony is "always a rite of connection for Updike," says Richard H. Rupp, who sees *The Centaur* especially rife with portentous (if comic) suggestions of that most ceremonial act—ritual sacrifice. His "John Updike: Style in Search of a Center" (*Celebration*, pp. 41–57) also betrays the curious assumption that if a work fails to yield the rich results of a special thesis, it fails to yield much of anything.

b. James Agee. "James Agee: The Elegies of Innocence" (*Celebration*, pp. 99–111) is, however, one of Rupp's better chapters. In a happy phrase, *Let Us Now Praise Famous Men* is described as "polemical pastoral," and there are also good interpretations of the fiction. Unable to believe in the "present reality of his celebrations," Agee embalms them in memory, a penchant for innocence that Rupp considers to be a death wish. Kenneth Curry follows up his fine study of the setting of *A Death in the Family* (see *ALS 1969*, pp. 246–47) with "Notes on the Text of James Agee's *A Death in the Family*" (*PBSA* 64:84–99).

Allen Shepherd, in "'A Sort of Monstrous Grinding Beauty': Reflections on Character and Theme in James Agee's *A Death in the Family*" (*IEY* 14[1969]:17–24), studies juxtaposed perspectives in point of view in this "internal monologue." He finds that throughout the novel Rufus is in the process of escaping from that "original self which his father despairs of recapturing."

c. Philip Roth. Scott Donaldson draws parallels between Roth's best novel and his 1961 essay calling for a tougher realism in American fiction in "Philip Roth: The Meanings of *Letting Go*" (*ConL* 11:21–35). The novel combines "Jamesian emphasis on psychological realism" with a "Dreiserian concentration on environmental forces."

Of the several post-*Portnoy* revaluations of Roth, Mordecai H. Levine's is the most solemn: "Philip Roth and American Judaism" (*CLAJ* 14:163–70) concludes that negative fictional views on Judaism reflect the author's bitter antagonism to his faith. J. Normand, in the course of his favorable reading of *Herzog* in "L'Homme mystifié: Les héros de Bellow, Albee, Styron et Mailer" (*EA* 22[1969]:370–85), dismisses *Portnoy's Complaint* as "un déshabillage narcissique."

Pierre-Yves Pétillon's "Philip Roth n'est pas mort" (*Critique* 26:821–38) is a Gallic romp through that novel and earlier ones as well as the whole "sideshow" of contemporary American culture. Through a lens supplied mostly by Alfred Kazin's memoirs, Pétillon places Roth in a larger tradition, one informed equally by Cotton Mather, Scott Fitzgerald, Edith Wharton, Bugs Bunny, and Flip Wilson.

d. **J. F. Powers and James Purdy.** In "J. F. Powers' *Morte D'Urban* as Western" (*WAL* 5:31–44), D. H. Stewart believes Powers's novel to be "the first satisfactory fictional statement of Catholic-WASP blending," the demonstration of which gets done only by much refraction of terms. The novel is a western finally because Powers faces "configurations of significance quite beyond narrowly American definitions." C. F. Burgess succinctly explicates one of Powers's most popular stories in "The Case of the Hen-Pecked Priest in J. F. Powers' 'The Valiant Woman' " (*Cithara* 9,i[1969]:67–71).

Bettina Schwarzschild has assembled some previously published essays and written new ones for *The Not-Right House: Essays on James Purdy* (Columbia, Univ. of Mo. Press, 1968). Most of Purdy's works have in common the figure of "the forsaken son" who dreams of a father to mend the defects in the cosmic machinery, but the most interesting account here is of *Eustace Chisholm and the Works.*

In "Playing House for Keeps with James Purdy" (*ConL* 11:488–510), a fine survey of most of the novels, Frank Baldanza also identifies the continuing theme of the lonely orphan searching fitfully for familial relationships. What he calls Purdy's "ur-fable" is a springboard for studying the major works as variations in genre: *Malcolm* as Kafkan allegorical fable, *The Nephew* as idyll, *Cabot Wright Begins* as satire, and *Eustace Chisholm* as tragedy. The essay is clear, sensible, and useful. James W. Grinnell's "Who's Afraid of 'Daddy Wolf?'" (*JPC* 3:750–52) is a note on the cereal-loving hero of Purdy's most popular story.

e. **Miscellaneous.** Raymond C. Palmer believes Kurt Vonnegut's views on God are behind "Vonnegut's Major Concerns" (*IEY* 14 [1969]:3–10), but the most substantial study of this author yet to appear is Tony Tanner's "The Uncertain Messenger: A Study of the Novels of Kurt Vonnegut, Jr." (*CritQ* 11[1969]:297–315). Tanner argues that the juxtaposition of settings real and imaginary suggests a preoccupation with the puzzling relationship between "facts we encounter" and "fictions we invent." "The point at which fact and fiction intersect is Vonnegut himself," a lying messenger who nevertheless acts on the assumption that "the telegrams must continue to be sent."

Granville Hicks's introduction to *Wright Morris: A Reader* (New York, Harper and Row) is a twenty-five-page summary of the achievement of an important writer. Especially useful are comments on Morris's characterization, his use of vernacular and cliché, and his imaginative use of artifacts as revelatory of man and his culture. Nalini V. Shetty, in "Wright Morris and the Territory Ahead" (*Indian Essays*, pp. 71–83), relates Morris's critical study to the ways in which he works himself out of a nostalgia for the American past. This essay, like Hicks's, is good in accounting for Morris's theories of cliché and the transforming ability of the imagination, especially as they shape the work after *The Field of Vision*.

In his pedagogical essay, "The Comic Christ and the Modern Reader" (*CE* 31:498–506), Richard B. Hauck argues for Christ figures consciously created as comic, including Ken Kesey's hero of *One Flew Over the Cuckoo's Nest*. John Bayliss argues for the importance of Willard Motley in "Nick Romano: Father and Son" (*NALF* 3[1969]:18–21,32); his great achievement was projecting himself into the white mentality, especially in *Knock on Any Door*. A good introduction to a young writer is R. H. W. Dillard's "The Wisdom of the Beast: The Fictions of Robert Coover" (*HC* 7,ii:1–11), a survey of two novels and a volume of stories. Dillard finds that Coover's writing combines a detailed naturalistic precision and the kind of freedom associated with Nabokov and Borges.

Nicholas Ayo, in "The Secular Heart: The Achievement of Edward Lewis Wallant" (*Crit* 12,ii:86–94), proposes that Wallant's fiction celebrates "radical incarnation," God's becoming man so fully that the emphasis is on the abusing of human flesh which must then be accepted without relief. Ayo is explicit in showing the "shadow side" of this writer's dialectic, but mostly asserts that Wallant's secular heart "earns" its reconciliation and insight.

In a helpful guide to a difficult novel, Donald J. Greiner, in "The Thematic Use of Color in John Hawkes' *Second Skin*" (*ConL* 11:389–400), concentrates not on the gothic vision of this novel but its structure, which is based upon "cross-references, parallels, and contrasts."

Colors provide frames of references for the often motiveless action and for the violent time shifts.

John M. Muste summarizes the achievement of a minor novelist in "The Second Major Subwar: Four Novels by Vance Bourjaily" (*Shaken Realist*, pp. 311–26). What Bourjaily says about violence in the modern world is a product of a thoughtful and imaginative mind; neither sociological nor psychological, his use of the war is nevertheless complex. In "John Cheever: The Upshot of Wapshot" (*Celebration*, pp. 27–39), Richard H. Rupp sees through and uses for his own purposes Cheever's wry, often sentimental, search for "appropriate forms." Using definitions by Mordecai Marcus, Kenneth W. Davis examines two Southwestern authors in "The Themes of Initiation in the Works of Larry McMurtry and Tom Mayer" (*ArlQ* 2,i:29–43).

John J. McLaughlin discusses style as well as the influence of the traditional prose satire and the pornographic novel in "Satirical Comical Pornographical *Candy*" (*KanQ* 1,iii[1969]:98–103). In "The Impact of Knowles's *A Separate Peace*" (*UR* 36:189–98), Peter Wolfe evaluates the premise of original sin in both that novel and *Indian Summer*, to find that "prime being" for Knowles means the "inherent savagery at the heart of man."

"Bradbury Revisited" (*CEA* 31,vi:4–6) is Willis E. McNelly's graceful profile of Ray Bradbury, "the only writer of science fiction respected by the academy" (if we exclude Vonnegut). And finally, Stanley Poss contributes "The Facts of Fiction: Interview with George P. Elliott" (*NWR* 11:62–84), in which the author gives his views on fantasy, science fiction, his doctrinal commitments, and the avant-garde.

Indiana University

14. Poetry: 1900 to the 1930s

Richard Crowder

Pound continued in 1970 to hold center stage, with Frost, Robinson, and Crane trailing after. In addition to the usual numerous articles there were biographies of Pound, Frost, and Sandburg and analytical studies of Crane, Lindsay, and Elinor Wylie. Two journals devoted all or most of an issue to Pound. Another was given over to Frost. Two books of essays on Robinson appeared (one, late in 1969; the other, a selection of reprints, with one exception).

There were no full-length general studies of the period. *Modern American Poetry: Essays in Criticism*, edited by Jerome Mazzaro (New York, David McKay Company) contains both reprinted and original essays. Those of concern here are on Robinson (H. R. Wolf), Pound (M. L. Rosenthal), Frost (Jan B. Gordon), Crane (Joseph N. Riddell), Jeffers (Robert Boyers), and Cummings (John Logan).

The *Explicator* (vol. 28) included brief analyses of Cummings's "I Will Be" (item 54), Robinson's "Richard Cory" (item 73), and Frost's "In White" and "Design" (item 41), "The Wood-Pile" (item 49), and "The Oven Bird" (item 64). Charles E. Merrill (Columbus, Ohio) published further *Checklists* and *Guides*—to Pound (Marie P. Henault), Cummings (Wilton Eckley), and Jeffers (William H. Nolte). These are useful chiefly to the tyro. Doctoral dissertations were fairly widely distributed: four each on Frost and Crane, two on Robinson and on Masters, and one each on Pound, Jeffers, Cummings, Sandburg, Wylie, and Amy Lowell.

i. Ezra Pound

In preparing to write *The Life of Ezra Pound* (New York, Pantheon Books), Noel Stock had full access to his subject's own library and papers for about a decade. Meanwhile he has published studies of Pound and his poetry, including *Reading the Cantos* (see *ALS 1967*, pp. 212–13). This present book is as close to a daily log of Pound's activities and contacts as is probably possible. Page 211, to take a typical example, accounts for "October 1917," "the second week in December 1917," "About 19 December," and "the end of December." Such careful chronological arrangement will no doubt be useful to Pound scholars, but it makes for a kind of stilted, disjointed, reference-card narrative. The index is inadequate. Dorothy Pound is sometimes mentioned in a passage not listed in the index. Edwin (called "Edward" in the text) Arlington Robinson figures on one page but does not appear in the index. The same goes for Lindsay. At least one reference to Masters is omitted, though three others are given. Nevertheless, Pound as subject is fascinating. As biographer Stock makes clear statements of fact and draws on heretofore unavailable letters and manuscripts. The story is brought to a close on June 18, 1969, the day Pound and Olga Rudge returned to Italy from a two-week visit to the United States.

Further biographical detail is supplied by Waller B. Wigginton in two items in *Rendezvous* 4,ii (1969). "The Pounds at Hailey" (pp. 31–68), supplemented by maps of "Hailey and Environs" and "Central Hailey in the 1880's" (pp. 29, 30), recounts activities of Pound's grandfather and father in Idaho. Wigginton draws his information from *Indiscretions*, deed records, newspapers, local histories, and biographies. The article is copiously documented, there being sixty-six footnotes as well as many parenthetical references. It relates Pound's family experiences in the West to passages in his poetry. Wigginton says that the *Cantos* are similar to the mountainous country around Hailey—"uncompromising, stark, separate, and completely, non-humanly alone" (a somewhat ambiguous comparison). The other Wigginton contribution is "A Homer Pound Letter" (pp. 27–29), addressed to Mrs. Susie Boice Trego, who had written Pound's father in 1925 asking for news of Ezra. Homer says that Ezra's home is now in Rapallo and that his musical compositions are being played in Paris. He encloses an advance notice of "16 *Cantos*."

Donald Gallup in "T. S. Eliot and Ezra Pound: Collaborators in Letters" (*AtM* 225,Jan.:48–62) has compiled a careful account of the assistance Eliot and Pound rendered each other from the time they first met in September 1914. Gallup had the full cooperation of Mrs. Eliot and Mr. and Mrs. Pound in the loan of letters and in the examination and analysis of the first manuscript version of *The Waste Land* before Pound's famous excisions. The article demonstrates

Pound's tremendous generosity, as well as Eliot's firm belief in Pound's genius as a poet.

William David Sherman's "The Case of Ezra Pound: A Documentary Play" (*AWR* 19, Autumn: 85–108) is in six scenes, the first in 1945, when Pound is arrested for treason. The succeeding scenes are in Pisa, Washington, and finally Spoleto in the summer of 1965. Sherman makes use of tapes and transcripts to create verisimilitude. Dorothy Pound is given very little to say, but her presence is felt constantly. At the end of the play Pound is reading from one of his poems about the impossibility of a secure peace.

In "The Pisan Cantos: The Form of Survival" (*Sense and Sensibility in Twentieth-Century Writing*, edited by Brom Weber [Carbondale, So. Ill. Univ. Press], pp. 118–29), Walter Sutton says that the two most important themes in the *Cantos* are quest and the poet's distinctive view of history. In the voyage of Odysseus Pound finds a symbol for his own quest for values. For him history amounts to the story of the decay of standards since classical times, though a certain few periods and personages have admittedly been models of the values he seeks. Sutton observes that each published group of *Cantos* further develops these two themes. The *Pisan Cantos* are more personal than earlier ones as the poet seeks to evaluate the standards he himself has regarded as vital. He has dropped his mask; he has established a definite sense of place. He is still the enemy of *usura*, but the reader detects a new note of humility. He actually describes the experiences of "Old Ez" as prisoner, and he reviews his past and catalogues his current views. In the midst of desolation he maintains self-discipline. He is definitely conscious of the sky and the birds. He leans on specific memories of past companions. Through it all he remains committed to beauty and particularly to poetry. Here "the belief in art is combined with a belief in the human capacity for endurance and love." The *Pisan Cantos* "focus on an irreducible personal integrity." More than in his earlier work, these poems give a sense of Pound's humanity. Some passages show him at the height of his lyric power.

In a forty-eight-page pamphlet, *Ezra Pound* (CWCP), Marion Montgomery looks at Pound from the Christian point of view. Chapters 2, 3, 4, and 6 are reductions of longer essays which have appeared in various journals. (The articles from which chapters 2 and 4 are taken were reviewed in *ALS 1969*, pp. 259–60.) Montgomery bases his argument on Pound's rejection of the Resurrection and his reliance on his own will for achieving Utopia. He explains Pound's so-called "arrogance" as a by-product of his determination to maintain poetic integrity—"an act of faith in his own powers, in the interest of action," for the achievement of wholeness. In the *Cantos* Pound records his "intense and fallible mind" as it works for a "wilfully anticipated end," his own desired end without the pattern and meaning that a Christian faith would give it. For Montgomery the effectiveness of the *Pisan Cantos* lies in the fact that Pound has come to realize that his intellectual position is not flawless. According to the author, Pound cannot after all be a whole man since he refuses the fulfilling potential of Christianity (reliance on something outside himself).

The anonymous reviewer of eight recent books on Pound in *TLS* ("Complete Poet's Poet," 21 Aug.:925–26) finds in them agreement that the *Cantos* are a poem of "open form" "in which time, religion and myth are of particular importance due to Pound's mystical inclinations." But, since they are also "intimately and inescapably a product of Pound's personal history and development," the reader's approach "*must* be thoroughly historicist." In much the same vein, Linda Welshimer Wagner, reviewing five books in "The Poetry of Ezra Pound" (*JML* 1:293–98), expresses dissatisfaction with Earle Davis (*Vision Fugitive*) since he limits himself to Pound's economics. On the whole, however, she finds the authors generous, willing to find out what the poet intended and then judge how well he achieved his aim. (All the books have been reviewed in one or the other of the last two issues of *ALS*.)

In "Ezra Pound—literaturnaja teorija, poèzija, sud'ba" (*VLit* 14, vi:123–47) A. Zverev states his belief that during the first decade of this century, when Pound was working for the destruction of subjectivism in poetry as well as dull rhythmic patterns and worn-out images, he was ironically moving in the direction of his own rigid theories of art. In fact, A. Alvarez answers the question of quality in Pound's poetry by saying that, in spite of his influence, he was outranked by Eliot and Yeats because his emotional range was narrow, his concerns were crotchety, his inspiration was spasmodic (*SatR* 53, 18 July: 27–39). According to John Wain, in "The Prophet Ezra v. 'The Egotistical Sublime'" (*Encounter* 33, Aug.[1969]:63–70), Pound's late work is deficient "because his grip on his own reality becomes weak." Joyce's art, on the other hand, broke down because he "bored in like a termite." Nevertheless, Pound's generosity remains an astonishment. In spite of a mutual disdain for each other's "system," Pound found truth in Joyce's early work. Pound himself stands out as "one of those men by whom the other men of their time instinctively measure themselves."

An ongoing problem in Pound criticism is the poet's relation to the symbolist movement. In "Ezra Pound's 'Approach to Paris' " (*SoR* 6:340–55), Patricia Hutchins proves by some letters published for the first time that Pound was interested in French poetry much earlier than most critics and biographers have said. Wallace Martin, however ("The Sources of the Imagist Aesthetic," *PMLA* 85:196–204), sees Taine and Theodule Ribot and other French psychologists and philosophers—and not the *Symbolistes*—as the chief influences on Pound and Hulme as they developed their ideas about the image. According to Martin, though some critics have considered Imagism the peak of Romanticism, it actually was this century's initial attempt at going beyond the dichotomy of subject and object by rational means. "In his desire to escape both subjective and objective irrelevance, [Pound] placed his faith in a scientific reductionism that has, despite reason, survived in our time."

As for other influential interests of Pound, 1970 produced articles on Marxism, Chinese literature, Fenollosa, James, and Dante. In "Ezra Pound and the Marxist Temptation" (*AQ* 22:714–25), William M. Chace sees Pound as caught between high aesthetic standards, on the one hand, and the pressures of politics, on the other. He suggests the practicality of studying Pound only after reading Karl Marx; otherwise, the poet is likely to be considered an inexplicable oddity in future histories of American literature. Sanehide Kodama, in "The Chinese Subject in Ezra Pound's Poetry" (*SELit* [Eng. No.]:37–62), provides an analysis of materials from Chinese literature that Pound found useful in his work. (Wai-Lim Yip has given full and adequate treatment of this information in *Ezra Pound's "Cathay"*, reviewed in *ALS 1969*, pp. 255–56.) D. B. Graham, in "From Chinese to English: Ezra Pound's 'Separation on the River Kiang' " (*LE&W* 13[1969]: 182–95), claims that this poem from *Cathay* has been carelessly treated by critics. Detailed analysis of Pound's *melopoeia* and *phanapoeia* here shows the poem to be "equally a translation and a new poem." For example, through the omission of certain localized references Pound has universalized the poem. The story—in Japanese—of Pound's discovery of the Fenollosa manuscripts is told by Jitsuei Kodama in "Pound no Naso to Fenollosa MSS no Hakken" (*EigoS* 115[1969]:234–37). According to Denis Donoghue, in "James's *The Awkward Age* and Pound's 'Mauberley'" (*N&Q* 17:49–50), the satiric chapters of James's novel may well have influenced the composition of "Hugh Selwyn Mauberley." The suggestion rises from Pound's long essay on James in two issues of the *Little Review* in 1918. In "Dante and Pound's Cantos" (*JML* 1:75–87), Edwin Fussell recognizes in the *Cantos* "simultaneously a secularized and a repaganized version of the *Commedia*." Pound alludes to Dante throughout his work, but, of course, transforms Dante's values and modifies his borrowings with allusions to and translations of the Greek epics.

Volume 1, number 1 of the *St. Andrews Review* contains seven articles on Pound—five of them biographical and reminiscent, two of them analytical. Lewis Leary's "Pound-Wise, Penny Foolish: Correspondence on Getting Together a Volume of Criticism" (pp. 4–9), analyzes the letters Leary received from Pound during the process of choosing the essays for a book about Pound. The poet's suggestions were both wise and kindly. Limited funds and Leary's self-termed "ignorance" prevented a total follow-through which would have resulted in a more brilliant collection. Likewise, Leary was unable to pursue the poet's suggestion that he (Pound) edit a series of textbooks on "relative values in writing" designed for freshmen and sophomores. The president of New Directions, James Laughlin, recalls, in "Pound the Teacher: The Ezuversity" (pp.17–18), his informal association, at age twenty, with Pound in Italy—brilliant conversation (chiefly monologue), attendance at the movies and concerts in Rapallo, tramps up the mountainside. Not least important to the young student were Dorothy Pound's readings aloud from Henry James. In an excerpt from his forthcoming book, Hugh Kenner ("Scatter—from *The Pound Era*," pp. 51–55) discusses details from Pound's activities between 1914 and 1920. The poet's interest in Wyndham Lewis, his influence in securing John Quinn's support for the *Little Review*, his unachieved intention to "translate" more Chinese poems and plays—all are given consideration. Kenner describes Harriet Monroe's refusal to publish *Homage to Sextus Propertius* entire and Pound's separation from *Poetry* as its foreign editor. In Kenner's view the decline and fall of *Vortex* was elegized in the Mauberley poems. Guy Davenport ("Il Vecchio," pp. 19–20) recollects visits to Pound's cell in St. Elizabeth's, where the talk was "rare, fine, and confusing." It was Davenport who brought the paper from Frost which, he asserts, began the action that finally freed Pound. In more recent years, the author observes, Pound has grown less talkative. His rare comments are "dramatically timed, perfectly apt." Harry Meacham ("I Remember Ezra," pp. 21–24) claims that Pound, not an insane traitor, earnestly sought "to educate the people of the United States." Meacham discloses that Robert Penn Warren, virtually alone, supported Pound as potential recipient of the Gold Medal of the National Institute of Arts and Letters. Pound also was recommended but never nominated to receive the Nobel Prize. Meacham knew Pound as a "generous, gentle, and understanding friend." Forrest Read ("'76: The Cantos of Ezra Pound," pp. 11–16) sees the spirit of '76 (revolution) as informing Pound's major work. The *Cantos* he classifies with Barlow's *Columbiad* and Whitman's *Leaves of Grass* as an American epic. With perhaps an excess of ingenuity, Read develops an elaborate analysis based on the number four. For example, he finds four "histrions"—Columbus (cantos 1–71, discovery), Tom Paine (cantos 74–84, colonization), Pound himself, with John Adams (cantos 85–109, founding), and Confucius (cantos 110–20, renewed civilization)—each of whom lived fourfold lives (for Columbus it was four voyages, for Paine, four books, and so on). The necessary brevity of the article makes the analysis seem arbitrary and imposed. One would hope that Read's book-length exposition (in preparation) would make all clearly justifiable. In "Pound and Confucianism" (p. 45), Akiko Miyake tries to demonstrate that the poet showed a common pattern in Eastern and Western cultures through a comparison of the Eleusinian mysteries and the Confucian history of China. This one-page article has the incomplete flavor of a dissertation abstract.

Sou'wester published an *Ezra Pound Birthday Issue, October 30, 1970*, edited by James Taylor. Eustace Mullins ("Ezra and America," pp. 3–5) points out that Pound's work is open-ended, not "dead" like Hemingway's, Fitzgerald's and Frost's. He has been crying out against pollution for sixty-five years. He has been truly American in always wanting to "make it new." "His work exists, not for the confounding of fools, but for the inspiration of those who believe in literature, . . . in America, . . . in life." This essay is impressionistic, and neither scholarly nor critical. In another excerpt from his new book, *The Pound Era*, Hugh Kenner ("Douglas," pp. 6–20) discusses the influence on Pound's thinking of Clifford Hugh Douglas (1879–1952). To Pound Douglas's principle of "Social Credit" seemed sound, since most of a country's wealth comes from processes and tools that are "the cultural inheritance of the community" (not "of the workers"). The idea of Social Credit was "an ordered view of what mankind was doing." A point of conflict was that present cost accounting does not know how to figure support for the time-energy expended by the sculptor or poet except to pay by piece or word. All shareholders in the community (i.e., everybody) should receive a State Dividend from the "absorbing energy" of production. R. P. Dickey, in an "Introduction to the Esthetic and Philosophy of the Cantos" (21–35), points out that Pound's aesthetic derives from Aristotle, the Imagists, and Chinese poetry. The poet's "philosophy" is practical and active. His basic metaphor uses light as the provenance of all that is good and creative. Finding sustenance for his faith in Confucius, Ovid, Neoplatonism, and "certain elements of Catholic thinking," he believes in a "permanence" even behind all the unproductive hypocrisy of modern life. Marion Montgomery's "Ezra Pound's Arrogance" (pp. 46–54) is identical with chapter 5 of his Eerdmans pamphlet, reviewed above.

Pound's long-time friend and student, Marcella Spann, published an essay in *Agenda* (8,iii–iv:40–43) entitled "Beauty in Fragments." She has here permitted it to be reprinted under the title "Ezra Pound: *Drafts and Fragments of Cantos CX–CXVII*" (pp. 55–58). Instead of continuing his struggle against usury and toward light, the poet here finds rest in beauty. He looks "straight into the heart" and finds the motives for action—the forging of "a world of permanent value." Through a careful study of the records of *The Dial*, Nicholas Joost ("Ezra Pound and *The Dial*—And a Few Translations," pp. 59–71) has discovered that Pound was not only this magazine's "very informal agent" and translator of European poets who was fired in 1923 and rehired in 1928, but contrary to the belief of some commentators "was paid, published, and publicized by *The Dial*" during the twenties. In other words these were not "forgotten years."

Through characteristic economy and vigor of language, variation in accent, and syntactical structures similar to haiku, Pound's "Separation on the River Kiang," in contrast with other translations, is

"an objectified drama of loss and realization of hope in an after life."
Such is the opinion of William J. Meyer in "The Imagist and the
Translator: Ezra Pound's 'Separation on the River Kiang'" (pp. 72–
80). (See the review of D. B. Graham's article above.) Randolph
Splitter relates canto 39 to the first six cantos ("Pound's Dream of
the Gods: A Baker's Half-Dozen of the *Cantos*," pp. 81–99). The early
cantos are structured on descent into "unconscious memory," "the
significant content of the dream" returning possibly more often than
seems necessary—for emphasis. Frequent metamorphosis leads to
ideogram. Then canto 39 caps the opening six as it returns to the
source of the dream—eros, "the ultimate ground of any dream."

Douglas L. Cooney ("Ezra Pound: A Study of His Prosody," pp.
100–17) gives chief consideration to cantos 1, 4, and 45, in which he
finds a dominance of accent based on the length of the sound of a
syllable (a quantitative mode). No general pattern emerges, but
rather a concern "with the musical phrase, and then with the canto,
and then with blocks of cantos, and finally with the total cumulative
effect." James Taylor, the editor of this issue, is caustic in "The
Typical Critic of Pound" (pp. 118–23). He blasts out at William Van
O'Connor, whom he sees as sterilely dismissing Pound as "the mad
poet." In his UMPAW essay (see *ALS 1963*, p. 176) O'Connor "failed
or refused to recognize [Pound's] . . . creativity and . . . genius."
Poems about Pound conclude the issue (pp. 125–38).

Renato Barilli's *Poetica e Retorica* (Milan, Mursia, 1969) is a
comparative study of the relation of rhetoric to poetry in the work
of Pound, Eliot, and five Italian poets, including Leopardi.

ii. Robert Frost

Without doubt the big news in Frost scholarship in 1970 was the
publication of the second volume of Lawrance Thompson's biography, *Robert Frost: The Years of Triumph, 1915–1938* (New York,
Holt, Rinehart and Winston). Awarded the Pulitzer Prize, it reads
like a novel, divided into thirty-four lively chapters, each with an
inviting title and an appropriate epigraph. The action extends from
the 1915 homecoming from England (including some extravagant
and delaying activities in New York and Boston before Frost's rejoin-
ing his family, sent ahead to Vermont) to the poet's "closing . . . out
of Amherst." Details show him as something of a monster, jealous,

egocentric, and cruel. The notes—kenneled in the rear—are given their own table of contents. They extend for 190 pages, some of them of considerable length. The elaborate index contains "sixty-three topical subheads which help illuminate the complicated and contradictory responses of Frost as man and as artist." The topics are widely varied: atheism, friendship, misunderstanding, pretender, style, utopia, and so on. Included in the book is a group of photographs from various of the years of the narrative. This is altogether a highly readable and extremely useful book.

Edward H. Cohen, in "Robert Frost in England: An Unpublished Letter" (*NEQ* 43:285–87) shows Frost, in a letter dated 27 February 1938, correcting Jessie Rittenhouse in the matter of the publication of *A Boy's Will*. He insists that he did not go to England to find either a publisher or an audience. Furthermore, he assures his correspondent that the book was in no way influenced by the Georgian poets with whom he consorted during his sojourn in England.

In *Modern American Poetry*, Jan B. Gordon ("Robert Frost's Circle of Enchantment," pp. 60–92) traces Frost's poetic development from his high school effusions in 1891 to *In the Clearing* (1962), exploring the poet's metaphor of the circle as a means of reducing alienation ("momentary stay") and at the same time of increasing a consciousness of its imminence. (Frost had his own "desert places.") Gordon draws an extended comparison between Frost's poems and the paintings of Andrew Wyeth: "In the art of both men there is a kind of airlessness that redeems the act on one hand and the poetry on the other, by just deflecting them from illustration." Among others, Gordon explicates "Home Burial," "West-Running Brook," and "Directive."

In "The Emersonianism of Robert Frost" (*ESQ* 57[1969]:61–66) William Chamberlain sees Frost as modifying Emerson's passivity to inspiration and faith in a poem's organic development with a pragmatism close to that of William James. Frost's "stay" is "a reorientation of the mind by which new departures are made possible" —his "way of believing the future into existence." Whereas Emerson believed that evolution reconciles fate and liberty, Frost shows his faith in "human resistance to chaos" in such poems as "After Apple-Picking" and "West-Running Brook." A close examination of "Directive" reveals Emerson-related ideas at work—especially the growth of form countering chaos and confusion, not imprisoning the poet but giving him an opportunity to move on, to create further: "his life is meaningful in the process of creation."

Also dealing with the problem of "A Stay Against Confusion" in *S&S* 33(1969):25–41, Annette T. Rubenstein thinks that Frost's "atheism" contrasts with Wordsworthian pantheism in viewing nature as totally indifferent to man. Frost differs further from Wordsworth in preferring "second-growth timber," that is, "unused roads, fields once cultivated but now overgrown with blueberries or woods, unclimbed mountains shadowing rocky pasture land." Nowhere does he "hint of the pathetic fallacy." There is still further contrast between Frost's pluralism and the monism of both Wordsworth and Emerson. Often, as in "Stopping by Woods on a Snowy Evening," he "holds two values quivering in a delicate balance." Time and again he resists the "invitation to succumb to the unconsciousness of nature."

Citing such poems as "Home Burial" and "West-Running Brook," Robert H. Swennes finds in such dialogue poems differing subject matter about domestic life but a recurring theme: how necessary it is, for a complete sense of union, to be open in expression of love and, for that matter, effective in all forms of communication ("Man and Wife: The Dialogue of Contraries in Robert Frost's Poetry," *AL* 42:363–72). That Frost is more *country* than *nature* poet is the contention of Theodore Morrison in "Frost: Country Poet and Cosmopolitan Poet" (*YR* 59:179–96). Because Frost creates his own kind of world, he will continue to be read despite the decrease in rural interest in our civilization. Morrison explicates several poems, including "All Revelation," which develops the idea that "the rural swinger of birches and the cosmopolitan poet" are identical. Reviewing the Trilling-Adams quarrel over Frost as "terrifying poet," Lloyd N. Dendinger ("Robert Frost: The Popular and the Central Poetic Images," *AQ* 21[1969]:792–804) discusses the question of Frost's popularity, in spite of his questioning of the materialism (the very heart?) of American social values and intents. He is widely read, probably because of his image as a "traveler through the natural world." He appeals to the basic American concept of "the solitary man confronting . . . the great American wilderness" and plays the role of an unpretentious, candid rural citizen. In a rather ingenious examination of Frost's point of view, Robert S. Vinson, in "The Roads of Robert Frost" (*ConnR* 3:102–07), has Frost (1) leaving the road (rejecting conformity, attempting to find meaning in nature), (2) returning to the road (defeated by a resisting nature, determined to focus on man), and (3) finding the road out (discovering, as in "Directive," that the meaning of life is in the human spirit).

With Scandinavian thoroughness, Johannes Kjørven has produced "Two Studies in Robert Frost," published in *Americana Norvegica* (pp. 191–218). The first study is a close reading of "The Road Not Taken," which Kjørven suggests might properly be expanded to "The Road Not Taken But Kept." He argues that the idea grows "from a creative recall"; hence, "kept." The view arrived at in the final stanza is an acquired "recognition of the matter of choice" and what may happen in the mind as a result. A true choice remains "permanently present in the inward eye," whereas a superficial decision or a "passive yielding" can never make such a lasting impression. The "sigh" must be read in the context of the entire poem: it is caused partly by regret that so much has been lost by the choice, but the choice testifies to the fact "that man is most free when he wills that which is his destiny." The final line expresses the poet's feeling of "awe and wonder" at freedom of choice and its consequences. Kjørven's second study is entitled "The American Poet in England." It is a review of English attitudes toward Frost from 1913 to about 1950. Fellow poets—Gibson, Aldington, Abercrombie—were among the reviewers of *North of Boston*. C. M. Bowra was his "first scholarly critic." Frost's reputation as something more than an "American poet" has increased with the years. He now appears to be "speaking to humanity at large."

D. S. J. Parsons reads "Once by the Pacific" as the "abstract of a tragedy" ("Night of Dark Intent," *PLL* 6:205–10). Reminded of *Othello* by the quotation, "Put out the Light," the author sees the entire poem in the light of the play: the threat, the dark irony, the hero's rage, which victimizes Desdemona. The poem Frost recited at the Kennedy inauguration is more complex than his hearers perceived. This is the opinion of Hamida Bosmajian in "Robert Frost's 'The Gift Outright': Wish and Reality in History and Poetry" (*AQ* 22:95–105). The poet permits his readers (hearers) to envision what they want to, and he shares their delight, but at the same time he criticizes the community, his attack going virtually unnoticed: he cannot communicate because the community remains "such as we were." His increasing complexity of style alienates his audience.

Frost, too, knows that the fulfillment of the American dream is highly unlikely because the people will not really work to achieve it.

The title of William H. Pritchard's article is from Frost's essay "'The Figure a Poem Makes': Wildness of Logic in Modern Lyric" (*Forms of Lyric*, pp. 127–50). Readers demand "wild lines out of private hearts" (an Emersonian idea). Yet often the most difficult thing to do in getting at a poem is to "imagine the speaking voice," for, even when we think we have succeeded, we must in all honesty ask "what it is we admire it *as*, delight in it *for*." Frost's own best poems are always "a little beyond our characterizing words," are always "wild tunes," always transform logic "into something else." Pritchard looks at works by younger poets—Lowell, Merrill, Wilbur, Jarrell—to see how they have followed Frost's proposal. The author's conclusion is that "the poet helps those readers who help themselves" in comprehending that the most moving logic is, indeed, wild.

BSUF devoted its Winter issue (11,i) principally to Frost. Lesley Frost Ballantine ("Somewhat Atavistic," pp. 3–6) reviews the influence Frost's mother had on her son's early reading and learning, but adds nothing to what Frost scholars already know. Dorothy Judd Hall ("Painterly Qualities in Frost's Lyric Poetry," pp. 9–13) offers such comments as a comparison of the poems to "a delicate Japanese silk-screen print" rather "than a riotous Matisse" except on rare occasions. She describes Frost's effects as the result of "diffused lighting," remarking also that he prefers purple and its lighter-hued variants. She admonishes readers to take the poet's injunction literally: "The poet's first job is to see."

In "Mother's Private Ghost: A Note on Frost's 'The Witch of Coös'" (pp. 16–20), Thomas R. Thornburg argues that the ghost of the woman's lover is not seen by the husband, who complies with his wife's hallucination in an effort to tranquilize her. Thornburg characterizes the poem as typically melancholy and quietly desperate. Keith Cox ("A Syntactic Comparison of Robert Frost's '. . . Snowy Evening' and 'Desert Places,'" pp. 25–28) finds that the first two stanzas of the poems have similar "basic sentence elements" ("noun-verb units"), but that they differ in predication, the sentences in "Desert Places" sounding incomplete. "Desert Places" also uses more "affixes," the result being longer words and longer rhythmic patterns. In "Rationalization in Two Frost Poems" (pp. 33–35), William B. Bache points out that "The Road Not Taken" becomes more meaningful and valuable as a poem when the reader is dramatically aware "that the speaker can qualify a lost past and . . . imagine a sad future." In "Two Tramps in Mud Time" "the speaker rationalizes his way out of an impossible moral situation."

In his sonnet "Why Did I Laugh Tonight?" Keats asks his question time and again. Robert F. Fleissner ("Frost's Response to Keats' Risibility," pp. 40–43) asserts that Frost, in "The Demiurge's Laugh," says he knows what the laugh means (though the reader may not be certain). At any rate, Keats appears to exult in death whereas Frost, almost pathetically, affirms life. Fleissner finds echoes of Keats throughout Frost. Sister Catherine Theresa's "New Testament Interpretations of Robert Frost's Poems" (pp. 50–54) records a number of echoes of the New Testament, both phrases and themes. Curiously, the author quotes from Bible translations obviously not the King James Version, which would have been the one Frost knew. William A. Sutton, in "A Frost-Sandburg Rivalry?" (pp. 59–61), reports that his survey of many people who should know proves that the two men were friendly, though given to "razzing and kidding" each other. By contrasting "Two Versions of a Poem by Robert Frost" (pp. 65–68), R. Glenn Martin finds eleven changes in the final version of "Our Hold on the Planet" from the first version—a Christmas greeting to members of a Harvard class (dated January 1941). There is a shift in the order of rhymes as well as some differences in typography and meter. The result is tighter structure.

iii. E. A. Robinson

Two more essays on Robinson by David H. Burton now come to our attention. "The Intellectualism of Edwin Arlington Robinson" (*Thought* 44[1969]:565–80) sets out to demonstrate that Robinson's poetry was prophetic of the turmoil of the 1960s, reminding us that our problems have deep roots. Burton directs attention to the poet's debt to Puritanism, shown in the way conscience works in many poems, in the sense of sin, and in the need for self-knowledge. Burton repeats what scholars know—that Royce's idealism, tempered by Emersonian transcendentalism, appealed to Robinson as a Harvard student. Repelled as he was by philosophic and scientific materialism, he nevertheless was affected by science itself in his realism and his devotion to character analysis, akin to the techniques of psychoanalysis. Robinson, too, was outspoken in his criticism of the direction democracy was going in the United States. In general, says Burton, the poet was sympathetic with the "growing disenchantment of many American intellectuals with the old order." There is nothing very new in Burton's essay. Nor does he advance far in his more recent essay on "E. A. Robinson and Christianity" (*Spirit* 37:30–35), which says again what he said in an essay reviewed in *ALS 1969* (p. 265)—that the poet was critical of organized religion but maintained faith in "the integrity of individual men." It was, however, his Christian tendencies that kept him "from ultimate despair."

In "E. A. Robinson and Henry Cabot Lodge" (*NEQ* 43:115–24), John W. Crowley publishes an exchange of letters between these two men from 1909 and 1924. Lodge proves to have been an enthusiastic and constant reader and rereader of Robinson's poems. Several letters deal with details of "On the Way." In one letter Lodge says that "Avon's Harvest" reminds him of Poe. Robinson encourages Lodge to keep the faith that the poetry of his son (George Cabot Lodge) will eventually receive its deserved recognition. In "The Poetry of Edwin Arlington Robinson" (*RMS* 13[1969]:132–47) John Lucas, reviewing the details of Robinson's emergence into the twentieth century, examines at varying lengths "Reuben Bright," "New England," "For a Dead Lady," "Mr. Flood's Party," and "Isaac and Archibald," and refers to others. Lucas judges Robinson a better poet than Frost because he was generous, fair-minded, and intelligently humble towards his characters. That he accepted the "mysteriousness" of even everyday people marks him as "one of the necessary poets." In an article not very well articulated, John Crawford ("Success and Failure in the Poetry of Edwin Arlington Robinson," *Rendezvous* 5:27–29) holds that, though the poet accepts failure as inevitable, "he finds life interesting, enjoyable, and worth living," but is under no illusion that "permanent happiness or success" is possible. Every man is accountable for his own failure—not through "vice and sin but by some error in his judgment." What successes there are have the color of skepticism and doubt. Robinson's brand of happiness lies in recognizing the coexistence and intermingling of failures with successes.

Francis Murphy edited *Edwin Arlington Robinson: A Collection of Critical Essays* (Englewood Cliffs, N.J., Prentice-Hall). Murphy's introduction (pp. 1–7) traces the poet's life and reviews the well-known traits of character—reticence, dedication, isolation—and the "defensive and slightly apologetic" tone of even his favorable critics. The editor draws most of his comments from Levenson, Dickey, Fussell, and other authors of essays in his collection. All of the selections are reprinted from other sources except the study by Josephine Miles, "Robinson's Inner Fire" (pp. 110–16), an examination of the poet's vocabulary. Professor Miles thinks of Robinson as a foreshadower of "the modern poet's connotative, implicative, nostalgic sense of beauty." Though he writes principally of "romantic natural beauty," he treats his material with the skepticism and unhappiness that makes him modern. "He praises with nostalgia and he blames with apprehension; many young poets today share his combination of attitudes and even his vocabulary of dismayed values."

H. R. Wolf has an essay in *Modern American Poetry* on "E. A. Robinson and the Integration of Self" (pp. 40–59). Wolf reads Robinson's shorter narratives in the framework of Freudian psychology. The inability of the characters to attain integrity of self results in "low-keyed psychic tragedies and elegies." For example, Wolf's interpretation of "Mr. Flood's Party," the Annandale poems, "Aunt Imogen," "The Gift of God," "Luke Havergal," and "Reuben Bright" is based on Freud's theory of mother-son attachment. "Aaron Stark" is structured on "an anal preoccupation." One must wonder here why Wolf misreads "unkempt" and "snarled" as "unkept" and "gnarled." He concludes that Robinson's work "must be approached . . . from a view of ego structure." Wolf's peremptory tone smacks a little of insecurity.

W. R. Thompson's "Broceliande: E. A. Robinson's Palace of Art" (*NEQ* 43:231–49) supports the thesis that hope of the world's salvation lies in imagination. Robinson intended Merlin to be presented as both counselor and as lover. It is too simple to think of *Merlin* as based solely on the idea that even an intellectual can be caught in the toils of passion. Thompson sees this poem as very complex (the method of composition differing entirely from that of the short poems). Camelot is a house built by reason; Broceliande is a palace of art in the realm of the imagination. Whereas Merlin's knowledge is the result of discipline, Vivian's comes from intuition. Merlin is able to see, however, that a world which denies the imagination is sterile. Robinson is telling his readers symbolically that the failures in this world are due to rationalism, that amelioration and liberation can be achieved only through the imagination. Specifically, for Robinson, the artist is alienated, not enmeshed. American culture needs the artist and his imagination if it is to survive as a total, unfragmented civilization.

For the centennial year, Ellsworth Barnard edited *Edwin Arlington Robinson: Centenary Essays* (Athens, Univ. of Ga. Press [1969]. The editor's essay, " 'Of This or That Estate': Robinson's Literary Reputation" (pp. 1–14), lists a number of causes for Robinson's decline in fame after the mid-thirties. His death was a contributing factor. Critics thought his last poems thin in plot, garrulous in dialogue, involved in syntax, relaxed in meter, and sparse in vivid imagery. Readers were more interested in reformation of society than of the individual. Macmillan failed to issue an inexpensive edition of his best poems. The poet had presented no "dramatic public image." Critics found no desirable "strangeness" in his verse. (He seemed to distrust the senses.) He was more interested in people than in symbolism. His anti-absolutist stance was unpopular. Now, however, in Barnard's opinion, there appears to be a modest revival. He does, after all, have a "way with words." He is a master of form in conjunction with theme. His vision is eternal, a vision of human character as it really is.

William J. Free considers "The Strategy of 'Flammonde' " (pp. 15–30). He finds the chief fault in Robinson's poetry to be the paucity of "fresh metaphors." The way the poet escapes from hackneyed abstraction is through "the objectivity of character." The portrait of Flammonde is very simple. The first four stanzas sketch out an image of aristocracy; the second four illustrate the image; and the third four destroy it. At the end we can accept Flammonde only as a mystery—a "substitute for light." Free defines the subject matter of the poem as the "ultimate failure of human perception." He thinks the poem works, then, because it embodies the idea in the skillful use of character.

David H. Hirsch examines " 'The Man Against the Sky' and the Problem of Faith" (pp. 31–42). First of all, the fire imagery is important for its various levels of meaning and for its unifying function. Hirsch notes that Robinson's fire does not purify, but may illuminate, though the goal is obscure. There is no ultimate revelation. The hill may be in hell. Certainly the "man" is internalized, that is, exists "in the imagination of the narrator." The questions at the end are the result of this internalization. For Robinson faith is persistent and, indeed, ineradicable. Hirsch does not think, however, that there is any necessary logic in Robinson's final argument that without knowledge or intuition of something beyond this world a man would choose suicide. He labels the poet's brand of faith "a source . . . of intensified anxiety." Scott Donaldson's "The Book of Scattered Lives" (pp. 43–53) looks at some of the New York poems. The men of the Calverly group—Clavering, Leffingwell, and Lingard—cannot cope with the world. Robinson's "clues" are characteristically of no value to the reader in understanding these men. "Veteran Sirens" and "The Poor Relation" are about women for whom he has "sympathy or empathy" but no devotion. In spite of these limitations, Donaldson detects more affection for the New Yorkers than for the New Englanders.

Robert D. Stevick analyzes "The Metrical Style of E. A. Robinson" (pp. 54–67). Robinson's greatest successes came through "verbal excitement" enclosed in ordinary (even rigid) meter and syntax. (Stevick contrasts the mediocre "The Unforgiven" with the superior "Eros Turannos.") In the beginning Robinson's meter followed pretty much the scansions of tradition. Later he turned frequently to a non-foot line based on "bulk" and certain features of syntax that mark line endings. At their best, the later poems are characterized by a "delicately subtle intellectual kind of aesthetic merit." The poet's letters to Josephine Preston Peabody form the basis for Wallace L. Anderson's "The Young Robinson as Critic and Self-Critic" (pp. 68–87). Robinson always stressed "naturalness, musicality, and economy of expression." It was bad practice to indulge in abstract philosophizing.

Charles T. Davis shows the influence of nineteenth-century versions of the Tristram legend on Robinson ("Robinson's Road to Camelot," pp. 88–105), but, though Wagner, Arnold, and Swinburne were an inspiration, Malory's *Morte d'Arthur* provided "a vast store of plots, characters, and situations." In reading about Robinson's Camelot, however, "we lose any sense of varied and motley origins." In "The Transformation of Merlin" (pp. 106–19) Nathan Comfort Starr pronounces Vivian the most original character in *Merlin*—no longer wanton, but "fascinating and capable," with "a good mind which she wants to improve." Not only does she possess common sense, but she is capable of stimulating Merlin intellectually. Merlin, on the other hand, is more derivative, though he is capable of vigorous action, fully aware of his two obligations—to Vivian and to Arthur. In general, if Vivian can be said to be centripetal, Merlin is centrifugal, for his prophetic vision has sometimes left him out of the difficulties of daily life. Starr reminds us that in this poem Robinson is unusually atuned to the sensuous surfaces of life. He paints Broceliande in lush colors. He also explores "the world of subtle sense impression and suggestion." The story is "a poignant account of a doomed love, acted out by living people . . . in a world which constantly suggests a dimension greater than Camelot."

Christopher Brookhouse, in "Imagery and Theme in *Lancelot*" (pp. 120–29), analyzes the nine sections of this book to show how the setting is metaphorically central to the structure of the story. Section 1 "suggests a false, mortal paradise." Section 9 at the Almesbury nunnery emphasizes the necessity for the lovers to find private salvation in eventual separation from the world of the material, to discover the need for endurance, and to strive for "spiritual vision beyond the garden of this life."

"A Crisis of Achievement: Robinson's Late Narratives" (pp. 130–56) is the subject of Jay Martin's article. After 1910, the author thinks, Robinson seemed more and more driven by a desire for "position, material success, and fame." Since American poets were having to write "either poems without content or poems without context" to meet the demands of American readers for either amusement or edification, Robinson's Arthurian poems lost the quality of myth while maintaining a mythic content. In his other poems Robinson balanced "scientific materialism" with the "science of mind." In the late narratives, beginning in 1921, Robinson moved toward defining "personality and reality" anew: he was interested in the individual on whom the world had had effect—not in ideas or truths. He was interested in responses, not causes. Hence, the common pattern of his poems is self-discovery and rebirth. "He thought of poetry as a way of preserving personality and thus civilization." J. C. Levenson's "Robinson's Modernity" (pp. 157–74) is a reprint. (See *ALS 1969*, p. 265).

The final essay in this collection is by Radcliffe Squires—"Tilbury Town Today" (pp. 175–83). Squires sees Robinson's style as coming "to seem more and more original, more and more brave," whereas the experiments of Pound, Eliot, and Crane have blurred "into a convention." His style is haunting, entreating, courteous, and quietly intelligent. The rhythms are inevitable, the rhymes inescapable. The content is clear and comprehensible, created within the poem, generally dramatic. If he insists on the survival of the individual beyond society, "as soon as he had saved a soul from society he wanted to return it to society." For example, "Eros Turranos" ends with a commentary by the town. He wrote "for all time," searching for health and survival. This essay is the exact opposite of Murphy's "apologetic."

iv. Hart Crane

It is good to have Brom Weber's *Hart Crane, A Biographical and Critical Study* (1948) reprinted by Russell and Russell (New York). Weber has prepared a new preface and has brought his facts up to date from the research of the last two decades.

A new book-length analysis of the poetry is R. W. Butterfield's *The Broken Arc: A Study of Hart Crane* (Edinburgh, Oliver and Boyd [1969]). This is a straightforward critical consideration of Crane's poems in the order in which they were written. The author makes use of biographical material, letters, reviews, and scholarly and critical studies to help in getting at the meaning of the works. He says Crane was motivated to write his early poems by a need to escape from the "squalor of matter" into "absolute beauty." He finds in "Black Tambourine" evidence of Crane's maturing interest in "words, images, and structure" as well as in increasing compassion with an accompanying feeling of alienation from the modern world. "Chaplinesque" is a step forward in developing the theme that all outside the inner self is hypocrisy—that bourgeois society is not "true in the spirit." Butterfield devotes an entire chapter to the composition and an analysis of "For the Marriage of Faustus and Helen," in which Crane's concern with beauty came to a climax in relation to the times. Like other responsible critics, the author concedes that in "Voyages" one finds some of the poet's very best work. He contributes serious consideration and frank opinions to the body of studies of these lyrics ("Voyages II" especially). He asserts that Crane's idealism receives its best statement here. *The Bridge* is the subject of three chapters—one on the protracted circumstances of the writing, the others on "A Meaning for the Past" and "A Vision for the Present." After seven years, "The man who completed the poem shared few beliefs and attitudes with the man who began it."

Except for "The Broken Tower," the shorter poems of 1926–1932 were unpolished though poignant, of more importance to biography than to criticism. "The Broken Tower" itself begins in fearful doubt but ends in a restoration to Crane of his feeling of "power to redeem the world with his word." The brief concluding chapter assesses the poet's achievement. The author relates Crane's "dark and light regions" to Poe and Whitman, but admits to his lack of emotional self-discipline "and his refusal to make any consistent attempt to understand the destructive and divisive forces at work in the material world." Though Crane was a "failure," he did leave some great lyrics and some exquisite and powerful passages in longer poems that "convey . . . the extremes of his emotional experience, the terror of his despair and the splendor of his vision." Appendices include an account of the early influence of Nietzsche and Plato, some relevant poems by Samuel Greenberg, an annotated list of analyses of "Voyages II," and an annotated catalogue of opinions of *The Bridge*. There is a selective bibliography. This book is readable, orderly, and sane. It should be very useful to students of Crane.

Letters written between January 1917 and May 1924 are given first publication by Thomas S. W. Lewis in "Hart Crane and His Mother: A Correspondence" (*Salmagundi* 9[1969]:61–87). They reflect Hart's efforts at "pleasing his mother" and her mistaken concern about his "falling in love." These letters are in the Butler Library at Columbia. Sy Kahn gives a narrative account of one of the poet's most important friendships in "Hart Crane and Harry Crosby: A Transit of Poets" (*JML* 1:45–56). Though the acquaintance lasted less than a year (ending with Crosby's suicide in December 1929), Crosby and his wife were enthusiastic readers of Crane's poetry in manuscript. The two men held the same view of "the nature and function of poetry," in spite of Crosby's loss of faith in any spiritual values in American life. Crosby was a true expatriate, whereas Crane was simply a traveler. The Crosbys encouraged Crane in the composition of *The Bridge*. Mrs. Crosby carried through their offer to publish it even after her husband's death. The article concludes with a summary of the remaining two and a half years of Crane's life and a catalogue of similarities between the two men: their attitudes toward death, their mysticism, their use of sun and sea as symbols, their conviction that absolutes exist, and their "quest for unitive and ultimate knowledge."

M. D. Uroff, in "Hart Crane's 'Voyages VI,' Stanza 6" (*ELN* 8:46–48) differs with interpretations of the "lounged goddess" as Eos (dawn) or Venus (love). She identifies her rather with Amphitrite (queen of the sea). Thus it is the sea which discloses to the speaker in stanza 6 the renewal and purification of life so that it becomes paradise. Malcolm Cowley, in "Hart Crane: The Evidence in the Case" (*SR* 78:176–84), amplifies former accounts of Crane's part in the publication of *Blue Juniata*. Cowley had sent to Crane the first inscribed copy of the book, which Peggy Baird was able to rescue from his stateroom the day following his suicide. J. A. Bryant, Jr. ("Hart Crane, Poet of the Sixties," *JML* 1:283–88) offers an explanation of the current interest in Crane: "his vitality, his Romantic interests, and his iconoclastic idiosyncracies." He suggests that the story of Crane's life has certain parallels with the lives of Marlowe, Chatterton, and Keats. In these relationships his "story is recognizable as a rare and ancient one." Crane's "visceral impact" differs from Rod McKuen's in being "a rare expression of subtle feelings." Crane's most important contribution to poetry was his exploring further than before the potential and challenge of language, which critics have only just begun to appreciate.

Minoru Hashiguchi, in "America no Homerostachi" (*Oberon* 30 [1968]:10–41), considers *The Bridge* and Williams's *Paterson* as epics, comparable in part to *The Iliad* and *The Odyssey*. Heinrich Ickstadt's *Dichterische Erfahrung und Metaphernstruktur: Eine Untersuchung der Bildersprache Hart Cranes* (Heidelberg, Carl Winter) analyzes the function of language and imagery in the poetry of Crane as a means of communicating the emotional experience, which is the matter of poetry.

v. Cummings, Jeffers, Lindsay, Sandburg

Wilton Eckley (in his *Merrill Guide to e. e. cummings*, Columbus, Ohio, Charles E. Merrill) compares Cummings to Thoreau, constantly attacking materialism, often through satire, but his lyrics are greater, based as they are on the theme of the necessity of love, both "physical and metaphysical." Eve Triem's *E. E. Cummings* (UMPAW 87[1969]) is a pedestrian categorizing of Cummings's work. She relates the poet to the absurd, since his transcendentalism is opposed by the current trend toward "dehumanized power." She catalogues (and illustrates) his literary devices: tmesis, spacings, eccentric punctuation, typographical design, word coinage, and so on. She says Cummings tries to awaken "the sleeping conscience" of his readers, though he "nearly always ends on a note of joy." She lists three points of concentration: sensory awareness; individual integrity as well as the necessity of brotherhood; and the discovery of *true* love. He makes an effort "to discover the true nature of the world." Miss Triem believes that Cummings grew "from poem to poem" and emerged as his true self, "and therefore as everyone."

To *Modern American Poetry* John Logan contributed "The Organ-Grinder and the Cockatoo: An Introduction to E. E. Cummings" (pp. 249–71). Logan says that the two purities in Cummings's verse are art and heart. The poems have followed the course set in *The Enormous Room*—experiment in language and expression of compassion. He suggests that a scholarly study would be helpful relating Cummings's "effects" to Freudian analysis of word play in dreams and jokes. He discusses the poet's "inventions" in typography, orthography, and grammar as efforts at exacting precision: the poet's "mentality" links him "to the Pythagoreans and their concern with the numerical roots of language" as well as to modern-day "Existentialists, with their concern for catching the quality of feeling in the subject" as against "the quality of intelligibility in the object." Logan declares that, of all the poets of his generation, "Cummings is the most provocative, the most humane, the most inventive, the funniest, and the least understood." Allen A. Metcalf, in "Dante and E. E. Cummings" (*CLS* 7:374–86), has discovered that the poet began early to refer to Dante as reinforcement for his own "satirical and negative vision of the modern world." It was the poetry following *Eimi* (which describes his trip through hell, i.e., Russia), however, that was more and more indebted to Dante's positive side—especially the *Paradiso* and the *Vita Nuova*.

Of the three issues of the *Robinson Jeffers Newsletter*, two present articles by Andrew K. Mauthe: "The Significance of Point Lobos in *Tamar*" (25:8–10) and "Jeffers' Inhumanism and Its Poetic Significance" (26:8–10). The third issue contains a brief discussion by Kamil Bednar on "Jeffers in Czechoslovakia" (27:8–9). William H. Nolte, in his *Merrill Guide to Robinson Jeffers* (Columbus, Ohio, Charles E. Merrill), in addition to rather full explication of many of the best-known poems, examines Jeffers's objections to Christianity and the influence on him of Nietzsche. However, "Whereas Nietzsche exhorted man to use his will to power so as to realize his god-like potential, Jeffers advocates a humility that seems almost Christian." But he differs from Christianity in supporting, not a rejection of "the world," but acceptance of man as "one of the infinity of phenomena, the totality of which composes the 'body' of God." Man "is in no broad sense a unique creation." This pamphlet, intended for beginners, explains the metaphors of incest, rock, and hawk, these latter two as substitute symbols for the self-immolation of the cross and the communal aggregation of the hive. Nolte gives us very little that is new, but his pamphlet is a useful summary. Robert J. Brophy sees parallels between Jeffers and Shelley. In " 'Tamar,' 'The Cenci,' and Incest" (*AL* 42:241–44), he suggests that the "mold-breaking, transcendental repercussions" of incest are part of the road toward ultimately "transhuman heights" for both Tamar and Beatrice. In both poems the degrading action becomes "a positive revelatory device." Karl Keller thinks it may be a mistake to read *Roan Stallion* for profound symbolism. In "California, Yankees, and the Death of God: The Allegory in Jeffers' *Roan Stallion*" (*TSLL* 12,iii:11–20), he claims to find more richness and meaning by reading the poem as allegory based in the poet's personal mythology, for by means of allegory Jeffers turns his didacticism into poetry. The metaphor of the death of God is necessary to Jeffers in explaining how depraved man now is. "The tragedy of man is that he is forever alienated from nature, the divine, power, beauty, and significance. This is the loss of God that is presumed by human experience."

In his preface to Vachel Lindsay's *Springfield Town Is a Butterfly Town*, with an introduction by Pierre Dussert (Kent, Ohio, Kent State Univ. Press, [1969]), Louis Untermeyer says that, though these recently discovered poems of Lindsay's are sometimes even callow and crude, they often remind the reader of "the poet who invented word-games, who championed what was considered strange and childish, and who believed" that all beauty must, in fact, be based in the strange. Dussert recounts the history of the verses and his own adventure in tracking them down. They show "children how to find and to love Beauty." Many of them consider children in the light of their future responsibility as citizens. The humorous pieces do not try to make a point: Lindsay simply is demonstrating with a wink how much he likes children. Now and then he invents a mystery, just for the fun of it. Van Meter Ames draws on his own recollections and on Lindsay's letters to Ames's father, a minister in the church of the Disciples of Christ (Campbellites), in "Vachel Lindsay—or, *My Heart Is a Kicking Horse*" (*Midway* 8,iv[1968]:63–79), to illustrate the poet's hope for a better—more beautiful, more democratic—America, relating it to his religious bent, nurtured in large part by the Disciples. The author cites the letters for evidence of the poet's interest in the movies as a medium for spreading his gospel of beauty.

Ann Massa's *Vachel Lindsay: Fieldworker for the American Dream* (Bloomington, Ind. Univ. Press) is not so much biography as a thorough analysis of Lindsay's purpose and accomplishment in bringing beauty to the citizens of a democracy. Quotations from the poems occur throughout the book, but Miss Massa's survey covers all of Lindsay's work—more prose than verse actually. The author organizes her material into eleven chapters divided into four large sections: "I. Lindsay's Gospel"; "II. The Golden Book of Springfield" (the book she describes as his "most original piece of writing and planning . . . in which Lindsay envisaged an American city in the year 2018 . . . "); "III. An American Entity" (America's past and present and her regions); and "IV. Art Forms and Society." Miss Massa concludes that "Lindsay was at one with his words." He formulated and held fast to "his convictions of promise and threat, dream and nightmare in an America [that] opposed him." Unsentimental, this study deals seriously with Lindsay's neglected contribution to the important American stream of idealism.

North Callahan's *Carl Sandburg, Lincoln of Our Literature* (New York, New York Univ. Press) is something else again. It is a superficial, journalistic narrative. Undated anecdotes are scattered throughout. The comparison with Lincoln is embarrassingly obvious and shallow. (Howells first used the phrase "the Lincoln of our literature" with reference to Twain—a more clearly deserved comparison.) Callahan reports conversations and correspondence with members of the family and cites a few letters heretofore unavailable, but very few facts are added to what we already know. There is no critical analysis of Sandburg's prose—chiefly tiresome summaries of the contents of the Lincoln biography, the novel, and the children's books. The chapter on the verse (only twenty-seven brief pages) is dominated by comments of reviewers. Callahan's comparison of Sandburg with other poets—Lindsay, Masters, "Edward" Arlington

Robinson—are derivative and sophomoric. For example, Sandburg and Robinson "both possess poetic imagery and both include many references, plain and subtle, to religion in their poems." This is an easy book to pass up.

On the other hand, with customary good humor, Roy P. Basler, the Lincoln scholar, in "Your Friend the Poet: Carl Sandburg" (*Midway* 10,ii[1969]:3–15), remarks that there is no need to apologize for Sandburg. Since he did not suffer from "psychoemotional dyspepsia," English professors have virtually ignored him. Whereas Williams and Eliot tried "to create, or re-create, a religiously, or . . . theoretically, valid world of myth and symbol . . . , Sandburg reverted to the primary poetic task of trying to apprehend by naming." Basler calls him a "pagan mystic," though without the credentials of a debt to the Hindus.

vi. Aiken, Ransom, and Others

Arthur Lerner is a professor of psychology. His book *Psychoanalytically Oriented Criticism of Three American Poets: Poe, Whitman, and Aiken* (Rutherford, N.J., Fairleigh Dickinson Univ. Press) is composed chiefly of critics' comments that he finds related to a psychoanalytical approach to the work of the poets. The chapter on Conrad Aiken (pp. 84–107) quotes Aiken himself as saying that the violent death of his parents when he was eleven years old determined him to live as consciously and meaningfully as possible. There are quotations from such critics as Roy Harvey Pearce, Joseph Warren Beach, George Whicher, and R. P. Blackmur to show that they have understood this attitude in the poet. Lerner calls Aiken healthily skeptic and creatively hopeful. This book is a rather plodding study built on a patchwork of quotations. "Due Lettere di Conrad Aiken," edited by Rosalia Ruffini (*SA* 14[1969]:451–54), presents two letters to the editor from Aiken in Savannah in which the poet explains that he has no orthodox religion but believes "in the evolution of consciousness." He discovers that he can still read Italian in 1969 after an interim of "sixty-odd years." He intends "The Crystal" to represent "the scientific . . . side" and to be "perhaps the final statement."

In 1968 David Mann and Samuel H. Woods, Jr., examined "John Crowe Ransom's Poetic Revisions" (*PMLA* 83:15–21). In "A Commentary on 'John Crowe Ransom's Poetic Revisions'" (*PMLA* 85:

532–34) there is an exchange between Walter E. Meyers (pp. 532–33) and the coauthors (pp. 533–34). Meyers concedes that Mann and Woods were "conscientious" in their collations and subsequent remarks on comparative effects of diction and meaning in early and late versions of Ransom's poems. He feels, however, that they were less sophisticated in their discussion of sound and syntax. He refers to their use of the phrase "sound cluster" as imprecise. Mann and Woods then defend themselves item by item, introducing terminology and referring to scholars of contemporary linguistics to support their approval of Ransom's revisions (such as "Soon must they all descend" for "So must the others drop").

Ward Allen pays tribute to a Vanderbilt colleague of Ransom's in "Donald Davidson" (SR 78:390–404). (Davidson died in 1968.) Allen traces the profound influence of Greek and Latin literature on Davidson's poetry. "The habit of reading the classics as a humanist left the clear marks of panorama and calm" on the man and his verse. Simple religious faith, akin to the myth of the ancients, characterizes his work, which, especially in *Lee in the Mountains*, tries the difficult task of disclosing God's mercy and justice. A former student of Davidson's, Robert Buffington, in "Mr. Davidson in the Formal Garden" (GaR 24:121–31), discusses some of Davidson's personal experiences in the classroom and with students outside. Davidson generally kept separate his social views and his pursuit of literature. He was more pragmatic than romantic. In his late poems social criticism from a traditionalist point of view is no longer his preoccupation. The shift is toward a "sense of continuity" replacing a "sense of crisis."

Claire Healy discusses "Some Imagist Essays: Amy Lowell" in NEQ 43:134–38. "The Imagists" is an attempt at definition, now familiar to all students of American verse of this period. "Two Imagist Poets" praises Richard Aldington and F. S. Flint. Miss Lowell "in her self-appointed role as spokesman for the Imagists . . . was as dauntless and inexhaustible as Pound had been before her." F. Cudworth Flint's *Amy Lowell* (UMPAW 82[1969]) describes her well-known connections with the Imagists and other innovators, considers her concept of "polyphonic prose," and reviews the contents of her books. Flint does not see her as a great poet but as an important figure in literary history. "She had a keen sense for whatever was beginning to be noticed, and a genuine interest in it. . . . Her work is thus a mirror of her time."

Thomas A. Gray's *Elinor Wylie* (TUSAS 165[1969]) is an odd book. The author devotes nearly all of the 140 pages of text to saying that his subject was a beautiful but vain and temperamental woman, a literary "figure" rather than a good poet and novelist. She was so occupied with matters of technique that she rarely said anything of importance. The basic conflict in her work is between the world and the self. Since she always considered the world as coarse and gross, she sought refuge in the delicate and rare. From the nineteenth century Gray finds the tone of Lionel Johnson's verse much like Wylie's. He plays down the resemblances with Shelley, in spite of her confessed adoration. Though she was acclaimed a "daughter of Donne" (as critics sought for seventeenth-century comparisons), Gray thinks her work is more like Crashaw's in some respects, Carew's in others. Amy Lowell grouped her with the "Lyrists," including Adelaide Crapsey and Sara Teasdale. The four novels, like the poems, strive for glamor and picturesque description. Gray selects about a dozen lyrics that may save her from being forgotten entirely, among them, "Velvet Shoes" and "The Eagle and the Mole," which convey her "desire for quality in human life."

Robert L. Johnson, in *The American Heritage of James Norman Hall, the Woodshed Poet of Iowa and Co-Author of "Mutiny on the Bounty"* (Philadelphia, Dorrance, [1969]), records his visit to Hall in Tahiti and Hall's account of his ancestry. Lawrence E. Mintz, in "Langston Hughes's Jesse B. Semple: The Urban Negro as Wise Fool" (*SNL* 7[1969]:11–21) characterizes "Simple" as "uneducated, but . . . not stupid." Joyce Kilmer's best-known poem is the topic of Paul Sawyer's "What Keeps 'Trees' Growing," (*CEA* 33,i:17–19). Since most readers discover this poem before critical faculties develop, it appeals to feelings not yet dissected by logic.

Purdue University

15. Poetry: The 1930s to the Present

A. Kingsley Weatherhead

i. General

Contemporary Poets of the English Language, edited by Rosalie Murphy and James Vinson (London, St. James Press), is a dictionary which provides biographical and bibliographical information concerning eleven hundred poets now writing in the English language. The poets included are those who are currently the most important and those who seemed most promising to the advisors and consultants for each country, themselves mostly poets, editors, or professors, who were asked, for this occasion, to "anticipate the judgment of history." In many cases, in addition to the objective data, poets have supplied their own comments upon their poetry and their careers; often those who are relatively unknown have named the articles about themselves that they consider most just and revealing; for about 300 poets, short critical articles have been specially contributed by a variety of poets and critics. There are over a hundred contributors. Neither the size of this achievement nor the extent of its usefulness needs any urging. The weaknesses are few: there are some omissions in the biographical data—the dates of birth of some poetesses, some details of education or career; the editors presumably had only what each subject supplied. Occasionally in the statement submitted, a poet, anticipating oblivion, has taken the opportunity to be obscene or cute or inordinately modish before a wider public than his own. Occasionally in the critiques, it being no simple task to epitomize a poet's work in a few lines, there are inevitable lapses into the pretentious or the merely silly: of one poet we read, "Disguised as a lion-maned nude, but never naked, this celebrant chants the body with the elegance of the average caryatid." Such nonsense is not common, however: for the most part entries are solid and informative. Dates of birth, details about schooling, marriage, children, pseudonyms, places of residence and travel, professions and jobs—whether farmers, poets-in-residence, mothers, or librarians—all this information, is, of course, interesting; it is the kind of book in which, on the way to ascertaining one small detail, one may spend an hour digressing among other curiosities. The critical essays are skillfully designed, the writers accommodating their material, one assumes, to space limits imposed by the editors: the best ones are exercises in economy. There is a closely packed statement of about 150 words by Edward Lucie-Smith on X. J. Kennedy which says much. At the other end of the scale there is Donald Hall's essay on Robert Lowell, breezy but hardly less terse, outlining the stages and styles in that continually evolving career: of *Lord Weary's Castle*, Hall says, that the "poems were formal, a tight decasyllable always rhymed; yet the violent energy of the diction—especially embodied in a series of monosyllabic verbs which were frequently tactile—hammered against the decasyllabic cage. Enjambment was violent, caesura eccentric, and the din deafening." In a number of entries, these articles make substantial summary statements on poets whose work has not yet been extensively subjected to critical study. There is, for example, pioneer work by Hayden Carruth on Adrienne Rich, by Ralph Mills on Stanley Kunitz, by Thom Gunn on Gary Snyder and so many others of the same quality and worth that it is perhaps misleading to single out individuals. These all present brief clear images of the poets, without resorting to generalization or cliché.

A work which generalizes about the poetry of this period is Monroe K. Spears's *Dionysus and the City: Modernism in Twentieth Century Poetry* (New York, Oxford Univ. Press), an excellent structuring of the forces of modern British and American poetry. Much of the book lies beyond the scope of this chapter, and with some Roman fortitude one must resist the temptation to praise all of it at considerable length. Lowell comes into the picture, however, as a poet of the city—the theme of the city appearing in Spears's rendition of the modern poetry scene as a complement to that of the dark powers of Dionysus. He appears again as the main figure in the second modernist revolution, for which Spears chooses the date 1957, largely because Lowell wrote his first "open" poem in this year. Spears outlines mid-century changes in painting and music that run parallel to those in poetry, in which, in general, "the change is a reaction against any form of aesthetic discontinuity, against the poem as in any sense autonomous, against any esoteric quality or unnecessary difficulty; against tight or elaborate forms; and against irony. The qualities newly emphasized are openness, simplicity, directness, colloquial language, the accents of psychological truth as the poet reveals (often) the most sordid, humiliating, and intimate details of his life" (p. 236). In this context Spears surveys Lowell's work from *Life Studies* on and makes a few selective observations about Roethke ("his lack of any real sense of the City is one way of defining his difference from Lowell") and John Berryman. Of the poets of the 1960s he reports on Ted Hughes in England and James Dickey in this country, the latter because his works respond to "the same pressures as the work of the anti-poets while not abandoning traditional requirements." Dickey's development, like the general movement of the day is toward open poetry, while his identification with animals is a Dionysian quality. One wonders whether Dickey's beasts are sufficiently primitive for this role.

The Survival of Poetry: A Contemporary Survey, edited by Martin Dodsworth (London, Faber and Faber), includes some studies of recent American poets (though hardly enough to justify the term *survey*)—Robert Lowell, John Berryman, Sylvia Plath, and Charles Olson and Edward Dorn. In his introduction, Dodsworth considers three kinds of poetry that may be produced as a response to the pressures of conformity and remarks the dangers of each: academic poems, like machines, amenable to explication, exemplified in James Dickey; translatable surrealist-imagistic poems that cultivate the inner life at the expense of the outer, exemplified in James Wright and Robert Bly; and the "projective verse" of Charles Olson, of which the dangers seem to be less than those attendant upon the others. The chapter has some interesting comparisons in it of English and American verse. So also does M. L. Rosenthal's "Dynamics of Form and Motive in Some Representative Twentieth-Century Lyric Poems" (*ELH* 37:136–44), which, in an argument it would be a disservice to attempt to summarize, makes a sensitive and unusually penetrating inquiry into the relation of formal poetic structures to freedom or involvement. From its own original angle this article studies poems by Denise Levertov, Robert Duncan, Galway Kinnell, and Thomas Kinsella.

An annual review of the previous year's poetry has been made by

Christopher Ricks in an article "Recent American Poetry" (*MR* 11: 313–39), which combines a great deal of bluff common sense with a wit which is caustic toward some and an ability to characterize a poet in a few quick strokes (for W. D. Snodgrass: "pained resignation flecked with repining"). Though Ricks may be a little hard to please, to see the exposing of pretentiousness in modern poetry is a pleasant novelty. Ricks quotes, " 'I walk back / toward the frog pond, carrying / the one letter . . .' " and comments, "Do you now?" He quotes, " 'I open my eyes and gaze down / At the dark water' " and says, "Such poetry has the right to take its time, but does it have the right to take mine?" " 'I strike a match slowly and lift it slowly'—you can say that again." But praise is also awarded. Most goes to John Berryman who "has clambered in to clobber Lowell" (a line Lowell himself might have written). For an apt description of the *Dream Songs*, Ricks lights on a remark of T. S. Eliot's about *In Memoriam* in which he finds, for all its obvious differences, remarkable parallels.

In another roundup, "American Poetry 1969: From B. to Z." (*MR* 11:650–86), Daniel Hughes touches on some twenty poets who published in 1969, and of many of them he makes generous quotation. His poets are mostly people more recent than those who became established in the 40s, but some of these appear—Wilbur, for example, whose traditional and academic style he has some difficulty in admitting, and Robert Lowell, to whom he devotes most space, reviewing *Notebook 1967–1968*: "Now that Frost is gone," he says, "Lowell's career has to be the likeliest place to look for greatness in American poetry."

In "Rhetoric and the Moderns" (*SoR* 6:380–97), A. T. Tolley finds that Eliot and Pound, being themselves stylists, made less of a break with the rhetoric of nineteenth-century poetry than did poets like Frost, Edward Thomas, Robert Graves, and William Carlos Williams. "The Poetry Wreck" (*LJ* 95:632–35) is an eloquent little jeremiad by Karl Shapiro in which he bemoans the degradation of American poetry, which has "plopped into the playpen" where "we are entertained with the fecal-buccal carnival of the Naughties and the Uglies."

A bird's eye view of the recent developments in American poetry is presented by Robert J. Bertholf in "The Key in the Window: Kent's Collection of Modern American Poetry" (*Serif*: 7,iii:52–70), an article of particular value for the publication details it gives of poems in small editions, in unknown presses, or in ephemeral journals.

There are two essays that concern poetry, written expressly for
Black Expression, edited by Addison Gayle, Jr. (New York, Weybright and Talley). In one, "The Future of Negro Poetry: A Challenge for Critics" (pp. 100–09), James A. Emanuel exhorts black
critics to study black poetry. He explicates sonnets by Gwendolyn
Brooks and Claude McKay. "Black Poetry" by Dudley Randall (pp.
109–114) is a brief survey of black poetry and poets.

ii. William Carlos Williams

Among the books on William Carlos Williams published during 1970,
is James G. Breslin's *William Carlos Williams, An American Artist*
(New York, Oxford Univ. Press) which, although it covers familiar
ground, consistently brings new details and makes new perceptions.
Breslin begins with two chapters that concisely describe the important influences upon the young poet—his parents, Keats, the medical
training, Whitman, the painters, Pound, and Imagism; then he briefly
places Williams in the modern movement, relating him to Eliot, Santayana, and T. E. Hulme. Then, again briefly, but with admirable
clarity, he epitomizes the poetic principles that lie behind the early
work: for example, on the question of meaning, he shows how Williams emphasizes the primary existence of the poem as sound and
rhythm, not arguing that it has no meaning, but believing that its
meaning, not at the surface, will be found "hidden in the minute relationships of the words." Breslin is perhaps to be faulted for quoting
the dicta of Williams without comment when, as not infrequently, they are bunk. And when he says of the method of the essays
which do not follow a single line of logic but leap from one insight to
the next that it "opens new possibilities in the form of the critical
essay" one deduces he has never read a freshman composition! The
author proceeds through Williams's work by genre—the lyric, *In the
American Grain*, the fiction, *Paterson*, and the final poems. He studies
selected parts of each but continually casts side glances upon the
works he is not centrally criticizing. In the chapter on the lyric, selecting *Spring and All* for close attention, Breslin contributes original
and useful observations on the still undeveloped subject of a poem as
a field of action. *Paterson*, he designates a "pre-epic" and calls somewhat spiritedly for an adjustment of critical approach to meet it on
its own ground. There is a familiar ring about Breslin's pleading that,

more than any "final" assessment, we need to "experience the poem in *its* terms, not *ours*." What is unfamiliar is his remark that *Paterson* is "a rough and profuse start from which some later summative genius may extract and polish," looking, it seems, for a latter-day Nahum Tate! The body of the chapter on *Paterson* selects passages for criticism and for all its relative brevity has a significant place among longer critiques on the poem. Breslin makes much of the divided nature of Paterson, the man: on the one hand, cold and aloof, going away to rest and write, and on the other the figure who yields to mythic forces and accepts disintegration as a phase of creativity; Paterson may be pompous or in turn ironic and comical. Breslin draws attention to his mythic descent for renewal and for the discovery of the source of beauty.

The opening chapters of *William Carlos Williams' "Paterson": Language and Landscape* by Joel Conarroe (Philadelphia: Univ. of Pa. Press) appeared as articles and were noticed in the *ALS* last year. After the good general introduction to the poem, Conarroe proceeds by studying five themes: the man / city, the river, the mountain, the economic motif, and the redeeming language. There has been only one other book devoted to the complete poem, and that is Walter Scott Peterson's *An Approach to "Paterson"* (see *ALS 1967*, pp. 244–45). Conarroe refers continually, of course, to other poems of Williams's. He has benefited from having had access to hitherto unpublished materials from the Lockwood Library in Buffalo and from the Collection of American literature in the Yale University Library, and the reader is correspondingly advantaged.

In *The Hieroglyphics of a New Speech: Cubism, Stieglitz, and the Early Poetry of William Carlos Williams* (Princeton, N.J., Princeton Univ. Press), Bram Dijkstra describes the impact of post-impressionist art on the first twenty years of Williams's poetry. There is persuasive documentation that the literary influences alone—Imagism, Whitman, and Ezra Pound—do not sufficiently account for Williams's development. These diminished from 1913 on and made way for his excitement about the visual arts, under the impulse of which he reformulated his means of expression following the newly developed theories about the visual reconstruction of reality on canvas. Imagism, says Dijkstra, simplifying matters somewhat, makes the image a metaphor for something else; in Williams the image becomes subject—self-supporting. Dijkstra describes Williams's acquaintance and relationships with the writers and artists in New York in the early decades of the century, some of whom were associated with the periodical *Others*, and also his relationship with Alfred Stieglitz, which Williams himself plays down in his autobiography. Dijkstra limits himself to describing the work and influences of the Cubists and of Stieglitz and his associates. The book has twenty-one photographs of art works, of Francis Picabia, Franz Marc, Charles Demuth, Charles Sheeler, Juan Gris, Stieglitz himself, and others. Williams's development was a "'progression from the concept, the thought, to the poem itself,'" which paralleled the talk of "sheer paint" on the part of the followers of Cézanne. Dijkstra discusses the abandonment of narrative sequence, the making of poems as visual units "lifted outside the movement of time," and the concept of simultaneism—"'the simultaneous representation of the different figures of a form seen from different points of view. . . .'" There is a rather startling parallelism between the poem "Spring Strains" and Franz Marc's painting "Tyrol," due to the common influence on both poet and painter of the work of Wassily Kandinsky and Picasso rather than to Williams's having rendered the painting into words. *Kora in Hell* is an example of the efforts to achieve simultaneity by presenting a "non-logically constructed sequence of direct sense impressions." Dijkstra discusses the photography of Stieglitz who focused on the American scene and found in its lines and textures qualities that would represent his feelings. Williams likewise, in such poems as "The Red Wheelbarrow" and "By the road to the contagious hospital," represented feeling in selected detail. In this good book, with competence in matters of both painting and poetry, Dijkstra most usefully clarifies an area of literary history that has hitherto been somewhat uncertainly documented.

In "Dimensionality in Dr. Williams's 'Paterson' " (*MPS* 1:98–117), Jerome Mazzaro is interested in relationships similar to those described by Dijkstra. He associates the use of prose in *Paterson* with the development of "synthetic cubism" which began "when Picasso carried 'the forward push of the collage (and of Cubism in general) *literally* into the literal space in front of the picture plane.'" Williams, for his part, incorporated parts of newspapers, documents, and letters into *Paterson*; and "one can say that art space begins to intrude on life space."

In *Intrepid 17* (Buffalo) Mazzaro introduces the first of two chapers with a discussion of Williams's emphasis on true language and his aversion to linear forms. Despite these, however, "a closer look at his poems reveals that they are generally constructed upon an unstated, unconscious mythic pattern"—a pattern of descent into hell. When writing himself out of despair, Williams invoked the figure of the wise old man, whose function, as C. G. Jung described it, is to muster together all the assets of the personality. The issue contains eight unusual photographs of Williams taken over a span of fifty years.

The genesis of *Kora in Hell* is the subject of Sherman Paul's chapter in *The Shaken Realist* (pp. 21–44). In "A Sketchbook of the Artist in His Thirty-Fourth Year: William Carlos Williams' *Kora in Hell: Improvisations*," Sherman Paul describes this work as having been written following Williams's dejection at the warm reception awarded to T. S. Eliot's *Prufrock* volume. Paul sees it as a descent to the sources of being: the Kora Williams pursues in hell is "his own creative self, his feminine secret nature." The book is less derivative from Rimbaud or other French sources than has been supposed. Inasmuch as it signifies the emergence of the poet's authentic self, on the other hand, it is related to Whitman's "Song of Myself."

A study of a work of Williams's is used by J. Hillis Miller in a discussion on the progress of poetry, "Williams' *Spring and All* and the Progress of Poetry," which appears in an issue of *Daedalus* (99:405–34) devoted to "Theory in Humanistic Studies." In the prose passages of *Spring and All*, says Miller, Williams rejects the art, the symbolism, and the subjectivity that stand between man and the present moment. He shows how Williams conceived of imagination, which is both creative and destructive, as the force that links man to nature. Here as elsewhere he goes beyond other critics in uncrumpling the difficult matter of the relation of words and meanings in Williams. In an article on the same work, "*Spring and All*: The Unity of Design" (*TSL* 15:61–73), Linda Wagner demonstrates that it is necessary to print the prose passages along with the poems. In "Poet as Dog in *Paterson*" (*TCL* 16:97–108), Thomas LeClair studies the dog images with a closer scrutiny than has previously been applied to them and offers new interpretations and some interesting new observations about the poem as a whole.

In *Testimony of the Invisible Man: William Carlos Williams, Francis Ponge, Rainer Maria Rilke, Pablo Neruda* (Columbia, Univ.

of Mo. Press) Nancy Willard has brought together four poets who
have written poetry based on the careful examination of concrete
things—"*Ding*-poets" as she calls them. Each frees his work from
ideas and also from his own personality, thus becoming an "invisible
man." The chapter on Williams has new observations to make both
on the matter of the local and the universal and on some of his individual poems.

iii. Wallace Stevens

Wallace Stevens: Poetry as Life (New York, Pegasus), by Samuel
French Morse, is about Stevens as poet, and he is quoted at the very
beginning as saying "'I have no life except in poetry.'" In fact, of
course, he had; and while the blurb claims that this book "delves into
every phase of Stevens' life," it does not delve very extensively, and
we would like much more than we get of the man—the "fat jocundus,"
the "burgher"—gardening, or listening to music or just doing this and
that. Perhaps what Morse says about the *Letters* is a clue to the
absence here of such details as make biography vital: "One hopes for
a somewhat less guarded edition later on." If, however, the book he
has written is thus threadbare, in other respects it is rich. Concentrating on Stevens's life as poet, Morse has described those things
related to it: the early predilections, definitions, aphorisms, and ideas
about poetry, and their relationship to philosophy; Stevens's acquaintance and relationships with Hi Simons, Ronald Lane Latimer, Stanley Burnshaw, Henry Church, George Santayana, and José Feo; and
the poetic influences on him. He relates Stevens's efforts to find his
own authentic speech in poetry. One of the earliest and longest philosophical influences was from the "superb figure" of Santayana, and
another came from Bergson. Morse traces the influences on Stevens
into particular features of poems, and his familiarity with the poet's
mind and his poetic life has provided him with a sound basis for
critical commentary on a number of poems. Speaking of "The Snow
Man" Morse complains somewhat acidly that for some readers "the
poem becomes the occasion for an essay on phenomenology, in which
Valéry, Heidegger, Georges Poulet, Merleau-Ponty, Ramon Fernan-
dez, Santayana, and Bergson, as well as the total canon of the poetry,
are rifled to 'prove' its 'viability' and 'dimensions,' as if anything less
would not do the poem justice" (p. 119). His protest is not untoward;

for while Stevens has indeed attracted some ostentatious scholarship, Morse's own solid common sense brings the criticism out of the clouds to dwell among men. His style is clear, discursive, and urbane; and all in all this book throws a great deal of light on Stevens's poetry.

Merle E. Brown is also interested in criticism, and in the opening pages of *Wallace Stevens: The Poem as Act* (Detroit, Mich., Wayne State Univ. Press), he gives more than passing consideration to it. He nourishes a lofty conception of the critic, who is as a performing artist, an actor or pianist, clarifying, defining and, a favorite expression for one stage or another of the whole poetic process, "bodying forth" the poem, articulating its poetic action, "translating its essence into existence." He voices strictures against the practices of the New Critics, which he says spoke of the poem as a finished object or, in a simile which should surely enter our critical vocabulary, as "an old dog bled dry." (In a piece noted below, Donald Davie remarks that we too seldom remember how few poems ever were written to be "mulled over excitedly" and "tugged this way and that.") The poem, as the title of the book suggests, is an act; in Stevens's phrase, it is "an act of the mind." It is not an objective action which can be observed: Brown says, "it must be participated in. It is a human gesturing, a human body in action, but only as that feels, from the inside, to the actor himself." The quotation epitomizes Brown's unusual angle of approach. He discusses at some length a number of the more important poems of Stevens as well as some less known ones. He includes "The Comedian as the Letter C," "Le Monocle de Mon Oncle," "The Idea of Order at Key West," "The Doctor of Geneva," "The Man on the Dump," "Asides on the Oboe"; to "The Man with the Blue Guitar," "Notes toward a Supreme Fiction," and "Esthétique du Mal," he devotes a chapter each. His approach is varied, but his consistent strategy is to present the poem as a living, documenting activity not abstracting an argument but following a movement: "The actual, vital movement of the poet's shaping, in the present, as it is and not as it was, is the absolute that makes Stevens's best poems the supreme achievement of modern American poetry." "Sunday Morning" and its commentaries being familiar to most, Brown's criticism of this poem will serve as an apt sampling. The pervading sense, he says, is that "one can experience beauty, can love a thing or person, only if he at the same time experiences the painful sense that the loss of that thing or person is imminent, that its mortality is a quality immanent in its living presence." The two conceptions of life the poem presents, the hedonist indulgence (life for sensuous immediacy) and the ascetic (life for the sake of a tedium of eternity), are both inadequate and both are presented in parallel syntax. But at the end of the poem the two are integrated into an earthly paradise: the movement of the pigeons, which "sink / Downward to darkness, on extended wings" in the last line, "occurs in the immediate present but is suffused with, haunted by, at one with, its very opposite, the sense of the endlessness of darkness, of death, of permanent stasis."

Richard Allen Blessing's *Wallace Stevens's "Whole Harmonium"* (Syracuse, N.Y., Syracuse Univ. Press) treats *The Collected Poems* as "a single, organic, and highly dynamic grand poem." The method is largely the explication of individual poems, especially those which need to be viewed in the context of Stevens's total output. This is not the first work of criticism to come at the poems as a whole; and in submitting his explications Blessing comes late into a field which others have all but ransacked. He has made much use of his predecessors, however, and has often improved upon their work and gone beyond it, presenting his new ideas and interpretations with creditable lucidity. Furthermore he is of considerable value as he summarizes the essential character of each of Stevens's volumes and demonstrates its place in the grand poem. His approach is less of a new departure than Merle Brown's, but the product is significant and useful.

In "The Impact of French Symbolism on Modern American Poetry" (*Shaken Realist*, pp. 165–217) Haskell M. Block summarizes the characteristics of symbolist poetry and lists the American critical studies of it. His account of its impact upon the poetry is extensive and thorough: there is affinity with Imagism only in general aim, and on Eliot the effect is found in his poetic theory of the twenties rather than in "Prufrock" or *The Waste Land*; *Four Quartets* however, contains an appreciable amount of Mallarmé. Allen Tate shows similarities to Valéry, Poe, and Baudelaire and uses synaesthetic metaphor. John Peale Bishop and Robert Lowell both reveal awareness of the Symbolists. In Wallace Stevens, however, Block finds many similarities in poetry, prose, drama, and dramatic theory, though Stevens himself wrote that if he had "picked up anything" from Mallarmé, Verlaine, Laforgue, Valéry, or Baudelaire, he had done so unconsciously. Some of the *Harmonium* poems make a parody or a statement or both of symbolist values; and though few are written in symbolist style, there are throughout such elements as conscious musicality, vague evocations of landscape, color symbolism, and Stevens's movement toward ambiguity and abstraction. In the later poems Block finds even more evidence of the force of the symbolist tradition to which Stevens comes close in the continual questioning of matters of being, the matters of the imagined and the real, the identity of self and so on. Block does not fail to observe also that there are striking differences and that Stevens's embodiment of the tradition "heightens rather than diminishes his originality." With no less concern to preserve the image of Stevens's originality, Doris Eder, in "Wallace Stevens: Heritage and Influences" (*Mosaic* 4,i:49–61), discusses his "elective affinities" and mentions a number of English and continental poets whose echoes can be picked up in his work, concentrating on those of the French Symbolists and, of these, Baudelaire and Mallarmé especially.

Previously unrecorded in these pages, Helge Nilsen's essay, "The Quest for Reality: A Study in the Poetry of Wallace Stevens" (*Americana Norvegica* (pp. 219–98), is a statement of some length about Stevens's thought, its development, its contradictions, and its inconclusiveness. Nilsen relates the ideas of Stevens to those of William James and Santayana; and the essay is rich in explications of poems. He occasionally takes issue with previous criticism: in particular, recalling the earliest animadversions on *Harmonium* as dilettantism, he takes issue with the generally accepted valuation of the poet, finding a division between man and artist and a lack of moral engagement, resurrecting the stern voice of Yvor Winters charging Stevens with hedonism.

Roy Fuller's "Both Pie and Custard" (*Shenandoah* 21,iii:61–76), a lecture, is a sensitive commentary on the life of Stevens, the two desserts named standing for alternative careers, of which the poet was able to choose both. It is a proper subject for Roy Fuller, himself both lawyer and poet; and he finds Stevens's tentative equation of poetry and reality most moving.

iv. Lowell and Plath

The purpose of Philip Cooper, in *The Autobiographical Myth of Robert Lowell* (Chapel Hill, Univ. of N.C. Press), is to demonstrate the unity underlying the variety in Lowell's work. He proceeds by relating the volumes of poetry to autobiographical facts and to each other. He is primarily interested in the opposing elements in the poems and in themes and leitmotifs that are repeated throughout the canon; but he ranges far, and his readings throw a good deal of light on individual poems. These readings are imaginative; sometimes Cooper out-Empsons Empson, and readers will not always follow him with commensurate zest: "the choice of the fourteen stanzas [for "Waking Early Sunday Morning"]—given the religious context of the title—suggests perhaps the fourteen stations of the cross . . . ." In "For the Union Dead" the words "a Mosler Safe, the 'Rock of Ages' " are parenthetically amplified, "the anal bank, the oral hymn." In "Eye and Tooth," Cooper reports, "the stuffed toucan of 'My Last Afternoon with Uncle Devereux Winslow' has become the American eagle—or hawk, whose 'asetic talon' is the bestial *lex talionis*." Elsewhere Uncle Charles is "bluecapped and bird-like" and Colonel Shaw in "For the Union Dead" is "also" bird-like. Occasionally the style too seems to be injured by excessive enthusiasm, as when Cooper says: "The recurrence of a radical thematic ambivalence, epitomized by what we may call Lowell's monster, and the ubiquity of its correlative formal principle, ambivalence as lyric structure, are like two threads of a single clue, to be followed in this study of Lowell's poems." It is enthusiasm, however, that sustains the fascination of the whole book, a critique of considerable interest.

In *Everything To Be Endured: An Essay on Robert Lowell and Modern Poetry* (Columbia, Univ. of Mo. Press) R. K. Meiners discovers in Lowell and also in Allen Tate "something very like an archetypal modern situation"—the sense of the poet as an isolated personality driven into a corner or back in upon itself.

In "Robert Lowell and the Classical Tradition," (*PCP* 4[1969]: 59–64), Thomas A. Vogler finds the poet seeking to identify a tradition and to join it. The *Imitations* manifestly shows this effort; *Lord Weary's Castle* shows it on a larger scale, with Virgil, Dante, Milton, Melville, and Christianity as models. Vogler reads "The Death of the Sheriff" for its parallels in the *Aeneid*. But, he says, nothing "*new*" is added: the experience of the poem is second-hand rather than visionary or inspired. Its "real subject reflects the modern man's spiritual predicament through the particular case of the poet as he learns that classics like morals are 'the memory of a success that no longer succeeds.' "

"Lowell's Marble Meanings," by Gabriel Pearson (*Survival of Poetry*, pp. 56–96; reprinted from *Review*) ranges into some fairly untrodden areas, in commenting on the volumes from *Lord Weary's Castle* to *For the Union Dead*. In addition to other various related issues, Pearson plays down the "openness" of *Life Studies*. He emphasizes the logic and the predetermined shape of the poems. Also, "The poem always exists somewhat after some fact, idea, or event; it is not itself a fact, an idea, or an event. It affirms some order which is its ground of being." Later, "the ultimate tendency of the poem is to insist upon its structure" and "there is an appeal to a transcending notion of literature through which this poem ["Memories of West Street and Lepke"] takes its place with other poems as part of an order."

Two or three critics this year wanted to qualify the label "confessional" that has been applied to *Life Studies*. Pearson says, "in explicitly treating his life as materials, he was not making his poetry more personal but depersonalizing his own life." W. D. Snodgrass has reservations about the classification: in " 'No Voices Talk to Me': A Conversation with W. D. Snodgrass," edited by Philip L. Gerber and Robert J. Gemmett (*WHR* 24:61–71), he says "the more you look at the poets you thought were quite impersonal—Eliot and Frost and so forth—the more you realized that they were writing exceedingly personal poems." Marjorie G. Perloff, in "Realism and the Confessional Mode of Robert Lowell" (*ConL* 11:470–87), describes confessional poetry as a literary convention and not merely confession and certainly not merely "personal catharsis." In *Life Studies* Lowell mythologizes his private life. The poem, "Man and Wife," which is studied in this article, has features in common with the romantic lyric, to which, however, its factual documentation is alien. But this constitutes a metonymic network of images around which the poem is organized. This article illustrates the use of metonymy by instances from Tolstoy, whose work Lowell admired for its ability to contain human richness in simple descriptive language.

In " 'Memories of West Street and Lepke': Robert Lowell's Associative Mirror" (*CP* 3,ii:23–26), George Lensing shows the poet defining himself through his cell-mates in the poem, which is more sophisticated and less of a cathartic confession than it is often taken to be.

Kenneth Johnson, in "The View from *Lord Weary's Castle*" (*The*

Forties, pp. 229–36), finds that Lowell is not a literary trailblazer: in form and content *Lord Weary's Castle* "is replete with echoes of many of the poets emphasized in *Understanding Literature*." He surveys a number of poems and identifies the main themes of the volume as the quest for salvation, the effects of war, and the spiritual meanings of the past. As the nature of *The Forties* no doubt determines, this is a brief, historically oriented, and summary discussion of a volume of poems of which the texture is extraordinarily rich and complex.

Among the new pieces in *Modern American Poetry* is one by Jerome Mazzaro, the editor, entitled "Robert Lowell's Early Politics of Apocalypse" (pp. 321–50), which, citing a number of works on this topic, describes in outline the apocalyptic idea and its status in the late 30s and 40s in this country and then proceeds to show its influence on the early poems of Lowell.

The Art of Sylvia Plath: A Symposium, edited by Charles Newman (Bloomington, Ind. Univ. Press), is the first volume of criticism to appear on this poet. The editor says he has tried to establish "that she speaks to our present condition in a manner which in no way depends upon the platitudinous despair and derivative techniques which have characterized so much American poetry of the last decade." The volume reprints earlier essays by Charles Newman, A. Alvarez, M. L. Rosenthal, Richard Howard, and others and includes newly commissioned articles by John Frederick Nims and Edward Lucie-Smith. Nims describes sound effects in the poems, rhymes of various degrees of matching, rhythms, metrics, and diction. He finds much that is traditional—surprisingly so: "I quote so much," he says, "because I expect incredulity. 'You mean Sylvia Plath is so *square*?'" Lucie-Smith, urging the unity of Sylvia Plath's work in opposition to the distinction Alvarez makes between the earlier and later, finds a consistent obsession with the sea, thought of as hostile and sometimes male, and a "watery death wish" throughout the poems. Her basic themes and basic materials were there from the beginning.

In "*Angst* and Animism in the Poetry of Sylvia Plath", on the other hand, an important article in the new *Journal of Modern Literature* (1:57–74), Marjorie Perloff emphasizes development: she describes the early poems as imagistic, or symbolic narrative, or ironic statement, while those after the fall of 1959, poems more appropriate to Miss Plath's "poetic vision," were of angst and animism (terms from

Northrop Frye), which render the human as merely material while imaginatively identifying humanity with the life of nature. Marjorie Perloff places Miss Plath in the tradition of oracular poets—Smart, Cowper, Collins, and Blake.

v. Moore, Berryman, Jarrell, Roethke, Tate

Donald Hall's *Marianne Moore: The Cage and the Animal* (New York, Pegasus) is a book of interlaced biography and criticism, devoting chapters to Miss Moore's childhood, her relationship with the *Others* group, her editorship of *The Dial,* and a chapter to each volume of poetry. The life is relatively uneventful; but the book is rich in anecdotes, and Hall's style is as honest and unpretentious as that of his subject. Sometimes the commentary on the poems is impressionistic—they may be "beautifully written" or "lovely." Mostly, however, it illuminates individual poems and also the general characteristics and the development of the poetry as a whole. Hall is keen to make the point that Miss Moore has so controlled and concealed the feeling in her poems that its very existence has been questioned or denied by criticism; and his concern to direct attention beyond the surfaces of the poems is marked by the subtitle, which is explained in the following: "There is enormous restraint, of course, but one should not be misled by it. Only the wildest animals need cages so carefully made." Images of the sea, the octopus, the sea-unicorns, he says, are related to the unconscious mind. But he claims also that the presence of feeling, or real imagination, or other reverberations from irrational sources in the mind is notified by otherwise inexplicable passages in the poems which, like music, resist paraphrase but communicate feelings: when "feeling seems deepest, meaning is most impenetrable. One *senses* the emotion." This may be broadly the case; but not all the examples adduced seem to be of the kind of impenetrability that should stop the critic in his habitual explicatory tracks.

Marianne Moore: A Collection of Critical Essays, edited by Charles Tomlinson (Englewood Cliffs, N.J., Prentice-Hall) contains reprinted material, a new bibliography, and one new essay in addition to the editor's introduction. The last addresses itself to the question as to how fact and imagination come to be united in the poetry and then, complaining at the injury this poet has endured from "lax adulation," gives instances of poems where she goes beyond her characteristic stylistic limit. "Two Philologists" (pp. 172–78), a gracefully written piece by Henry Gifford, compares Marianne Moore with Emily Dickinson, finding them united in their "practical interest in the capacities of the English language." The title of a review-article by Larry P. Vonalt, "Marianne Moore's Medicines" (SR 78:669–78) refers to the struggle in which she has been consistently engaged against such human "diseases" as affectation, arrogance, materialism, and selfishness. There are fresh views here on her themes and techniques.

"Conversation With Berryman," reported by Richard Kostelanetz (MR 11:340–47), contains some interesting incidental information about Berryman's poems, some of which no doubt, should be taken with a grain of salt: Henry " 'is a very good friend of mine. . . . He doesn't enjoy my advantages of supervision; he just has vision. He's also simpleminded. He thinks that if something happens to him, it's forever; but I know better.' " Henry does not have self-understanding. He suffers; and his friend, Mr. Bones, is a Job's Comforter.

William J. Martz's *John Berryman* (UMPAW 85[1969]) manifests the difficulties a critic faces when treating a writer in small compass, which often precludes the documentation of general statements and leads to clichés. Martz attends in detail to some poems: he contrasts one of Berryman's Sonnets that doesn't "work" with one that does, rather overstating the case for each, and he discusses *Homage to Mistress Bradstreet* at some length, which, along with Roethke's "North American Sequence," he considers one of the two long poems that "emerge as great" in American poetry following World War II. He also compares one of the *Dream Songs* from the early books with a passage from one of the later ones, evaluating each.

In his introduction to *The Achievement of Randall Jarrell* (Glenview, Ill., Scott Foresman), the late Frederick J. Hoffman comments on the separate volumes of this poet and identifies various themes—the dream, the ironies of freedom, the gap between knowledge and experience—with an occasional penetrating glimpse into the essence of this elusive body of poetry. " 'Trading Another's Sorrows for our Own': The Poetry of Randall Jarrell," by Jane Donahue (LWU 2 [1969]:258–67), is a survey of Jarrell's poetry, brief but with valuable insights, among them the perception that Jarrell was "a man unconscious of his own past and unable to find a viable personal tradition—a poet with too much negative capability."

Much of Roethke's poetry, as if following the prescription of Wallace Stevens, resists the intelligence almost successfully; and good criticism is rare. One example of it is "Theodore Roethke and the Failures of Language" (*MPS* 1:73–96), by Jerome Mazzaro, who finds pronouncements in Jung that describe with some accuracy certain practices in Roethke's early poems. In *Open House* language failed to mediate between the inner and outer worlds of the poet; it fails later inasmuch as it mediates only what in childhood the reader had in common with the poet.

"Will and Vision: Allen Tate's *Terza Rima* Poems" (*SR* 78:543–62) by Radcliffe Squires is an essay that embodies a general comment on Tate's poetry and the period to which it belongs in a study of three poems, written in the mid-fifties as parts of an unfinished long poem, "The Maimed Men," "The Swimmers," and "The Buried Lake." These reveal a pattern that repeats itself in Tate's poetry, that of the one successful poem, here "The Swimmers," in a context of others that fall short. Tate was aware of the new drift of poetry in the 50s: in a fine perception, Squires remarks that " 'The Buried Lake' . . . belongs in a category of poetry which brings a literary movement to an end," and "it takes as high a talent to finish an age as to begin one."

vi. Ginsberg, Olson, Snyder, Kinnell, Warren, Merwin, and Others

Allen Ginsberg by Thomas S. Merrill (TUSAS 161[1969]) is a full account of the poet and the poems. It offers first a shrewd and balanced discussion of the Beat background, its attitude to society, to religion, et cetera, and considers also the general artistic principles to which the Beat poets adhere, mentioning Zen art, which provides a compromise between control and spontaneity. Many of Ginsberg's poems lend themselves unwillingly or not at all to analysis, being often enough spontaneous acts of mind. But Merrill's commentary consistently performs important functions: he describes the provenance of poems, quoting the poet's remarks and adding his own. He gives considerable space to *Howl*, quoting Ginsberg as to the occasions of the respective parts and discussing the famous line length. *Kaddish* is also discussed at length. Later Merrill pays more than passing attention to "The Change," which he calls "a document of a crucial turning point in a man's life." He is useful also in his consideration of techniques, distinguishing indebtedness to W. C. Williams, Jack Kerouac, Whitman, and others and noticing how Ginsberg's procedure measures up against the precepts of Charles Olson.

Olson's own work, *The Maximus Poems*, is reviewed in "Antipoetic Fisher of Men" (*TLS* 13 Nov.:1315) by an anonymous critic who finds the work not to be in his line of country at all. Olson has many admirers, he says. "The unhappy few," however, "who listen for lines that engrave themselves on the tablets of memory, for rhythmic subtlety or the undeniably right choice of words, for grace of sound or felicity of perception, for a fresh, true insight into the human condition—in other words, for significant art—will feel generally thwarted." One may sympathize with such taste and yet be more grateful for an essay, also originating in England, that contains the best critical introduction to Olson that has yet appeared. In "The Black Mountain Poets: Charles Olson and Edward Dorn" (*Survival of Poetry*, pp. 216–34), Donald Davie distinguishes the Mountaineers from such academic poets as Eliot, Tate, and Lowell, linking Olson and Dorn with Pound and, surprisingly, Milton. They use Pound to "bypass Eliot" and Donne and Marvell, who are also "stumbling blocks" (it all seems like a parody of the old pronouncements of Eliot on Milton), in order to reestablish contact with Whitman. The key with which Davie comes to *The Maximus Poems* is geography, in the curious byways of which he discovers the local and general relevance of details in the poem and in Olson's other work that at first glance seem purely fortuitous.

Two books ought to be noticed. One is on James Dickey, *Self-Interviews*, edited by Barbara and James Reiss (New York, Doubleday), a tape-recorded monologue in which the poet speaks of his career, expresses some of his opinions about literature, and says some things about his poems and their backgrounds. *The Man in the Sycamore Tree: The Good Times and Hard Life of Thomas Merton, An Entertainment, with Photographs*, by Edward Rice (Garden City, N.Y., Doubleday) gives an account of the life of the poet and his thought, generously documented with quotations from his prose. The photographs are excellent, and their lengthy legends provide a summary of the adjacent narrative.

The *Iowa Review*, launched in 1970, is quickly making its mark as a medium for studies in recent American poetry. Paul Ramsey, "Louise Bogan" (1,iii:116–24) writes with the warmth of admiration of this poet's work in general and particular, discussing themes and their implications and looking with especial care at their rhythms. Donald Davie, in "The Poetry of Samuel Menashe" (1,iii:107–14), introduces this work, discussing mostly the significance of the Jewishness of the author.

The review is most noticeably hospitable, however, to criticism of the work of young emerging poets. Richard Howard, in "John Wieners: 'Now Watch the Windows Open by Themselves'" (1,i:101–07), insisting on the genuineness, in a world of the counterfeit, of this poet's depravity, briefly sketches the features of his poetry, noting a curious parallel to Rilke's. Sherman Paul, in "From Lookout to Ashram: The Way of Gary Snyder" (1,iii:76–89; iv:70–85), supplies such guidelines as the average occidental reader will welcome in approaching the work of this poet, the poetry and the journals, which bear the impress or indeed the shape of oriental thought, showing at the same time similarities with Thoreau. Some of Paul's observations may assist the reading of work other than Snyder's and not necessarily influenced by the East: "We are given objective fragments, but even in this simplest entry they are arranged and placed on the empty space of the page. Like a haiku poem, they work by means of the art of omission, by what they suggest." Or, "Each entry [in the journal] is a formal design, a field of experience." Paul's sympathetic reading of the poems should serve to introduce this writer to many to whom he has hitherto been unknown. Martin Dodsworth, in "Body Rhythm," a brief review of Snyder's *Earth House Hold* (*Review*, 23: 55–60), describes the special response that Snyder calls for, in comments resembling those that have been made about William Carlos Williams: "Poems work at the level where words become action, in the sense of rhythms felt bodily." They re-create for us a "sense of the wilderness" and also "the sense of *having to do* and *doing* with the wilderness, registered in the body through rhythm . . . ."

This year a number of critical articles on miscellaneous poets have paid more or less attention to the various moves toward openness that have been made in American poetry since Lowell's celebrated turn. "A Reading of Galway Kinnell," by Ralph J. Mills, Jr., (*IowaR* 1,i:66–86;ii:102–22), combines skilled and sensitive interpretation of single poems with the categorization of Kinnell's work as a whole and its development. In addition, Mills places Kinnell in the context of the sweep of contemporary American poetry: the first collection

(1960) is one of the poetical works of the period that embody departure "from the witty, pseudo-mythic verse . . . of the 1950's [and] arrive at the more authentic, liberated work of the 1960's." Kinnell shows a progressive stripping off of illusion and moves toward a loose structure. Mills quotes the poet's intention to make " 'a poem without scaffolding or occasion, that progresses through images to a point where it can make a statement on a major subject," and says that this description is good also for the poetry of Robert Bly, Louis Simpson, W. S. Merwin, Frank O'Hara, Donald Hall, and John Ashbery, among others.

The common concern of the new poets, Mills says, is "the creation of a poetry which relies less and less upon logical or narrative structure, upon the representation of external events . . . but which develops around a highly suggestive grouping of images whose source is inward experience, memory, dream, or vision." This strategy comes under some discussion in an essay, "The Present State of American Poetry: Robert Bly and James Wright" (*ES* 51:112–37), by G. A. M. Janssens, who is also concerned to note changes in direction taken by American poetry in the 50s. He names Olson's "Projective Verse" essay, which enjoyed "disproportionate success," as an influence running counter to that of the New Criticism and quotes at some length the introduction to the Penguin anthology, *Contemporary American Poetry* (1962), where Donald Hall quotes lines from Robert Bly and Louis Simpson to show that a "new imagination" is at work. Janssens proceeds to outline a controversy in the *Southern Review* in which Cleanth Brooks was taken to task for saying that "the structure of the two poems cited by Hall [looked to him] as old as that of Wordsworth's Lucy poems." This discussion about the new poetry introduces a comparison of the work of Bly and Wright in which the characteristics of each are brought out.

A review article, "The Latest Poetry of Robert Penn Warren" (*SR* 78:348–57), is a brief but informative study by Monroe K. Spears, who observes among other characteristics that the style of the poet has taken a direction similar to that noticed above—the open and confessional. In Warren, this is a development of tendencies present from the beginning; and his work avoids the faults of formlessness, exhibitionism, and sentimentality, to which the new poetry is prone.

In a pleasant, anecdotal piece, "A Portrait of W. S. Merwin" (*Shenandoah* 21,ii:3–14), which surveys the poet's career to date,

Frank MacShane records miscellaneous comments by Merwin about his abandonment of punctuation, the dreamlike quality of some of his poems, the aim of transparency in language, and the dominance of Pound's influence on his work. Kenneth Andersen, in "The Poetry of W. S. Merwin" (*TCL* 16:278–86), notes that Merwin begins as an alien artist whose skepticism about the validity of myth doesn't preclude him from using it. His later poems are epigrammatic, with metaphysical conceits, and the latest lack punctuation, "making the thought more open-minded and suggestive." Andersen emphasizes the importance of metaphor throughout, quoting an early poem, "all metaphor . . . is magic." Harvey Gross, in "The Writing on the Void: The Poetry of W. S. Merwin" (*IowaR* 1,iii:92–106) studies this poet from the point of view of rhythm and, again, of metaphor: "A poet's rhythm," he says, "articulates his ways of feeling; his metaphor projects his *Weltanschauung*." Gross surveys Merwin's career, aspects of it at least, up to and including *The Lice*, demonstrating its development. One of the many observations in this sensitive essay, which the author modestly calls "notes," is that the poems of *The Moving Target* and *The Lice* "delineate the eerie quality of behavior and feeling in a post-apocalyptic world: after the end but before another beginning." Another is: "Merwin is a symbolist in a world emptied of God: where symbols are no longer believed but merely *interpreted*."

University of Oregon

16. Drama

Walter J. Meserve

i. Bibliographies, Histories, Anthologies, Dissertations

During 1970 bibliographers of American drama produced several volumes of definite value for the scholar's bookshelves. Although E. Hudson Long's Goldentree Bibliography, *American Drama from Its Beginnings to the Present* (New York, Appleton-Century-Crofts) is brief (seventy-eight pages) and geared to the demands of a survey class in American drama, it has value within its limitations as an annotated reference work. After the listing of basic references, the organization of this book by period, region, genre, and theme dictates some of its limitations. There are also some omissions such as Helen Deutsch and Stella Hanau's *The Provincetown* (1931), and sections on library collections and dramatic criticism would have been helpful. A second work and one of greater use to the researcher is Carl J. Stratman's *American Theatrical Periodicals, 1798–1967* (Durham, N.C., Duke Univ. Press). The listing for each periodical includes the title of the periodical, its place of publication, the number of issues published with inclusive dates, present holding locations, the editor, and title changes. Although one misses the listing of such nineteenth-century periodicals as the *Knickerbocker, Literary World, Port Folio,* or *Something*—all of which contain good theatre criticism—such limitations necessarily imposed by the project objectives do not seriously detract from this aid to scholarship in American drama.

Helen H. Palmer and Jane A. Dyson's *American Drama Criticism, Supplement 1* (Hamden, Conn., Shoe String Press) updates the initial work to January 1969, includes material previously omitted, and adds some thirty playwrights to their list. Mainly these newly listed playwrights are quite minor contributors to American drama, but the criticism on Paddy Chayefsky, Charles Rann Kennedy, and John Steinbeck certainly adds to the value of the bibliography. This supplement includes a list of works indexed but lacks an index of critics.

Another reference book which should be noted is the *Chicorel Theater Index to Plays in Anthologies, Periodicals, Discs and Tapes*,
volume 1 (New York, Chicorel Library Publishing Co.) edited by
Marietta Chicorel.

There were a few books which dealt with some historical aspect
of American drama and theatre. As a brief introduction, Bernard
Hewitt's *History of the Theatre from 1800 to the Present* (New York,
Random House) presents succinct commentary on the theatre of
England, the Continent, and America from the "Romantic Revolt"
through the movements of Realism, Symbolism, and Expressionism
to Epic and Absurd theatre. It is a scattered treatment that America,
perhaps necessarily, receives, however, and one does not get a clear
picture of American contribution to world theatre from this text. Of
very little value to the student of American drama is Emory Lewis's
Stages, The Fifty-Year Childhood of American Theatre (Englewood
Cliffs, N.J., Prentice-Hall, 1969). This is a personal and somewhat
nostalgic view of a New York theatre critic. Presenting his scattered
thoughts against a cultural and historical background, he indulges
himself in language that is predominantly more vivid than convincing. For him American drama was born in 1915 and presumably has
not yet achieved adulthood. Mainly (two-thirds of his book), he
deals with drama since 1960 and is at his best in his chapter on critics,
"Fatheads and Cretins," while his prejudices show in judgments such
as that on Lillian Hellman's *My Mother, My Father and Me*, which
he found a high point in the theatre of the 1960s.

There is one section in Ronald E. Mitchell's *Opera, Dead or Alive:
Production, Performance, and Enjoyment of Musical Theatre* (Madison, Univ. of Wis. Press) which is particularly applicable to America.
In part 1—"On Stage with Musical Theatre"—he makes occasional
reference to America, but on pages 269–82 in "The Range of Musical
Theatre" he discusses American musical comedy as "the rebel child
of European operetta" and presents extended analyses of *Oklahoma!*
and *Kiss Me, Kate*. Mitchell also includes a very interesting glossary
of terms. Although Bernard Beckerman's *Dynamics of Drama Theory
and Method of Analysis* (New York, Knopf) is not a book on American drama, it does involve a distinctive approach to drama which
may inform or irritate the teacher of drama. Drama, he explains,
"occurs when one or more human beings isolated in time and space
present themselves in imagined acts to another or others." Through

concentration on "the dramatic segment," Beckerman explores a structural approach to drama.

Finding a dissertation topic and getting it approved has always been something of a problem even for the best of graduate students. With the increasing number of drama and theatre departments as well as English departments now offering Ph.D.'s, the choice of a topic should perhaps be more carefully scrutinized. Just what should a Ph.D. dissertation represent? Some are certainly as meaningless in their generality as others are in their detailed concern for the insignificant. Can a Ph.D. candidate satisfy the research and scholarship requirements through a dissertation on "John Gassner: Play Anthologist" (two dissertations having treated Gassner as a critic) or the study of a single Albee play or the stage history of a single contemporary pageant drama? There is also repetition in topics—two dissertations this year, for example, on the tent repertory theatre. On the other hand, there were some interesting topics listed. Along with the names one might expect—Williams, Miller, O'Neill, Wilder, Hellman, Albee—there were dissertations on Henry DeMille, Dan Marble, James N. Barker, and Edward Harrigan. Other dissertations on vaudeville, dramatic criticism, the Negro, and partisan or political drama in the nineteenth century suggest something of the scope of scholarship still open to the imaginative degree candidate searching for a topic.

ii. The Beginning to 1915

For the historian of American drama and theatre the name Hallam is of particular significance. In "The British Background of the American Hallams" (*TS* 11,i:1–35) Philip Highfill, Jr., provides a well documented history of the family. While he freely admits to an "erratic chronological progress" in his essay, one must, however, shudder at his wandering and unselective presentation while still admiring his detailed research. Another essay, "Early Theatres in Rhode Island" (*TS* 11,ii:167–86) by Donald C. Mullin, tells of the activities of the Douglass-Hallam company in Rhode Island during the early 1760s and the 1790s while locating the theatres in Newport and Province during those years.

One of the major figures in the early drama and theatre of America is William Dunlap. Robert H. Canary's *William Dunlap* (TUSAS

164) is an interestingly written and informative biography. More historian than drama and theatre critic, Canary places Dunlap well among the Federalists and comments upon his several careers. He does not, however, present an adequate picture of Dunlap as a theatre manager, nor does he discuss in a knowledgeable fashion the structure of the plays he analyses. Generally, he provides plot summaries of Dunlap's major works but is distinctly inadequate in his commentary on such plays as *Yankee Chronology*, *André*, and *The Glory of Columbia*. His evaluations of *The Father* and *Leicester* are more effective, however, and his discussion of Dunlap's use of morality is an outstanding aspect of the book. The limitations of space in this series is always a problem for the writer, and that may explain why the final assessment in this book strikes the reader as more favorable than the previous commentary suggested. Yet it is, in all, a welcome book on a generally neglected but significant figure in American drama. Dunlap's successful translations of Kotzebue's plays have long been noted, and now Alfred Behrmann traces the history of Kotzebue's plays in America: "Kotzebue on the American Stage" (*Arcadia* 4[1969]:274–84). Don B. Wilmeth's "An Index to *The Life of George Frederick Cooke* by William Dunlap" (*TD*, 2,i–ii [1969–70]:109–20) clarifies Dunlap's association with this successful English Actor. Another essay by Wilmeth, "The Posthumous Career of George Frederick Cooke" (*TN* 24:68–74) explains what happened to Cooke's body after he died. The career and contribution of one of Dunlap's contemporaries, theatre manager John Sollee, is very effectively assessed by Julia Curtis, "John Joseph Stephen Leger Sollee and the Charleston Theatre" (*ETJ* 21[1969]:285–98).

As the years pass, the drama and theatre of nineteenth-century America are attracting more attention, and this is at least an encouraging direction for drama scholarship even though the books are sometimes disappointing. Cortland P. Auser's *Nathaniel P. Willis* (TUSAS 132[1969]), for example, is not too well written, but it does have a lot of well-documented ideas concerning Willis as editor, poet, sketch writer, and journalist. His plays, however, are treated in four and a third pages without critical evaluation and without reference to his participation in a developing theatre and drama. Joseph Leach's *Bright Particular Star, The Life and Times of Charlotte Cushman* (New Haven, Conn., Yale Univ. Press) is not always an easy book to read and lacks a critical evaluation of her acting or much contemporary criticism of her stage appearances. It is, instead, a rather full picture of Miss Cushman—her headstrong early years in New England, her stage career in America, the several women who were so vital a part of her emotional life, the theatrical and social life in England that brought her in close contact with the Carlyles among others, her place among the American literary figures in Florence, and her later days as a reader upon the stage.

Dion Boucicault was the subject of a well-researched article by A. Cleveland Harrison and a book by Robert Hogan. Harrison's "Boucicault on Dramatic Action: His Confirmation of the Poetics" (*QJS* 56:45–53) analyses Boucicault's essays to discover that the dramatist followed Aristotle's concepts in a quite thorough manner. Hogan's volume, *Dion Boucicault* (TUSAS 163[1969]) is written in a lively manner which sometimes suggests the author's inability to believe in Boucicault's work. He sees mainly "the Pseudo Work of Art," omits commentary on Boucicault's theoretical writings, and reserves his best comments for the Irish plays. Essentially, the book adds little to existing scholarship and remains a brief introductory volume.

There were also a few scattered articles dealing with various aspects of nineteenth-century drama. Most valuable for drama and theatre historians is Alfred H. Srnka's "An Index to *Personal Recollections of the Stage* by William Burke Wood" (*TD* 1,ii[1969]:51–73). A very pertinent essay on dramatic criticism is Tice L. Miller's "John Ranken Touse: The Last of the Victorian Critics" (*ETJ* 22:161–78) which shows how the *New York Evening Post* critic fought for more than fifty years to defend his Victorian tastes and his "moralistic and conservative views." Arthur N. Kincaid's "Italian and English Sources of Boker's *Francesca da Rimini*" (*ATQ* 1[1969]:91–100) offers little that is surprising but puts it all together for the interested student. In a very well-documented and interestingly written article, Alan W. C. Green—" 'Jim Crow,' 'Zip Coon': The Northern Origins of Negro Minstrelsy" (*MR* 11:385–97)—discusses the Negro character in American drama prior to the establishment of the minstrel show in the mid-nineteenth century. David Grimsted's "*Uncle Tom* from Page to Stage: Limitations of Nineteenth Century Drama" (*QJS* 56:235–44) compares the novel and the play and makes a number of carefully phrased or qualified assertions. For example, *Uncle Tom's Cabin* "was the principal American play staged for over a half century that dealt seriously with a controversial issue without smothering it under melodramatic conventions." *Principal* and *smothering* are problem words which might, one suppose, eliminate a number of plays from *Neighbor Jackwood* (1857) to *The Reverend Griffith Davenport* (1899). At any rate this essay does not show the best of scholarship. In the "Early Recognition of Gordon Craig in American Periodicals" (*ETJ* 22:78–86), Norman Myers contends that Craig was accepted merely as a designer trying to reform the current stage, not as a man laying the foundations for a totally new theatre.

iii. Between the Two World Wars

In recent years there have been a number of fine essays on American drama appearing in books published in India or in Indian journals such as the *Literary Half-Yearly* in Mysore. Three books of essays were published in 1969—*Indian Essays in American Literature* (Bombay, Popular Prakashan), *Perspectives in American Literature* (Ludhiana, Lyall Book Depot), *The Experience of American Literature* (New Delhi, United States Educational Foundation in India)—and T. R. Dutta's "The Human Image in Modern American Drama" (*Indian Essays*, 261–66) may serve as good introduction to this section. American drama, Dutta writes, is "the symbolic chronicle of the human struggle for survival and 'prevalence,' for identity and purpose, for meaning and promise."

a. **Eugene O'Neill.** In studying this "chronicle" critics invariably find a lot to say about Eugene O'Neill. Egil Tornqvist in *A Drama of Souls, Studies in O'Neill's Super-naturalistic Technique* (New Haven, Conn., Yale Univ. Press, 1969), employs an interesting approach without writing a book that will impress many scholars. Using "supernaturalism" as a focal point for analysis—O'Neill's term for Strindberg's "behind-life" position in *The Dance of Death*—Tornqvist emphasizes the variety of theatrical and literary devices that O'Neill uses to achieve his objectives. He discusses scenery, costumes, masks, action, sound and language to try to shed some light on O'Neill's attempt to give expression to those "forces behind life." Another critic, P. S. Sastri (*Indian Essays*, 55–59), proposes "One Approach to O'Neill" by selecting a half dozen plays to show that O'Neill has simply modernized Euripides' themes and arguments. His argument, however, is not effective.

A number of the O'Neill essays dealt with particular plays. In "The Alienated Ape" (*LHY* 11,i:53–69) Mrs. P. N. Das discusses the play in terms of the word "belong" and O'Neill's concern for belonging and alienation. The writer wanders from her analysis of the play somewhat and sees man's attempt to cope with his machines as a reduction of man to an ape-like existence. She further warns modern man that machines must not be worshipped as a "modern substitute for God." Another Indian critic, Shashi Gujral (*"The Hairy Ape—*Disintegration of the American Dream," *Perspectives,* 383–88), weakly argues that the play is a symbolic nightmare and O'Neill's pessimism typically American. Two essays on *The Iceman Cometh* add nothing to O'Neill scholarship. N. S. Predham (*"The Iceman Cometh* and the Theatre of the Absurd," *Perspectives,* 389–96) compares the play to Absurd Theatre but to no purpose. Delma E. Presley's "O'Neill's Iceman: Another Meaning" (*AL* 42:387–88) briefly notes the underworld meaning of the word *ice-man,* for whatever value it may have. On the other hand, in a very carefully written essay based on O'Neill's extensive notes, John H. Stroupe, "O'Neill's *Marco Millions*: A Road to Xanadu" (*MD* 12:377–82), shows O'Neill's approach to writing the play, his interest in satire, and his own nature as it is revealed in the play. In a much less effective essay, "O'Neill's Lazarus: Dionysus and Christ" (*AL* 41:543–54), Egil Tornqvist asserts without much logic or substantiation that Lazarus resembles both Dionysus and Jesus and that O'Neill "felt it a matter of particular concern that Jesus and Zarathustra . . . somehow be found 'one and equal.'" In another essay of limited value Jere Real emphasizes the pessimistic view that man's "selfish possessiveness" makes him prostitute himself for material gain—"The Brothel in O'Neill's *Mansions*" (*MD* 12:383–89).

Four other essays are on more general approaches to O'Neill. Emil Roy, "The Archetypal Unity of Eugene O'Neill's Drama" (*CompD* 3[1969–70]:263–74), argues in that vague and sometimes meaningless language of the myth and rite critic that O'Neill is at his best creating "individual fantasy expressing symbolic action" that brings "an order in artistic design and coherence." In a rather brief essay Egil Tornqvist, "Personal Addresses in the Plays of O'Neill" (*QJS* 55[1969]:126–30), explains what should be obvious—that personal addresses indicate "mental relations between the characters." Another slight and questionable point is made by Orley I. Holtan,

"Eugene O'Neill and the Death of the Covenant" (*QJS* 56:256–63), who maintains that O'Neill's inability to complete his eleven-play cycle resulted from the failure of his dream of seeing the United States become the most successful country in the world. One of the more substantially written essays on O'Neill, whatever value one attaches to the subject, is Lewis W. Falb's "The Critical Reception of Eugene O'Neill on the French Stage" (*ETJ* 22:397–405). Of the plays performed in France—about one-fourth of O'Neill's productivity—O'Neill's experimental work was generally unsuccessful with the French, who were most appreciative of his theatrical qualities.

b. **Dramatists of the South and Southwest: Green, Wolfe, Riggs.** In the Southwest Writers series of Steck-Vaughn there are now long introductory essays on three more Southern writers. Generally uneven in value, particularly on the better-known writers, the series is certainly significant for bringing minor writers into better focus in a developing American drama and literature. Not surprisingly, Ladell Payne's *Thomas Wolfe* (SWS 9[1969]) allows only a single paragraph to list some of his plays and does not mention his relationship with the theatre designer, Aline Bernstein. Nor is Walter S. Lazenby's *Paul Green* (SWS 10) a satisfactory volume, either in the writing style or the material presented. Lazenby's best work is shown in his rehearsal of the plots of the early plays, while his evaluations of Green's better-known plays are very slight. On the other hand, Thomas Erhard's *Lynn Riggs* (SWS 29) is a fair, economical, and revealing presentation. The work is well written, provides interesting commentary on Riggs's little-known productivity and, while indicating the poverty of critical evaluation, tries to assess Riggs's contribution to drama in the Southwest and in America.

c. **Robert Sherwood.** There were two books this year on Sherwood. John Mason Brown's *The Ordeal of a Playwright* (New York, Harper and Row) is the second volume of his biography—cut short by his untimely death. The charm of this volume (as with his first volume) is in the bias of this exuberant biographer who kept "finding wonderful new things about Bob Sherwood" in the vast Sherwood papers which he alone was allowed to use. This book, which includes the text of *There Shall Be No Night* to fill out the proper length, tells the story of the writing of this play, starts Sherwood in his wartime job with FDR, and skips to 1945. There is nothing on the war years, nothing after Sherwood's reaction to FDR's death. The second book is Walter J. Meserve's critical biography, *Robert E. Sherwood, Reluctant Moralist* (New York, Pegasus Press), which assesses the careers of Sherwood as film critic, playwright, and ghost writer for FDR, emphasizing his contribution to the developing American drama between the two world wars. Meserve presents not only a man whose considerable gifts for theatrics and words won him fame and fortune during a period when such achievements were necessary to the development of an art and the welfare of a nation but also a man whose emotional reaction to the joys and suffering of humanity seriously intruded upon his attempts to be profound.

d. **Maxwell Anderson.**   A close friend of Sherwood's and a fellow founder of the Playwrights' Company, Maxwell Anderson was the subject of a special issue of the *North Dakota Quarterly* (38,i). Of the collected essays the most significant is Laurence G. Avery's "Maxwell Anderson and *Both Your Houses*" (pp. 5–24). Working with an unpublished 1939 revision of this play, Avery shows how Anderson revised his drama in order to distinguish between man and the institution of government and to defend American democracy. Although slight in words, the change is dramatic in Anderson's thought development, and Avery's work is extraordinarily good. Arthur T. Tees's "Legal and Poetic Justice in Maxwell Anderson's Plays" (pp. 25–32) is a brief, effective essay examining the legal injustice and the poetic justice which he found to be the usual juxtaposition in Anderson's work. Throughout, Tees contends, Anderson feels that poetic justice occurs despite the weaknesses of man. In "Mio Romagna: A New View of Maxwell Anderson's *Winterset*" (pp. 33–43) Robert L. Gilbert argues with considerable cogency and, contrary to past critics, that *Winterset* is not a revenge play and that Mio is logically and carefully presented and his reversal thoroughly foreshadowed. Jackson K. Hershbell, "The Socrates and Plato of Maxwell Anderson" (pp. 45–59), concerns himself with Anderson's interpretation in *Barefoot in Athens* of politics in Athens and Sparta. Generally, he feels that Anderson was more accurate in his essays on the subject than in his play, but though he quarrels with Anderson as historian and philosopher, he does not question the effect of the play. Randall J. Buchanan, "A Playwright's Progress" (pp. 60–73), deduces twenty-five rules for playwriting from Anderson's essays and with these rules in mind analyzes *Saturday's Children* and *High Tor*, concluding that by 1937 Anderson had his dramaturgy well under control. Although his essay is only partially related to Anderson's work, Masanori Sata tries with moderate success to survey a theme in American drama— "*Superstition* (1824) to *Winterset* (1935): Romeo-Juliet theme kara no kosatsu" (*ELLS* 6[1969]:131–46).

e. **Barry, Connelly, Wilder, Rogers.** Far too little has been written about Philip Barry, especially that part of his work where he struggled with overwhelming questions concerning man, freedom, reality, truth. In "Philip Barry: A Dramatist's Search" (*MD* 13:93–99), Walter J. Meserve traces Barry's progress toward answering these questions from the early *You and I* through *Second Threshold*. John L. Phillips, "Before the Colors Fade: *Green Pastures* Recalled" (*AH* 21:28–29,74–76), explores Marc Connelly's memory concerning the writing and the stage history of his famous play. N. S. Subramanyam, "Wilder's *Our Town*—A Study" (*The Experience of American Literature*, 281–98), writes an interesting if general essay suggesting the importance of *Our Town* to Indians. Although Will Rogers is hardly concerned with the drama, an essay by Walter H. Eitner, "Will Rogers: Another Look at His Act" (*KanQ* 2,ii:46–52) emphasizes Rogers's belief in "common sense" and "home folks attitude" at a time when one might say the stage appreciated these qualities.

iv. After World War II

Divisions and categories of American drama are either too easy or too difficult to determine, and the twenty-five odd years since World War II may still suffice as a recognizable period of progress in drama.

a. **Arthur Miller.** Benjamin Nelson's *Arthur Miller, Portrait of a Playwright* (New York, David McKay Co.) is particularly good on the early plays and their relation to later works. He provides a well-written, well-documented, critical evaluation of individual plays. There is, on the other hand, no thesis approach to the dramatist, no developing analysis or final interpretation of his contribution to the drama. The emphasis, as stated, is on the playwright. Darshan Singh Maini, "The Moral Vision of Arthur Miller" (*Indian Essays*, 85–96), sees Miller as a moralist in both Puritan and Hebraic traditions, frustrated or bothered by the problems arising from public issues and private conscience. It is a well presented essay and a good piece to read with Eleonore Hombitzer's "Die Selbstentfremdung des modernen Menschen in dramatischen Werk Arthur Millers" (*NS* 69:409–16), which suggests that Miller wants people to become idiots in the sense of the Greek word *idiotes*: people who have a feeling of self and who refuse to let themselves be completely planned or programmed. In another broadly based, inter-genre essay Edmond Schraepen, "Arthur Miller's Constancy: A Note on Miller as a Short Story Writer" (*RLV* 36:62–71), relates *All My Sons, Death of a Salesman*, and *After the Fall* to themes in his short stories. Although Robert H. Martin in an interview with Miller, "Arthur Miller and the Meaning of Tragedy" (*MD* 13:34–39), talked primarily about *After the Fall*, their comments are revealing. Miller observes, for example, that man's awareness of human nature may force him to conclude that "it's all pretence at some kind of faith" and that the dramatist is left with "a kind of sad comedy when we try to do tragedy." One general item adds to the existing list of bibliographies: Harriet Ungar, "The Writings of and about Arthur Miller: A Check List, 1936–1967" (*BNYPL* 74:107–34).

Among the essays that dealt with particular plays, two treated different approaches to *The Crucible*. Relating the play to McCarthyism of past and present, Robert J. Willis, "Arthur Miller's *The Crucible*: Relevant for all Times" (*FJ* 1,i:5–14), maintains that Miller believed both in mitigating circumstances which minimize evil and in people dedicated to the pursuit of evil. In the second essay, " 'The Interior of a Heart': *The Crucible* and *The Scarlet Letter*" (*UCQ* 15,iv:27–32), Herbert Bergman compares the obvious features of both works because they are read in general education, English, Humanities, and drama courses. Neither essay reveals much critical enlightenment for the reader. Assuming a Quentin-Miller identity, Baldev Raja goes over the old ground of "search for self-knowledge" and "recovered innocence" in "Arthur Miller's *After the Fall*—A Study in Quest Innocence" (*Perspectives*, 397–407). Although the title of the following essay is a bit painful, C. W. E. Bigsby's "What

Price Arthur Miller? An Analysis of *The Price*" (*TCL* 16:16–25) places this drama quite effectively in the Miller canon.

b. Tennessee Williams. In addition to rather slight essays on "The Function of Gentlemen Callers: A Note on Tennessee Williams' *The Glass Menagerie*" (*NMW* 2:83–90) by Elmo Howell and "Tennessee Williams' *Kingdom of Earth*: A Sterile Promontory" (*D&T* 8:90–93) by Alfred E. Halson, there were good studies of Williams's religion and women. Sister M. Carol Blitgen, "Tennessee Williams: Modern Idolator" (*Renascence* 22:192–97), claims that Williams is a theist with an "Old Testament mind-set" who believes that "God exists when He can be humanly communicated." John J. Fritscher, "Some Attitudes and a Posture: Religious Metaphor and Ritual in Tennessee Williams' Query of the American God" (*MD* 13:201–15), finds religion everywhere in Williams's plays. *Streetcar* he sees as a parody, a "metaphorical translation of the Episcopalian Mass." Equating Williams's plays with his life, Fritscher describes Williams as a believer whose characters see God both in terms of the Old Testament wrath and the New Testament need-guilt. Louis Blackwell in "Tennessee Williams and the Predicament of Women" (*SAB* 35,ii:9–14), categorizes Williams's women into four groups and discusses his plays in terms of these women. Although such categories sometimes tend to diminish the value of the characters, this study is enlightening in discussion and organization of the four-pronged thesis. Another essay dealing with characters is Leland Starnes's "The Grotesque Children of *The Rose Tattoo*" (*MD* 12:357–69). Starnes finds the characters, particularly Serafina, pushed to comic incongruities touching upon the grotesque and, as a consequence, more effective and poignant in the special ethnic world of these wild, emotional people.

c. William Inge and Archibald MacLeish. The two essays on Inge suggest, sadly, the end of his prominence on the American stage. Jordan Y. Miller, "William Inge: Last of the Realists?" (*KanQ* 2,ii:17–26) traces Inge's attitudes back to Ibsen and discusses Inge's four major plays as unique contributions to the modern theatre in America before noting that both Inge and his style have disappeared. The second essay illustrates the attitude of some critics who feel that the

similarities in technique and subject matter of any two writers are
worth a comparison. Edwin J. Hamblet compares *Le temps des lilacs*
and *Picnic* for no particular reason in "The North American Outlook
of Marcel Dubé and William Inge" (*QQ* 77:374–87).

There was another comparison essay—one with greater logic behind it—concerned with MacLeish's affirmation of life and T. S. Eliot's
early pessimistic view as expressed in poetic drama. Unfortunately,
the approach is confused and the conclusion inconsistent as the author, N. S. Subramanyam, both asserts and denies tragedy in "Mac-
Leish's *J.B.*: A Tragedy of Affirmation" (*Indian Essays*, 223–31).
John H. Stroupe very carefully forges his thesis that through the use
of masks and the metaphor of acting MacLeish's *J.B.* demonstrates
the impotence of the Deity and the exercise of choice by J.B. which
establishes his superiority to God. For Stroupe, J.B. is an existential
work in which the suffering of man provides man with awareness of
both his masks and his gods—"The Masks of MacLeish's *J.B.*" (*TSL*
15:75–83).

d. **Edward Albee.** Another source has now declared that the American theatre is removed from real life—N. A. Anastas'ev, "Profile
amerikanskogo teatra" (*VLit* 13[1969]:139–59). Part of the blame
for this removal from life is attached to the Absurd Theatre in America and its leading dramatist, Edward Albee, who, though not anti-
humanist, has elements of dehumanization in his plays. Other critics
were not as severe with Mr. Albee, and one, James E. White, "An
Early Play by Edward Albee" (*AL* 42:98–99), provided a new view
with a brief comment on *Schism*, an Albee play written at Choate
Prep about "a young person's flight from religious dogmatism and
conformity." In "Illusion and Betrayal: Edward Albee's Theatre"
(*Studies* 59:53–67), A. Robert Lee looks at Albee's plays solely in
terms of his ability to dramatize states of betrayal. After treating
most of Albee's plays, he concludes that a pattern of betrayal and
illusion may be Albee's greatest achievement. No critic of Albee's
plays was startling in his revelations, although most were definite in
their statements. John J. von Szeliski—"Albee: A Rare Balance" (*TCL*
16:123–30)—felt motivated to discuss *A Delicate Balance* simply because he found it Albee's best play, a "truly major drama" and the
best recent "expression of the peculiar loneliness of our time." Mary
Elizabeth Campbell's "The Tempters in Albee's *Tiny Alice*" (*MD*

13:22–33) is a more convincingly written essay, and it does provide a certain enlightenment. She sees the play in terms of the morality "struggle of Vices and Virtues," Butler, Lawyer, and Miss Alice pitted against the hero. *Tiny Alice* was also used as a prime illustration in Paul Witherington's contention that the form and language of Albee's plays are the characteristics of modern Gothic literature— "Albee's Gothic: The Resonances of Cliché" (*CompD* 4:151–65)—an interesting approach but without a strong point.

e. **Black Drama.** Drama / theatre in America now seems to be compensating for whatever neglect it may have caused blacks in the past. This year a number of books appeared which describe this activity, for, in the world of theatre art, "being black" is allowed an increasingly important emphasis. *On Being Black, Writings by Afro-Americans from Frederick Douglass to the Present* (Greenwich, Conn., Fawcett Publications) is edited by Charles T. Davis and David Walden. Except, however, for an essay on the dramatic dialogue in Jean Toomer's story, "Kabnis," and LeRoi Jones's essay on "Myth of Negro Literature," which has some comment on the drama, there is little in this volume that is relevant to the drama. *Five Black Writers*, edited by Donald B. Gibson, reprints old essays on Wright, Ellison, Baldwin, Hughes, and Jones except for one essay by William Miles, "Isolation in Langston Hughes' *Soul Gone Home*" (pp. 178–82), a fantasy with the theme of isolation forced upon blacks. These two collections follow a general trend in the social world as well as the publishing world. The following two books, however, indicate the serious direction of work in black drama. Of considerable value for the teacher of black drama and theatre is William Reardon and Thomas Pawley's *The Black Teacher and Dramatic Art* (Westport, Conn., Negro Universities Press). More questionable in its importance for the student of black drama is James V. Hatch's *Black Image on the American Stage, A Bibliography of Plays and Musicals, 1770–1970* (New York, Drama Book Specialists). Hatch lists all plays that contain at least one black character, or were written by a black, or have a black theme and were produced in America during the two hundred year period. Understandably, nearly half of the volume deals with the post-1940 period; it is more difficult to discover what scholarly use the volume has.

In "Telling It Like It Is: An Experiment of Black Theatre as Rhetoric" (*QJS* 56:179–86), W. A. D. Riach assesses black drama not so much as drama "but to ascertain what Black drama reveals of the movement of which it is an expression and what the Black political movement is saying rhetorically to America through the Black Theatre." In this manner he discusses the artist and his society through his plays: LeRoi Jones and *Dutchman,* Jimmy Garrett and *And We Own the Night,* Ben Caldwell and *The Militant Preacher,* Marvin X and *Take Care of Business,* Joseph White and *Old Judge Mose is Dead.* Another discussion of this theatre was explored by Mario Fratti in an "Interview with Ellen Stuart" (*D&T* 8:87–89). After a survey of Negro parts in American plays from the Revolution to the Depression, A. Cleveland Harrison, "Negro Actors: The Added Dimensions of Color" (*SSJ* 35,i[1969]:16–27), discusses the importance of Negro actors in the casting of modern plays.

Mainly, however, the majority of essays on black drama focused upon the work of LeRoi Jones. From "Archetypes in LeRoi Jones' *Dutchman*" (*SBL* 1,i:66–68), briefly noted by Tom S. Rock, to "Myth, Magic, and Manhood in LeRoi Jones' *Madheart*" by Charles D. Peavy (*SBL* 1,i:12–20) and on to Stephan Brecht's "LeRoi Jones' *Slave Ship*" (*TDR* 14,ii:212–19) Jones's drama is considered from several points of view. Consistent with the new critical approach to black drama, Brecht feels that *Slave Ship,* a spectacle play of exhortation "devoted to showing the evil done" and set in a black-white scene that is invisible to Euro-Americans, is addressed solely to the Afro-American community. It becomes increasingly evident that this dramatist has become, as Daphine S. Reed explains, "LeRoi Jones: High Priest of the Black Arts Movement" (*ETJ* 22:53–59). In this essay the writer gives Jones credit for starting the Black Arts Movement, for providing a spiritual unity, and for showing blacks the way to reject the white world and rediscover their own glory and prestige.

v. New Directions

Just where is American drama heading? Although the period of time since 1945 is easily taken as a unit, there should be some lines drawn, some new attitudes suggested, for the new directions being taken. Although it may take the historical critic another generation to determine exactly what is happening, changes are being made. As time passes, however, it becomes obvious that no one dramatist has made a sufficient contribution to have his work mark a definite change.

Albee might be so designated by some, but the Theatre of the Absurd has not been that effective in America. Perhaps it may only be said that change in American drama and theatre has permeated the sixties. Alan S. Downer very acutely observed one direction of the change in "More Strange Than True: Notes on the New York Theatre, 1968–69" (*QJS* 55[1969]:225–36) when he noted the "increasing theatricalism" of the New York productions which deliberately subordinated the playwright. Like others, Downer bemoaned the thinness of commercial theatre, whether wrought by principle or expediency, and described the contemporary drama as "more strange than true, servant-monster in the fair." Certainly, *The American Theatre, 1968–69* (New York, International Theatre Institute) bears out some of Downer's fears as it describes the theatre season from the Off Broadway and Off-Off Broadway erotica through black drama and the contributions of Chinatown to New York conservatism and on to educational and regional theatre. Another approach to the changes in American drama may be suggested by *The New Underground Theatre* edited by Robert J. Schweder (New York, Bantam Publishers, 1968). This editor sees a new drama springing from "a commitment to non-commitment," plays that are anti-tradition, anti-establishment. Yet other critics such as C. W. E. Bigsby have found "commitment" basic to drama of the sixties, while more than vestiges of an older drama obviously remain. Yet the scholarship this year indicates something about this slow conversion of American drama and theatre to meet the needs and dreams of modern America. William Inge and his realistic drama are looked upon as part of the past. Seemingly no new and exciting dramatists have appeared since Edward Albee; more critics seem interested in the security of research in the nineteenth century (although it must be said that the needs in this area are great); and a sense of revolt from the traditional way of searching for truth fills the drama / theatre atmosphere.

For a significant number of drama / theatre people something is seriously lacking. One critic thinks that it is *intelligence*—in both playwrights and their characters. In "Reactionary Notes on the Experimental Theatre" (*MR* 11:101–16) Oscar Mandel bluntly exclaims that T. S. Eliot, the "only absolutely intelligent playwright America has begotten," fled to England and that "in the entire body of the successfully staged American drama, there are not five intelligent characters to be found." Such broad statements necessitate careful hedging, but there are also critics who do not agree with this attitude toward intelligence. George Ralph, "History and Prophecy in *Benito Cereno*" (*ETJ* 22:155–60), provides a full and convincing discussion of this play's communication, "visually, verbally, intellectually, emotionally." Another critic, Jerome Mazzaro, in "Robert Lowell's *The Old Glory*: Cycle and Epicycle" (*WHR* 24:347–58), has encouraging words for the work being done at the American Place Theatre which produces only the plays of living American playwrights. For the historian-critic the emphasis of this theatre upon well-written and experimental plays suggests a definite vitality being infused into American drama—a drama in which language may be increasingly important. Certainly, this should be a hopeful sign for those who share Alan Downer's concern. And perhaps there is another hopeful sign in the activity of the academic theatre where beginning playwrights are getting more and more opportunities. In *The Carolina Playmakers, The First Fifty Years* (Chapel Hill, Univ. of N.C. Press) Walter Spearman traces the history of an academic theatre which has contributed substantially to the development of American drama and theatre. The author's wandering style ebbs and flows, perhaps symbolically indicative of progress in an academic theatre, but the achievements both for the Carolina Playmakers and the academic theatre at large cannot be denied.

Indiana University

17. Folklore

John T. Flanagan

Folklore bibliography appeared in a variety of places in 1970. Abu Saeed Zahurul Haque compiled "A Bibliography of Mississippi Folklore—1968" (*MFR* 4:28–36), which lists material chiefly from Mississippi newspapers, although some national magazines are cited too. Brief annotations are included. The annual listing in the *American Quarterly*, by James H. Penrod, Warren I. Titus, and Cratis Williams, includes some forty-three items (22:346–49). *The Negro in America*, originally the work of Elizabeth W. Miller, appeared in an edition revised by Mary L. Fisher (Cambridge, Mass., Harvard Univ. Press). Folklore items are scattered through some twenty pages (75–96) under such subheads as Negro authors, literary criticism, and music. The last item includes material on jazz, blues, soul music, and spirituals. Volume 8 of *Abstracts of Folklore Studies*, edited by Richard E. Buehler and a corps of associates, provides somewhat eccentric coverage of a number of magazines, some of the items listed going as far back as 1963–1964. The arrangement is by the periodicals reviewed, an awkward plan, but citations are gleaned from such unlikely sources as *Craft Horizons*, *Phylon*, and the *Beaver*. A substantial amount of folklore material, taken frequently from the folklore journals, appears in a bibliographical appendix to Duncan Emrich's attractive volume, *The Nonsense Book* (New York, Four Winds Press). The references correspond to the main divisions in the text: riddles, game rhymes, autograph albums and memory book rhymes, tongue twisters, and nonsense in general. This is a most useful compilation.

Sparse folklore material appears in Lewis Leary's *Articles on American Literature, 1950–1967* (Durham, N.C., Duke Univ. Press), but there is no folklore subhead among the twenty-six divisions; anyone seeking relevant articles would need to know the author or the theme in order to use the book profitably. The listing in the 751-page compilation is alphabetical by author within the various subheads. The *1969 MLA International Bibliography* (1:43–46, 119–20) includes some eighty odd items divided among theory, ballad and folksong, folk drama, folk narrative, linguistic folklore, and myth. The listing is alphabetical by authors. There is no annotation and the coverage at times is thin.

As the title indicates clearly, Katharine M. Briggs's *Dictionary of British Folk-Tales in the English Language* (Bloomington, Ind. Univ. Press) concentrates on material from Great Britain but it requires citation here because of the American relevance of many of the items listed. After providing a useful bibliography of books quoted or consulted, the editor includes an index of tale types and story titles, and then proceeds to discuss five kinds of tales: fables and exempla, fairy tales, jocular tales, novelle, and nursery tales. A folk narrative is here defined as fiction told for edification, delight, or amusement, and folk legends are considered to be stories once accepted as true.

Judith C. Ullom's excellent *Folklore of the North American Indians* (Washington, Library of Congress) appeared in 1969. Some 152 items are listed and helpfully annotated, and the material is arranged by North American culture areas. Editions or anthologies especially suitable for children are grouped at the end of each division.

Once again specialists in folklore will find paramount utility in Merle E. Simmons's compilation in the *Southern Folklore Quarterly* (34:149–313). The most recent edition of this annual collection follows the familiar plan: books and articles appearing anywhere in the world and dealing with the folklore of the United States, Latin America, Spain, Portugal, and other parts of the Luso-Hispanic world. The ten basic categories of previous lists are retained here, the arrangement is alphabetical by author, and there is a useful index of contributors. Since material about the folklore of the United States is not segregated, users of this bibliograhpy must first choose the appropriate subhead and then scan the included materials; but the coverage is impressive. Thus the section on material culture includes discussions of lace-making, ceramics, penitente buildings in New Mexico, carving, weaving, folk architecture, pottery, Indian beadwork, and Navajo squaw dresses. Here is certainly God's plenty.

i. History and Theory

Folklore theory has always appealed to those specialists who wish to make a unique discipline out of folklore study rather than accept it as a multidimensional approach to a subject with many facets. Occasionally the theories expressed clarify problems and point out fruitful directions for further study, but often they are so burdened by pretentious jargon that the very points expressed seem invalid.

Stith Thompson in his essay, "Unfinished Business: The Folktale" (*Medieval Literature*, pp. 213–21) covers a large territory in a few pages. He points out the existence of both oral and literary narrative, reviews folktale theory and collecting procedures, alludes to the great indexes that he himself helped to develop, and suggests areas still to be explored. Richard M. Dorson, in "Esthetic Form in British and American Folk Narrative" (*ibid.*, pp. 305–21), observes that the folktale, unlike the ballad, has never been fully admitted to the canon of British and American literature and contends that it can reveal a narrative skill which well deserves study. He then quotes three examples, a legend about the battle of Culloden, a tall tale about a poor Negro lad in the Mississippi football stadium, and an altercation between two bruisers in Michigan's Upper Peninsula. All three items are dramatic, present character, and employ language dexterously. They represent the craft of individual narrators working within an admirable tradition.

William O. Hendricks in "Folklore and the Structural Analysis of Literature" (*Lang&S* 3:83–121) reviews the work of Vladimir Propp and Axel Olrik and argues that a science of literature should be concerned with technical rather than evaluative considerations. Thus a folkloristic approach to literary analysis can place criticism in a cross-cultural perspective. Although his essay yields some interesting points, it is repetitious and opaque (thus he can speak of the "complementarity of syntagmatic and paradigmatic narrative analysis").

In an essay-review of David C. Fowler's recent book on balladry, *A Literary History of the Popular Ballad*, W. Edson Richmond places the study in the framework of ballad criticism and notes that the book implies that textual changes stemming from oral transmission are almost always degenerative. Richmond's essay, "The Development of the Popular Ballad: A New Theory" (*Genre*, 3:198–204), points out the value of Fowler's book as a stimulus to close reading of the ballads but deplores its lack of clear structure and its aberrant speculation.

Although Brian Sutton-Smith's essay, "Psychology of Children:

The Triviality Barrier" (*WF* 29:1–8), seems defensive, his point is a good one. He discusses the activity of children's groups—games, riddles, rhymes, jokes, pranks, torments, codes, gang lore, and so on— and observes that children engage in such behavior chiefly because it is fun but also because it is singularly expressive. Folklorists and social scientists would do well to concern themselves with such material. "The further understanding of the formal and functional nature of these phenomena is then the research focus of the psychology of childlore."

Certain theoretical discussions touch on material folklore. Cortland P. Auser in "The Viable Community: Redirections Through Applied Folklore" (*NYFQ* 26:2–13) pleads for a greater knowledge of objects and artifacts and uses his museum experience to demonstrate the need for more extensive exhibition of such items. Henry Glassie in "Artifacts: Folk, Popular, Imaginary and Real" (*Icons of Popular Culture*, edited by Marshall Fishwick and Ray B. Browne, Bowling Green, Ohio, Bowling Green State Univ. Press, pp. 103–22) distinguishes among the various levels of culture and draws a sometimes tenuous distinction between the folk and the popular. Corn knives, he points out, were originally folk products, then became popular imitations of folk originals, and finally in the South evolved into folk imitations of popular models. The reader, straining at times to follow the argument, is not always convinced that the distinction is worth making. Taking a somewhat wider frame of reference, Roger T. Trindell in "American Folklore Studies and Geography" (*SFQ* 34:1–11) links the study of non-verbal folklore with scientific geography. He feels that geography can contribute much to folklore and that the study of covered bridges, agricultural fairs, and classical toponyms, to mention no others, can be immensely rewarding. Trindell ends his essay with an apposite quotation from Don Yoder to the effect that folklife is "the totality of the verbal, spiritual, and material aspects of a culture."

ii. Ballads

Ballads emanating from both sides of the Atlantic Ocean continue to attract the attention of scholars. Basing his study on the first two volumes of the famous Francis J. Child collection, Harry B. Campbell in "The Multiple Effects of the Tragic Event in the Child Ballad"

(*NYFQ* 26:14–41) asserts that the tragic hero of the traditional ballad is often hard to identify. "Glasgerion" or "Fair Annie" or "The Lass of Roch Royal" are good examples. For this reason the chief culprit sometimes avoids punishment and the group or community represents the fallen figure. Moreover, the author contends that the disgraced hero can experience two kinds of affliction: death, or psychological and emotional pain.

Studies of individual ballads represent a wide focus of interest. Faith Hippensteel in " 'Sir Hugh': the Hoosier Contribution to the Ballad" (*IF* 2:75–140) observes that some twelve variants of the ballad in question have been recovered in Indiana, all belonging to a single type. Both texts and music are given, and the author provides illuminating comment on the distribution of the ballad as well as its historical tradition, textual variations, and aesthetic qualities. A more incisive study is that made by E. Flatto of "Lord Randal" (*SFQ* 34:331–36). This particularly memorable ballad reveals all the traditional traits: incremental repetition, dramatic dialogue, a refrain, but it is also singularly emotional. The author points out that we are told nothing about the motivation behind the poisoning and that there is no indication of the hero being at fault. Lord Randal is indeed the victim of inverted hospitality: poisoned food. This ambiguity does not detract from the ballad, however, but "helps it create the sense of a mysterious, terrifying external world, where man strays from his home to be robbed of his fondest hope and illusions."

Kendrick Smithyman in his study of "The Little Mohee" (*NYFQ* 26:64–70) admits that this familiar American ballad may descend from the British broadside, "The Indian Lass," but claims that it is probably a whaling song rather than a mainland song and that Mohee is either a reference to the Hawaiian island of Maui or a corruption of a Polynesian word. The author reviews all of the critical authorities and presents the disputed points logically but offers essentially nothing new. Another treasured American ballad with a British source is the subject of Roger L. Welsch's "A 'Buffalo Skinner's' Family Tree" (*JPC* 4:107–29). Beginning with the old ballad "Caledonia," familiar in the eighteenth century, Welsch surveys the ballad in its adaptations to the Canadian woods, to the Texas cattle ranges, to North Dakota and Mexico. Its tangled history involves John Lomax, J. Frank Dobie, and Carl Sandburg, and the text provides interesting shifts from the milieu of Canadian lumbering to Southwestern buffalo hunting. Extensive notes and a bibliography support the author's efforts to establish a genealogy for the ballad.

A more difficult problem interested John Quincy Wolf as his title, "Who Wrote 'Joe Bowers'?" (*WF* 29:77–89), implies. One of the best known and most famous American ballads, "Joe Bowers," probably represents a fictitious Gold Rush figure and its authorship is generally disputed. The "facts" of the ballad have never been verified even though the hero was supposdly a Missourian from Pike County. Wolf contends that this "most popular song in the West," though it may be doggerel, was the work of an itinerant singer named John Woodward about 1850 and that its composer made it familiar in the dance halls and theaters of the West.

A Kentucky horse race in 1878 produced a ballad about two race horses which survived in popular tradition for a long time. Jean H. Thomason in "Ten Broek and Mollie: New Light on a Kentucky Ballad" (*KFR* 16:17–34) points out similarities between this song and an Irish import entitled "The Noble Skewball" and prints a version sung by an eighty-year-old Kentucky farmer in 1970. Much less familiar is a ballad about a stage driver for Ben Holladay, who, according to tradition, refused to stop for a band of road agents and lost his life in the process. In "Tune for 'Baldy Green'" (*SFQ* 34:12–17) Ben Gray Lumpkin comments on the four-stanza ballad and claims that it was sung by Edward Burnett, a Wyoming pioneer, in the 1880s. The closing lines are succinct:

> "The road agents they've got Baldy,
> But Baldy saved the gold."

Two essays by Austin and Alta Fife deal with women and cowboys in western balladry. In "Pug-Nosed Lil and the Girl With the Blue Velvet Band" (*AW* 7,ii:32–37) the authors observe that women in the songs of the West represented not only mothers, sweethearts, and wives but also prostitutes and camp followers. Among the texts provided to support their claim are "No Use for the Women," "Belle Starr," and "Pug-Nosed Lil," the last frankly a burlesque with a sophisticated use of clichés. "Spurs and Saddlebags" (*AW* 7,v:44–47) gives a succinct account of the cowboy, his character, habits, and attitudes. Cowboy ballads, the authors contend, are in general nostalgic and reminiscent, although their themes may be quite diversified. Prof. and Mrs. Fife are also the editors of *Ballads of the Great West*

(Palo Alto, Calif., American West Publishing Co.), a collection of some 113 Western ballads arranged in four categories, although the cowboy theme seems to dominate the book. Some unusual texts of familiar ballads have been utilized, the headnotes are satisfactory, and the sources are scrupulously identified. But many of the choices are conventional and the editors have included obviously literary ballads from the pens of John Hay, John Antrobus, Charles Badger Clark, Jack Thorp, and Joaquin Miller.

American balladry with quite a different slant is the subject matter of two analytical articles. Frederick E. Danker in "Towards An Intrinsic Study of the Blues Ballad: 'Casey Jones' and 'Louis Collins,'" (*SFQ* 34:90–103) pleads for a more intensive study than any heretofore made of the "blues ballad," which is less narrative than commentary or celebration. The blues ballad is loose and repetitious but does emphasize situation and delineate character. The two examples Danker cites are versions of "Casey Jones" and "Louis Collins" by the late Mississippi singer John Hurt, who recorded both of them. Robert D. Bethke in "Narrative Obituary Verse and Native American Balladry" (*JAF* 83:61–68) traces the development of funeral elegies, which appeared throughout the seventeenth century in New England as broadsides, and comments that during the Revolution political and topical broadsides proliferated. Numerous printing presses in the major Northern cities and a constant shortage of paper elsewhere caused a concentration of these productions in a few places. Murder pamphlets provided ample data for ballad writers and their work occasionally entered oral tradition. Bethke believes that a large number of native American broadsides owe something to this funereal narrative tradition.

iii. Popular Song

Interest in popular song is if anything even more lively and diversified than interest in balladry with attention being increasingly focused on the milieu and preparation of the singer. The geographical and social variation of popular song becomes continually more apparent.

William R. Ferris, Jr., in "Railroad Chants: Form and Function" (*MFR* 4:1–14), deals with the railroad chants once familiar to bridge gangs and section crews. In Mississippi especially the chant flourished and was led by vocally gifted section hands who drew the same wages as the laborers but did little physical work. Cal Taylor's chants, simple and monotonously repetitious, provide good examples. Taylor worked out of Memphis and lived much of his life in a railroad car.

At least two authors probed further into the currency and dissemination of the rhymes sung by children at play. Mac E. Barrick in "Jump-Rope Rhymes" (*PF* 19,iv:43–47) collected rhymes from a Harrisburg family and described the actual procedure of jumping rope. He points out that most such games are endurance tests, the jumper (usually a girl) striving to set a record before she misses. Ed Cray in "Jump-Rope Rhymes from Los Angeles" (*WF* 25:119–27) presents examples of rhymes collected a dozen years ago in California from girls in the eight-to-twelve age bracket.

The autograph album continued to interest W. K. McNeil. In "From Advice to Laments Once Again: New York Autograph Album Verses, 1850–1900" (*NYFQ* 26:163–203) he surveys the verse written in albums over a half century and notes the changes in tone from serious to humorous. Quotations also tend to become briefer. McNeil discerns thirteen themes, the most popular being pleas for remembrance, congratulations, bits of advice, admonitions, and laments (with an occasional parody).

Two articles by R. Serge Denisoff represent a serious attempt to analyze the origins and trends of popular music. In "Protest Songs: Those On the Top Forty and Those on the Street" (*AQ* 22:807–23) he disputes the commonly accepted thesis that popular songs can readily alter public opinion. Songs can produce an impression only if they are closely linked with some political movement such as Populism or the IWW. Although the Weavers, the Beatles, and folksinging groups like the Kingston Trio have had their impact, the effect has been emotional rather than productive of social action. Even Sloan's "The Eve of Destruction," a best-selling record of 1965, produced mixed impressions among the youthful group it was particularly addressed to. In "The Religious Roots of the American Song of Persuasion" (*WF* 29:175–84) Denisoff argues that the propaganda song originally appeared within the framework of organized religion. Although the Puritans sanctioned only hymn and psalm singing, John Wesley and his followers encouraged singing for emotional and religious purposes (as an early reformer pertinently inquired, "Why should the devil have all of the good tunes?"). Camp meeting devices were adopted by Grangers and Populists, and the *Little Red Song Book* played its role in the organization of the IWW. It is well known that Negro spirituals included thinly veiled laments or social protest ("Steal Away" and "No More Auction Blocks For Me" are good examples); and serious attempts were made to incorporate spirituals in organizational activity in the South.

Several writers dealt with the musical culture of the blacks. In "Two Negro Folk-Poems" (*MFR* 4:98–104) Gordon Weaver describes the familiar black poem of insults, "The Signifying Monkey" (with its variant, "The Pool Shooting Monkey"), and shows how it probably emanated from Negro prisoners in army stockades after World War II. Weaver provides no text, probably to avoid printing obscenities, but he does describe the poem and explains the monkey hero as a weak animal who overcomes his adversaries by chattering insults. In "Folk Tradition, Individual Talent: A Note on the Poetry of Rock" (*MR* 11:385–97) Gene Bluestein considers the folk tradition and the symbolist movement in American poetry (using Emerson, Whitman, even T. S. Eliot) and then stresses the importance of Woody Guthrie and Bob Dylan as folk composers. The retention of symbolism links popular music with the main American literary stream, in Bluestein's view, and the vogue of rock confirms the influence of black style in contemporary music. Robert Ladner, Jr., in "Folk Music, Pholk Music and the Angry Children of Malcolm X" (*SFQ* 34:131–45), refutes the notion that black culture is all derivative. He remarks that Negro rhythms are surprisingly complex and that many of the American Negroes came from such African tribes as the Yoruba and Ashanti, who were notable for their religious systems and a developed musical culture. Consequently, black folk music, especially spirituals, blues, and work songs, has become a vehicle for racial pride and group cohesiveness, no longer merely a means of survival. David Evans in "Afro-American One-Stringed Instruments" (*WF* 29:229–45) considers the one-stringed instrument, often called a "jitterbug," which is usually played as a solo accompaniment for singing. Made of the crudest materials—broom wire, baling wire, wooden blocks, pill or snuff bottles—and played with a bottle neck or knife blade, it was often fastened to a wall or played on one's lap. The jitterbug often led to adult playing of the guitar or drums. Few recordings of songs accompanied by jitterbugs have been made, but Evans points out that at least in Mississippi the device is familiar.

D. K. Wilgus in "Country-Western Music and the Urban Hillbilly" (*JAF* 83:157–79) traces the evolution of country-western music over a period of three decades. He considers the basic instruments, the media of communication, and themes and styles. Fiddle and banjo were eventually supplanted by the guitar; the phonograph record, the radio, and television became the essential links between performer and audience; sin, sex, and booze replaced maudlin songs of love and domesticity. By mid-century the influence of jazz, the blues, and especially bluegrass music became apparent; and musicians like Bill Monroe, the Carter family, Jimmy Driftwood, Roy Acuff, Jimmie Rodgers, and Earl Scruggs had permanent impact on country-western music. Wilgus's highly informative article is supported by a discography scattered among the footnotes.

In 1969, Harry Oster published his *Living Country Blues* (Detroit, Folklore Associates), a remarkable volume not previously noticed here. Oster recorded his songs at the Angola, Louisiana, penitentiary between 1959 and 1961, a prison with some 3000 Negro inmates, many of them "lifers" and almost all of limited education, drifters, fugitives from broken homes. The blues sung by such singers as Hogman Maxey and Robert Pete Williams deal with themes like farming, gambling, nostalgia, the lure of the open road, and inevitably sex. Although extremely repetitious and even monotonous, their simplicity is often deceptive; Oster points out that the metaphors which throng the lines are both sophisticated and poetic. He contends too that the blues are ultimately optimistic, a quality aided by spirited guitar accompaniments, a cheerful vocal tone, wry good humor, and exuberant bodily movements that even prison life cannot contain.

A compilation of a different kind also first published in 1969 is Ed Cray's *The Erotic Muse* (New York, Oak Publications), the first annotated collection of bawdy songs in the English language "offered for public sale without asterisk, dash, or similar emendation of words considered offensive." Cray's preface considers the authorship and currency of such songs, changes in verbal taste which now permit the publication, and editorial policies. Cray was not averse to conflating texts in order to produce a better song. He also defines a folk song as any ditty which has passed from one generation to another, an innocuous definition until one realizes that he means a college generation (four years), a miner's generation (six to ten years), a schoolchild's generation (seven years). Many familiar songs appear in Cray's collection and the frank texts are given without subterfuge. It might be added that many of the songs have little merit beside their vulgarity.

Individual folk singers who have become the subject of scholarly research vary considerably. Susan Braudy in "James Taylor, A New Troubadour" (*NYTM* 21 Feb:28–29,88–92) summarizes the career to date of a young singer who went from the academic world to almost instant success as a folk-blues singer. He has sung at the Newport festival and has signed a contract with the Apple Record Company of the Beatles. In an article entitled "He Hewed His Own Path" (*SLitI* 3:37–63) Loman D. Cansler provides a biographical study of William Henry Scott, a Missouri Ozark railroad tie maker and homesteader who in the midst of a long life not only sang traditional ballads like "Lord Lovel" and "Fuller and Warren" but composed his own songs. Despite little formal education Scott was well informed about the world around him but he was never an economic success. Another hinterland bard named Scott, this time from Maine, is the subject of Edward D. Ives's monograph, "A Man and His Song" (*Folksongs and Their Makers*, edited by Henry Glassie, Edward D. Ives and John Szwed, Bowling Green, Ohio, Bowling Green Univ. Popular Press, pp. 71–146). Joseph William Scott, born in New Brunswick but for most of his life a Maine lumberjack, wrote a number of ballads between 1896 and 1901 which became familiar in the Maine logging camps and which Scott himself printed as broadsides. Although he wrote "Howard Carey" and "The Norway Bum," Scott was best known for his sentimental ballad about his own unfortunate love affair, "The Plain Golden Band." Ives's study is carefully detailed but a reader might well ask whether the subject is worth the effort. Another folk composer worked within the black sacred harp tradition. In an article called "Judge Jackson, Black Giant of White Spirituals" (*JAF* 83:446–51) Joe Dan Boyd traces the career of a self-educated Alabama farmer who compiled *The Colored Sacred Harp* in 1934 and included some seventy-seven songs. The book has been understandably neglected.

The famous Almanac Singers provided the theme of R. Serge

Denisoff's essay " 'Take It Easy, But Take It,' " (*JAF* 83:21–32). This is a close study of the group which came together in 1941 and included originally Pete Seeger, Lee Hays, Millard Lampell, and Pete Hawes (later Woody Guthrie affiliated with them). The author asserts that collectively they were in the Stalinist orbit but that not all were Communists. In their primary function of supplying propaganda to produce social change they were not conspicuously successful; even their famous album "Talking Union" had a limited impact. To Denisoff the Almanacs were "a synthesis of the rural organizational campaigns and the intellectual-radical concerns of the Red Decade." Blackballed eventually by the entertainment world, they perhaps could ascribe their lack of success to a limited appeal and to a basic isolation from mass values. Denisoff credits them, however, with the introduction of the hootenanny and with being a model for the later Weavers.

Two very different singers are evaluated by Roger D. Abrahams in "Creativity, Individuality, and the Traditional Singer" (*SLitI* 3:5–34). This is both a personal analysis and a milieu study. Abrahams deals with Almeda Riddle, now 71, of rural Arkansas, and Marybird MacAllister of Albemarle County, Virginia, deceased in 1965 at 84. Although belonging to the same generation and deriving from similar cultures, the two women differed materially in their singing practises. Mrs. MacAllister learned her songs as a girl and would sing anything, fragmentary or not. Mrs. Riddle sought out songs throughout her life and preferred to sing complete song units, which she at times altered for greater comprehensibility and impact. Both sang familiar traditional ballads like "Barbara Allen," "The House Carpenter," and "Will the Weaver." Abrahams observes that Mrs. Riddle consciously distinguished between *presenting* a song and *performing* it; she would present a Child ballad but perform children's songs. Abrahams's study is careful and revealing. But he fails to remark that Mrs. Riddle's quavering soprano is painful to listen to, especially in the course of a long ballad like "The Brown Girl" (Child no. 73).

The best study of a popular singer published during the year is Richard A. Reuss's "Woody Guthrie and His Folk Tradition" (*JAF* 83:273–303). Reuss believes that Guthrie has still been accorded insufficient attention, that he played various roles during his lifetime, and that his significance as a folk figure is not limited to his singing and creation of folk ballads. Guthrie, largely self-educated, was a rustic sage and philosopher, a Dust Bowl minstrel, and a people's artist. His best work, written between 1939 and 1942, fuses his folk heritage and his left-wing social consciousness. After Guthrie came to New York City about 1942 his themes changed considerably and he turned from traditional narratives to mass media. He is undeniably the most prolific and most important American folk composer, yet oddly enough none of his songs have become fixed in oral tradition.

iv. Folk Tales and Legends

Interest in folk narrative produced articles and collections ranging in focus from the tales of the Brothers Grimm to legends associated with West Virginia and the Santa Fe country. Michael C. Kotzin, for example, in "The Fairy Tale in England, 1800–1870" (*JPC* 4:130–54) discusses in particular the English reputation of the Grimm stories. He claims that most of the fairy tales current in England were imports from the continent with such notable exceptions as "Jack and the Beanstalk" and "Dick Whittington and His Cat." Although Kotzin's article is centered on England, many of the tales alluded to are equally familiar to American readers. Incidentally a famous Grimm story, "Rapunzel," is the theme of Lynn Rosen's article (*TQ* 13:51–53), in which she contends that "Rapunzel" might well have been the source of the popular novel and motion picture "Rosemary's Baby." At least the witch motif and the covenant idea are common to both.

Ben Gray Lumpkin discusses "The Fox and the Goose" and "The Hawk and the Buzzard" in separate issues of *North Carolina Folklore* (18:90–94;144–47). Versions of both stories were derived from the oral narratives of George Coffin Taylor. Lumpkin provides analogies, index numbers, and analyses of selected details. A more ambitious study is C. E. Schorer's "Indian Tales of C. C. Trowbridge: 'Thrown Away'" (*SFQ* 34:341–52), which incorporates the text of an early tale collected from Michigan Indians. Schorer discusses the idea of the abandonment of a child, a theme central to the story but common to many cultures, and points out that the narrative reveals the survival of the repudiated boy and his eventual replacement of his father as chief of the village. In "Variations on a Theme: Some Northern California Indian Horror Studies" (*WF* 29:257–67) Doris E. Marrant examines some ninety stories from northern California Indian tribes and analyzes them thematically. Her arbitrary divisions include the overcoming of dangerous spirits, acquisition of power from such spirits, encounters with demons, and abductions by monsters. She draws from various collections to support her analysis but seldom tells much of the individual stories. One cannot disagree with her conclusion, however, that "mythmaking or talemaking is one of a continual re-sorting and re-combining of familiar materials."

At least one anthology of Indian tales appeared during the year, Louis Thomas Jones's *So Say the Indians* (San Antonio, Tex. Naylor Company). Some of the narratives, arranged by tribal geography rather than by tale types, are interesting, but most seem trivial and the editorial comment is both banal and inaccurate.

A particularly interesting study of a single folk tale is the essay by D. K. Wilgus and Bruce Rosenberg, "A Modern Medieval Story: 'The Soldier's Deck of Cards'" (*Medieval Literature*, pp. 291–303). This familiar variant of the Thompson type 1613 refers to the soldier who was apprehended in a church with a deck of cards and who won his freedom by expounding the cards in terms of biblical tradition. Each of the numbered cards refers to some Old Testament incident in the soldier's interpretation while the queen is the Queen of Sheba, the King is the heavenly monarch, and the Knave is the constable who made the arrest. This story has become a staple in certain folk sermons although the specific attributions are not always constant.

Negro narrative forms are the subject of a short and superficial article by Mary Arnold Twining, "An Anthropological Look at Afro-American Folk Narrative" (*CLAJ* 14:57–61). She cites tales, toasts, jokes, reminiscences, and memorats as examples and remarks that West African folk narratives sometimes become folk sermons in the New World. In her estimation some ten percent of Afro-American folklore is influenced by the folklore of the Dark Continent.

In *Positively Black* (Englewood Cliffs, N.J., Prentice-Hall) Roger Abrahams deals with the stereotypes of blacks held by whites and challenges many of them as a result of his own experiences living in South Philadelphia and field collecting in Texas. Abrahams quotes many tales and anecdotes, as well as some toasts, to prove his contention that Negro lower-class culture is basically unfamiliar to whites. He also uses folklore to confirm his point that Negroes retain their own black stereotypes, the "cat" versus the "gorilla" for example, or the country boy versus the preacher. Although Abrahams repeats some previously collected data, his book is a valuable contribution to the understanding of our most important minority group, and it relies largely on folk evidence: jests, anecdotes, toasts, as well as excerpts from blues and popular songs.

Rural storytellers provided the subjects for two essays. Einar Haugen in "Thor Helgeson: Schoolmaster and Raconteur" (*NAS* 24:3–28) gives biographical material about a Norwegian teacher and writer who imigrated to the United States in 1862 and spent much of his life in the Scandinavian settlements of Wisconsin. Helgeson's repertory abounded in anecdotes reflecting his experiences of frontier life, but also preserved stories from Norway in which witches, devils, and trolls appeared. George G. Carey's article " 'And Everyone of Them's Gone But Me': Another Look at Tangier Island's Oldest Inhabitant" (*SLitI*,3:73–87) introduces once more Captain George A. Wheatley of Tangier Island, Virginia, an old waterman, fisherman, and oyster catcher. At the age of ninety-two he can still remember tall tales, legends, and anecdotes of long ago.

A rather unusual collection of folk tales is Ruth Ann Musick's *Green Hills of Magic: West Virginia Folk Tales from Europe* (Lexington, Univ. of Ky. Press). These seventy-nine tales recorded from European-born miners in the West Virginia coal fields are divided into fourteen categories by content: evil spirits, dragons and giants, efforts to outwit death or the devil, wise and foolish folk, etc. They are presented in a drab, undistinguished style, and many are little more than anecdotes. Only one tale has a possible American connection, although all were derived from immigrants to the United States. Miss Musick has provided notes on her informants, indications of sources, and motif and type numbers.

In *Living Legends of the Santa Fe Country* (Denver, Green Mountain Press) Alice Bullock compresses into twenty-three brief chapters assorted tales of the area around Taos, Albuquerque, and Santa Fe. From the time of Coronado's invasion to the era of the cattle magnates the country produced its legends and superstitions, ranging from accounts of lost mines and ancestral curses to mysterious visits and haunted mansions. An enthusiast for the region, Mrs. Bullock personally visited most of the sites described and is always ready to provide the necessary atmosphere in reputable chamber of commerce style. The book is pleasantly written and amply illustrated; the folklore may be at times synthetic but much of the material is basically traditional and remains very much alive.

One of the most famous American legends stimulated a new examination of the evidence by William Hartley. In "Mormons, Crickets, and Gulls: A New Look at an Old Story" (*UHQ* 38:224–39) he reconsiders the cricket war of 1848 and points out that sea gulls were not unknown in Utah even prior to the famous cricket infestation. Yet many contemporary records (diaries, letters, memoirs) fail to mention the "miracle of the gulls." Sober analysis suggests that Mormon crops in 1848 had been damaged before the crickets appeared and that the birds had returned at other times. Nevertheless, popular belief persists that the sea gulls came at an opportune time because of a divine decision to aid the Latter Day Saints.

v. Folk Speech

The flexible category of folk speech can be extended to include discussions of vocabulary, etymology, onomastics, and riddles and jokes, all of which interested scholars during the year. Like folklore itself, the subject reaches beyond a single discipline.

Thus E. N. and Marja L. Anderson in "The Social Context of a Local 'Lingo,'" (*SFQ* 29:153–65) return to the subject of "Boont Ling," the peculiar speech characteristic of Boonville, California, which has already become established in American folklore. As the authors point out, this language is ordinary English deliberately mispronounced or changed by substituting a localism for a common word. The result is funny and to an outsider confusing. On the other hand, James E. Spears in "Notes On Negro Folk Speech" (*NCarF* 18:154–57) provides a brief but valuable analysis of the language of Southern blacks in which he deals with vocabulary, phonology, and syntax. He makes the useful point that since Negroes were in the past generally illiterate they rarely saw their own speech in print. Among his examples are the tendencies to drop final letters, duplicate plurals ("womenz"), and omit auxiliary verbs ("she gone to town").

Arthur H. Lewis's book *Carnival* (New York, Trident Press) is primarily a history of carnival shows along the eastern seaboard and stresses the operation of ferris wheels, motordromes, and freak or girl shows. But Lewis could not avoid discussing the victims ("marks") of these itinerant carnivals or the idiom of the professionals. The carnies live in a marvelous world of their own, and if the "three sheets" (posters) are familiar to the "fuzz" (police) the patrons are seldom aware that a "patch" (fixer) is necessary before a kootch show can be staged without interruption and that alibi agents and shills are essential for the survival of these travelling circuses. Lewis's book is a fascinating lexicon of carnival lingo.

The history of the oil industry in the United States by Mody C. Boatright and William A. Owens, *Tales from the Derrick Floor* (Garden City, N.Y., Doubleday), also exemplifies the idiom of a particular occupation. Most of the book is historical. But a chapter entitled "Oil-Field Lingo" is rich in the jargon of the workers. One soon discovers that terms like "boll weevil," "Christmas tree," "crumb boss," "mudder," and "starved owls" have connotations quite different from their literal meanings. Boatright and Owens also observe that divining rods and doodle-bugs were once common in the oil fields and that a half century ago clairvoyants, fortune tellers, and spiritualists did a thriving business among those committed to seeking a fortune beneath the ground.

One of the most valuable books published during the year is Bruce A. Rosenberg's *The Art of the American Folk Preacher* (New York, Oxford Univ. Press), a study of the oral sermons of Negro preachers, particularly in Oklahoma and California. The book has two main parts, a discussion of the contents and structure of the sermon, and a presentation of specific sermons such as "The Deck of Cards" or "God's Plowboy." Rosenberg distinguishes between the manuscript preacher and the spiritual preacher, the latter generally chanting his sermons. To Rosenberg the oral chanted sermons are folk art: "The sermons almost never rhyme, they seldom alliterate, the imagery is meager, yet they are poetic." The Negro preachers are imperfectly educated but they believe in intuition, song, and a divine mission. On paper the sermons may seem monotonous and stale; in the proper setting their effect is often electric. Similar material though in briefer form appears in Rosenberg's "The Formulaic Quality of Spontaneous Sermons" (*JAF* 83:2–20). Negro preachers like D. J. McDowell and Rubin Lacy provided many of the texts.

One aspect of folk speech is exemplified by the joke fads which periodically sweep the country—moron jokes, elephant jokes, and inevitably the ethnic jokes which are often as cruel as they are funny. In "Racial Riddles & the Polack Joke" (*KFQ* 15:3–15) Mac E. Barrick remarks that ethnic jokes ridiculing various minorities have always been common with the victims changing from Irish to Italians to Jews. Currently the Poles bear the brunt of this unkind humor. Barrick presents a collection of such jests from Pennsylvania and demonstrates that brute strength, lack of intelligence, uncleanliness, and want of ambition are the traits of Polish-Americans frequently ridiculed. Two examples will surely suffice: "Why are there no Polish elevator operators? They cannot learn the route"; and "What do you call 144 Polacks? Gross ignorance." Similar material is used by Jan H. Brunvand in "Some Thoughts on the Ethnic Riddle Jokes" (*IF* 3:128–42). He observes that the characters victimized in ethnic jokes are generally numbskulls with a long tradition behind them. In actuality "the riddle joke Polack is a concept, not a living reality," although admittedly that assertion can give the sensitive immigrant small consolation. Jokes relating to "kikes" or "niggers" these days are more emotionally charged than jests about immigrants of Polish descent.

But jokes can also depend on religious or social attributes, as Brunvand shows in another article, "As the Saints Go Marching By: Modern Jokelore Concerning Mormons" (*JAF* 83:53–60). Brunvand contends that Utah is a veritable folklore laboratory, even though some of the old stereotypes have vanished. Today religious joke themes circulate in Utah in the form of nicknames, wisecracks, graffiti, and parodies. This folklore is not always a survival from the past nor is all of it good-natured. Moreover, among contemporary Mormons themes other than sexual predominate. There is probably no more typical Mormon jest than the following question: "Did you hear about the hippie who didn't know LSD from LDS? He went on a mission instead of a trip."

Proof that riddles are not obsolete in modern American culture is supplied by Richard Bauman's article, "The Turtles: An American Riddling Institution" (*WF* 29:21–25). In order to join the group known as the "turtles" one must submit to initiation rites. Ambiguous questions are asked and part of the fun is the supposition that every "turtle" is supposed to be the owner of a donkey. Bauman suggests that the group is a burlesque or parody of esoteric groups that still perform some public function.

Two articles by Robert M. Rennick touch on proper names. In "The Folklore of Place-Naming in Indiana" (*IF* 3:35–94) he goes into considerable detail to describe types of place names and gives suitable illustrations. Names of places can be derived from popular heroes, from other locations, from literary, classical, or biblical sources. Nicknames given early settlements sometimes survive (Yankeetown, Lickskillet) and infrequently the aspirations of early citizens are preserved (Harmony, Needmore, Onward). The famous post-office name, Santa Claus, needs no gloss. In "The Inadvertent Changing of Non-English Names by Newcomers to America" (*NYFQ* 26:263–82) Rennick touches again on a subject which previously held his attention and reveals what can happen to immigrants with a limited command of English when they reach Ellis Island or other entry ports. Lacking necessary documents, often unable to spell their own names, these unfortunates are often saddled with patronymics that they can not shake for generations and that often misidentify them completely. Often they give occupations instead of names (hence the many Jews named Cantor) or are baptized Ferguson because the immigration inspector cannot understand "Schon vergessen" or have their names translated for convenience (Koch to Cook). Some mute arrivals, terrified by their strange surroundings, even emerged from the inspection with entirely new names suggested by helpful immigration men.

vi. Folk Heroes

Despite the deliberate tendency to glamorize figures in other occupations or fields, bandits and desperadoes still seem to provide paradigms of the popular hero. Two articles are illustrative.

Helena Huntington Smith, in "Sam Bass and the Myth Machine" (*AW* 7,i:31–35), gives a summary account of Bass's life, which was brought to an end by a posse at Round Rock, Texas, in 1878. Tradition paints Bass as a major outlaw, but in actuality he was singularly inept and unlucky. To call this man, who died largely as the victim of his own gullibility, a hero is according to the author a distortion of the word. In similar fashion Kent L. Steckmesser debunks the Georgia-born Pretty Boy Floyd. In "The Oklahoma Robin Hood" (*AW* 7,i:38–41) he admits that legend has made Floyd the hero of a Woody Guthrie ballad, of a Hollywood cinema, and of a cycle of Oklahoma folk tales. Yet Steckmesser insists that he was "a bragging, overbearing desperado, responsible for the murder of at least four law officers" and a remorseless killer who made a career of bootlegging and robbery. Tradition transformed him into an Oklahoma Robin

Hood after his death and even today Floyd remains alive in folk memory. Probably the "havenots" whom he left unmolested are responsible for this apotheosis.

vii. Beliefs and Superstitions

Despite improved literacy and the replacement of a simple pragmatism by scientific knowledge, beliefs in folk medicine remain widely prevalent. A 1969 volume by Dr. W. W. Bauer, *Potions, Remedies and Old Wives' Tales* (Garden City, N.Y., Doubleday) is a fascinating compendium of misinformation or only partly valid information about illness and cures. Bauer discusses medicinal plants, poisons, and general therapy. The ninth chapter, "Grandma Is Not Always Wrong," suggests that old-time panaceas still retain some value while at the end of the book the physician lists some 200 fallacies of popular medicine. Among the delusions he ridicules are the beliefs that boils purify the blood and that according to the old adage one must feed a cold and starve a fever. Evidence that doctors sometimes disagree is Bauer's scorn for the vinegar-and-honey cure that has recently received much publicity.

Robert and Martha Cochran in "Some Menstrual Folklore of Mississippi" (*MFR* 4:108–13) extract from interviews with both high school students and older women some of the peculiar traditional lore about menstrual periods. Girls during this time must under no circumstances go swimming or wash their hair. Picking up heavy objects is also a taboo.

John Q. Anderson's *Texas Folk Medicine, 1,333 Cures, Remedies, Preventives, & Health Practices* (Austin, Encino Press) shows the close connection between nostrums and superstitions. Anderson's informants believe in the transference of ailments to animals and in verbal magic; they accept madstones as efficacious and regard ritual healing as essential. Simple items familiar on the frontier often figure in the remedies cited: turpentine, vinegar, soda, wood ashes, soot. Whiskey is a common ingredient, but axle grease, chicken manure, asafetida, and human urine are also employed. Anderson's compilation is arranged alphabetically by ailments without identification of informants; the sections on warts, colds, and hiccups are the longest.

In "A Study of the Use of Madstones in Oklahoma" (*CO* 46[1969]: 433–49) Kenneth L. Ketner traces the evolution of the idea of a madstone (an animal calculus, frequently secured from a deer). Applied directly to a wound (the bite of a mad dog or of a poisonous snake) it supposedly absorbs the poison; boiling in milk can restore the stone to its original hue and permits reusage. Evidence from Oklahoma suggests that the madstone was held to be efficacious.

In contrast, Marcia Westkott in "Powwowing in Berks County" (*PF* 19,ii:2–9) reports that faith healing or *Braucherei* is still known and practiced in rural Pennsylvania. Active powwowers are of both sexes and are convinced that they possess the power of healing; among the afflictions they treat with confidence are erysipelas, headaches, warts, fevers, and gallstones (unless they become too large). No fees are charged patients since the healers are fearful of being accused of practicing medicine without a license but "donations" are accepted. Biblical quotations and Christian symbolism are an essential part of the ritual.

Wayland Hand in "Hangmen, the Gallows, and the Dead Man's Hand in American Folk Medicine" (*Medieval Literature*, pp. 323–29) calls attention to the gruesome belief that the corpse of a hanged man or even the executioner's body has some therapeutic efficacy. He reports evidence from Pennsylvania, Illinois, and California but admits that this is a notion more common in Europe, perhaps according to the Latin dictum, "in medio vitae mortuus sum." In "Magerou, the Greek Midwife" (*UHQ* 38:50–60) Helen Z. Papanikolas tells the story of a Greek woman who emigrated to Utah early in the century and became locally famous as a midwife and healer. She delivered children with consistent success but also employed simples to cure infections, relieved backaches and set broken bones, and in particular combated the Evil Eye with a combination of burning incense, holy water, and saliva. A favorite proverb exemplified her practical life code: "Too much *Kyrie Eleison* wearies even God." An interesting article by Elsie H. Booker and her son Curtis Booker, "Patent Medicines Before the Wiley Act of 1906" (*NCarF* 18:130–42), recites the surprising number of ailments which the makers of patent medicines prior to 1906 claimed they could relieve or eliminate: from dyspepsia to jaundice and from anemia to cholera. Some nostrums were equally effective for animals and humans. Patent medicine promotion incidentally was aided by decorative talents, with barns, fences, and even outhouses providing the necessary media. Marijuana can hardly be regarded as a panacea but Eve C.

Mitchell in "Folklore of Marijuana Smoking" (*SFQ* 34:127–30) lists some of the euphemisms employed for "grass," comments on the methods of smoking, and describes the often lamentable effects. The evidence comes mostly from college students.

In an article which turns out to be more sociology than folklore, Ellen J. Stekert analyzes the beliefs and practices of Southern mountain women who migrated to Detroit. "Focus for Conflict: Southern Mountain Medical Beliefs in Detroit" (*JAF* 83:115–47) reports some eight in-depth interviews. These women are suspicious of hospitals and male doctors, whose services in Detroit they utilize less than Negroes do. Actually they prefer to give birth at home. In the mountains asafetida, turpentine, paregoric, and castor oil were common medications; children's fingernails were bitten off rather than cut off; nosebleeds were stanched by cobwebs. Old names for diseases lingered too: hives could be "bold" or "little red" or "stretch." Miss Stekert observes that in the Southern mountains women were the prime transmitters of medical lore and that they still regard physicians as greedy and cold.

Collections of superstitions appeared in various journals. Anna Lett in "Some West Tennessee Superstitions About Conjurers, Witches, Ghosts and the Devil" (*TFSB* 36:37–45) reports the beliefs of an old Negress, Mama Mollie, of Jackson. Typical are various conjure spells, tokens by which witches can be recognized, and the fiddle and banjo as devil's instruments. One spell is revealing:

> Take seven hairs from a blood snake, seven scales from a rattlesnake, seven bits of feathers from an owl, and a hair from the head of the person you desire, and a bit of nail paring, and cook these for seven minutes over a hot fire in the first rain water caught in April. Sprinkle the concoction on the clothes of the first person to be charmed. It cannot fail.

In "Witchcraft and Ghostlore in the Great Smokies" (*TFSB* 36:1–6, 31–36) Joseph S. Hall reports on material gleaned from four counties. Witches are commonly charged with causing a cow to give bloody milk, transforming humans into animals, and producing serious illnesses. They can be identified by their staring or rolling eyes and by their possession of hair balls. Witch spells can be broken by the use of metal objects, sprinkling salt around a house, drawing blood from the supposed witch, and placing a Bible beneath one's pillow. In "North Carolina Folk Beliefs and Superstitions Collected in California" (*NCarF* 18:117–23) Wayland Hand provides some 145 items derived largely from former residents of North Carolina. Among the less familiar examples are these: "Two people with false teeth should not marry," "Babies come from magnolias," and "If you wash acne in urine, you will be cured."

The entire January issue of *North Carolina Folklore* is given over to Joseph D. Clark's "North Carolina Popular Beliefs and Superstitions" (18:2–67). The 1683 entries are divided into thirteen categories, the largest number relating to birth, infancy, childhood, and the human body. As always one finds oddities among the familiar cures and proscriptions. Onion juice would not seem to be the ordinary medication for burns nor sassafras tea for eye infections. Monogamy is apparently encouraged by the axiom: "If you marry three times, your liver automatically turns white." One is warned against kissing a red-haired person lest fever blisters ensue and one is advised that only an elderly woman can properly make sauerkraut.

A cursory article by Louis and Carol Winkler, "Thousands of Years of Halloween" (*NYFQ* 26:204–15) surveys the lore concerning the ancient festival and comments on the practices associated with it: divination, masking, the lighting of bonfires. The authors consider the origin of the holiday and select excellent examples to support their generalizations.

One issue of the *Kentucky Folklore Record* (16:41–68) is a memorial to Gordon Wilson (1888–1970), who spent so much of his time collecting the superstitions and beliefs of the people living in the vicinity of Mammoth Cave. A posthumous article by Wilson in the same journal deals with the origins and surnames of Mammoth Cave residents (16:73–78).

viii. Literary Use of Folklore

Diligent research continues to document the frequent use of folklore by American writers. The material varies from proverbs and folk speech introduced into dialogue to folk incident and characterization employed in the narrative.

Two articles by Florence Healy French deal with James Fenimore Cooper's use of proverbs. In "Cooper's Use of Proverbs in the Anti-Rent Novels" (*NYFQ* 26:42–49) she claims that the trilogy of *Satan-*

stoe, *The Chainbearer,* and *The Redskins* contains some 206 proverbs derived by the novelist from both literary and oral sources. Moreover Cooper deliberately used proverbs to support his Jeffersonianism. Folk similes like "quick as lightning" and "as honest as light" appear frequently while the dialogue contains vigorous metaphors or effective euphemisms ("No man should be above his business," "Many men, many minds," and "Take time by the forelock"). In "Cooper the Tinkerer" (*NYFQ* 26:229–39) material from the Anti-Rent trilogy proves that Cooper sometimes changed the original proverbial form. Like Franklin he altered the word order but in so doing often made the expression less colloquial. Thus "Easy come, easy go" is transformed into "What came easily, went as freely"; and "Like calls to like" appears as "The upright recognize the upright."

In "Hawthorne's Folklore and the Folklorists' Hawthorne: a Reexamination" (*SFQ* 34:34–52) David J. Winslow reviews Hawthorne's use of folk material. He argues that the novelist's contact with the folk was limited. Hawthorne was a highly sophisticated artist who levied on folk material for purposes of mood, background, and historical authenticity. Folk themes such as witchcraft, the compact with the devil, and the search for the elixir of life certainly appear in Hawthorne's fiction but they are substantially Gothic elements to which the writer gave New England garments. Winslow admits, however, that Hawthorne's use of folklore was highly effective.

The local colorists were often closer to their material. Ormonde Plater in "Before Sut: Folklore in the Early Works of George Washington Harris" (*SFQ* 34:104–15) deals with the early sketches of Harris which appeared for the most part in the *Spirit of the Times.* Harris was drawn to such themes as the trickster and the tricked, as well as to sex humor; his early work includes tall tales about animals, satirical skits about country bumpkins, and folk scenes linked with quarter races, quilting-bees, and corn-shucking contests. Erotic elements often appear. Geoffrey Allan Grimes in "'Muels,' 'Owls,' and Other Things: Folk Material in the Tobacco Philosophy of Josh Billings" (*NYFQ* 26:283–96) comments on Henry Wheeler Shaw's famous essay on the mule, notable for its cacography and exaggeration, and points out the wide popularity of the comic aphorisms in the *Old Farmer's Allminax.* The contention that Shaw also drew folk sketches of the Yankee or the frontier boaster is not always adequately supported. Tommy W. Rogers in "The Folk Humor of Joseph B. Cobb" (*NMW* 3:13–35) deals with the author of *Mississippi Scenes*. As plantation manager, newspaper editor, and legislator, Cobb had ample opportunity to observe people. But he was neither prolific nor comprehensive so that none of his rustic figures won the recognition accorded Simon Suggs or Sut Lovingood. Somewhat later in the century a Hoosier writer better known for his dialect verse occasionally tried his hand at prose. In "Folklore in the Prose Sketches of James Whitcomb Riley" (*IEJ* 4:3–19,27) Ronald L. Baker shows that Riley made extensive use of Indiana folk speech before systematic collections of Hoosier folklore existed. Riley employed traditional proverbs, superstitions, tales, and games, all of which confirm his familiarity with farm or domestic life. Although Riley wrote relatively little in prose, his use of folk medicine beliefs and weather lore suggests his closeness to his sources.

Two brief articles provide more evidence for William Faulkner's dependence on folk material. George W. Boswell in "Note On the Surnames of Faulkner's Characters" (*TFSB* 36:64–66) observes that such men as Quick, Bunch, Gowrie, Armstid, and Sutpen have names with colloquial or local connotations, while the Rev. Tooleyman (obviously from Tout le Monde) takes on an allegorical or onomatopoeic significance. Boswell adds that Sartoris may well derive from Mr. Sartoris who taught high school in Sardis, Mississippi. Elmo Howell in "William Faulkner's Chickasaw Legacy" (*ArQ* 26:293–303) discusses Indian material in "Red Leaves," "A Justice," "Lo!", and "A Courtship." Faulkner's aboriginal stories came either from history or from his imagination, but the novelist was guilty of distortion in making his Indians cannibals or participants in ritual murder. Howell also claims that Faulkner's Indian dialect was foredoomed to failure. Yet "Red Leaves" is an artistic triumph because it reveals the novelist "working in harmony with that natural law which underlies all system and governs alike all created things."

A philosophic article by Norine Dresser, "The Metamorphosis of the Humor of the Black Man" (*NYFQ* 26:216–28) suggests that in the course of a century Negro humor has changed materially and reflects in sequence black experiences of segregation, integration, and nationalism. Thus old master stories and Negro preacher tales are supplanted in the course of time by Civil War anecdotes and eventually by stories involving Malcolm X or Martin Luther King. At the moment the Negro is emancipated enough culturally not only to glory in a new freedom and status but even to laugh at himself.

ix. Material and Miscellaneous Folklore

As students of material folklore continue to multiply, the subjects of their research diversify accordingly. Such unlikely themes as corn knives, Easter eggs, and shapes of barns were dealt with in articles during the year.

Michael Owen Jones in "Folk Art Production and the Folklorist's Obligation" (*JPC* 4:194–212) contends that the folklorist-collector has a duty to help the craftsman market his products. Despite the danger that this practice might introduce commercialism and destroy spontaneity, Jones argues that craftsmen like the Appalachian chair-makers with whom he is especially concerned need such aid. To him folklorists can be of vital service in making the products of folk artists known to museum personnel and the American public in general. Mary Ganim, turning her attention to children's games, develops the thesis in "A Study of Children's Games" (*NYFQ* 26:50–63) that games are not merely trivial pastimes or expiring customs. She points out that sex roles in games are rapidly changing (boys jump rope, girls play football) and that since freedom and permissiveness are important today the "it" character representing authority in games is growing less popular. Thus children's folklore can not only reflect the contemporary social structure; it can also function psychologically for the individuals involved.

The artist and craftsman have always employed a variety of media. Guy T. Hollyday in "The Ephrata Wall-Charts and Their Inscriptions" (*PF* 19,iii:34–46) discusses the "frakturs" still visible at the famous cloister at Ephrata, Pennsylvania, and remarks that only the smaller ones remain. These large charts or wall hangings were done with elegant penmanship, usually in ornamental Gothic letters, and are virtually ink paintings. Their texts usually came from scripture or early hymns. A very different kind of art distinguishes the once familiar chapbooks. Robert D. Bethke in "Chapbook 'Gallows-Literature' in Nineteenth Century Pennsylvania" (*PF* 20,i: 2–15) describes the flamboyant pamphlets which formerly appeared at the time of public executions. They were copiously illustrated and written in a heavily didactic prose. Clergymen often moralized in these chapbooks and criminals spoke their last "good nights." Easter eggs also provided the craftsmen with artistic opportunities. In a long article entitled "Slovak and Ruthenian Easter Eggs in America" (*JPC* 4:155–93) Andrew Cincura discusses the tradition imported by immigrants settling in Cleveland. The reader is informed about the methods used in ornamentation, the ingredients and the tools, and the designs employed. Natives of Bohemia and Moravia brought with them such patterns as chains, rosettes, garlands, swastikas, triangles, hexagrams, and crosses, all of which were imposed on egg shells by painting, embossing, or inlaying. Today, although American ingredients and tools are used more frequently, the traditional custom endures.[1] Inscriptions of a different kind are carved on trees, a practice discussed by Joseph M. Gray in "The Folk Tradition of the Sweetheart Tree" (*PF* 19,ii:14–17). The campus of Grove City College in Pennsylvania possesses deciduous trees on which romantic couples have incised various symbols and initials. The durability of the carving depends largely on the strength of the boy and the sharpness of his penknife.

Whittling too is a viable skill. Earl F. and Ada F. Robacker in "Whittling: Dumb Dutch Pastime" (*PF* 19,iv:2–9) comment on the remarkably competent Pennsylvania carvers and itemize the wooden objects which have become the prizes of collectors: butter molds, cream scoops, bowls of all kinds, stools, toys. An expert like William Schimmel became widely famous for his carvings of eagles. Youngsters too can become adept at whittling as Rosalie B. S. Daniels demonstrates in "Folk Toys and Amusements of Rural Mississippi Children" (*MFR* 4:68–75). With ingenuity and skill children could "carve" or fashion toys out of such intractable materials as corn cobs, broomstraws, dried vines, and wheels salvaged from discarded farm vehicles. In many ways these folk toys proved more satisfactory than those glittering on store shelves and commanding impossible prices.

Toni Fratto's "Cooking in Red and White" (*PF* 19,iii:2–15) belongs more properly in a cookbook than in a discussion of material folklore, yet her account of South Philadelphia Italian cookery is

---

[1] In *An Egg at Easter* (Bloomington, Ind. Univ. Press) the English folklorist Venetia Newall has written an erudite study of egg decoration and egg symbolism. Little American material is involved but some of the beliefs and practices described have indeed crossed the Atlantic Ocean.

full of traditional recipes. Basic ingredients are the two sauces: red
sauce with a tomato base, white sauce made with garlic and olive
oil. The author observes that American tastes have modified this imported folk cookery; organ meats are no longer preferred and the
use of garlic is declining. Clement L. Valetta also pays considerable
attention to food and drink in "Friendship and Games in Italian-
American Life" (*KFQ* 15:175–87), an account of Italian immigrants
in Roseto, Pennsylvania. But he is equally interested in showing how
close social bonds develop among people unrelated by blood but
thrown together by physical proximity. Cookery as well as certain
rituals are the basis of Philip Tilney's article, "The Immigrant Mace-
donian Wedding in Ft. Wayne" (*IF* 3:3–34), an eyewitness account
of several wedding ceremonies with their foods, dancing, and
symbolism.

In "Pensylvania Corn Knives and Husking Pegs" (*KFQ* 15:128–
37) Mac E. Barrick discusses the various shapes of one of the truly
indigenous American folk tools and shows how its function has modified its form. Roger L. Welsch, on the other hand, deals in two articles with folk architecture as revealed by barns and houses. In
"Nebraska's Round Barns" (*NH* 51:49–92) he identifies and describes a number of round barns constructed in the early part of the
century. The basic model seems original in the United States, perhaps
deriving from early forts or Indian wigwams. Its merits outnumbered
its disadvantages; superior wind resistance, use of less wood, extra
loft space, and a good ratio of interior spaces to wall length. The
folk architect possibly had an old maxim in mind too: a round barn
would keep the devil from lurking in the corners. In "Sandhill Baled-
Hay Construction" (*KFQ* 15:16–34) Welsch explains that Nebraska
farmers used baled-hay as well as sod to construct their prairie homes
usually adding concrete foundations and wood or concrete floors.
The area called the Kinkaid Sandhills was particularly rich in such
dwellings. Still another kind of rural building interested Beulah M.
D'Olive Price. In "The Dog-Trot Log Cabin: A Development in
American Folk Architecture" (*MFR* 4:84–89) she comments on the
origin of the double log cabins with a breezeway between them.
Early log cabins in the lower Mississippi Valley were crude and
quickly built. Simple tools such as the broadaxe, auger, cross-cut
saw, knife, and frow sufficed for the purpose. Double cabins were
the result of expanding families.

Miscellaneous objects drew the attention of several scholars. Angus K. Gillespie in "Graveyards and Ostentation" (*PF* 19,ii:34–43) deals with semi-rural cemeteries in eastern Pennsylvania. The graveyards maintained by different denominations over the years reveal a tendency to use smaller and more horizontal stones and to reduce the length of the inscriptions. Yet "grief therapy" (the need to erect memorial stones to make up for neglect during one's lifetime) still operates in cemeteries. David C. Winslow in "Trade Cards, Catalogs, and Invoice Heads" (*PF* 19,iii:16–32) considers early advertising devices, especially in trade catalogs, and emphasizes their importance as evidence on material aspects of folk cultural phenomena. Illustrations can help identify implements, tools, early vehicles, as well as changes in dress. Trade cards and invoices carried pictures of barrels, grindstones, chairs, churns, and baskets.

Reference to an article by Richard M. Dorson, "Is There a Folk in the City?" (*JAF* 83:185–216), might well conclude this appraisal. Dorson contends that the folklorist working in a city atmosphere must consider ethnic cuisine, folk religion, artifacts, dances, musical instruments, and personal histories as well as the familiar tales, ballads, and superstitions. In Gary and East Chicago, where the steel industry is the basic economic factor, the workers are to a large extent Negroes, Serbs, Croatians, Mexicans, and Puerto Ricans. Dorson found few responses to a request for folk tales but a wealth of material about the Evil Eye, fantastic cures, regional rituals imported from the Old World, pamphlets and books relating to national groups, and reminiscences about personal experiences. Moreover, deep-seated ethnic and regional animosities, some of which seemed to grow more implacable when transported to the shores of America, became immediately apparent. Dorson demonstrates that folklore exists in quantity in the cities, but that to collect it the researcher must change his sights and widen his collecting net.

University of Illinois

18. Themes, Topics, and Criticism

G. R. Thompson

In this year's chapter I shall examine recent issues and trends in the study of black writers. It is a decision imposed in part because of the crippling effect of the delayed 1970 MLA International Bibliography but, more happily, because of the timeliness of the subject.[1]

i. A Second Black Renaissance: Black "New Criticism" and a Black Aesthetic

The awareness of and the study of black literature in America have begun to produce a more and more coherent body of significant critical concern, and the serious student of American literature and literary criticism must not allow himself to be put off by a certain shrill repetitiveness nor by what often seems an undue brevity or an apocalyptic tone. For, like the early nineteenth-century cry for a uniquely "American" literature, the present cry for a uniquely "black" literature is often purely defensive. Indeed, there are a number of instructive parallels between the Black Renaissance and the American Renaissance (in Matthiessen's use of the phrase). An accidental one, perhaps, is its two stages: black American literature may be said to have had its first creative renaissance in the Harlem writers of the 1920s and 1930s. Now it seems to be undergoing a second critical renaissance similar to the socially and politically oriented criticism of the 1920s and 1930s, exemplified by such figures as H. L. Mencken and Van Wyck Brooks, and recently surveyed by Richard Ruland in *The Rediscovery of American Literature* (Cambridge, Mass., Harvard Univ. Press, 1967). Another, more central, parallel is the strong

1. I wish to acknowledge a grant-in-aid from the Research Committee of Washington State University and the assistance of Doris J. Richardson, a black student, who helped in collecting, abstracting, and selecting much of the material presented here. She has also aided me in better understanding black attitudes, though she is not, of course, to be held responsible for the attitudes expressed here.

quality of polemic in the concern for something exclusively this or that, one thing or another, whether Americanness or blackness. A sign of this critical rediscovery of black literature is the flood of case-books, extensive reprint projects, and, more significantly, the expansion or initiation of scholarly journals devoted to black studies—as well as, by my informal count, the publication of over two hundred critical essays from 1967 to 1970. A few examples, of course, will have to suffice.

The McGrath Publishing Company (College Park, Md.) is re-printing a series of "classic" works on black literature, black writers, black art forms, black folklore, and so on, including such works as Frederick W. Bond's *The Negro and the Drama*, Henri Gregiore's *An Enquiry Concerning the Intellectual and Moral Faculties and Literature of Negroes,* John Herbert Nelson's *The Negro Character in American Literature.* The McGraw-Hill Book Company has begun a series of casebooks and paperback reprints of both creative writing and critical studies, called "The Black Experience: Materials By and About Black Persons." Not limited to literary and artistic matters, the series includes such works as Eldridge Cleaver's *Soul on Ice,* Whitney Young's *Beyond Racism: Building an Open Society,* Frank Willett's *Ife in the History of West African Sculpture,* and a sequence of films and tapes on the history and culture of black people in Africa and America. (McGraw-Hill is also issuing a second series called "The Third World: Materials By and About Ethnic Groups," of which "The Black Experience" is to be an integral part.)

Among the many casebooks that have begun to appear, only a very few seem to be carefully done. Indeed, many, perhaps most, are rather obvious commercial exploitations of the current surge of in-terest in things black. Representing the range are *From A Black Perspective: Contemporary Black Essays,* edited by Douglas A. Hughes (New York, Holt, Rinehart and Winston); *Black Literature: Essays,* edited by Darwin Turner (Columbus, Ohio, Charles E. Mer-rill), the third of a series; *Early Black American Poets,* edited by William A. Robinson, Jr. (Dubuque, Iowa, William C. Brown, 1969); and *Black Literature in America: A Casebook,* edited by Raman K. Singh and Peter Fellowes (New York, Crowell), a useful anthology which collects a representative range of poetry, fiction, nonfiction prose, and drama, followed by a series of recent critical essays on black writing. Perhaps the most interesting of recent casebooks, from a critical perspective, is *Black Expression: Essays by and About Black Americans in the Creative Arts*, edited by Addison Gayle, Jr. (New York, Weybright and Talley, 1969), for Gayle's focus is on the creative act and he offers a wide range of provocative selections organized into four sections on folk culture, poetry, drama, and fiction, followed by twenty critical and theoretical essays, from the twenties to the present. (Six of these, counting Gayle's useful introduction, are original pieces written expressly for the volume.)

New journals include the *Black Scholar*, apparently modeled after the *American Scholar*, and the *Negro American Literature Forum*, generated by teachers of literature and largely focused on pedagogical problems, though essays on black culture, history, and art, and critical examinations of black writing are also major features, along with a continuing series of reviews and bibliographies. *Negro Digest* meanwhile has become *Black World*; although continuing to restrict contributions to the shorter and the note-length articles in the manner of *Reader's Digest*, the editors are much more culturally oriented and show great interest in the debate over the so-called black aesthetic. *Studies in Black Literature*, founded in 1970, unfortunately came to my attention too late for more than brief mention here.

The more than two hundred articles appearing in these publications and elsewhere tend to fall into three or four groups: the most extensive group is comprised of studies of individual figures (largely covered elsewhere in *ALS*); the others include studies of the black heritage, polemics on revolution, and polemics on the black aesthetic. "Blackness" as a central quality of life and art rather than an attribute of person is doubtless still a somewhat alien concept to most of us. And the call for a black aesthetic, while a positive and corrective counter to the myth of black inarticulateness or black inferiority, is likely also to seem a severely limiting factor, for it represents, at present, a segregationist attitude.

And yet, for whites, the idea of blackness as an "aesthetic" quality is, it seems to me, more unclear than alien. Paradoxically, the alienating effect embodied in the cry for a black aesthetic is apt to be felt more by humanists than others. The typical white person would probably be more than happy to acquiesce in the idea that there is some vague Negro "style," or "soul," or whatever—and then dismiss it. The humanist, however, is generally unwilling to be, especially by edict, excluded from human experience of any kind, to be told that there is something beyond his comprehension that he need not inquire into further. Indeed, most humanists have been reared on the concept of the ultimate brotherhood of man.

But for certain black writers and critics, it isn't necessarily so. Typical of the extremist stance is a short polemic on "The Black Aesthetic" by Ameer Baraka (presumably this is LeRoi Jones) in *Negro Digest* (18,xi[1969]:5–6). He declares very simply that the black aesthetic is nothing less than total commitment to revolution, which black artists must persuade black people collectively to carry forward as total war against the white world. Although such an unremitting segregationist attitude is not wholly typical because of its extremism, it does bluntly express a recurrent theme in recent black criticism. Not only do we see a moderate and "positive" version of this segregationism manifested as special courses in black literature in our universities, but also there is at work an increasingly rapid development of a black "mythos" in literary criticism that sometimes seems only a little removed from the position taken by Ameer Baraka.

Eugene Perkins, for example, in "The Changing Status of Black Writers" (*Black World* 19,viii:18–23,95–98) maintains that any serious effort by a black writer to become accepted in the American literary mainstream is obstructed by "the refusal of white America to acknowledge the Black Experience as a legitimate frame of reference for developing a meaningful literature." He sees charges that black writing does not possess the "universality" necessary for good literature as a "racist disguise" designed to impose white America's norms and values. (Contrary to this supposition, let me remark that a useful aspect of the essay for the white reader is Perkins's roll call of new writers in the black movement.) Mari Evans in "Contemporary Black Literature" (*Black World* 19,viii:4,93–94) claims that the "most significant and rigorous components" of black writing are "oppression, containment, denial, suppression." But people operate on different levels of consciousness, Evans acknowledges and goes on to make an interesting distinction between the "Negro writer" and the "Black writer." The former is one whose focus is inward upon himself rather than outward toward the "Black family / nation." The latter, then, is one who understands the reality of blackness as a "primary, inescapable involvement." For the present, the black writer must be "revolutionary": he calls for his people to view the nature

of their oppression, he identifies the oppressor, and he advocates
freedom by whatever means may be necessary. Carolyn Rodgers in
"The Literature of Black" (*Black World* 19,viii:5–11) admonishes
blacks not to leave European language—the "colonizer's language"—
as it is. It is itself a form of "oppression" that should be remodeled
after black patterns, for black words conjure up black images that
whites do not share: white critics "do not, never will, understand
what—or how—it is."

Such attitudes, be it confessed, have for the sympathetic white
reader a dark allure that tends to obscure the intrinsic anti-literary
quality of such a segregationist attitude. The implication is clearly
that literature itself has failed to render human experience under-
standable and vivid to those finding themselves in different circumstances, when one of the traditional functions of literature has been
to make such "alien" conditions real and comprehensible. As Charles
I. Glicksburg in "The Alienation of Negro Literature" (see *Black
Literature in America*, pp. 238–49) well observed fully twenty years
ago, a perverse duplicity hovers about the attempt to create a black
mythos. His remarks stand almost as an ominous caveat: "The whites
are delighted to welcome any contribution which can be conspicuously and generically labeled 'Negroid.' By stressing the 'Negroid'
quality of his art, the whites strengthen the dualism in the heart of
the Negro writer. After pushing him into a Black Ghetto, they say:
'Go to it, boy. That is your distinctvie racial talent. You will succeed
best to the extent that you are most truly yourself: a Negro.'" Thus
the black writer is encouraged to fix his eyes broodingly on "one
sector of experience, the suffering of his people, the fatality of 'color,'"
so that he can think and write of nothing else. Whites make the black
writer "drink his cup of gall and wormwood to the lees," and then
they dismiss his work as the shrill incoherence of an obsessional
neurosis.

But militance, one soon becomes convinced after reading recent
black criticism, is indeed a necessary stage in the acceptance of
blackness by both whites and blacks. Although unfortunate from one
point of view, it is at present an essential and valid quality of black
life. Any white reader who has read with any understanding Toomer,
Hughes, Wright, Jones, Ellison, Cleaver, knows that literature has
not "failed." For no matter how removed the white reader may be

originally, he comes from such writers a changed man. Moreover, we have "militant" statements from black critics that are often measured and temperate. Two brief examples may be useful here.

John O. Killens in "The Artist and the Black University" (*BS* 1,i[1969]:61–65) reviews the leadership role of black artists in the black power movement and notes that, when artists were at first denied any kind of role, a group that included Ossie Davis, Ruby Dee, Max Roach, James Baldwin, Louis Lomax, Odetta, and himself, got together to declare a "cultural revolution" designed to "de-brainwash" people. But the Association of Artists for Freedom, as they called themselves, found that even black universities were resistant to cultural change; and they had, therefore, to urge a "Black Communiversity" to be held on the sidewalks of the black community to bring black people back to their "black commitments." Killens really blames neither white nor black in the course of his discussion.

Addison Gayle, Jr., in "The Critic, the University, and the Negro Writer" (*NegroD* 16,iii[1967]:54–58) observes that university English professors determine literary standards, by and large, and that their standards often do not apply to works by Negro authors. Moreover, the professors are often beset with a polemic of their own: the desire to dispute any changes brought against American society. When university teachers do treat black literature, they usually offer only a token piece of Negro writing, generally Wright, Baldwin, or Ellison. Thus, it is clear, in Gayle's view, that American society is not yet ready to look at Negro literature "through glasses cleansed of 150 years of prejudice." Such "militant" criticisms can hardly be called unreasonable.

Indeed, there is a reasonableness and sanity amidst the militancy of the best black criticism. Two such discussions are brief essays by Addison Gayle and Hoyt W. Fuller in Gayle's *Black Expression*. In his preface (pp. vii–xv), Gayle discuses the "invisibility" of the black critic, which derives from three white attitudes: Negro literature has never been considered an integral part of American literature; white critics consider themselves as capable of a more objective and un-biased evaluation of Negro literature than Negroes themselves; Negroes are supposedly unconcerned with aesthetics. Gayle then weighs the insistent demand by Negroes that literature at bottom be "moral." This demand, he observes, is no more than a variation on

Dr. Johnson: "a clamor for men to do justice and avoid evil." None
of America's minorities, Gayle movingly asserts, "believes more in
the American creed; none has staked more upon the Constitution;
none has depended more upon man's natural instincts for justice and
tolerance; and none has shouted with more patience, with more passion, with more eloquence—white man, listen!" A criticism based on
an amoral aesthetics of form alone is irrelevant, just as is one based
on metaphysical themes, to a "Negro community daily confronted by
the horrors of the urban ghetto, the threat to sanity and life in the
rural areas of the South, and the continual hostility of the overwhelming majority of its fellow citizens."

Hoyt Fuller in "Towards a Black Aesthetic" (*Black Expression*,
pp. 263–70) remarks on the white reception of such movements as the
Organization of Black American Culture, which has sponsored a
writer's workshop in Chicago that encourages black writers deliberately to "invest their work with distinctive styles and rhythms and
colors of the ghetto" on the premise that there is a black style that
is part of a different life experience, from dress, to bearing, to speech.
But such a movement, he acutely observes, is bound to be "reviled
as 'racism-in-reverse,' and its writers labeled as 'racists,' opprobrious
terms which are flung lightly at black people" with no apparent sense
of irony. (Is one merely indulging in a faddish "white guilt" if he
remarks to himself, "guilty," at this point?) Fuller discusses what is
now for black critics a notorious 1963 review of Gwendolyn Brooks
in which the reviewer (himself a well-known poet) noted a certain
limitation of subject matter (her poetry presents "some lively pictures of Negro life") and observed that "if being a Negro is the only
subject, the writing is not important." Fuller remarks that "the history of American race relations is contained in that appraisal": on
the one hand, civilized, urbane, gentle, elegant; on the other hand,
arrogant, condescending, presumptuous, racist. "To most white readers," Fuller writes, the reviewer's "words, if not his assessment, seem
eminently sensible; but it is all but impossible to imagine a black
reader not reacting with unalloyed fury." Black critics, then, have
the "responsibility of approaching the works of black writers . . .
with the knowledge that white readers—and white critics—cannot be
expected to recognize and to empathize with the subtleties and significance of black style and technique. They have the responsibil-

ity of rebutting white critics and of putting things in the proper perspective."

ii. The Black Mythos: Black vs. White

The major characteristics of the black mythos, then, seem to be four. First, there is the prevalent tone of militancy often combined with an almost violent despair that yet has overtones of hope for eventual black equality—or in some cases black dominance through some final apocalyptic confrontation. A major facet of this militancy is a deep-grained distrust of any white interest in black art, though in most cases humanistic scholars and critics stress harmony, reconciliation, and even integration after the validity of blackness is once acknowledged. Second, there is the already mentioned mystique of some sort of all-black aesthetic, a configuration of truly unique expressive forms that reflect black life and black consciousness and black sensitivity. The constant implication is that this black aesthetic is something conceptually different from other approaches to literature, that black experience is expressed in such a way that whites do not, can not, indeed, *shall* not understand. But, as far as I can tell, what the black aesthetic is, really, is simply the call for a recognition that the form and pressure of life as lived by a black person and as spoken of by a black person have their own integrity. At present the black aesthetic is undergoing a segregationist phase; and this leads to the third point. A recurrent theme in black criticism is the tension between an all-black aesthetic and "universality," which leads us back to that militant distrust of anything white. Yet there are many voices that call for an art and a literature that reveals the universal bedrock of human existence at the same time that it presents an individualized (if racialized) particularity to temporal, physical, and psychological experience in this country. The fourth characteristic is directly related: this is the attempt to rediscover a viable and respectable black tradition or heritage, both African and American, valid in and of itself and in which the contemporary black American artist can take pride. This too is militantly asserted.

Thus, the white reader may well keep reminding himself that if whites are not yet ready to look at black writing "through glasses cleansed of 150 years of prejudice," neither have black writers and

scholars yet gone "beyond anger," no matter how peculiar an institution a segregationist black aesthetic may seem. Instructive, and reas-
suring, is the impeccable restraint of *The Militant Black Writer in
Africa and the United States* (Madison, Univ. of Wis. Press, 1969),
a gathering of two longish essays: "African Voices of Protest" by
Mercer Cook and "Survival Motion" by Stephen E. Henderson. Cook
points out that early nineteenth-century attempts at social justice in
African colonies were aimed at the humanitarian, Christian conscience of the European. Among blacks, writers tried to inculcate a
sense of "self-respect and solidarity, a desire for education, progress,
and self-government." African writers and the African Church in
their rejection of Europeanism are the sources of African nationalism.
In the 1930s a new African consciousness combined scholarship and
militancy with the authentic voice of African humanism—a movement led by such people as Jomo Kenyatta, Nnamdi Azikwe, Leon G.
Dumas, and Aime Césaire. In modern African poetry and fiction,
according to Cook, two themes dominate. The main ingredients of
the "civilize the savage" theme (usually treated ironically) are violence and European greed, arrogance, hypocrisy, injustice. The
other main theme is the New Africans' belief that they must achieve
their own identity and self-respect by refusing to align themselves
with either of the two biggest power blocs. Cook claims that Africans
are less militant than American blacks because the Africans are a
majority and therefore have time on their side.

In "Survival Motion," Henderson first asserts that it is redundant
to call a black writer militant because the assertion of blackness is
a militant act in itself. The role of the black writer, he suggests, is to
warn the people and save them from the mainstream of American
life so as to prepare them for the upcoming confrontation. The black
poet is "baptised in blackness" when he rejects white middle-class
cultural values and affirms his black selfhood. The black writer
should reject Broadway, National Book Awards, and Pulitzer Prizes.
Henderson then turns to another recurrent theme in black criticism,
the struggle against the unconscious, culturally determined prejudices of the white power structure as manifest in language itself.
White culture traditionally equates the color black with evil; and
this, he suggests, affects both blacks and whites in a peculiar way,
resulting in blacks having two contradictory concepts of black con-

sciousness, love and hate of oneself. (Even the "dozens" and the "blues" evidence black hatred of self.) All this sounds gloomily segregationist. But, Henderson continues, when these two contradictory impulses are fused and held together by passionate imagination, we have the power of the new black poetry and new black consciousness. Thus Henderson's final point actually affirms the validity of literature for blacks and whites both. To understand the revolutionary black literature, we need to understand as one the people to whom it is addressed, earlier black writers, and those presently engaged. For black people are not only the poets and the audience, they are themselves the "poems."

Francis Ward and Val Grey Ward come at the problems of militancy in a different way in "The Black Artist—His Role in the Struggle" (*BS* 2,v[1971]:23–32). They observe that the writers of the Harlem Renaissance defined their work in terms of their particular black conditions and in such a way that implies that blackness imposes certain responsibilities and limitations on the artist. They suggest that there are only two relevant critical positions to take: one is to view art as art for art's sake; the other is to see art as a reflection of the cultural and social context of the artist, that is, as a reflection of the current conditions of the artist's actual existence. The black struggle today, they suggest, does not offer the familiar political "leaders"[2] so much as it offers revolutionaries in a somewhat uneasy alliance with writers, and the present role of the black artist must be to serve not only as creator and critic but also as propagandist, activist, social critic, hero figure to the young, and even as fund raiser. "With the advent of the black power movement," they write, "the black artist became the re-interpreter of the black past, the re-definer of the black present, and the analyst of the black future." If the white reader should wish to participate in this experience, as a first step he must accept the primary importance of blackness and even of anti-whiteness.

Although he discusses the "universality" of black writing, Floyd Gaffney in "Black Theatre: Commitment and Communication" (*BS* viii:10–15) defines the black writer's role purely in terms of "black expression" as "protest, identity, achievement, revolt, and freedom," all clearly polemical in nature. The black playwright, and the black

2. See in this connection Marcus H. Boulware, *The Oratory of Negro Leaders, 1900–1968* (Westport, Conn., Negro Universities Press, 1969).

artist generally, has a responsibility to mirror black "lifestyles through drama that possesses both literary and theatrical merit—but from a non-white perspective."

This call for a culturally infused criticism, rather than a sterile and possibly racist aesthetic formalism, is evident in two articles calling for a true "black perspective" by the poet Don L. Lee. In "Black Critics" (*Black World* 19,vi:24–30), Lee argues basically that "true art is as much a part of the culture as is the critic who judges it." The black writer is black, first, and a writer, second, contrary to claims by certain black writers (notably Ellison). Lee forcefully states the prevailing black attitude by means of a clever twist. "I, as a Black man / critic," he writes, "cannot possibly accurately judge or assess . . . Chinese literature," since

> first, I can't speak the Chinese language (which means I can't read the literature in the original); second, I never lived among the Chinese people—so that I know very little about their daily life style; third, my only knowledge of Chinese religion comes from what I read—which puts me at the disadvantage of accepting someone else's interpretation, which is always dangerous; fourth, my knowledge of Chinese music is terribly limited; fifth, my knowledge of Chinese folklore and dance is negligible; and finally, I've never been to China, so would be unfamiliar with many of the references used in the literature. [p. 26]

Although this is a reductive denial of man's ability to learn anything through "reading," it does highlight some of the problems whites face in reading what is at least akin to a foreign literature: the problem is that white readers refuse to admit that the black language and the black experience is foreign to them. In "Directions for Black Writers" (*BS* xii[1969]:53–57), Lee remarks that when critics call on black writers to be "universal," they are asking that these writers be "white" and "western." But the black writer should instead be concerned with the various internal racist levels of American society because, again, he was black before he was a writer. The black writer must therefore offer black direction and love of black self. And critics will just have to see "universal" implications within the particularities of the black situation, if they are to see any universality at all.

James C. Kilgare in "The Case For Black Literature" (*NegroD*

18,ix[1969]:22–25,66–69), takes up similar problems from a more moderate perspective. He writes that literature primarily should mirror the "humanity" in its readers, but that what is traditionally considered "American" literature is a mirror of white life only. The aesthetic experience should be broad enough to encompass the reflection of all the "peopled hills" of America. Black literature therefore should not be taught as a separate course but as part of the American literature course.[3]

Joseph R. Keller, in "Black Writing and Editorial Unbelief" (*NALF* 3[1969]:35–40), addresses himself to two aspects of one question: is there really any such thing as black literature, and, if so, how can it be identified? Keller directed these questions to journal editors as those who determine academic attitudes. Answers varied from total denial of the existence of black literature to the acknowledgment that black literature exists as a kind of sub-level of American literature. *No one* was willing to acknowledge the existence of a black literature with an integrity of its own. Keller suggests that black literature is identifiable in its obsessive motifs of black identity and white oppression, and concludes that what is needed is a more careful reading of the body of extant black literature by white editors and an understanding of black motifs. Keller also suggests that an important step in removing unconscious prejudice would be university courses in black *language* for young whites. In a follow-up article, "Black Writing and the White Critic" (*NALF* 3[1969]:103–10), Keller continues his discussion of white prejudice embodied in the very forms of our language. "Color" words are learned at a very early age by both blacks and whites, according to their particular environment. Some of the same words are used by each group, but with different connotations that are difficult to shed. The white critic's attempt to understand Negro color words (if possible) must be a first step toward understanding Negro attitudes.

A similar essay on unconscious white prejudice as institutionalized by our culture is Addison Gayle's "Cultural Strangulation: Black Literature and the White Aesthetic" (*NegroD* 18,ix[1969]:32–

3. A similar "postive" as opposed to an "anti-" stance is found in Kilgare's "Toward the Dark Tower" (*Black World* 19,viii:14–17), where he observes that there are almost no poems about a black man's love for a black woman. Rather than detailing the songs of "evil or wronged" women, he suggests that black writers need next to learn to respond to the human beauty of black people, to show that black means beautiful by honoring black femininity.

39). Gayle gives a short history of what he calls the "white aesthetic," beginning with Plato. Plato, he remarks, defines two kinds of symbols: natural and arbitrary. Natural symbols are the reflection of a divine form of absolute beauty; arbitrary symbols are those assigned to an object by man. White critics act as though their perceptions were natural rather than arbitrary; but their symbols, as well as symbols which govern black artists, are arbitrary. White critics therefore cannot presume to set standards for good black writing. Acceptance of the phrase, "black is beautiful," as a valid symbolic statement is the first step in the destruction of the old "truths" and laws of the white aesthetic.

A closely related study is Carolyn F. Gerald's "The Black Writer and His Role" (*NegroD* 18,iii[1969]:42–48). Gerald claims that image making is central to man's self-definition. The image maker shapes our view of reality "because the images the words conjure up when they are put together artistically provoke an immediate emotional response in us and dim out of our consciousness all the untold other points of view at our disposal." Man projects his cultural and racial images on the universe. He defines himself in terms of others like him. Since the black man is living in a white world where white images are projected, it is easy to see how the black man sees himself in terms of "zero images." The artist thus must be the guardian of the image, the myth maker of his people. The black artist, as the guardian of black images, must reject the white man's attempt to portray black reality. Negative images of black life have to be wiped out and new, positive ones asserted by black writers by a kind of reverse symbolism.

Related to such assumptions are two studies of white treatments of Negro characters. In "The Negro in Southern Fiction: Stereotype and Archetype" (*NALF* 2[1968]:3–6), Nancy M. Tischler writes that of nineteenth-century white Southern writers who came closest to breaking away from unconscious stereotypes, Mark Twain was the most successful.[4] But other Southern writers (except Faulkner) even today are trapped by cultural clichés. A distinguishing characteristic of Southern literature as opposed to Northern is that Southern literature focuses on the rural Negro as a "primitive and superstitious literary character who embodies folk traditions." Because the study

4. See also Tischler's *Black Masks: Negro Characters in Modern Southern Fiction* (ALS 1969, p. 228).

of Southern fiction uncovers the dominant attitudes of the region and period, she adds, it is part of Southern intellectual, social, and cultural history. She concludes with a comment on the universality of black literature; we should look for the "archetype" even in black protest literature as a layer of meaning underlying strictly racial meanings. Nanelia S. Doughty in "Realistic Characterization in Post-bellum Fiction" (*NALF* 3([1969]:57–62) observes that although most nineteenth-century writers have characterized Negroes by stereotypes, there have also been those who presented Negroes as believable human beings, but these writers tend to be overlooked in the "flood of distorted portraits." Among the works Doughty cites as giving believable portraits of Negroes are Samuel Clemens's *The Gilded Age* and *Pudd'nhead Wilson*, DeForest's *Miss Ravenal's Conversion*, Cable's *Grandissimes*, *Silent South*, and *John March, Southerner*.

What at first glance looks like it ought to be the single major work of the last five years in the critical study of black literature, turns out to be less than stunning. Still, it is a major contribution, and if the interested reader has time for only two books, then he should add to his reading of Addison Gayle's *Black Expression* the two-volume collection of essays, *The Black American Writer*, edited by C. W. E. Bigsby (Deland, Fla., Everett/Edwards, 1969). Bigsby has collected a large number of fair to good essays (most of them original) and organized them into sections on "The Critical Dilemma," "The Black View," and the genres of fiction, poetry, and drama. A dozen are on larger themes and topics, and represent something of a synthesis of the themes and concerns detailed in the foregoing pages. Although Bigsby seems to have a real concern for black literature, I, for one, am not at all sure he understands very well what is going on. For example, in his introductory essay, "The Black American Writer" (1:5–34) Bigsby tries to define "Negritude" and claims that it has been superseded by a "new sense of cultural universality." He claims that, contrary to American Negroes, native Africans did not have to bolster their self-image because they were not threatened by an alien white culture. So far as I can tell, these observations (besides being in sheer error about the lack of a white threat in Africa) run counter to everything now being written. Moreover, Bigsby seems to be critical of "disagreements" among black writers, as if they should all form a solid monolithic front. But let us survey the general essays.

Jean-Paul Sartre in "Black Orpheus" (2:5–40) also discusses the concept of "Negritude." The mere fact that poets have to communicate in the language of an alien country, he observes, is a hazard to "Negritude." For example, when a Negro declares in French that he rejects French culture, there is an obvious contradiction in his very use of the French language. So also the Afro-American suffers a loss of Negritude when he considers that he is part American; America and American whites are an automatic obstacle to the Afro-American's Negritude. In an effort to rid himself of some of the handicaps of speaking the enemy's language, the Negro must try to "regurgitate" the whiteness out of words by using them in unusual contexts and with unusual connotations.

On this note, let it be mentioned that many of the essays are on black suspicion of white interpretation of black literature. Loften Mitchell, for example, in "On the 'Emerging' Playwright" (2:129–36) argues that the white concept of the Negro dramatist as "emerging" is just another aspect of the effort to deny cultural maturity in non-white groups. In "Contemporary Negro Fiction" (1:229–44), Hoyt W. Fuller suggests that whites are now labeling Negro literature "protest literature" in an effort to prevent it from really touching the white consciousness. Whites do not want Negro literature to deal honestly with Negro life because this would necessarily mean direct exposure of white failures. An interesting aspect of Fuller's discussion is his feeling that black writers, because they have been excluded from the mainstream of American life, have not partaken of its perversions to the extent that whites have; blacks have been able therefore to maintain a vision of a society constructed on principles of justice and equality that whites have let fade.

Richard Gilman in "White Standards and Negro Writing" (1:35–50) makes a distinction between Negro writing and that writing which happens to be done by people who are also Negroes. Negro writing is concerned with a definition of self and contains "truths and valuations different from white concepts," though these differences are never very clear. In the second part of his essay, Gilman tries to defend himself against the charge of racism, for he had in an earlier work suggested that white critics are not qualified to judge Negro literature. His critics suggested that if this were so, then Gilman is not qualified to judge the writings of Genet or Lessing on the same basis on which he refuses to judge Negro writing; for just as he cannot participate in the world of the Negro so he cannot participate in Genet's world of homosexuality or Lessing's world of "woman." Gilman replies that the world of the Negro is on an entirely different level from that of Genet and Lessing—the black world being a "real" world as opposed to an "imaginary" one! The distinction is intriguing, having as its implicit basis some sort of hierarchy of significance, but it is not at all made clear by Gilman.

Another treatment of the relation of black critic and white is the essay, "Harold Cruse: An Interview."[5] Cruse remarks that it is whites who have set the tone for Negro writing; black perception of black experience is shaped by white perception of black experience. Moreover, the black writer's view of white life is also limited because of his shallow view of black life. Cruse views with suspicion any attempt of blacks to interest themselves in movements other than black, such as the Jewish cause.

Although James W. Tuttleton, in "The Negro Writer as Spokesman" (1:245–60), seems to resent the constant attempt of whites (both "liberals" and "racists") to speak for the Negro, he yet feels that the white critic has to deal with Negro writing because, as critic, that is his job, and because, as a man, he should be concerned about the quality of human life reflected in his culture. After all, he argues, the black idiom is only a variant of our mother tongue; so the white critic should be capable of treating black writing. Moreover, because the world created by the black writer is a world of imagination, the white reader can participate in it vicariously. But Tuttleton never really comes to grips with the felt experience of being a black man in a white man's world, and thereby, in his focus on "language" and the "imagination" is guilty of what most blacks would consider typical blindness to the essential qualities of black literature. Related is Larry Neal's discussion of "The Black Arts Movement" (2:187–202), wherein he points out that for LeRoi Jones, the "leader" of this movement, ethics, and aesthetics are the same. Therefore any concept of the artist that separates him from his commitments to his community is pernicious.

In "Our Mutual Estate: The Literature of the American Negro" (1:51–62) Theodore L. Gross maintains that the Negro writer's audience is all America. The American Negro's work is prompted by the

5. See 2:227–39. Cruse is the author of *The Crisis of the Negro Intellectual* (London, Allen, 1969).

friction in American society and is a moral indictment of America, but when the artist decides to become a "spokesman" for his people, he restricts himself unduly and thereby sacrifices his art. A variation on this theme is John A. Williams's "The Literary Ghetto" (1:65–70). Labeling Negro writing with phrases like "beautiful anger," "black hatred," "painful rage," "exquisite protest," and the like, deprives the writing of value for mankind, including Negroes. Such categories for black writers limit the expansion of their talents, making them "spokesmen" for one set of values, and allowing but one name at a time to emerge. Langston Hughes, in an essay written in 1963, "Problems of the Negro Writer" (1:65–69), discusses what were then intense problems of getting a "Negro book" published in America, some measure of how times have changed. In "The Negro Writer: Pitfalls and Compensations" (1:71–78), after commenting that a restricted vision and a quality of bitterness are the black writer's major handicaps, William Gardner Smith goes on to suggest that his compensations are greater, including emotional depth, a sense of social reality, and resistance to capitalism even after a disappointing flirtation with communism.

The black interest in communism as an alternative to capitalistic exploitation in the Western world is discussed by Wilson Record in "The Negro Writer and the Communist Party" (1:217–28). He cites several reasons why the party is no longer popular with black writers. It is an old organization with ties to other older organizations that have failed in dealing with race relations. Whites continue to dominate the party, and blacks feel that they are being used in a game of "tokenism," while simultaneously Jews have become influential in the party and Negroes are growing increasingly anti-Semitic. Another reason is that the Soviet Union has not developed programs that completely avoid racial and ethnic discrimination—indeed, the Soviets have a poor record over the last half-century. Finally, intensified race consciousness emphasizing black nationalism and separatism condemns integrationist movements and organizations. At the heyday of its influence among Negroes (in the thirties and forties), the party offered the black writer a publishing outlet and a ready-made audience through its magazines and presses; but writers were forced to write on themes that were not central to the black experience.

Several essays in Bigsby on what might be called the black tradition may be discussed together. Gerald W. Haslam (2:41–51) in

"The Awakening of American Negro Literature 1619–1900" gives a survey of the development of black literature in America. Oral literature, he points out, was the forerunner of the written literature of Negro slaves such as Lucy Terry, Jupiter Hammon, Briton Hammon, Phillis Wheatley, and Gustavus Vassa in the eighteenth century. In 1827, *Freedom's Journal*, the first Negro newspaper, was founded and began to publish abolitionist writings; along with the abolitionist movement in general, a flood of spoken and written protest literature appeared. Oral literature remained the basic form of black literature during the period of slavery until the emergence of such writers as Paul Laurence Dunbar, Charles W. Chesnutt, W. E. B. DuBois, and Booker T. Washington.

In "The Black Playwright in the Professional Theatre of the United States of America 1858–1959" (2:113–28), Darwin Turner offers several reasons for the scarcity of Afro-American playwrights, all economic. For one thing, Negro life has been generally considered "exotic," and producers have feared that plays on Negro themes would have a very limited audience. For another, directly related, drama is more expensive than the other arts, and playwrights have traditionally depended upon acquaintance with people who have money, an obviously severe limitation for a black writer. Turner points out that the first serious Broadway production was a one-act play by Willis Richardson in 1923 called *The Chip Woman's Fortune*. Two full-length plays followed shortly afterwards, *Appearances* by Garland Anderson and *Meek Mose* by Frank Wilson. *Mulatto* by Langston Hughes had the longest Broadway run (in 1935) of any play by a black dramatist before Lorraine Hansberry. The depression of 1929 accounts further for the relatively small number of black playwrights.

In "Claude McKay and the New Negro of the 1920's" (2:53–65) Wayne Cooper suggests several reasons for the change in the spirit of the Negro in the twenties. They were inspired by the self-assertion of other Negroes such as W. E. B. DuBois; their old servile patterns of life were disrupted when Negroes began to migrate Northward; they believed that if America could fight for the cause of democracy abroad, perhaps it could do something about democracy at home as well. McKay is worthy of attention today as one of the first to express the spirit of the "New Negro." In a related essay, "Poetry in the Harlem Renaissance" (2:67–76) Gerald Moore argues that the Har-

lem Renaissance was hampered because there was no Negro audience for the writers and because the writers were overwhelmed at
being "discovered." Moreover, the writers were trying to use an
idiom that was outmoded. McKay and Cullen tried to model their
poetry after the Elizabethan sonnet, the Keatsian ode, and the Tenny-
sonian ballad. Although there is a world of real anguish and desire
struggling to find expression in these poems, Jean Toomer and Langston Hughes are much more powerful because they did not have an
improper reverence for an alien tradition but instead sought a natural
language adequate to their black experience.

iii. A Black Heritage: Afro-American Traditions

A group of black scholars attending the 1969 African Studies Association national conference in Montreal walked out of what they
considered a white-oriented, white-controlled meeting and formed
their own group, the African Heritage Studies Association. This new
black group, which defines itself as an organization of "scholars of
African descent," held its first meeting at Howard University in May
1970 and put together a manifesto dedicating themselves to the unity
of all black peoples and the repossession of the native heritage for
all black people. (This document is reprinted in *Black World* 19,ix:
20–24).

Several recent studies of the black "heritage" may be singled out.
Eugene B. Redmond, in "The Black American Epic: Its Roots, Its
Writers" (*BS* 2,v[1971]:15–22), makes what at first seems an ingenious argument seem quite plausible and offers in the process a
clear example of the temper of new black consciousness in quest of
a usable past. He reminds the reader of two general characteristics of
the epic: the epic carves the specific details of a people's life style
through a "collective" eye and mind; and the protagonist of the epic
is an heroic, personified embodiment of the best characteristics of
his people. Using Margaret Walker's *For My People* to illustrate his
argument, Redmond suggests that the "Black American Epic" fuses
physical Africa and the southern United States. The hero may be an
accumulation (mentally and physically) of the most desirable traits
of the race, but he emerges as a single man—a sort of classic tragedy
figure. In the black epic, significantly, the hero often embodies traits

considered criminal by the larger society. Redmond goes on to suggest that the five hundred to six hundred "spirituals existing today in written form, and the numberless others living on the tongues of old folk" constitute the "first Black American Epic." Old-time preachers become in his view the first black American poets; and Langston Hughes he sees as the greatest modern epic writer because of his work with the black language as the embodiment of the range, power, and endurance of his people.

In "The Slave Narrative: An American Genre," the introductory essay to *Great Slave Narratives*, edited by Arna Bontemps (Boston, Beacon Press, 1969), Bontemps observes that the focal point of the great number of "slave narratives" in existence before the Emancipation Proclamation of 1863 was Negro suffering under white oppression and the consequent attempt to relieve it by flight to some imagined promised land of freedom. "The disappearance of the slave narrative, unlike the phasing out of the minstrel show, deprived black people in the United States of a medium of self-expression for which there was no ready substitute. Decades of relative silence followed, insofar as protest was concerned; and this silence paralleled a growing hostility against Negroes." Booker T. Washington tried to stem this tide of hostility through conciliation, in direct opposition to W. E. B. DuBois, who became, Bontemps claims, the true spokesman for his people. "As long ago as the Negro Renaissance of the 1920's, perceptive scholars and bibliophiles were bracketing Negro slave narratives with Negro music as the two most notable examples of the black man's contribution to American culture. From the spirituals came the cadences as well as the words and images that awakened later poetic genius. From the narratives came the spirit and the vitality and the angle of vision responsible for the most effective prose writing by black American writers from William Wells Brown to Charles W. Chestnutt, from W. E. B. DuBois to Richard Wright, Ralph Ellison, and James Baldwin." Bontemps cites Briton Hammon, Jupiter Hammon, Phillis Wheatley, Olaudah Equiano (Gustavus Vassa), and John Marrant as among those who set the mold for the genre and singles out Washington's *Up from Slavery* and DuBois's *Souls of Black Folk* as masterworks of the genre. Interest in the slave narrative was at its peak in the abolitionist movement, where it was hoped that reprintings of works by such writers as Phillis Wheatley and Benjamin Banneker would simultaneously inspire Negroes and shame those white critics who wished to minimize the Negro contribution to American society.

Robert E. Fleming carries the search for the black tradition to a reassessment of a classic work in "Contemporary Themes in Johnson's *Autobiography of An Ex-Coloured Man*" (*NALF* 4:120–24). Fleming writes that Johnson's *Autobiography* is still worth reading not only because of its value as a cultural artifact, but also for the perspective it can give the reader on later fiction by black American writers. Fleming points up several themes in Johnson that are still present in black writing. First, there is the theme of racial self-hatred: blacks, constantly told that they are inferior, may come to believe or fear that it really is so, as illustrated in Ralph Ellison's *Invisible Man*, William Demby's *Beetlecreek*, James Baldwin's *Go Tell It On the Mountain*. Second, there is the theme of namelessness: modern blacks are the inheritors of the loss of identity suffered by slaves stripped not only of their names but also of their language and life patterns, as illustrated in Ellison's *Invisible Man* and Baldwin's *Nobody Knows My Name*. Third, there is the ambiguous role of the black mother: whereas Johnson portrays family life as matriarchal, with the mother warm, loving, devoted to her children, later black writing shows that the mother may be destructive, as in Wright's *Black Boy* (a work such as Ann Petry's *The Street* bridges the gap between Johnson's portrayal of the mother and Wright's, for the mother in *The Street* is torn between love for her child and the reality of their situation). Fourth, there is the characterization of the white "patron" or the white "liberal": the liberal is usually treated with suspicion; he is believed to have selfish motives for all his deeds, as portrayed in Wright's *Native Son*, Baldwin's *Another Country*, and John A. Williams's *The Man Who Cried I Am*.

The Negro in American History (3 vols., Chicago, Encyclopaedia Britannica Educational Corp., 1969), edited by Mortimer J. Adler and Charles Van Doren, attempts to recapture the historical past by collecting a large number of original documents and moving backwards: volume one is titled *Black Americans, 1928–1968*, volume two *A Taste of Freedom, 1854–1927*, volume three *Slaves and Masters, 1567–1854*. Many of the documents are literary and cultural, such as, in the third volume, Emerson's essay on "The Fugitive Slave Law," Frederick Douglass on "The Mexican War," the "Confession" of Nat Turner, passages from the journal of Gustavus Vassa, and so on.

Charles R. Larson, in "African-Afro-American Literary Relations: Basic Parallels" (*NegroD* 19,ii[1969]:35–42), suggests three characteristics and a five-step evolutionary process shared by black African writing and black American writing: South African writing is a "depressing mirror image of race relations in the United States"; the quest for "Negritude" derives from African black nationalism; and present-day African novels exhibit a great number of similarities to what is now called "Afro-American" writing. Five stages in the historical development of African literature have exact parallels in this Afro-American literature: (1) portrayal of a reaction to initial stages of colonization; (2) educational themes on the difficulties of adjusting to Western patterns; (3) portrayal of the African leaving the rural back country for the city; (4) political themes of black power; and (5) themes of a more individualized nature, bordering on the problems of personality and psychology. Larson concludes that for a proper evaluation and understanding, literature must be seen from an international perspective.

John Henrik Clarke in "The Origin and Growth of Afro-American Literature" (*NegroD* 18,xi[1967]:54–67) goes back first to the oral tradition in West Africa. He then cites Ahmed Baba as a notable example of the African scholar; Baba was the last chancellor of the University of Sankare, which existed from the fourteenth century to 1591, and wrote more than forty books. During the period of the Moorish occupation, however, there was a decline in West African intellectual activity; and when Europeans arrived soon after, they mistakenly assumed that "nothing of order and value existed in these countries," an impression that lasted for four hundred years! In the American tradition, Clarke sees the following order as the historical development of forms. The slave narrative, as illustrated by Gustavus Vassa, was followed by the development of poetry as illustrated by Phillis Wheatley and Jupiter Hammon; then came a genre of "petitions," exemplified by the West Indian writers Prince Hall and John B. Russwurm; this was followed by the rise of journalism, of which Frederick Douglass is the prime example. About 1887 the black short story developed, as represented by Charles W. Chesnutt and Paul Laurence Dunbar. Then came the "Harlem Renaissance," characterized by a new Negro consciousness, portrayed by such writers as

Claude McKay, Zora Neal Hurston, Eric Walrand, Rudolph Fisher, who were greatly influenced by W. E. B. DuBois, James Weldon Johnson, and Alain Locke of the preceding generation.

Joyce Nower, in a rather conventional article, "The Tradition of Negro Literature in the United States" (*NALF* 3[1969]:5–12), observes that "there is a body of literature by black writers which does what literature has always done, namely, it reflects the unique experience of writers within their own culture"; but much of this literature, while embedded in the particulars of a group experience, transcends that group experience and partakes of the universal situation of man. Nevertheless, Nower identifies a black literary tradition in America that dates from the publications of a slave poet, Jupiter Hammon, in 1760. Protest literature in this black tradition can be traced back to George Horton in 1829 with the publication of two volumes, *Hope of Liberty* and *Naked Genius*. William Wells Brown became the first black novelist in 1854 with *Clotel*. Nower goes on to trace certain themes (the search for identity, social invisibility, and so on) through to Demby, Wright, Ellison, Baldwin, LeRoi Jones, and Ronald Fair. This black literary tradition, Nower concludes, has been obscured because it attacks the racist assumptions of American society.

In "America Before 1950: Black Writers' Views" (*NegroD* 18,x [1969]:26–34,67–69), James A. Emanuel remarks that the phrase "protest literature" has observed the two-hundred year tradition of black American writing. He proceeds then to survey the development of the novel, short story, poem, suggesting sub-types within each. Although "between the eighteenth century and 1950 . . . black writers of fiction and poetry . . . suggested such a complex, varied picture of America that no single impression emerges," there is yet a pattern worth noting. Before the Civil War, black writers mounted an attack on slavery and prejudice. Afterwards, to 1900, they replaced stereotypes with heroic figures or humanized folk Negros. Then they turned to the psychological and economic effects of racism. From 1900 to 1930, black writers were less self-conscious, more cosmopolitan, and satirical; this was also a time of great poetical achievement. The Depression saw the development of social novels of black life; Emanuel sees seven types: war novels, folkway novels, historical novels, proletarian novels, college novels, family history novels, migrant worker novels. From 1940 to 1950, black writing was confined less rigidly to "black" subjects.[6]

iv. The Black "New Criticism": A Final Word

One of the most judicious and balanced essays on recent black criticism is Darwin Turner's "Afro-American Literary Critics" (*Black World* 19,ix:54–67). Echoing Addison Gayle, Jr., Turner points out that, with a few exceptions of those who have become known as creative writers, and despite the recent interest in black literature by whites, the black literary critic is still the "invisible man" of the black movement. If one really wishes to understand the literature of black people, however, to be alert to what is really going on, he must read the "ablest interpreters of that literature" rather than relying on white critics, who are "equally distant from the Black experience." Turner then surveys black critics by what he calls an over-simplified categorization into six groups: (1) Afro-Americans who have written on traditional white figures and are primarily identified with mainstream American culture (William Stanley Braithwaite, Benjamin Brawley, Philip Butcher, Esther Merle Jackson, Nathan A. Scott); (2) black historians who have described literary achievements as part of their broader study of Afro-American culture (William Wells Brown, W. E. B. DuBois, Alain Locke, John Hope Franklin, Margaret Just Butcher, Ernest Kaiser); (3) black essayists who have made some memorable statement or another (usually scathing) about a writer or a group (Harold Cruse, James Baldwin, Eldridge Cleaver); (4) creative writers who are incidentally critics (James Weldon Johnson, Countee Cullen, Wallace Thurman, Langston Hughes, Richard Wright, James Baldwin, Ralph Ellison, Arna Bontemps); (5) academic critics (Benjamin Brawley, Sterling Brown, Saunders Redding, Nick Aaron Ford, Hugh Gloster, John Lash, Blyden Johnson); and (6) the black "New Critics" who are either returning to a revaluation of black writing or who argue for a black aesthetic (James A. Emanuel, W. Edward Farrison, Addison Gayle, Jr., Stephen Henderson, George Kent, Hoyt W. Fuller, John Henrik Clarke; and LeRoi Jones,

6. For a useful survey of and introduction to thirty-five more contemporary black writers as they see the present literary scene, see the symposium "Black Writers' Views" (*NegroD* 17, iii[1968]:10–48).

Larry Neal, Clarence Major, Carolyn Rodgers, Sara Webster Fabio, Cecil M. Brown, Ed Bullins).

During the course of his discussion, Turner sketches the major works and attitudes and subjects for each critic he names. He concludes that "despite 50 years of criticism of Afro-American literature, criteria for that criticism have not yet been established": some readers judge black literature according to "its moral value, a few for its aesthetic value, most by its social value, and too many according to their response to the personalities of Black authors." He sees some hope for a greater coherence from the "New Critics" who demand that literature be judged according to an aesthetic grounded in African and Afro-American culture. Although most of these critics, including the academic critics (who seem to be his real hope for a mature criticism), are now involved in the revolutionary cause of black liberation, the best of their criticism is not merely a polemic against white oppression, it is also a reinterpretation of black experience.

This is not to say that black New Criticism does not have serious faults. Indeed, Turner suggests two major faults: a tendency to denounce older writers while lauding anyone or anything new; and the constant devising of prescriptive literary theories prior to the existence of any literature that it describes (in fact, calling upon writers to write the literature that will show the excellence of their theories).

Significant as the development of the new black criticism is, Turner laments the fact that this writing is not well known; in part, it is not because black critics do not attempt to publish in journals subscribed to predominantly by whites, but instead in *Black World, Journal of Black Poetry, Cricket, Black Scholar, Black Theater*. But Turner feels that as the number of black instructors increases in universities, they will produce increasing numbers of critical books on both black and white writing. And, as "some of the present ferment subsides," the new black critics will look more closely at current black writers and evaluate their works "more carefully on aesthetic bases." Thereby, they may soon expand American critical theory "to a degree at which Americans can more fully appreciate poetry which depends on oral presentation and can appreciate drama which involves less physical action than has been the custom in the Anglo-American theater."

Here in brief outline, then, is the shape of black literary criticism in America over the last three years. Of all the facets of the new black consciousness, the quest for a usable past and a viable literary tradition is probably the easiest for the white reader to get hold of. A good beginning is simply a roll call of important black American writers and critics, and such a framework as that offered by Turner provides a useful orientation. Much as I think I understand the present necessity for insisting on an anti-white aesthetic, its purely literary theory runs counter to all my experience in the reading of literature. I would conclude, therefore, on an optimistic note with the assertion that white readers can and will try to understand and feel and assume the integrity of black writing. Turner also would like to be optimistic, but his skepticism is evident:

> The chances are great that unless America changes drastically within the next few years, most American readers will continue to look at literature through the eyes of the white critics rather than the Black. Full awareness of Black critics will develop only when publishers make greater effort to look beyond the prestige colleges for authors of scholarly books and when the literary public learns to look beyond the prestige journals for literary scholarship. And full appreciation of the criticism of Afro-American literature will develop only when all readers perceive that a thorough knowledge and understanding of the Afro-American experience, culture, and history is a prerequisite for an individual who wishes to be a critic of that literature. [p. 67]

Washington State University

Index

This index gives references to literary and historical figures who are referred to throughout the book, as well as to authors of the literary scholarship therein surveyed. Works are cited only for those authors given chapter coverage. Literary movements and genres are not indexed as such, since the organization of the book makes pertinent pages clear for most such studies.